SUCCESSFUL SMALL BUSINESS MANAGEMENT

MOM'S FOOT
LONGS
GRAND OPENING
THE BEST DOGS IN TOWN

JIM JONES
COMPANY

FORREST H. FRANTZ

Successful Small Business Management

PRENTICE-HALL, INC., Englewood Cliffs, New Jersey 07632

Library of Congress Cataloging in Publication Data

FRANTZ, FORREST H
Successful small business management.

Includes bibliographical references and index.
1. Small business–Management. 2. Small Business–Finance. I. Title.
HD69.S6F7 658′.022 77-14385
ISBN 0-13-872119-X

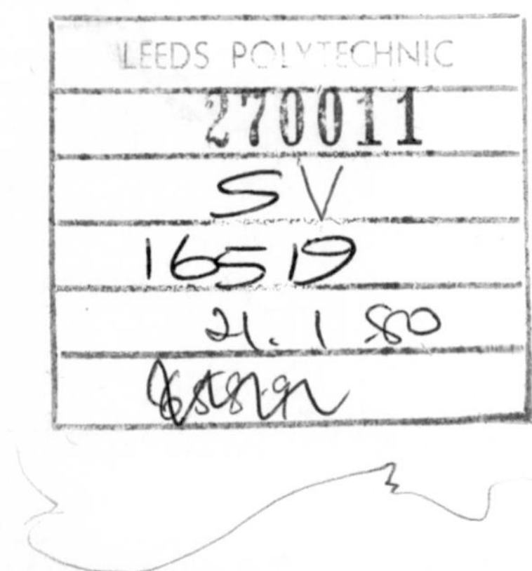

Printed in the United States of America

10 9 8 7 6 5 4 3 2 1

PRENTICE-HALL INTERNATIONAL, INC., *London*
PRENTICE-HALL OF AUSTRALIA PTY. LIMITED, *Sydney*
PRENTICE-HALL OF CANADA, LTD., *Toronto*
PRENTICE-HALL OF INDIA PRIVATE LIMITED, *New Delhi*
PRENTICE-HALL OF JAPAN, INC., *Tokyo*
PRENTICE-HALL OF SOUTHEAST ASIA PTE. LTD., *Singapore*
WHITEHALL BOOKS LIMITED, *Wellington, New Zealand*

CONTENTS

PREFACE *xiii*

STUDY AND BUSINESS PREPARATION AIDS *xv*

THINGS TO DO NOW TO OBTAIN SUPPLEMENTARY MATERIALS FREE IN ADVANCE TO AID YOUR STUDY *xvii*

FEDERAL GOVERNMENT INFORMATION *xix*

1
You and Your Own Business 2

OPPORTUNITIES IN MINI BUSINESS;
Mini Business Is Different;
The Advantages of a Business of Your Own; Mini-Business Successes;
Failures Too—and Why; *Review Exercises 1-A;*
THE ATTRIBUTES OF SUCCESSFUL SMALL BUSINESSPEOPLE;
The Surefire Success Attitude; Goal Setting and Planning; Organization;
Direction; Control; How to Overcome Problems and Obstacles;
The Objectives of Business; *Review Exercises 1-B;*
SUITABILITY AND SPECIALIZATION; Your Suitability;

Business Demands on Owners; The Difference;
Try to Enjoy Yourself; *Review Exercises 1-C;*
CAPITAL, RESOURCES, AND PROFIT;
Capital and Other Resources; Profit Expectations;
Time Required to Reach Profitability; *Review Exercises 1-D;*
THE DOOR IS OPEN; SUMMARY; *KEY TERMS;*
QUESTIONS AND PROBLEMS;
FIELD INVESTIGATIONS AND PROJECTS

2
Going into Business for Yourself–an Overview 30

FORM OF BUSINESS ENTITY; Definitions; Proprietorships;
Partnerships; Corporations; *Review Exercises 2-A;*
DEVELOPING THE CONCEPT; Steps in Concept Development;
Minimizing Cash Requirements; Other Requirements;
Review Exercises 2-B; FEASIBILITY STUDY; Location;
Market Survey; How to Assess Competitors; *Review Exercises 2-C;*
START-UP: FINAL PLANS AND ACTION; Final Analysis and Planning;
Financing and Banking Arrangements; Commitments and Action;
Work Ahead; Sources of Information; *Review Exercises 2-D;*
PLANT, SHOP, STORE, AND OFFICE LAYOUT;
The Manufacturing Plant; Repair Service Shops; Retail Stores;
Wholesale Houses; Service Offices; *Review Exercises 2-E;* SUMMARY;
KEY TERMS; QUESTIONS AND PROBLEMS;
FIELD INVESTIGATION AND PROJECTS

3
Going into Business for Yourself–a Further Exploration 54

START OR BUY? Why Buy? Money-Maker or Bargain? Search;
Investigation and Analysis; Negotiation; *Review Exercises 3-A;*
COOPERATIVE ARRANGEMENTS, FRANCHISES, AND
INVESTMENTS; Cooperative Arrangements; Franchises;
How to Investigate Franchises; Investment and Appreciation;
Review Exercises 3-B;
THE SPECTRUM OF BUSINESS OPPORTUNITIES; Service Businesses;
Retail Businesses; Wholesaling, Brokerage, and Agency;
Manufacturing and Construction; Entrepreneurial Approaches;
Review Exercises 3-C; SUMMARY; *KEY TERMS;*
QUESTIONS AND PROBLEMS;
FIELD INVESTIGATION AND PROJECTS

4
Marketing and Sales 80

MARKETING; What Marketing Is All About;
Market Research Simplified; Market Forecasting;
Marketing Strategy and Tactics; Specialization and Diversification;
Some Terms and Definitions; *Review Exercises 4-A;*
SELLING: PRIMARY KEY TO BUSINESS SUCCESS;
The Selling Process; Prospecting; How to Put "Sell" in Your Business;
Steps to Surer Sales; Selling Pointers–Handling Objections;
Suggestion Selling; Proposals and Bids; *Review Exercises 4-B;*
CASE: MARKETING AND SELLING; *Review Exercises 4-C;*
SUMMARY; *KEY TERMS; QUESTIONS AND PROBLEMS;*
FIELD INVESTIGATION AND PROJECTS

5
Advertising, Promotion, and Public Relations 108

ADVERTISING; Media, Costs, and Results; The Principles of Ad Writing;
Headlines That Attract Readers; Ad-Writing Suggestions;
Layout, Position, and Size; Classifieds; Result Measurement;
Review Exercises 5-A; PROMOTIONS; Events Suitable for Promotions;
How to Make Promotions Successful; Special Services;
Ten Sales Promotion Ideas; *Review Exercises 5-B;*
PUBLIC RELATIONS AND PUBLICITY; Definitions; Image; Publicity;
Daily Relations; Public Service and Community Relations;
Review Exercises 5-C; CASE: ADVERTISING AND PROMOTION;
Review Exercises 5-D; SUMMARY; *KEY TERMS;*
QUESTIONS AND PROBLEMS;
FIELD INVESTIGATION AND PROJECTS

6
Accounting, Credit, and Collections 138

DOUBLE-ENTRY BOOKKEEPING SIMPLIFIED;
The Elements of the System; Cash Sales; Charge Sales;
Payment Received on Account; Expense Paid;
Expense Invoice Received, Not Paid; Accounts-Payable Disbursement;
Review Exercises 6-A; EXPANDING THE SYSTEM;
The Accounting Equation; Required Accounts; The Accounting Cycle;
The "Books"; Starting Entries; Operating Transaction Entries;
The Work Sheet; *Review Exercises 6-B;* INTERNAL CONTROL;
Internal Control Policy; Bank-Balance Reconciliation;
Cash-Drawer Reconciliation; Petty Cash; Other Precautionary Measures;

Review Exercises 6-C; CREDIT AND COLLECTIONS;
Credit—a Sales Tool; Credit Policy and Evaluation; Collections;
Review Exercises 6-D;
OTHER APPROACHES TO MINI-BUSINESS ACCOUNTING;
CASE: A RETAIL AND SERVICE BUSINESS MISADVENTURE;
Review Exercises 6-E; SUMMARY; *KEY TERMS;*
QUESTIONS AND PROBLEMS;
FIELD INVESTIGATION AND PROJECTS

7
Financial Analysis and Management *180*

PROFIT AND WORTH; THE INCOME STATEMENT;
Developing the Income Statement; Gross Profit; Expenses; Net Profit;
Review Exercises 7-A; MEASURES OF PROFITABILITY;
Net Profit Margin; Return on Equity; Gross Margin;
Percentage Income Statements; *Review Exercises 7-B;*
THE BALANCE SHEET; Assets; Liabilities; Owner's Equity;
Review Exercises 7-C;
MEASURES OF FINANCIAL POSITION AND ACTIVITY; Liquidity;
Leverage; Activity; Return on Assets; *Review Exercises 7-D;*
CASE: THE RETAIL FORECLOSURE; *Review Exercises 7-E;*
COMPARISONS; SUMMARY; *KEY TERMS;*
QUESTIONS AND PROBLEMS;
FIELD INVESTIGATION AND PROJECTS

8
Financing Your Own Business *204*

CAPITAL AND FINANCING; How Much Will You Need? Computations;
Long-Term Financing; Off-Balance Sheet Financing;
Short-Term Financing; Customer "Out-of-the-Business" Financing;
Review Exercises 8-A; LOAN TERMS AND LENDERS; Collateral;
Interest Rates and Computations; Other Terms; Sources of Debt Capital;
Renewals and Refinancing; *Review Exercises 8-B;*
HOW TO BORROW MONEY; The 5 C's of Credit; Loan Request Preplan;
Approaching the Lender; Banks and Bankers; *Review Exercises 8-C;*
CASES: LOANS; Case: The Refusal; Case: Loan Granted;
Review Exercises 8-D; SUMMARY; *KEY TERMS;*
QUESTIONS AND PROBLEMS;
FIELD INVESTIGATION AND PROJECTS

9
Reporting, Taxes, and Tax Planning *232*

TAXES, RECORDS, AND REPORTS; Sales Taxes; FICA, Withholding, and Tax Deposits; Unemployment Taxes; Other Taxes; *Review Exercises 9-A;* FEDERAL INCOME TAX; Filing and Forms; The Basic Tax Formula; Rates and Schedules; Where to Get Information and Help; *Review Exercises 9-B;* FEDERAL INCOME TAX PLANNING; Depreciation; Investment Credit; Other Ways to Minimize Tax Liability; *Review Exercises 9-C;* CASE: INCOME TAX PROBLEMS; *Review Exercises 9-D;* SUMMARY; *KEY TERMS; QUESTIONS AND PROBLEMS; FIELD INVESTIGATION AND PROJECTS*

10
Law, Regulation, Risk, and Insurance *260*

BUSINESS LAW; Contracts; Agency; Form of Entity and Entities; Property; Sales; Negotiable Transactions; Security; *Review Exercises 10-A;* REGULATION; Federal Regulation; State Regulation; Local Regulation and Licenses; *Review Exercises 10-B;* RISK AND INSURANCE; Risk; Insurance; Coinsurance and Deductibles; Policies and Forms; *Review Exercises 10-C;* CASES; Business Law; An Insurance Claim; *Review Exercises 10-D;* SUMMARY; *KEY TERMS; QUESTIONS AND PROBLEMS; FIELD INVESTIGATION AND PROJECTS*

11
Pricing, Planning, and Budgeting for Profit *282*

PROFIT RATIONALE; An Elementary Analysis; Activity Segregation; The Retail and Wholesale Business; The Manufacturing Business; The Service Business; *Review Exercises 11-A;* COST, VOLUME, AND PROFIT; Fixed and Variable Costs; Break-Even Analysis—Graphical; Computational Techniques; Effects of Fixed and Variable Costs; *Review Exercises 11-B;* PRICING, PROFIT, AND STABILITY; Pricing Economics; Pricing for Profit; *Review Exercises 11-C;* PLANNING AND BUDGETING; Basic Planning and Budgeting; Income and Cash Flow; Cash Budget; *Review Exercises 11-D;* CASE: AN INVESTMENT DECISION INVOLVING PRICING AND PROFIT; *Review Exercises 11-E;* SUMMARY; *KEY TERMS; QUESTIONS AND PROBLEMS; FIELD INVESTIGATION AND PROJECTS*

12
Purchasing, Inventory, and Expense Control *308*

PURCHASING; How to Find Sources; Shopping and Negotiating; Factors Affecting Price; Special Deals; Paperwork; *Review Exercises 12-A;* INVENTORY; Cost of Inventory; Ordering Computation; Inventory Records and Management; Inventory Turnover; *Review Exercises 12-B;* EXPENSE CONTROL; Interim Income Statement Signals; Cutting Location and Utility Costs; Cutting Wage and Salary Costs; Other Expense Reductions; *Review Exercises 12-C;* CASE: SPECULATION IN PURCHASING; *Review Exercises 12-D;* SUMMARY; *KEY TERMS; QUESTIONS AND PROBLEMS; FIELD INVESTIGATION AND PROJECTS*

13
Management *332*

MANAGING YOUR BUSINESS; Planning; Organizing; Directing; Controling; *Review Exercises 13-A;* OTHER FUNCTIONS OF MANAGEMENT; Innovation and Creativity; Coordinating; Representing; Budgeting and Reporting; *Review Exercises 13-B;* CASES: TYPICAL SMALL-BUSINESS MANAGEMENT PROBLEMS; Diversifying the Ice Cream Store; The Small Manufacturing Company Turnaround; *Review Exercises 13-C;* BEHAVIORAL APPROACHES TO MANAGEMENT; SUMMARY; *KEY TERMS; QUESTIONS AND PROBLEMS; FIELD INVESTIGATION AND PROJECTS*

14
Human Resources *358*

BRINGING EMPLOYEES INTO YOUR BUSINESS; Recruiting; Selection; Conducting the Interview; Other Selection Action; Placement and Pay; Temporaries, Moonlighters, and Others; *Review Exercises 14-A;* WHEN YOU HIRE AN EMPLOYEE; Paperwork; Job Descriptions and Specifications; Employee Development; Performance Evaluation; Incentives, Fringe Benefits, and Promotions; *Review Exercises 14-B;* WORKING WITH AND THROUGH PEOPLE; Approaches to Leadership; Communications; Motivation; *Review Exercises 14-C;* CASE: A LESSON IN HIRING; *Review Exercises 14-D;* SUMMARY; *KEY TERMS; QUESTIONS AND PROBLEMS; FIELD INVESTIGATION AND PROJECTS*

15

Economics, Business Cycles, and the Growth of Your Business 390

HOW ECONOMIC CONDITIONS AFFECT BUSINESS; Local Conditions; National Conditions; Monetary and Fiscal Policy; *Review Exercises 15-A;* BUSINESS CYCLES; The Nature of the Business Cycle; The Upswing; The Peak; The Downswing; The Trough; Indicators; Harnessing Business-Cycle Knowledge; *Review Exercises 15-B;* YOUR GROWING BUSINESS; The Growth Cycle of a Business; Changes in Requirements; Development of Continuity; Mergers and Acquisitions; *Review Exercises 15-C;* CASE: PROFITING FROM THE BUSINESS CYCLE; *Review Exercises 15-D;* SUMMARY; *KEY TERMS; QUESTIONS AND PROBLEMS; FIELD INVESTIGATION AND PROJECTS*

PREFACE

If you want to–

- Learn a lot about business fast
- Acquire the practical business skills needed to start (or buy) and operate your own business
- Update or refresh your business knowledge and skills

this book was written for you. It began with the suggestion of Professor Leon Pleasant of Eastfield College, Mesquite, Texas that a brief, practical business text was needed for students of auto mechanics, electronics, refrigeration, air conditioning, the building trades, and other disciplines–in short, anyone who might wish to harness his/her special knowledge and skills in a business of his/her own.

Others cited additional needs for a practically oriented introduction to business with emphasis on small-business and small-unit operation. These needs included small-business classes, adult education classes, mid-management programs, and other specialized programs in which a practical, working knowledge of business principles and skills would be essential, or at least advantageous. Hence, students of food and hotel management, real estate, insurance, transportation, retailing, and secretarial science should find this book useful. Friends in industry suggested that the book would also be useful for technical professionals who were becoming increasingly involved in business and management.

Everyone consulted expressed the desire for simplicity in presentation without dilution of essential material. The writing effort has been directed toward meeting these requirements. If it has succeeded, it is because of the suggestions and reviews of countless people in education, small businesses, industry, and the financial community.

The first three chapters will help you assess your suitability for a business of your own and show you how to get started. Chapters 4 through 12 present the basic skills essential to *mini-business* (fewer than five employees) success. Chapters 13 through 15 show you how to manage and staff a growing business. (See "Study and Business Preparation Aids," immediately following the preface, for further information on the book and its approach.)

The text does not stop at "how to." It contains the essential *principles* and *theories* of business and management to establish a sound foundation for the operation of a successful business. It will be useful to you if you elect to pursue further business education or go to work in someone else's company. It provides a broad solid base to build on, and you can build as high as you want to.

Thanks go to Donna Cone for her typing and patience; my wife Marie for much coordination; Sally Bird of SBA's Dallas office for information; and Fred Stitzell of American Petrofina, and Professor Robert W. Smith of the University of Houston for preliminary reviews and suggestions. The in-depth reviews of Professors Stephen I. Winter, Orange County Community College; George N. Freedman, Dutchess Community College; Edwin A. Giermak, College of DuPage; Richard J. Huber, Waukesha County Technical Institute; Edward T. Hamilton, Wayne Community College; and Eugene Britt, Grossman College provided valuable steering for the project, and their help is gratefully acknowledged. Thanks to Prentice-Hall's Stephen Cline, Ron Ledwith, Charlotte Leonard and William Gibson, who played key roles in seeing this book to print. Finally, thanks to many others, too numerous to name, who have been helpful in this project.

This book is intended for both men and women. Long-time usage of such terms as "businessman" belie the fact that women are involved in business, many in businesses of their own. An effort has been made to present a nonsexist view, but in the interests of readability both masculine and feminine pronouns have not been used everywhere. "Him," as used in this book, means "him or her."

FORREST H. FRANTZ

STUDY AND BUSINESS PREPARATION AIDS

This book contains these aids to help you learn the material faster with greater understanding and to begin planning for your own business:

1. *A list of things to do now* (immediately following this section) which will put free supplemental materials in your hands for use as you progress through the book.
2. Liberal use of *examples, figures, mini cases* and *point summaries* throughout the text for clarity and easy retention.
3. *Review exercises* at the end of each section (three to six sets per chapter). Do these as you complete each section.
4. *Cases* at the end of Chapters 4 through 15 for your study, practical problem solving, and classroom discussion. Some of these cases are discussed in *detail*, some contain *contrasts*, some *reach conclusions and require you to provide the computations and reasoning*, and some of the cases are *open-ended, leaving the solution to you*. A set of review exercises provides guidance for using the cases most effectively. *All of these cases are founded on factual small-business problems and experiences.*
5. End-of-chapter *summaries, key term* lists, and *questions and problems.* A substantial number of the questions and problems are practical "hands-on" business problems.

6. End-of-chapter field investigations and projects designed to stimulate research and give "hands-on" experiences. One or more of these in each chapter is designed as a step in developing your plans, gathering information, establishing contacts, and otherwise preparing yourself to enter your own business.
7. Concentration on the problems encountered, the skills and knowledge needed, and their application to the *mini business* (fewer than five employees) throughout the first twelve chapters; you learn how to do things yourself with minimum help before you learn how to preside over a larger company. Then, Chapters 13 to 15 show you how to manage the larger business to which yours should grow. These chapters also provide background on external influences and growth problems.

THINGS TO DO NOW TO OBTAIN SUPPLEMENTAL MATERIALS FREE IN ADVANCE TO AID IN YOUR STUDY

1. See page 47. (a) Order free literature cited from Small Business Administration (SBA). (b) Write Bank of America for Business "Profiles" and "Operations" lists.
2. See page 53, project 2, part (b). Write to several companies for copies of their Annual Reports. This material can also be used for project 1, p. 203.
3. See page 107, project 1. Write to SBA for Small Marketeer's Aids, no. 156, *Marketing Checklist For Small Retailers*.
4. See p. 231, project 1. Write to SBA for information on SBA loans.
5. See Chapter 9. Order the following from the Internal Revenue Service (IRS):

   Forms SS-4, 940, 941, 501, W-2, W-4, 1040 (with schedules A, B, C, D, E, and R), 1040 ES, 1065, 1120, 1120S
   Circular E, Employer's Tax Guide
   IRS Publication 334
   IRS Publication 17

6. Order information on your state's sales taxes and sample sales-tax forms from the state comptroller or other similar officer in your state.
7. See p. 307. Order SBA's *Small Marketeers Aid* No. 146.

FEDERAL GOVERNMENT INFORMATION

Offices of the various government agencies are located in Washington D.C. and most are represented in each of ten regional cities as follows:

Region I	Boston
Region II	New York City
Region III	Philadelphia
Region IV	Atlanta
Region V	Chicago
Region VI	Dallas-Fort Worth
Region VII	Kansas City
Region VIII	Denver
Region IX	San Francisco
Region X	Seattle

If you are located in or near any of these regional cities, you can obtain SBA, IRS, and other government agency information quickly by placing a phone call. IRS has fifty-eight district offices, so you may be near one of these even if you're not located near a regional city. The agencies are listed under U.S. Government in telephone directories.

If you aren't located in or near a regional city, write the appropriate agency in Washington, D.C. You can obtain Washington addresses of agencies by consulting the *United States Government Manual* (published annually). The Washington address of SBA and IRS are:

Small Business Administration
1441 L St. N.W.
Washington, D.C. 20416

Internal Revenue Service
1111 Constitution Ave. N.W.
Washington, D.C. 20224

Publications of the SBA and other agencies for which there is a charge may be obtained at U.S. government bookstores located in the federal building in each of the ten regional cities, or they may be ordered from:

U.S. Government Printing Office
Washington, D.C. 20402

SUCCESSFUL SMALL BUSINESS MANAGEMENT

You and Your Own Business

1

You're reading this book because you want to know more about starting (or buying) and operating your own business. You're taking a step that will increase your chances of success. Approximately 10,000 *known* business failures and discontinuations occur each year;[1] many more are unrecorded. The number of failures and discontinuations would decrease significantly if all business starters entered a program of business study as you are doing.

This mention of success and failure may raise several other questions. Here are a few that you might be asking yourself right now. This chapter will help you find some of the answers. You'll know the answers to all these questions and many more by the time you finish the book.

1. What kinds of business can I get into?
2. What are my chances of success?

[1] *Statistical Abstract of the United States* (Washington, D.C.: U.S. Department of Commerce, 1975), p. 507. The number of failures ran from 10,000 to 17,000 per year between 1955 and 1967; between 1967 and 1974 failures were in the 9,000 to 11,000 range. Note that this includes only *known* cases of businesses that went into bankruptcy, were otherwise out of business, or made compromises with creditors. It does not include businesses that voluntarily threw in the towel and quit business. There are no statistics available on this kind of discontinuation.

3. How can I increase my chances of success?
4. What are the attributes of a successful businessperson?
5. Am I emotionally suited to own or operate my own business?
6. Do I have any special advantages or disadvantages?
7. How easy—or tough—will it be to get started?
8. How much capital (money, equipment, and inventory) will I need?
9. What can I do to better prepare myself for starting and operating my own business?
10. Can I get my business started part-time while I enjoy the security of regular employment?

Look for answers to these questions as you study this chapter.

OPPORTUNITIES IN MINI BUSINESS

There are 13 million businesses in the United States. Many of these were started by a person like yourself. They were generally begun as *proprietorships* (owned and often managed by one person), rather than as corporations (which usually have several owners and hired management). There are more than 10 million proprietorships, about a million partnerships, and less than 2 million corporations in the U.S. The number of proprietorships has increased by 3 million over the last twenty-five years.[2]

Mini Business Is Different

The small proprietorship, ranging in size from the owner as the only worker to as many as four or five employees, is quite different from larger businesses. This is how most businesses get started. A business of this size is generally lumped into the category of "small business." The Small Business Administration classifies a manufacturing company as small if it employs 250 to 1500 (depending on the industry) or fewer people. Similarly, retail businesses doing less than $1 to $5 million in sales and wholesalers doing less than $5 to $15 million in sales are classified as small businesses. This definition encompasses businesses that must be considered quite large in contrast to most newly started concerns, which usually employ one to five persons (and more often one to two). We'll define our very small business with less than five workers as a *mini business*.

Mini business is quite different from big business, and it's quite different from even a medium-sized small business. Most texts and courses in small business deal with the broad spectrum embraced by the Small Business Administration (SBA) definitions. In doing so, they fail to address the different nature, viewpoint, and knowledge needs of the person going into business for the first time with limited funds. This book answers those needs and attempts to build a firm

[2] Ibid., p. 490.

base for growth and success in the business world from mini businesses to large corporations. If you grasp the principles of starting and operating a mini business, you can readily make the transition to big business.

A mini business can operate more efficiently than larger businesses. Lost motion, time spent in communicating, misunderstandings, waste, and costly errors are reduced when fewer people are involved. Smaller investment in equipment per worker is generally possible in a mini business. The owner's investment of "sweat equity" reduces the dollar capital needs for start-up. Finally, the owner-worker is usually motivated to work much harder for each dollar earned than is a hired manager.

POINT 1-1: A mini business (five or fewer workers, more often one or two) is quite different from a large or even medium small business. A mini business is owner-operated, usually starts with limited capital, and the owner has broad responsibilities.

The owner of a mini business must be a very flexible manager and worker. He (or she) does not have specialists to do his bidding at every turn. Consequently, he must be a jack-of-all-trades. He'll be better able to find the time to do all of the tasks he must do if he understands them. In that sense, the owner will be more likely to succeed if he (or she) is a specialist in mini-business skills and techniques.

Skills and techniques that contribute to mini-business success are scattered in the fields of finance, accounting, promotion and advertising, marketing, business law, industrial management, administrative management, and personnel management. The bulk of the knowledge in these fields deals with big business and often isn't presented in a form easy to adapt to a mini business. *Lacking the specific knowledge in these fields needed for starting and operating a mini business can be at least limiting and at worst disastrous.* The limitation is evidenced by the fact that nearly 80 percent of the 10 million proprietorships in the U.S. have annual sales of $25,000 or less.[3] That's hardly success! The worst, bankruptcy, culls about 10,000 businesses, and there are probably more than 100,000 voluntary liquidations and closings each year.

You can say these unsuccessful businesspeople had inadequate working capital, managed poorly, didn't pay attention to business, or whatever. It usually boils down to the fact that they didn't have the specific knowledge that it takes to start and operate a mini business—or if they did, they didn't apply it.

POINT 1-2: You're much more likely to succeed in your mini business if you learn the business techniques and skills that are specifically essential to mini business—and apply them!

[3] Ibid., p. 491.

The Advantages of a Business of Your Own

There are numerous advantages in owning your own business. The primary advantages are

1. Unlimited earning power. You can earn as much as your wits, skill, training, willpower, and capital allow. You're not limited to a salary or hourly wages.
2. Freedom of action. You set your own policies, procedures, and mode of operation. You make your own decisions, and you can make them quickly without exhaustive conferences and approvals. You're constrained only by law and the demands of your customers.
3. You have opportunity for greater and faster personal financial growth in your own business than you do as a salaried or hourly employee.
4. You can generally experience greater personal satisfaction and sense of accomplishment in a business of your own.

The coin is not one-sided. You can fail and lose your investment. Many who start don't make it. It has been estimated that out of every ten businesses started, eight ultimately fail. (Precise, all-inclusive statistics are not available for reasons to be cited later.) The people who do make it are a special breed. A large portion of this chapter will be devoted to defining the pedigree of the winners. Often, a special skill is the launching pad of a mini-business winner.

Mini-Business Successes

Special skills often form the basis of a service business. Service businesses may deal in personal services, business services, repairs, amusement and recreation services, hotels and lodging services, and professional services (such as medical, legal, accounting), to mention a few broad categories.

A typical successful start was made by Joe, an electronics technician in the aerospace industry. He began to service television sets part-time in 1964 when color television sales started to boom. Few technicians really understood color sets or how to service them then. Joe boned up on color TV, got service contracts with most of the furniture stores and some of the appliance stores in town, and placed classified ads offering his services. His part-time venture grew into a full-time business within a year.

Henry came to the United States in 1960. He went to work for an air-conditioning firm and simultaneously took a night course in the subject. He went into his own air-conditioning service business in 1965 and by 1976 owned two mechanical contracting companies and an air-conditioning service company.

Mary was a beauty operator who had worked in someone else's shop for five years. In 1973 she opened her own shop. Now she has fifteen operators working for her and has added a ladies' clothing store to her business activities.

Bob was an auto mechanic. He started a customized recreational vehicle business in 1974. Now he's doing over $250,000 a year gross (total) sales.

Some people start businesses part-time and retain the security of a regular job. Others make a clean break from their jobs and devote all their time to business right from the start. Either way, there's a lot of investigating, planning, organizing, and preparation that can be done before the smart person quits his job or starts investing his money. Preplanning and advance work prevent missions that abort on the launching pad.

We've mentioned service businesses; let's expand our list of mini-business categories to include

Service
Investments and franchises
Retailing
Wholesaling, brokerage, and agency
Manufacturing
Construction

Within each of these categories, there are many specific kinds of businesses that can be started and operated by one or a few persons.

Some manufacturing businesses are started with a new product idea or an invention. Businesses that start as service businesses sometimes develop products that put them into manufacturing.

Bill was in the upholstery business. He developed a substantial enterprise with apartment owners. He realized that if a standardized couch and chair of his design were used in apartments, he could mass-produce covers at lower cost and increased profit. He started manufacturing his own standard couches and chairs and sold them with guaranteed reupholstery cost 20 percent below the rate for nonstandard jobs. Thus, he got into the furniture manufacturing business and had a captive market for furniture sales as well as for his mass-production reupholstery service.

POINT 1-3: A business should have a basis such as owner's special skill, an invention, an innovative idea, previous experience, a service to meet a new need or supplement a scarce supply, or some other basis over and beyond the desire for gain.

Products must flow from manufacturers to consumers. They generally flow through a number of *middlemen.* These middlemen include *wholesalers, distributors, brokers, agents,* and *retailers.* In treating middleman businesses in this book, we will deal with the wholesaler, broker, agent, and other quantity sellers between manufacturer and retailer as a group, and we'll deal with retailers as a group.

I'm sure you know some retailers. Acquaint them with your interest in going into business for yourself, and they'll be glad to tell you how they got started, some of the problems they encountered, and how they solved them.

A typical example of a success in the wholesaler-broker-agent category is that of George, a manufacturer's agent. *A manufacturer's agent is a functional middleman; he does not buy goods and take title to them* as a merchant middleman (e.g., a wholesaler) does. An agent merely negotiates the sale of the goods between the manufacturer and the next middleman in the distribution chain. He is usually paid a commission on the sales he negotiates. George acquires lines to sell by writing several hundred letters to manufacturers. He specializes in photographic equipment and supplies, and he calls on camera stores and volume users of photographic supplies and equipment. He traveled most of Texas, originally, and didn't do too well in the first two years. In the third year his business prospered. Now he has four men traveling for him in four states. His earnings are substantial!

POINT 1-4: There are many profitable businesses that do not require substantial investment in equipment and inventory (goods for sale), and they're very attractive if your nest egg is small. Look for low overhead, shared rent and other expenses, and minimum capital investment.

Failures Too—and Why

There have been more than 100,000 known business failures over the last ten years.[4] A "known business failure" is a bankruptcy or other withdrawal from business with known losses to creditors. Many businesses, unable to pay their bills, fold without sufficient fanfare to make compiled statistics. Many more businesses close their doors simply because the owners cannot earn as much as the salary or wages they could earn working for someone else. The degree of nonsuccess ranges from low profitability to insolvency.

A business is *insolvent* when its *liabilities* (payables—what it owes to others) "due now" exceed its *assets* (inventory, receivables, equipment—what the business owns). Hence, it cannot fully satisfy its obligations even if all its assets are sold. Note that a business may have a negative value, but may be technically solvent because its obligations are not due.

A business may fail because it is *illiquid;* that is, because it's short on cash it cannot pay some of its bills when they fall due. A business is liquid if it has the cash to cover bills when they are due. Thus if a business owes $5,000 and has pledged all of its assets valued at $15,000 to secure the $5,000 obligation, it may be forced out of business because it doesn't have $5,000 in cash to settle the obligation on the due date. A distress sale of the assets might bring only $5,000. Then it has nothing to work with. Hence, lack of liquidity can cause an otherwise solvent business to become insolvent.

A business may be liquid and yet have such a low earning level that it doesn't

[4] See footnote 1.

give the owner fair return on his investment, fair wages for his work, and some profit for his enterprise. It is important that your business

1. *Give you a fair return on your investment.* If it costs 8 percent to borrow, and if you put $10,000 in your business, the business should earn $800 a year to compensate you for the use of the money you've invested.
2. *Compensate you for your work.* If you are earning $12,000 a year working for someone else, your business should earn $12,000 to compensate you for your work.[5]
3. *Earn a profit for your enterprise.* The money you invest in your business should earn more than the interest on a well-secured loan. It should earn "venture profit," since you are investing at greater risk. Let's say it should be $2,000 a year in this case.

Thus, in this example, your business should earn $800 as the cost of money, plus $12,000 in wages, plus $2,000 in profit for your enterprise and management, or a total of $14,800 a year. While you might not be able to reach this earning level during your first year in business, the venture should show potential of reaching this level in two to three years.

POINT 1-5: Your business should compensate you with interest on your capital, a salary for your labor, and a profit for your enterprise.

The list of causes of business failure is a long one. Ranking of the most frequent causes varies among analysts. Some cite inadequate financing as the most frequent cause of failure, others cite poor management, and so on. It generally boils down to lack of business knowledge or previous working experience in a similar business, or having it and not using it. If you know your business, you won't be inadequately financed, and you'll know how to manage. However, you may mismanage even if you know how to manage. Why? You may not be willing to work hard enough. You may keep inadequate records or you may commit other business sins. So, poor management appears to be the major cause of business failure. This is confirmed by Dun & Bradstreet statistics. Dun & Bradstreet's *The Business Failure Record 1975* lists the following four causes accounting for 92.9 percent of the 1975 business failures:

Incompetence	41.2%
Unbalanced experience	21.1%
Lack of managerial experience	13.7%
Lack of experience in the line	16.9%
	92.9%

[5] Most business starters are willing to accept some loss in personal earnings during the first few years as part of the price to own their own business. Nevertheless, mouths must be fed and household expenses must be met. Don't overlook this!

Unbalanced experience refers to weakness in experience in one or more of the following areas: sales, finance, purchasing, or production on the part of the manager or the management team. All four of the causes listed boil down to poor management.

REVIEW EXERCISES 1-A

1. (a) How is a mini business different from a medium-sized small business?(b) Discuss the advantages of the mini business. (c) Can you think of disadvantages in a mini business?
2. I implied that $25,000 a year sales resulted in unprofitable operations in most businesses. (a) What kind of business can be very profitable on this volume? (b) What kind of business might just break even on this volume? (c) What kind would probably lose money on this volume?
3. Why might you want to start or buy a business of your own? Explain.
4. What should you have as a basis for your business besides a desire to make money?
5. Explain the difference between a merchant middleman and a functional middleman.
6. What three factors must be compensated out of the earnings of a business and why?

THE ATTRIBUTES OF SUCCESSFUL SMALL BUSINESSPEOPLE

Successful small businesspeople are a breed apart. They move in an exciting world where possibilities for profit and growth are great. Their attributes include willingness to invest long hours and hard work; willingness to master a broad array of knowledge, skills, and disciplines; single-minded, iron-willed determination to succeed; willingness to make personal sacrifices; and the faith and belief that they will succeed. They set goals, plans, organize, staff, direct, and control the activity that leads to attainment of their goals. They know what's most important in dealing with most situations, and they're usually looking ahead to spot opportunities and to avoid problems. They're generally respected in their communities and they're generally happy, although they often go through a lot of trauma in building big successes from mini business starts. You can enhance your chances of success in your own business by studying and developing the attributes of successful small businesspeople. The pointers that follow represent a lot of lessons in the school of hard knocks. They're the distilled experience of many lifetimes. Note them well.

The Surefire Success Attitude

The surefire success attitude is *the belief that you can do anything you make up your mind to do.* It doesn't follow that because you make up your mind to accomplish something, it will automatically happen. But it does follow that if you

1. Make up your mind to do something
2. Find out what you have to do to make it happen
3. Do what you have to do to make it happen

it usually will happen. In other words, you can do anything you make up your mind to do if you work to make it happen. The first part of this attitude is *faith. Determination, planning,* and *work* turn your dreams and desires into *results.*

POINT 1-6: A lot of determination, a little investigation, and a lot of directed hard work can make the almost-impossible a reality.

The functions of management are planning, organizing, staffing, directing, and controlling. We'll examine these functions briefly as they relate to you in succeeding topics.

Goal Setting and Planning

You have to decide what you want to do in order to do it. Your chances of getting to Los Angeles from Dallas are slim unless you decide you want to go to Los Angeles. You have to pick a target or you're not likely to hit it.

Set goals in your personal life and business endeavors so you'll know which direction to take. Businesspeople often set interim goals to guide the way to their ultimate goals. When you and your associates know what you're going for, you're more likely to achieve it.

POINT 1-7: Decide where you're going; set goals and subgoals along the way.

Goals are often called *objectives* in the business world. Concentrate on one objective at a time. Channel all your resources on this objective. If you try to pursue several objectives simultaneously, your resource limitations may cause your efforts to be diluted. Consequently, you may dilute and exhaust your finances, your equipment, and your personal energy—pursuing three objectives without attaining any one of them. And yet, you might readily attain first one, then the next, and finally the third objective by taking them on in a *concentrated* one-at-a-time effort.

Some people call this "single-mindedness." No matter what you call it, it pays off.

POINT 1-8: Concentrate your efforts.

After you have determined and stated your objective (always put it in writing), the next step is planning the way to achievement. Before you leave Dallas on an auto trip to Los Angeles you pull out a roadmap and *plan* your itinerary. If you take that much trouble over an automobile trip, doesn't it make sense to plan a business project on which you've staked thousands of dollars—or even your whole future?

Plans begin as rather broad concepts for getting the job done. Then they're expanded in detail and refined repeatedly till all the bugs seem to be eliminated, and the *who, what, when, where, why,* and *how* are all spelled out.

You're more likely to succeed if you have detailed plans.

POINT 1-9: A written plan is a roadmap for reaching a goal.

Planning can be overdone. Good planning calls for *perspective*—the ability to distinguish the relative importance of things. The more important an objective is, the more thorough the planning should be. Your sales plan for the next year is more important than choosing the carpet for your office. You may devote 50 to 100 hours to your sales plan, at most 30 minutes to choose the carpet. Perspective is the key.

Another key to good planning is *practicality*. This is the ability to perceive whether ideas and plans are workable. If you spot an unworkable idea or plan *before* it eats up hours and dollars, you'll conserve your resources for the winners.

Vision, the ability to forecast, to see what is likely to happen in the future based on past experience, trends, and present information is another important attribute of successful businesspeople. If you have some idea about what is going to happen, you can plan accordingly. This applies equally well to the *business cycle* (the ups and downs of the economy), and to changes in lifestyles. Watch the business cycle; look for trends in business, social life, habits, and buying patterns. Apply vision to your planning, decision making, and business operations.

POINT 1-10: (You fill it in.)

Organization

Successful small businesspeople are usually good organizers. They organize their time, their work, their tools, their desks, their employees, their trips, and everything else. As their companies grow they develop organization in their businesses to encourage and support the attainment of objectives. *Organization in business deals specifically with the division of functions and the assignment of responsibility of these functions to specific individuals.* The organization diagrammed on an organization chart shows who is responsible for each function and who reports to whom in the organization. The present discussion will be confined to personal organization.

As a small businessperson, time is your most valuable resource. You can convert it into money-making plans, ideas, and productive work. A person who squanders time on aimless conversations, unproductive work, hunting tools in a cluttered workshop or hunting business papers in a disorganized office, is blowing dollars out the window. A person who makes a trip to the east side of town, then to the west, and back again to the east when both calls on the east side could have been made on the same trip is paying for extra fuel and lost time.

POINT 1-11: (You fill it in.)

These things may seem obvious, yet most people who fail in business do so because they make obvious mistakes. Other common mistakes that involve loss of time and inattention to business include making business hours too short (for example, closing on Saturdays to hunt, fish, or take a trip), irregular business hours (posting 9:00 to 6:00 business hours and closing at 4 or 5 o'clock several times a month), and failing to keep appointments (for example, on a service call or a collection date). Daydreaming and constant reploughing of the same furrows are also time-wasters. Once a plan is made, execute it, revise it as required, but don't rehash it without having productive intentions; put your time into making your plans work. *Plan the work; work the plan.*

POINT 1-12: (You fill it in.)

Direction

If you're running a one-person show, you have to direct yourself. If you have employees, you have to direct them. It may be easier to direct employees than it is to direct yourself. You can look at their work from a detached viewpoint, give them help and counsel, and show them better ways to do the job. Alas, when you look at yourself, it's hard to find what went wrong, how to direct and help yourself to do things better, and how to spot your own imperfections and errors.

During the early stages of growth of a one-person business, you may hire special services and part-time help. This puts you in the position of directing other people. Directing includes training, supervising, and motivating. Direction should not be a brute-force process. It requires tact, finesse, and an understanding nature. The results that you get from the part-time workers that you employ and from specialized services that you contract for will be related to your ability to direct. As your work force grows, the ability to direct the work grows in importance.

Control

A plan is useless if it isn't made to work. The only way you can know if it isn't working is to set checkpoints and standards. A *checkpoint* indicates a date when a defined part of a job is to be completed. For example, if you're manufacturing a refrigerated vault, your production schedule shows completion dates for the framework, electrical wiring, cooling coils, the interior and exterior covering, and the connection and test of the compressor unit. *Standards* set the amount of time and the cost of material planned for each step in your schedule. If results don't match checkpoints, you need to determine why they haven't and what must be done to bring the project back on plan. If actual production costs exceed standards, you'll need to determine why and correct the situation.

Dollars in sales or profits, number of units completed, percentage of a job completed, and similar measurements indicate amount of progress and whether the project meets the plan. For example, if you project $30,000 sales by mid-year and your reporting system tells you that actual sales are only $20,000, you know you're off target. The next question is why? Perhaps not enough advertising, slow deliveries, customer loss of confidence, or inadequate equipment. Once you determine *why*, you put your finger in the dike by increasing advertising, finding new suppliers, making personal sales calls on customers, or procuring better equipment, as the case may be.

> POINT 1-13: Control is the process of setting standards or goals, having a reporting system that shows "misses," finding the reason(s) for the miss(es), and providing fixes. (Measure, detect, analyze, fix.)

Some comments on personal control are in order. Personal control is one of the most outstanding traits of the successful businessperson. Good self-control minimizes time wasting, keeps you on course, and enables you to work your plan. Personal self-control causes you to tune out bad habits that might dilute your efforts or jeopardize your health. When we speak of self-control, we're really speaking about willpower. If you have strong willpower, you'll have self-control.

Control doesn't stop with control of habits relating to health or getting things done. A strong-willed person has control of his (or her) emotions and personal conduct. Such a person controls his temper and his mind.

How to Overcome Problems and Obstacles

Business isn't always pleasant and orderly. There are frustrations, setbacks, and seeming defeats at times. These frustrations and setbacks can cause useless worry, loss of sleep, and consequent degradation of operations and profit. The weaklings just up and quit.

Recognize that you're human, that you'll make mistakes, and that one mistake is not the end of the world. You can't venture and succeed without some minor setbacks. One mistake should provide the experience so you can avoid making it a second time. Sometimes you'll make the same mistake the second time, but if that doesn't happen often, you're not a hopeless case.

The best way to overcome problems and obstacles is to address them logically. Again, the *who, what, when, where, why, how* can help you pinpoint problem areas and set your mind moving in constructive directions. Remember that you can get on the other side of a wall by going through it, over it, under it, or around it. There are several possible solutions to most business problems.

Sometimes business problems require more than thought, a good idea, or a better solution. The problem may be in the human relations area, and the solution may be *tact, understanding, kindness, apology,* or a combination of these. Sometimes the answer lies in outside counsel or assistance. Remember: *As the owner of your own business, you may seek help from anyone you feel you can afford.* Fortunately, there's plenty of good counsel (and some not so good) available at no cost or at affordable prices.

> POINT 1-14: When you feel like you're losing, try to figure out how to win. Use your head—and other people's heads too.

The Objectives of Business

Now, let's get down to the brass tacks of what business is all about. Why do you want to go into business for yourself? Sure, you want to make money, and you think you can make more that way than you can on somebody's payroll. That's *profit* you're talking about.

To make a fortune is number two. That's *growth* you're talking about. The net worth of a business builds up as profits are ploughed back into the business and as the sales grow.

Fame next! You're talking about *leadership.* You achieve fame as your business becomes the leader in its field. At first your leadership may be confined to your locale. As your business grows, your leadership can expand geographically. To achieve leadership you'll have to produce an outstanding product or service at an acceptable price. And you'll have to tell the world about it in the right way.

You can achieve these objectives by providing quality products and services. Remember: *Customers don't buy from you because they are interested in your welfare! They buy from you because they believe you're giving them quality and service at a competitive price!*

POINT 1-15: Your customers pay you for *service.* Give them what they want, and they'll give you what you want—*profit, growth,* and *leadership.*

REVIEW EXERCISES 1-B

1. Why is it important to set goals?
2. What is the purpose of planning?
3. What is the *business cycle?* (You may have some difficulty answering this at this point.)
4. What are some of the common mistakes that can lead to business failure?
5. Explain the meaning of control. How can you apply self-control to improve your chances of success?
6. What are the three dominant objectives of a business venture? Are there any others? Discuss them.

SUITABILITY AND SPECIALIZATION

A commitment to start your own business, or to enter any career, for that matter, is best made with long-term pursuit in mind. You will lose ground by frequent goal switching. Since a long-term commitment is implied, it's a good idea to answer these questions:

1. Are you suited for a business of your own?
2. Can you—and do you want to—cope with the demands a small business makes on an owner?
3. Do you have a special skill or talent that will make you better suited for a particular kind of business?

Your Suitability

At this point in your study it may not be easy for you to evaluate your suitability to business. But you can get some indications of fit and misfit. If there aren't too many misfits you may be able to clear them up if you still feel inclined to start a business of your own. Take the suitability test, Figure 1-1. Avoid the tendency to give yourself the benefit of doubts; you're looking for weaknesses that may cost you time and money if they aren't recognized.

Business Demands on Owners

Are you willing and able to cope with the problems and details of a mini business? Are you willing to work long and hard when the business requires it? Are you willing to deal with seemingly trivial and excessive demands of your customers and government regulatory and tax agencies? Are you willing to do the record keeping that a mini business requires?

The owner of a mini business must cope with situations, problems, and experiences that never bother the hourly or salaried employee. We often call these the "headaches" of operating a small business, although they're not really headaches if you take them in stride. These are some of the headaches:

1. You have to tend to many details in a small business. You're manager, bookkeeper, salesperson, advertising manager, production supervisor, shipping and receiving clerk, purchasing agent, and janitor, to mention only a few of the jobs you may have to cover. Since many of these duties do not produce direct dollar income, you sometimes wish you didn't have to perform them. But if you can't afford employees to do these jobs, you'll have to do them yourself if you want to keep your business going.
2. Customers often make seemingly unreasonable demands such as "service now" when you have eight calls ahead of them, a "blue chair" when you have green, brown, red, and gold chairs in stock, "free service" beyond the scope of your guarantee, "precise bids" on jobs that you find difficult to estimate, "maximum and prolonged attention" demands for trivially small purchases, and calls for "service now" at unreasonable hours.
3. Laws and regulations that seem trivial but make large time and dollar demands on you and your capital must be complied with. Typical examples are requirements stemming from income tax laws, building codes, health laws, licensing, and record-keeping requirements.
4. Changes in the business cycle that cause your business to fall off when you most need sales, run interest rates up when you most need to borrow, and run material costs up when you most need to be competitive are part of the business experience.
5. "Slow pays" and deadbeats don't honor their obligations and cause you to devote considerable time (and perhaps even incur legal costs) in collecting. Sometimes you can't collect at all!

This is by no means an all-inclusive list of the headaches. When you're work-

FIGURE 1-1 Small-business suitability test

WORKSHOP FOR PROSPECTIVE SMALL BUSINESS OWNERS --- WORKSHEETS

Rating Scale for Evaluating Personal Traits Important to the Proprietor of a Business

INSTRUCTIONS: Place a check mark on the line following each trait where you think it ought to be. The check mark need not be placed directly over one of the guide phrases, because the rating may lie somewhere between the phrases.

Trait				
Initiative	Additional tasks sought; highly ingenious	Resourceful; alert to opportunities	Regular work performed without waiting for directions	Routine worker awaiting directions
Attitude toward others	Positive; friendly interest in people	Pleasant, polite	Sometimes difficult to work with	Inclined to be quarrelsome or uncooperative
Leadership	Forceful, inspiring confidence and loyalty	Order giver	Driver	Weak
Responsibility	Responsibility sought and welcomed	Accepted without protest	Unwilling to assume without protest	Avoided whenever possible
Organizing ability	Highly capable of perceiving and arranging fundamentals in logical order	Able organizer	Fairly capable of organizing	Poor organizer
Industry	Industrious: capable of working hard for long hours	Can work hard, but not for too long a period	Fairly industrious	Hard work avoided
Decision	Quick and accurate	Good and careful	Quick, but often unsound	Hesitant and fearful
Sincerity	Courageous, square-shooter	On the level	Fairly sincere	Inclined to lack sincerity
Perseverance	Highly steadfast in purpose; not discouraged by obstacles	Effort steadily maintained	Average determination and persistence	Little or no persistence
Physical energy	Highly energetic at all times	Energetic most of time	Fairly energetic	Below average

SBA Form 593 9–69 PREVIOUS EDITIONS ARE OBSOLETE.

(Source: Small Business Administration)

ing as a paid employee, there are buffers to problems outside of your responsibility area–other people to take care of the problems. When you're in business for yourself, there are no buffers. You have to face and cope with all of the headaches yourself.

POINT 1-16: The demands on the owner of a mini business are many, varied, and at times disturbing. You'll have to be willing and able to cope with hard work and adapt to changing demands in a business of your own.

The first year of business sometimes ends in frustration at income tax time. Fred, a new businessman, has had a successful year of operation, had made a reasonable profit, and has drawn $1,000 a month from the business to support his family. He has $2,000 in the bank, and he's doubled his inventory. He's made three quarterly income tax payments of $500 each. But he owes $3,500 (in addition to the $1,500 he's paid) for income taxes. What happened?

In spite of the fact that the business was profitable, Fred did an inadequate job of planning and record keeping. He underestimated his earnings. He made about $22,000 in taxable income, but he failed to realize it. He put about $12,000 of his profits back on his shelves in the form of inventory. By increasing his inventory too rapidly, he consumed cash that should have been held in reserve for income tax obligations.

You may have a distaste for book work and record keeping. If you want to have a business of your own, you'd better acquire a taste for keeping books and records in a hurry. You'll need to keep books and records (and understand them) to measure the profitability and growth of your business. You also need to keep records to discover areas of unusual profit or loss so that you can make adjustments to cut losses and put more emphasis on the more profitable parts of your business. You need to keep and understand records to forsee future cash requirements, such as changes in income tax liability. You need to keep records to make your business run smoothly. For example, if you don't keep tabs on your inventory you may lose business because you're out of stock. Or you may go to the opposite extreme and tie up excess amounts of cash in overstock.

Finally, you have to keep records to satisfy legal, regulatory, and tax-reporting requirements. These requirements include sales tax, income tax, and personal property records for all businesses. If you have employees, you'll need payroll, withholding, FICA, and unemployment tax records. Specialized businesses may have additional record-keeping requirements such as federal excise taxes, federal firearms, and automobile sales and transfer record requirements.

POINT 1-17: You have to keep records to make your business run smoothly, to keep score on your progress, to be sure you don't run short of cash, and to satisfy tax and regulatory requirements.

The Difference

Why are some people highly successful, others mediocre, and some failures? The one fundamental thing that they all have in common is that they are *different.* Does the difference make a winner or a loser? Not necessarily so. *The winner capitalizes on his difference.* He competes in races where he has a chance to win. He sharpens his difference to make it more valuable. If you can put your skills and abilities to work in a way that makes your products and services more attractive to the public, you'll harness *differential advantage.*

So, how are you different from other people? What traits, skills, or talents do you possess that are different or a little better than most? How can you sharpen these characteristics to increase your chances of winning? What's the best track for you to compete on? Regarding personal traits, you have a guide to work with in the results of the suitability test. Now, let's see if you have a special skill that suits you for a particular business.

Are you an auto mechanic, cook, air-conditioning technician, electrician, electronic technician, plumber, carpenter, computer programmer, florist, pharmacist, painter, real estate salesman, writer, bookkeeper, chemist, clothing designer, credit manager, interior decorator, secretary, printer, entertainer, or one skilled in some other specialty? If you are, consider a business in which you can employ your skill and experience.

Suppose you're an auto mechanic. What are your options? You can: start a general automotive repair; take an automotive repair concession in a filling station or automotive accessory store; start a do-it-yourself garage facility and automotive supply store (you rent out tools and working space, provide advice, and sell required parts to do-it-yourselfers); start a specialized service, such as a transmission shop, automotive electrical service, front-end shop, body and paint shop, engine overhaul shop; start a truck and/or heavy equipment service shop (there are a number of options in specialized automotive and internal combustion equipment); start a fleet service shop; start a mobile service shop for small fleet operators (you carry hand tools, basic test equipment, and a small assortment of parts in your truck and do the less complicated jobs in the customer's garage); start a tire sales and service shop; or take any one of many other options that you can think of.

Put on your thinking cap. Develop a list of options open to you because of a special skill you have as a result of training, experience, or a hobby.

POINT 1-18: A special skill or an unusual approach to business may give you a distinct edge on success in a particular business. Analyze the possibilities of your work experience, education, and hobbies.

Try to Enjoy Yourself

You don't go into business with enjoyment and fun as goal number one. But enjoying what you do is an important factor in your personal motivation, your chances of success, and your personal satisfaction. It's especially important in view of the long-term implications of a decision to go into business.

REVIEW EXERCISES 1-C

1. (a) What are some of the "headaches" encountered in a small business? (b) How can you cope with them?
2. Most states have sales taxes. The merchant collects these taxes and submits them to the state periodically with a report. What are some of the possible consequences for a small businessperson who has poor financial records and controls?
3. List your special skills. Then develop lists of businesses in which each particular skill would give you special advantages.

CAPITAL, RESOURCES, AND PROFIT

The questions and reservations that are usually uppermost in your mind when you're anxious to get into a business of your own concern the amount of capital needed to get started, where to get the capital, and how much can be made. Detailed help in answering these questions comes later. Right now, we're going to establish a base of fundamental knowledge concerning capital, resources, and profits.

Capital and Other Resources

When you think of capital, you generally think of money. There are money equivalents that are also classified as capital. Before we pursue this discussion further, let's examine all of the resources employed in business.

Economists speak of *the factors of production.* They include land, labor, capital, and entrepreneurship, sometimes designated by other terms. *Land* refers to natural resources such as the land itself, mineral deposits, timber, and water. In other words, the term *land* includes all basic unprocessed raw materials and the land itself.

Capital refers to facilities, tools and machinery for the production of *capital goods* (tools and machines), and *consumer goods* (goods bought for use without further production potential). Capital goods are not used up quickly; they are put to work and are gradually used up during their productive lifetimes. Thus capital includes manufacturing plants, machinery, tools, transportation equipment, power plants, and office equipment. We speak of money as *finance* or *investment capital,* because money can be converted into capital goods.

Labor refers to the hired workers in a business. Land and capital cannot produce without labor.

Entrepreneurship involves the organization and combination of the other factors of production into a productive entity. Some authors refer to this factor as management. The entrepreneur is more than a manager. He (or she) is an innovator and a promoter as well.

Now, let's apply these concepts to your mini business. First of all we'll assume that we're talking about a one-person business. That means you're the entrepreneur and the labor force. Unless you go into the mineral extractive, timber harvesting, or agricultural fields, you're not directly concerned with the land, except as a patch of ground on which your store, shop, or factory is situated.

That brings us back to capital. The important thing to realize about capital is that it encompasses more than the idea of "cash" that most laypersons associate with the term. This is important to you because, if you're thinking about going into a repair service business and you own a station wagon or a truck that you can use for making service calls, you can avoid an outlay of *capital cash;* you have the capital in the form of a potentially productive capital asset. If you have equipment and tools that you can use in your business, this constitutes additional available capital. If you own a business building, or if you can conduct the business from your home, using your garage as a workshop and a corner of your kitchen or den for an office, you further reduce the amount of capital required in the form of cash.

The point should be clear. In assessing your starting capital needs, you should think in terms of the dollar costs of capital equipment required. In comparing your *available* starting capital to the *needs,* you should attribute cash values to capital equipment that you own and can use in your business.

POINT 1-19: Starting capital can take the form of cash, equipment and fixtures, usable inventory, and buildings. Land, capital, labor, and entrepreneurship are combined to form a business.

Profit Expectations

What kind of profits can you expect? What level of sales will you need and how readily can you achieve it? These are some of the primary questions in the minds of men and women who are about to embark on their own business ventures. Simply put, *net profit before taxes equals sales minus cost of goods sold minus expenses.* Net profit after taxes is what's left after you subtract income taxes. These ideas can be expressed in equation form, and in the process we'll introduce the idea of gross profit.

Gross Profit	= Sales – Cost of Goods Sold
Net Profit	= Gross Profit – Expenses
Net Profit	= Sales – Cost of Goods Sold – Expenses
Net Profit After Taxes	= Net Profit – Income Taxes

If you require a net profit of $10,000 a year and your merchandise costs are 60 percent of your selling price (that's 40 percent gross margin on sales) while expenses are $5,000, you can compute sales needed as follows:

(Net Profit)	=	(Gross Profit)	–	(Expenses)
$10,000	=	0.4 X Sales	–	$5,000
$10,000	+	$5,000	=	0.4 X Sales

$$\frac{\$15{,}000}{0.4} = \text{Sales}$$

$$\text{Sales} = \$37{,}500$$

You'll need to have sales of $37,500 to make a net profit of $10,000 under the conditions cited.

Time Required to Reach Profitability

Few new businesses are profitable at the outset. It takes time to become established and build sales. Meanwhile, fixed expenses like rent, utilities, insurance, and salaries, plus your personal needs to support your family, continue to eat cash.

Consequently, as you assess your capital needs for starting (or buying) and operating your own business, you'll have to take into account

1. The required capital investment including start-up costs
2. Capital needs to cover operating losses till the business reaches profitability
3. The personal financial requirements to support yourself and your family until the business is able to support you

Many new businesses fail because the founder failed to consider these factors. One way to meet the pressure of the third requirement is to start your business on a part-time basis while you're employed elsewhere. Another way to meet this requirement is for your spouse to work in another job until the business is established.

You can't pinpoint the time it will take to reach profitability. You're likely to reach profitability faster if you get into a business in which demand for products or services (in contrast to the supply of products or services) is great. The demand for reliable repair services has been great in the past two decades, and people who start repair service businesses usually can achieve profitability in a short time.

Another factor in minimizing the time that it takes to make a business profitable is adequate homework and preplanning before the business is launched. For example, if you're going to start a manufacturing business, preplanning can minimize start-up time; advance selling can put you into profitable operation at the start. Similarly, if you're going to function as a merchant middleman, orders taken in advance of your formal opening can put you way ahead on the road to profitability. Preliminary advertising and public relations work with a grand opening sometimes launches a retail business into an immediately profitable start.

POINT 1-20: Starting capital must at least cover cost of equipment, inventory, working capital, and start-up plus expenses and a salary for yourself for the anticipated time to profitability.

REVIEW EXERCISES 1-D

1. Name and discuss the factors of production.
2. A business has sales of $40,000 a year. Expenses are $10,000 and cost of goods sold is $25,000. What is the *gross* profit? What is the net profit?
3. A merchant's monthly sales are $8,000. His gross margin is 30 percent. What is the cost of goods sold? What is his gross profit? If expenses are $1,000, what is the net profit?
4. What factors are involved in determining the capital needed to start a business? Discuss.

THE DOOR IS OPEN

The door is open for you to start a business of your own whether you're white, black, brown, yellow, Jewish, Catholic, Protestant, male, or female. The door is open to you if you have a physical disability. And age is no barrier.

Differences that may be viewed with prejudice in a "work beside you" or "live beside you" situation by prejudiced persons disappear in the marketplace. When it gets down to converting money into a product or service, people buy where they feel they get the best value in spite of any prejudices they may have. And prejudiced customers dealing with you over the years tend to lose their prejudice as they equate the value of your services with your ability as a person. This had been happening for centuries in the field of international trade. Marco Polo set a typical early example.

Disabilities usually don't pose any different problems in running your own business than those encountered in working for someone else. Actually, since you can pick and choose from a broad array of business endeavors, you can probably find a business that minimizes the handicap of a physical disability.

You may be 15 years old or 75 years old or somewhere between. Neither end of this age spectrum eliminates your chance to start your own business. Many youngsters under 15 start part-time businesses and earn respectable incomes. Many persons retire several times, first from a job at age 55 to 65, then from their first post-retirement business at age 65 to 70. Then some go on to start yet another business!

SUMMARY

A business of your own is within your reach. Most small businesses begin as proprietorships. You have unlimited earning power, freedom of action, opportunity for faster and greater financial growth. You can generally experience greater personal satisfaction in a business of your own than you can working as an hourly or salaried employee.

There is chance of failure as well as success. But you can increase your chances of success by learning the specific fundamentals of mini business start (or purchase) and operation in detail. Other ways to assure your chances of success are to enter a business in which you can employ your skills, traits, and aptitudes, and to learn and acquire the attributes possessed by successful businesspeople.

The fundamental objectives of a business are to make a *profit, grow,* and achieve a *leadership* position in its field. In pursuing these objectives you'll have to meet legal and regulatory requirements which include obeying the law, keeping records, and making mandatory reports. Record keeping is essential to business success because your records can show you where you're making money, where you're losing, and how to improve operations.

We'll classify businesses as

1. Service
2. Investments and franchises
3. Retail
4. Middleman
5. Manufacturing
6. Construction

Service businesses are usually easiest and least costly to start. Franchises sometimes provide advantages, but you have to pay for them.

Middlemen are classified as *merchant middlemen* (they take title to the goods they sell) and *functional middlemen* (they do not take title to goods, but merely negotiate for transfer of title from seller to buyer). Merchant middlemen are usually called wholesalers, distributors, or jobbers. Functional middlemen are usually called brokers, agents, or manufacturer's representatives.

The attributes and principles that lead to success in business are

1. Faith in your own ability to accomplish anything you set out to do
2. The practice of setting goals (objectives)
3. *Planning* to achieve established goals
4. *Organizing* for orderly operation and goal achievement
5. *Directing* work to ensure *accomplishment*
6. *Controlling* the work and pursuit of objectives to avoid deviations from the plan

Projects, work, and product costs are controlled in well-run businesses. Projects are controlled with respect to completion time with *schedules* and *target dates.* Costs are controlled by comparison of results to *standards* of time and cost determined for each job.

If you want to go into business for yourself, you'll have to be ready to work long hours and cope with a broad array of problems, nuisances, and irritations; and you'll sometimes feel that you're working more for the government, your suppliers, and your employees than you are for yourself. *If you don't have the temperament and disposition to cope with these things, you're not well-suited to operate a business of your own!*

The key factor in being able to succeed in a business of your own is learning to sense changes in the business cycle—when good times are ahead, and when recession looms. Here *vision,* the ability to look ahead, to discover trends, comes into play.

The factors of production are *land, labor, capital,* and *entrepreneurship.* In order to start your business successfully you'll need to plan on enough capital to meet initial capital requirements including start-up costs, losses that may be incurred until the business becomes profitable, and your personal support requirements.

Gross profit is sales minus the cost of goods sold. It is also the percentage gross margin times sales. *Net profit* is gross profit minus expenses, or sales minus cost of goods sold minus expenses. *Net profit after taxes* is net profit minus income taxes.

Perhaps the most important point of all is that *the service you provide is what people pay for!* (I'm using services as a general term here to mean the satisfaction and benefits you deliver.) You're providing your customer with a service when you save money for him or her, when you save a customer's time, provide convenience, improve his or her living standard, or reduce his or her worries. Spoil your customers with service, quality, attention, and convenience. They'll come back again and again and again, because to them you're the best.

KEY TERMS

Key terms will be listed at the end of each chapter. Review these terms and strive to understand them well; subsequent subject matter builds on these terms. Most of the terms in this chapter are defined in the summary; this will not necessarily be the case in the subsequent chapters.

Business cycle
Capital
Controlling
Directing
Entrepreneurship
Functional middleman
Gross profit
Growth
Labor
Lands
Merchant middleman
Net profit
Net profit after taxes
Organizing
Planning
Profit
Service
Standards
Vision

QUESTIONS AND PROBLEMS

1. What are the advantages of operating a business of your own? The disadvantages?
2. Discuss factors peculiar to a service business.
3. Discuss the difference between merchant middlemen and functional middlemen.
4. What are some of the most common causes of business failure?
5. Differentiate between solvency, liquidity, and profitability.
6. A business has assets of $15,000 (which includes $1,000 in cash and in the bank), and has liabilities (obligations) of $10,000 (of which $2,000 is due now). Is the business solvent? Is it liquid? Can you tell whether or not it's profitable?
7. Another business has assets of $15,000 (which includes $5,000 in cash and in the bank) and has liabilities of $16,000 (of which $1,000 is due today and an additional $2,000 will be due over the next year). Is it solvent? Liquid? What else can you say about it?

8. A new interior decorating business was started with $10,000 capital by a woman who had previously earned $12,000 a year working for a major department store. The $10,000 investment could have earned 8 percent if it had been invested otherwise. She figures that the net return for her enterprise should be $5,000. What should the net profit for the business be if she doesn't pay herself a salary? If she pays herself $6,000 a year? If she pays herself $12,000?
9. If the net profit of a business has to be $20,000 to satisfy the owner, what must his gross profit be if expenses are $15,000?
10. Assume the facts of Question 9. If gross margin is 40 percent, what value must sales achieve?
11. Assume the facts of Question 9. What is the cost of goods sold?
12. What are the attributes that most successful people, particularly businesspeople, possess?
13. Why are goals and planning important in business?
14. Discuss the statement, "Plan the work; work the plan."
15. What are some of the obstacles and problems small businesspeople encounter that hourly workers generally don't encounter?
16. Discuss the statement, "I quit working for the other fellow to become my own boss. Now I have everybody for my boss."
17. What are the major and foremost objectives of business?
18. You have opened a TV repair shop. You are hiring a man who is willing to work either for $6 an hour or half of the labor billed. Discuss the pros and cons of each approach. Which would be most advantageous to you initially?
19. What can you do to minimize the cash capital requirements for starting your new business?

FIELD INVESTIGATIONS AND PROJECTS

One or more projects in each chapter are asterisked. These projects involve work toward starting your own business. If you do each of these, you will have a well-developed, detailed plan for starting your business and you will have the ammunition for a venture capital proposal to lenders and/or investors.

Some of the projects are double-asterisked. These projects pertain to specific approaches, such as a franchise, or to businesses other than retail, such as manufacturing. The applicable projects will give additional depth to your planning.

*1. Interview several small businesspeople in retail, service, middleman, and franchised businesses. Organize your questions in advance to conserve their time and yours. Here are a few suggested questions to get you started:
a. How did you get started in your own business?

b. How long did it take for your business to become profitable?
c. To what principal factors do you attribute your success?
d. What were the biggest problems in getting started?
e. What mistakes should I try to avoid making when I start my own business?

Going into Business for Yourself –an Overview

2

You'll be best equipped to plan your start in your own business after you've acquired the business knowledge tools presented in subsequent chapters. However, those chapters will be easier to understand if you have a feel for the steps involved in starting a business. This chapter will present a broad overview of the business starting process. It is not intended to give you the immediate know-how to start your business. It is simply an introduction to the process. Chapter 3 and succeeding chapters will give you the skills and knowledge to buy or start and operate your business.

Look for answers to these questions as you read this chapter:

1. What is the best form of entity to use for my business? (An entity is a distinct and independent body. Most business texts speak of "form of organization." I believe "form of entity" is a better term for this concept.)
2. What steps must I take to start a business?
3. How can I determine what kind of business to go into?
4. How can I determine equipment needs?
5. How can I find a location?
6. When should I order equipment and inventory for my store, factory, or service business?
7. Is there anything I can do to speed the time to profitability?
8. Where can I get more information on starting a mini business?

FORM OF BUSINESS ENTITY

Before you lay plans, you should choose the form of business entity you'll use. The choices in the form of common business entities are *proprietorship, partnership,* and *corporation*. There are variations such as the limited partnership, the trust, and the Subchapter S Corporation. We shall be concerned only with the three basic forms.

What we refer to as "the form of business *entity*" has long been called "the form of *organization*" in business texts. We'll use the term "entity" throughout the book.

Definitions

A *proprietorship* is a business owned solely by a single individual. It is usually managed by the owner. Its income is taxed to the owner, not to the business.

A *partnership* is a business owned by two or more individuals. The partnership shares need not be equal. It is usually managed by one or more of the partners. Its income is taxed to the owners, not to the business.

A *corporation* is recognized as an entity by agreement between the state and those who form the business. It is owned by a number of people who receive shares of stock as evidence of ownership. The owners are represented by an elected board of directors who set major policy and strategy, and who hire the key operating management. A corporation is taxed as an entity and submits its own tax return.

Small businesses usually start as proprietorships, and the text assumes that most of you will utilize this form of entity to start your mini business. However, some of you, because you're forming a larger business or for some other valid reason, will want to go the partnership or corporation route. Those of you who start with a proprietorship will want to know when it becomes advantageous to switch to another form of entity.

An entity is recognized as a distinct and single body in business. However, when it gets to matters of liability and the law, the distinction is not so clear-cut. This section will spell out the potential pitfalls and advantages that accrue to each form of entity.

Proprietorships

These are the advantages of a proprietorship:

1. A proprietor is his own boss; he answers to no one
2. Since he answers to no one, he doesn't waste a lot of time and effort "conferencing" or "consulting" partners
3. Formation (and dissolution) costs are practically zero
4. Regulation and reporting are simpler, less time-consuming, and less costly than for the corporate form

5. There are tax advantages when profit is small (something like $30,000 a year or less)
6. The proprietorship is a tax conduit—that is, a proprietorship is not taxed; the profit is shown on the owner's individual tax return (IRS Form 1040)

These are the disadvantages of a proprietorship:

1. The owner has unlimited personal liability—that is, his nonbusiness assets (not protected by exemption and homestead laws) may be taken to satisfy deficiencies of his business
2. It's usually more difficult for a proprietorship than for a corporation to raise capital
3. The life of a proprietorship is limited to the life of the proprietor; hence, there is a lack of continuity

Figure 2-1 is a graphic summary of the trade-offs.

Partnerships

The advantages and disadvantages of the partnership are the same as those of the proprietorship, with these exceptions:

1. The partnership puts two or more minds and bodies to work, and should give the business greater impetus
2. The pooled capital of two or more persons should be greater than the capital of only one; credit should also be greater
3. There is some loss of unanimity of action since two or more people are involved
4. Compatible partners are hard to find; personal friction may develop between the partners and lead to failure of the business

The most common form of partnership is the *general partnership*, in which all partners have the capacity and authority to act for the business and have full liability. Another form of partnership is the *limited partnership*, which may include one or more general partners and at least one limited partner. A limited partner does not have the authority to act for the business and takes no part in the control of the business. His liability is limited to his capital contribution. *However*, if the limited partner becomes active in the control of the business, he is liable to the same extent he would be as a general partner.

Partnerships usually are most successful when the partners have different skills and interests. Thus, a good technical person and a good businessperson usually make good partners because neither cares to do what the other likes to do. This minimizes conflicts and brings the best skills to bear on specific aspects of the business. A written partnership agreement should always be drafted for a partnership, but it is not required by law. The partnership contract

FIGURE 2-1 What form of business entity?

Single proprietorship

Advantages	*Disadvantages*
1. Low start up costs	1. Unlimited liability
2. Greatest freedom from regulation	2. Lack of continuity
3. Owner in direct control	3. Difficult to raise capital
4. Minimal working capital requirements	
5. Tax advantage to small owner	
6. All profits to owner	

Partnership

Advantages	*Disadvantages*
1. Ease of formation	1. Unlimited liability
2. Low start up costs	2. Lack of continuity
3. Additional sources of venture capital	3. Divided authority
4. Broader management base	4. Difficulty in raising additional capital
5. Possible tax advantage	5. Hard to find suitable partners
6. Limited outside regulation	

Corporation

Advantages	*Disadvantages*
1. Limited liability	1. Closely regulated
2. Specialized management	2. Most expensive form to organize
3. Ownership is transferrable	3. Charter restrictions
4. Continuous existence	4. Extensive record keeping necessary
5. Legal entity	5. Double taxation
6. Possible tax advantages	
7. Easier to raise capital	

(Adapted from Wendell O. Metcalf, *Starting and Managing a Small Business* [Washington, D.C.: Small Business Administration, 1973] p. 24) should be prepared by a lawyer and should spell out all facets of the partnership arrangement, including names of firm, partner, and location; nature of the business; term (duration) of the agreement; each partner's contribution to capital; profit distribution, salaries, and draws; duties and authority of each partner; the mechanics for adding partners and dissolving the partnership.

Corporations

There are many advantages to the corporate form of entity:

1. Liability is limited to the amount of the stock issued
2. Life is unlimited
3. Ownership is easy to transfer
4. Capital is easier to raise, and larger amounts can be raised than in the case of the proprietorship or the partnership
5. Specialized hired managers usually operate corporations
6. There are tax advantages for the larger entity
7. The corporation is viewed as an entity by the state and is taxed directly

The disadvantages of the corporate form include the following items:

1. Formation and organization cost is higher than that of the other forms
2. There is more government control and regulation than for the other forms
3. A corporation's charter may restrict activities, but this usually isn't significant
4. Since the corporation is taxed directly, and since dividends paid to owners are taxed, distributed profits are taxed twice–this is double taxation
5. Extensive record keeping and reporting is required; also, there is more red tape than for the other forms of entity.

The corporation form of entity is ideal for a one-person business when profit exceeds a minimum of about $55,000 a year.[1] This critical minimum varies with changes in tax laws and regulations. In 1975 through 1978, for example, the critical minimum was about $30,000. Then a corporation paid a total of $10,500 tax on $50,000 profit, while a proprietorship paid about $17,000 tax on a joint return (over $20,000 on an individual return) before personal deductions and exemptions. The corporation tax on the same amount in subsequent years will probably be $17,500. The corporation income tax in years after 1978 is 22% on all income with a surtax of 26% on all income over $25,000. Hence everything over $25,000 is subject to a total tax of 48%.

If you decide to incorporate, obtain the services of a lawyer. He or she will be familiar with the laws of your state and will be able to obtain a charter for you.

[1] See Chapter 7 for ordering information on current tax regulations and schedules from the Internal Revenue Service (IRS).

The corporate entity is usually preferable to the partnership when more than one person has ownership in the business. The limited liability and easier transferability of ownership provide a measure of protection and flexibility that the partnership doesn't offer. While this may seem contradictory to a preference for the proprietorship, it isn't. You have control in the proprietorship that you don't have in a partnership. When partners have major disagreements, or if one of them heads down the drug, booze, or gambling trail, the business can be ruined in short order.

The *Subchapter S Corporation* (sometimes called a tax-option corporation) is a special form of corporation added to the IRS code in 1958. A corporation can form or switch to Subchapter S status with the consent of all shareholders and a valid election not to pay corporate tax on income, but instead to have shareholders pay tax on income. Taxes on the corporation's income must be paid by the shareholders even if the income is not distributed; they can also deduct their share of corporate losses. Hence, individuals with large personal incomes can shelter part of that income with losses incurred in a Subchapter S Corporation. A Subchapter S Corporation may not have more than ten shareholders.

The Subchapter S Corporation does not provide any outstanding benefits for you unless you or some of your investors have large additional personal incomes, and the business obviously will lose money for the year. The big plus for you is that you can attract outside investment because of the shelter aspect of the Subchapter S Corporation on large personal incomes in the event of corporate losses. There is also an advantage if there are corporate profits and the personal incomes of the shareholders are quite low.

Tax laws are complex and ever-changing. The Tax Reform Act of 1976 made substantial changes in the tax laws. Continuing reform and minor year-to-year changes make the laws difficult to follow. You should have some knowledge of income taxes to be an effective businessperson, but you will do well to avail yourself of competent tax accounting and legal counsel.

POINT 2-1: The proprietorship form of entity is the most generally used form for a new mini business. If ownership is divided, the corporate form is generally preferable to the partnership. As a business grows, it reaches a size that makes the corporate form advantageous.

REVIEW EXERCISES 2-A

1. What are the advantages of the proprietorship? the disadvantages?
2. Why is the proprietorship the usual form of entity chosen for a new business start?

3. At what point in the growth of your business would it be most advantageous to switch from the proprietorship entity to the corporate form of entity?

DEVELOPING THE CONCEPT

The first step in planning a new business is to develop the concept of the business.[2] This involves determining the *kind* of business it will be, *how it will be different* from businesses in the same field, and *its general requirements.*

Steps in Concept Development[3]

You may have chosen the type of business or venture that you want to start. Some of the steps that will be presented may cause you to turn back and reconsider. It's better to make a change before you make a considerable investment in money, time, and other resources than to make the commitment and find that you've made a bad choice. Develop the concept of your business and then study the field. If the field does not look productive, turn back and try another route.

In what area or areas do you intend to serve?

Bill Jackson, a clerk for a large insurance company, initially felt that he wanted to start an insurance agency. But he decided to examine other opportunities too. He examined these ten types of activity:

1. Creative/technical (such as research, writing, invention, electronic design)
2. Service (TV repair, janitorial services, motor repair)
3. Construction (home building, commercial building, road construction)
4. Manufacturing (furniture, bric-a-brac, electronic devices)
5. Selling (retailing, insurance, wholesaling)
6. Trading (stock market, commodities, TV sets, air conditioners, tools, factory machines)
7. Finance and investment (real estate, stocks, businesses, lending)
8. Rentals (homes, apartments, commercial properties, tools, automotive equipment, machinery)
9. Natural resources (prospecting, mining, timber, resort properties)
10. People resources (secretarial, sales, manufacturing, personnel contracts)

[2] There may be some debate as to whether the concept or the feasibility study comes first. These activities intermesh. You have to know what kind of business you're conducting the feasibility study for and determine the market, yet the feasibility study may show that the concept of the business must be altered to meet market needs. Concept and market needs must mesh to make the business feasible.

[3] This material borrows from the author's *Big Time Opportunities and Strategies That Turn Pennies into Millions* (West Nyack, N.Y.: Parker Publishing Co., Inc., 1973).

Bill finally decided to consider these possibilities in addition to the insurance agency opportunity:

Selling–retail (he worked in a men's clothing store after he graduated from high school)

Finance and investment–real estate (one of his former classmates was doing well in new-home sales)

When you've decided on the endeavor, determine what special features about your business will tend to make it more successful than any others in the field. What are the "pluses" that you will have to offer?

1. Experience (as a salesperson, accountant, manager, plumber, electrician, engineer, artist, or ?)
2. Personality (outgoing–salesperson-oriented; or ingoing–research-, planning-oriented; or handwork-, machinery-, physical result-oriented)
3. Sincerity (the striving to satisfy)
4. Reputation (recognized for a specific capability, such as solving electronics, manufacturing, or insurance requirement problems)
5. Wide acquaintanceship (recognized as a community leader, know all of the people in town, or know all of the people in a specific industry)
6. Large following (lots of people think you're tops in a specific field)
7. Location (downtown, near other businesses of the same kind, easy to find)
8. Convenience (on the route to many activities, home service, open evenings, or ?)
9. Credit (30-day open account, easy credit, or a bank financing plan)
10. Delivery service (daily pick-up and delivery)
11. Fast service (in at 10, out at 4)
12. Economy (low prices, cost discounts)
13. Guarantees (180-day unconditional guaranteed service)
14. Quality (the best, made to last)
15. Easy-pay plan (bank or finance company financing plan)
16. Diverse array of products or services (one-stop service or sales)
17. Higher quality of life (more leisure, less bother, greater comfort)

Bill Jackson decided that his experience fitted him for any three of the opportunities he was considering. His experience, personality, sincerity, reputation, and wide acquaintanceship would help. Because people associated him with insurance, he stuck to his original choice. He also decided to work as a real estate agent, since insurance business is associated with property sales. When he checked into real estate sales, he found he'd have to take out a real estate "salesperson's" license and serve under a licensed broker for a year. He found one who would let him sell insurance from his office as well.

Bill ended up with a free office, a ready-made insurance market on the real estate sales of the broker and his other salespeople, and the chance to make real estate sales commissions himself!

What did he stress–besides his experience? One-stop insurance and real estate service.

The list above includes just a few of the possible benefits that might differentiate your business from the other businesses in the pack. You don't have to offer them all, but you must offer something to be different and better.

Minimizing Cash Requirements

Bill Jackson's case is unique. He performed most of the start-up operations quickly once he decided on the business he was going to enter. He landed a very low-overhead operation requiring very little starting cash.

Can you get off to a similar low-overhead, low-cash start? Possibly. If you're going into a repair service that requires that you do the work in the customer's home or that you bring the work to your shop, you can operate from your home and use your garage as a shop. Other businesses that you might operate from your home are a manufacturer's representative agency, an advertising agency, a publishing company for a small trade paper, a mail-order business, a bookkeeping and tax service, a wedding service, a home improvement service, and many more. As long as you can get your business by phone, mail, or by making personal calls, you shouldn't have a problem. If you can avoid the use of a sign and heavy traffic in and out of your home, you shouldn't have a problem with zoning laws.

There are other ways to reduce cash starting and operating requirements. In Chapter 1, I listed a number of possible businesses an auto mechanic could enter. Several of these involved operating in someone else's facility. This is what Bill Jackson did.

> POINT 2-2: You can minimize cash requirements by resourceful choice of operating mode. This includes operation from your home or from another business and anything else you can do to reduce start-up and operating costs.

Other Requirements

Are you going to have to be located downtown, or can you operate from a low-traffic location? If manufacturing is your business, you don't need "downtown." If most of your business is done by phone, you don't need "downtown."

Take a look at your equipment requirements. What are you going to need in the way of tools? Machines? Automotive equipment? Handling equipment? Are you going to need any specialized test instruments?

Once you've pinned these things down, take a look at your inventory requirements. How much inventory do you need? Will it cost \$100, \$1,000, or \$20,000? What kind of variety do you need? Will 10 items do it, or do you need 10,000 items? Where can you obtain the inventory that you need? Locally, from New York, or where?

Are there employee requirements? What kind of skills are needed? What will you have to pay? Can you work with part-time help or will you need full-time help?

What are the other requirements? What about licensing? Permits? Zoning? Do you have an accountant? A lawyer? Do you have friends who can give you additional ideas on starting your business? Investigate all of these. It's very important that you take them into consideration at this point in your program.

POINT 2-3: Start-up planning includes a host of details and requirements. Explore every possible requirement and use lists to avoid overlooking anything.

Wally Wilson has decided to go into automotive automatic transmission repairs. He will work from a garage in a low-rent area (that is zoned for business) because most of his business will be by phone in response to Yellow-Page listings and ads, and by referrals from filling stations and general garages that don't work on transmissions.

Wally needs $1,000 worth of equipment and $200 worth of inventory. He has decided to start as a one-man shop. He finds he doesn't need any special license, so he is ready for the next step.

At this point Wally should go back and look over the requirements that he has determined thus far. Then he should list his estimated start-up costs. He'll have one-time-only (non-recurring) start-up costs such as machines, equipment, permits, and initial layout.

He'll also have recurring overhead costs, such as rent, telephone, advertising, employee costs, office supplies, stationery, restroom and janitorial supplies, and others that are expense items but that are not direct-cost items. He must analyze direct-cost items. When a person enters a service business, some of the employee costs will be direct costs. In the case of retailing, the cost of merchandise is a direct cost. Wally will need an initial inventory. He must take all these factors into account and estimate his start-up and operating costs.

Wally has determined his start-up costs (exclusive of equipment and inventory) to be $200 for last month's rent, $50 for signs, $50 for utility and phone deposits, and $75 for "grand opening" advertising. Start-up costs for his transmission shop will be $375 plus $1,200 for equipment and inventory, or $1,575. (He considers last month's rent as a start-up cost because he has to pay it in advance.) His monthly operating costs will be:

Rent	$200
Phone	30
Advertising	50
Utilities	30
Office supplies and miscellaneous	20
Monthly operating expense	$330

Wally decides he needs a total of $2,235. That includes $1,000 for equipment, $200 for inventory, $375 for start-up, and $660 in cash (two month's expenses) for operating cash. Actually, Wally is cutting it pretty close.

At this point you should have a pretty good general feel for the costs of start-up and operation. They may change some as you develop your plan further.

POINT 2-4: Develop a feel for start-up and operating costs early in your planning. Your minimum capital needs are cost of equipment, starting inventory, start-up costs, and operating cash.

REVIEW EXERCISES 2-B

1. Discuss the factors that you should consider in developing your business concept.
2. Make a list of other ways to reduce start-up and operating costs besides those cited in the chapter.
3. How should you determine your equipment and inventory needs and costs?
4. What is the difference between direct and operating (sometimes called "overhead") costs?

FEASIBILITY STUDY

After you've developed the concept of your business, you'll probably be all fired up and ready to go. You'll probably feel that you have a sure winner. But the rest of the world may not feel that way at all. And there may not be a big enough world in your business area. So, you'd better find out if your concept is feasible for the chosen locale.

Location

If you haven't already selected a tentative location, that comes next. Wally Wilson decided he didn't need a downtown location since most of his business came by referral or through Yellow-Page ads. Generally, repair services have wide options on location. However, they too may gain advantage from location. For example, a TV repair service located among a number of stores selling TV sets and other electronic entertainment products may benefit from the location.

Location is not too critical for manufacturing plants as long as they are reasonably located with respect to a source of employees and shipping facilities. Wholesale locations are not too crucial either, but ideally should be near the center of their customer population. Industrial parks or downtown industrial districts usually work well for either. A rail siding or truck dock accommodation may be essential.

The location for a retail business is more crucial. It must be near the center of a reasonably large segment of population that buys its products, or it must be located in a high foot-traffic area. For example, an arts and crafts shop is not likely to do well in a blue-collar neighborhood with young families, while a discount food or department store might do quite well. The age group of the population in the store area, the group's affluence, and its buying habits are prime considerations. If they don't match the store's products, image, price class, and mode of operation, you'd better look for another location.

To select a retail location, you can begin by narrowing down to a specific town, a given area in town, a given location (site), and then determining whether you have enough people in the store trading area and whether their profile fits the business. Or you can take the approach of choosing the city, area, and general location by analyzing population, growth trends, buying habits, automotive and pedestrian traffic levels, and other factors. Once you've narrowed the desired location down to an area of several blocks or a block, you can look for an available location. The latter approach is the preferred one. Figure 2-2 illustrates the selection process.

The selection of a location is an important and difficult task involving many variables. Location may make or break you.

POINT 2-5: Location selection involves different factors for different kinds of businesses. Location often isn't crucial for manufacturing, repair services, and most wholesale operations. It is particularly crucial for retail businesses. You can't sell without customers.

Market Survey

Once you've picked a tentative location, you'll want to determine if your type of business can prosper there. Besides learning whether there are enough customers who will patronize your kind of business, you'll need to determine how much of the business you might get. To do this, determine how many competitors you'll have, and estimate what part of the market will be left to you after they get their share.

You can estimate the market in a number of ways.[4] Probably the most common approach is to take the number of families in the trade area (usually available from city or chamber of commerce data) times the estimated annual expenditure for your kind of products per family.

[4] Chapter 4 enlarges on methods and sources of data for estimating markets.

FIGURE 2-2 Selecting a site

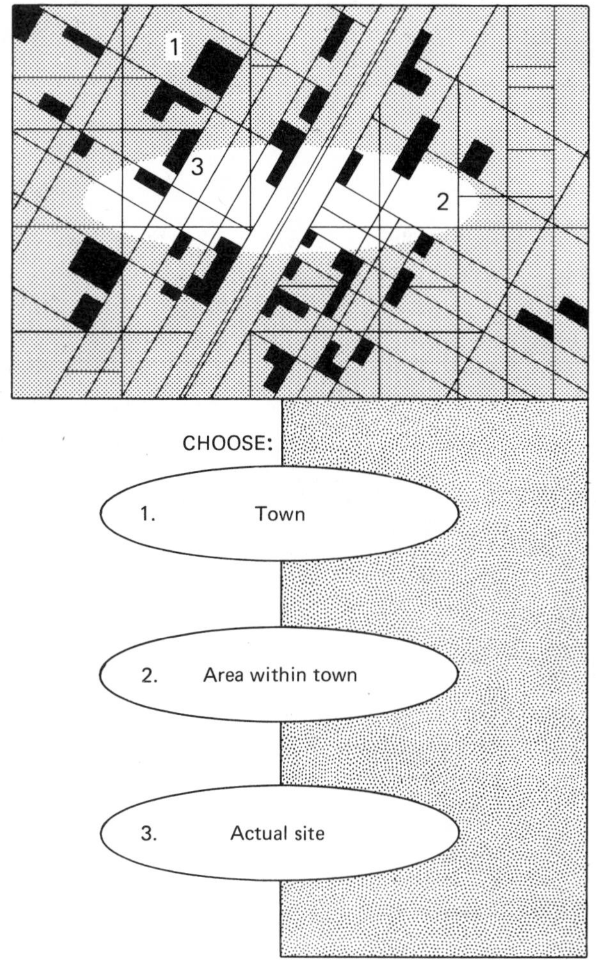

(Source: Wendell O. Metcalf, *Starting and Managing a Small Business* [Washington, D.C.: Small Business Administration, 1973] p. 29)

Then, determine who your competitors will be (by checking the Yellow Pages, city directory, chamber of commerce, or by a tour of the area). Next you can try to assess the portion of the market that each competitor will have by observation and try to determine how much you'll be able to get.

Another approach is to obtain an estimate of the inhabitants per competing store by dividing the population by the number of competitors (including yourself). Then, you can compute the estimated sales per store by multiplying inhabitants per store by annual expenditure per inhabitant for that kind of product. For example, if there are 10,000 people in the store trade area who spend an estimated $150 a year for the product, and the number of competitors in the area (including yourself) are to be twelve:

$$\frac{\text{Sales}}{\text{Store}} = \frac{\text{Population} \times \text{Annual Purchases Each}}{\text{Number of Stores}}$$

$$= \frac{10{,}000 \times \$150}{12} = \$125{,}000$$

You shouldn't assume $125,000 to be your market share since you're new and the competitors are established. You can try to arrive at an estimate of how much of that $125,000 you can get by observing your competitors and comparing the pull you expect your proposed business to have.

This kind of survey is relatively crude, but it beats guessing—especially if you're as enthusiastic and optimistic as most new business starters.

POINT 2-6: Determine that your possible share of the market is adequate before you make a final commitment on location. Make a sales-per-store computation based on total sales for your product line in the area.

How To Assess Competitors

Visit the locations of businesses that will be competitive with you. Observe their traffic and level of business. Walk in and get a feel for the way they do business and the way they treat customers. Be prepared to ask about a specific product or a specific service in order to learn more about the way they operate.

After leaving make notes of your impressions of the firm. When you have completed your rounds, put your information together. Determine whether there is room for a new competitor in the field. Work the business from the other end, too. Talk to friends and neighbors and determine their feelings about needs for the products or services you'll offer.

You don't have to make the kind of sophisticated, formal market survey the big companies make. A formal market survey often involves considerably more effort than the result is worth. But at least a simplified market survey is essential.

You can make additional comparisons by comparing the statistics on businesses in your locality against national figures. You can obtain statistics on businesses from trade associations, government publications, and trade magazines, to name only a few. One government publication that is especially helpful to an entrepreneur is the *Statistical Abstract of the United States,* published annually and available from the U.S. Government Printing Office, Washington, D.C. 20402 or its stores (usually located in the federal building in major cities). The *Statistical Abstract* will be a valuable addition to your library because it contains approximately 2,000 statistical tables, many of which deal with business and enterprise. At least, acquaint yourself with this publication in your library.

POINT 2-7: Enhance your chances of succeeding in business by sizing up your immediate competitors, and by examining national sales statistics.

REVIEW EXERCISES 2-C

1. What is the purpose of a feasibility study?
2. What are the factors to consider in choosing a location for each of the following types of businesses: (a) manufacturing, (b) wholesaling, (c) retailing, (d) repair service, (e) real estate sales, (f) a rooming house, (g) a mail-order business.
3. What is the purpose of a market survey? Explain.
4. The *Statistical Abstract* shows that there were 26,400 hardware stores in the U.S. in a recent year. They did $3,957 million in sales and had payroll of $490 million. Population was 208 million residents. Compute: (a) sales per store, (b) sales per resident, (c) residents per store, (d) percentage of payroll to sales.

START-UP: FINAL PLANS AND ACTION

At this point decisions on the concept of the business and location are firm. An estimate of anticipated sales has been made. There is still quite a bit of analysis and planning to do. And after that, there's a lot of work.

Final Analysis and Planning

Your next step is to determine your capital needs. You first determine your equipment and inventory requirements in detail and determine the total cost of each. You can get help on this from your suppliers. Then, determine other costs associated with opening such as store redecoration or factory equipment installation, signs, and grand opening costs. Total all of these costs.

In addition to these costs, you'll need to firm up your recurring costs. Using these with your anticipated sales and your gross profit margin, prepare a cash-flow projection.[5] Your cash-flow projection shows how much extra cash you'll generate or need each month. Don't forget to include a salary for yourself if you have to live out of the business.

The total capital required is at least the cost of fixed assets (equipment and fixtures), plus special start-up costs, plus inventory, plus the cash deficiency (if

[5] See Figure 11-5, Cash Budget, and accompanying text.

one exists, and it probably will) on the first year's operations, plus working capital (which we'll define in a succeeding chapter).

Some of the capital must be your own, and some must be borrowed.

You'll learn how to perform all of these steps in succeeding chapters of the book.

Financing and Banking Arrangements

Your next step is to gather your own capital (owner's equity) and arrange to borrow the needed balance.

Your owner's equity may come from savings; the sale of equity in a home, boat, antiques, jewelry; or other assets you own.

Your borrowed money may come from an insurance company (against your insurance policy), a bank, a relative, the Small Business Administration, suppliers, or any of numerous other sources.

Regardless of where the bulk of your borrowed money comes from, you'll still need to establish banking connections.

When you go to see your banker you should have a personal balance sheet (which shows your net worth), a projected income statement (which shows what you feel your business will earn), your cash-flow projection, your estimate of capital needs, and a résumé (which will show your experience). You should be able to ask for precisely the amount of money you want to borrow and show how it will be used in the business. You'll learn more about how to work effectively with bankers in a later chapter.

Establish a checking account for your business, and use it for business purposes only. Don't let personal transactions flow through this business account!

> POINT 2-8: Set up a business checking account for your business. Deposit all receipts in it, and disburse all but the most trivial payments by check. Keep your personal transactions away from this account.

Commitments and Action

Assuming your financing is all taken care of, it's action from now on. You have to nail down your location with a lease. (If you aren't familiar with leases, find out about them.) Read it thoroughly. If there's any question, have your lawyer look it over.

Next, place orders for your equipment, inventory, signs, stationery, business forms, utility service, and phone service. Meanwhile, start any redecoration or remodeling you'll have to do at your location. Concurrently with this, get plans started for your grand opening.

You'll also have to set up your accounting books. Make arrangements for such permits and licenses as may be required and insure your inventory and equipment. Get liability insurance to protect yourself. If you're going to have any employees, you'll need to advertise for them and start hiring. You'll also be working on arrangements for advertising and conducting your grand opening.

Meanwhile equipment and merchandise is coming in. It has to be installed and the shelves have to be stocked. You'll be a very busy person.

POINT 2-9: You get awfully busy as the opening date for your business nears. The only way to avoid slips is to plan thoroughly and do as much work as possible in advance.

Work Ahead

If you're employed, you'll be smart to do your survey, analysis and planning work while you're still receiving a paycheck. You can work all the way up to the point at which you have your financing and have a signed lease on your location. At that point, pull all stops and get your business into operation.

Other work that can be done before you quit your job is image planning, preliminary ad copy, choosing a name for your business, business form selection, letterhead design, sales planning, equipment and inventory order preparation, and applications for licenses and permits. These steps can be time-consuming and delaying. The more you have done before you open the doors for business, the sooner your business will become profitable.

Sources Of Information

The Small Business Administration (SBA) was created by an act of the U.S. Congress in 1953. The SBA assists small business in numerous ways. A major assist is the publication of educational and informative literature for small businesspeople.

Four free SBA publications deal with start-up planning for small businesses: *Small Marketers Aids, Nos. 150, 153, 218, and 221*. They deal with retailers, small service firms, small manufacturers, and small construction firms, respectively. You may obtain these by calling the SBA field office nearest you or by writing Small Business Administration, Washington, D.C. 20416. I suggest you request them immediately. Also ask for SBA 115-A and SBA 115-B. These are lists of free (115-A) and "for sale" (115-B) SBA publications.

Bank of America publishes the *Small Business Reporter*, a series of reports which consists of *Business Profiles*, which concerns specific kinds of businesses, *Business Operations*, which deals with specific business subjects, and *Professional Management* reports, which deal with starting professional practices. For information write Bank of America, Dept. 3120, P.O. Box 37000, San Francisco, California 94137, or ask at any Bank of America community office.

SBA publishes a *Starting and Managing* series on specific businesses. These books are for sale by the U.S. Government Printing Office, Washington, D.C. 20402, or its book stores, usually located in the federal building in regional cities. (You'll find them listed under the "U.S. Government" head, "Government Printing Office" subhead, and "Book Store" fine print in phone directories.) Watch for publication dates on these because many are quite old. Some of the older ones may contain outdated statistics or deal with businesses that are declining and no longer have the luster they once had.

REVIEW EXERCISES 2-D

1. Why should you include a salary for yourself in business expenses?
2. Capital may be either cash or an asset usable in your business. (a) What assets do you own that can be used in your business? (b) What effect will this have on the amount of cash you'll need?
3. Can you think of any ways that you can reduce the amount of cash you need for necessary equipment that you don't already own? Discuss them.
4. List as many reasons as you can think of for keeping personal transactions out of your business checking account.
5. Why should you have a lease on a building you rent for business purposes?
6. Why is prior planning and advance work on your business "money saved"?

PLANT, SHOP, STORE, AND OFFICE LAYOUT

The physical layout of your business is important because it has a bearing on the efficiency and effectiveness of your business. Layout is a complex subject, and every situation is different. The discussion in the limited space afforded here will focus on general rules and problems in layout for typical types of businesses.

The constraints on layout are physical size, physical shape, location of shipping and receiving facilities (in the case of manufacturing, large wholesale, and large repair service operations), frontage and window display (in the case of retail businesses), to name a few. Structural and utility features such as columns, points of availability of electrical power, water, and drainage may constrain you in developing your layout for an existing building.

The Manufacturing Plant

In large-volume proprietary product operations, the layout is generally by *product* with an assembly line for each product. In a custom manufacturing operation where a large variety of products are manufactured in small quantities, the layout is generally by *process*. Medium-volume plants handling several different products often have a *hybrid product-process* layout. The fundamental plant layout rule is that raw materials should proceed from receiving into processing and assembly and then to shipping in a continuous motion. Figure 2-3 shows the concept. When shipping and receiving are separate—often the case in the larger plant—the layout for flow shown in Figure 2-3 (a) can be used. In a smaller plant, the same person usually handles the shipping and receiving function, and the flow shown in Figure 2-3 (b) is often used. Where parts must be fabricated and then assembled, the layout might take the form shown in Figure 2-4.

The custom manufacturing plant layout might take the process layout form shown in Figure 2-5. Individual routing is prepared for each order. These continuous-flow arrangements reduce handling costs and time.

Manufacturing clerical personnel should have their desks stationed near the center of the area in which they're functioning. The same applies to supervisory personnel, although they are often located in a central supervisor's office on the plant floor.

FIGURE 2-3 Layouts for production flow

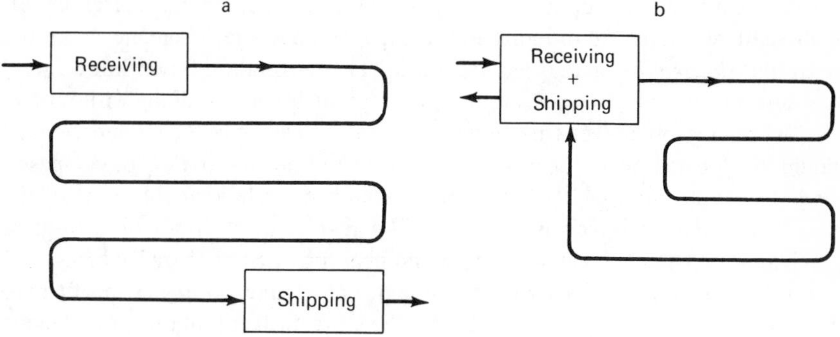

FIGURE 2-4 Layout for production flow

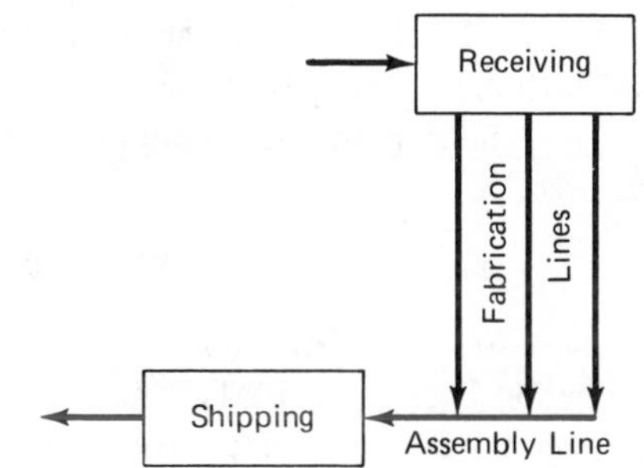

FIGURE 2-5 Flexible layout for production flow in a job shop

Receiving + Stock Room	Machine Shop	Welding Shop	Electrical Harness Shop
Shipping + Storage	Assembly Shop	Paint Shop	Electronic Circuit Shop

Repair Service Shops

Repair service shops where large items such as furniture and appliances are trucked in and out should be laid out for continuous flow from shipping to receiving just as manufacturing plants are. There should be a clear separation between incoming and outgoing storage to make it easy to know what is where.

Retail Stores

An important layout rule for small retail stores is to have incoming shipments and warehouses at the rear if at all possible; all other nonselling activity such as offices and restrooms should be at the rear of the store. There are several schools of thought on what kind of merchandise ought to be where. There are two types of traffic, *destination* and *shopping* traffic. The destination buyer knows what he wants and wants to go right to it. The shopping buyer is looking without any specific buying objective. One opinion is that convenience items and services should be located near the rear of the store so the destination buyer passes goods he would miss seeing if he could make his purchase at the front of the store. Thus, the pharmacy is located at the rear of most drug stores. Impulse merchandise is usually located up front and near high customer-traffic areas.

Another opinion is that front space is most valuable, so highest-profit merchandise should be located at the front of the store. Still another line of thinking is that the shopper circulates to the right (counterclockwise around the store), while the destination buyer goes to the left (clockwise), so convenience goods should be on the left-hand side of the store to allow destination shoppers to make purchases quickly. Since every kind of retail business is different, your best bet for developing layout ideas is to visit a number of successful stores in the same business as your own.

Wholesale Houses

A wholesale house should follow a continuous flow from incoming to receiving such as that described in Figure 2-3 (b). Fast-moving merchandise should be located nearest the shipping-receiving dock to minimize handling, with slowest-moving items near the back of the warehouse. Motion can also be saved by placing shelves and bins perpendicular to the shipping-receiving dock. Handling can be facilitated through the use of conveyors.

Service Offices

Service offices such as insurance agencies and real estate offices generally have a reception area with a reception desk, chairs, and couches at front. The receptionist usually doubles as telephone operator and typist. The agents are usually grouped in individual offices close to the reception area, and clerical workers are to the rear. Files that must be used by agents as well as clerical workers should be grouped in a location convenient to both.

POINT 2-10: Lay out your facility for continuous work flow from receiving to shipping. In the case of a retail business, strive for maximum customer exposure to all of your goods. In the service office, locate commonly used files conveniently for all who use them.

REVIEW EXERCISES 2-E

1. What are some of the common constraints in layout?
2. What are the general rules of layout concerning work flow?
3. Discuss retail store layout and objectives.
4. Why is it desirable to have a receptionist-telephone operator in a service office with five agents and ten clerical workers?

SUMMARY

The three common forms of business entity are the proprietorship (single owner), partnership (more than one owner), and the corporation (one to many owners). The proprietorship and partnership are not taxed directly on income, are easy to form and dissolve, and provide considerable freedom of action, but the owners are fully liable for the acts and debts of the business. The corporation is taxed directly on income and is subject to considerable regulation and red tape, but the owners' liability is limited to owners' investment.

The following are the steps involved in forming a new business:

1. Choose a form of entity
2. Define the "specific business" of the business
3. Decide how the business will be different from other businesses in its field
4. Develop the concept of the mode of operation of the business
5. Investigate avenues for keeping start-up and operating costs down
6. Determine broad location parameters[6]
7. *Estimate* fixed equipment, inventory, start-up, and operating costs
8. Pick a suitable location, keeping feasibility in mind
9. Conduct a simple but reasonable market survey and analysis to estimate anticipated sales
10. Get *detailed figures* on your fixed equipment, inventory, start-up, and operating expense costs

[6] A parameter is a specifying term and can be thought of as a boundary or constraint. Thus, location parameters might include (but not be limited to) (a) a population of 50,000 people within a radius of two miles, (b) location on a well-traveled street, (c) adequate parking, etc.

11. Using anticipated sales, the gross margin on sales, and your operating expenses, prepare a cash-flow statement and a pro forma income statement (a statement of expected revenue, expense, and profit)
12. Using the data of Points 10 and 11, determine your capital needs
13. Determine how much owner's equity you can raise and which assets you'll have to convert to raise it
14. Make debt arrangements with lenders to obtain the additional needed capital
15. Establish a checking account and a set of accounting books
16. Lease your location; order utilities, phone, equipment, inventory, signs, business forms, stationery, and office supplies
17. *Plan* a grand opening
18. Apply for needed licenses and permits; get insurance
19. Redecorate or remodel business site as required and install fixtures and equipment
20. Hire employees as required
21. Stock the shelves
22. *Hold* grand opening!

KEY TERMS

Concept of the business
Corporation
Entity
Feasibility study
Limited partnership
Market survey
Nonrecurring costs
Owner's equity
Parameter
Partnership
Partnership agreement
Proprietorship
Recurring costs
SBA
Start-up costs
Subchapter S Corporation
Tax advantage

QUESTIONS AND PROBLEMS

1. A proprietorship has profits of $60,000 a year. Should the owner change the form of entity? Discuss.
2. What results can you achieve by studying and evaluating several possible businesses?
3. Do you think Bill Jackson was smart or lucky? Explain.
4. Make up a list of businesses (excluding those listed in this chapter) that can be started from your home.
5. Do you think Wally Wilson's estimated expenses are realistic? Discuss each item.

6. What is the purpose of a feasibility study?
7. Discuss the relative merits of these locations for a beauty salon: (a) downtown shopping district, (b) community shopping center, (c) industrial district, (d) neighborhood shopping strip.
8. Would a discount clothing store prosper best in an affluent suburban location or a low-income area?
9. List as many kinds of retail businesses as you can. You may use references. Which references would you choose?
10. List as many service businesses as you can using the ground rules of Question 9.
11. What's the point of having a business checking account? Why not just use cash or use your personal checking account?

FIELD INVESTIGATION AND PROJECTS

*1. Pick a type of retail business in which you have particular interest. Find out how many stores are in this type of business in your neighborhood. (What references can you use? Whom can you question?) Then determine the number of residents for that type of store nationally. Is your neighborhood oversaturated with stores of that type? Finally, determine the sales per store nationally. Are your neighborhood stores getting more or less than the national average? Explain your conclusions.

2. Some of the prominent big-business periodicals you'll find in your library include the *Wall Street Journal, Fortune, Business Week, Dun's Review,* and *Forbes*. Scan them. (a) What are your impressions about the differences between big business and mini business? (b) Write to five companies among the advertisers, or call if they're local, requesting their *annual reports*. When the reports arrive, scan them and jot down your impressions. Scan them again after you have finished Chapter 6 and Chapter 7, jotting down your impressions each time.

*3. If you have a retail or service business in mind that is especially interesting to you, call or visit several wholesalers who supply that type of merchandise or parts, and tell them that you're interested in going into business. Ask them what kind of gross margin the merchandise carries, how they might work with you financially, how they might help on advertising, what promotion aids they furnish, and so on. The objective is to find out what kind of help you can expect from suppliers. Organize your conclusions in a short report.

4. A formal approach to a business case study might include:
   1. Summary of case
   2. Analysis (including possible alternatives)
   3. Statement of the fundamental problem(s)
   4. Your recommended action(s) (decision)
   5. Justification (rationale) of your decision

   Prepare a formal case report on the Bill Jackson case. Do not limit yourself to Bill's solution if you feel there is a better option.

Going into Business for Yourself —a Further Exploration

3

You've been exposed to the problems of starting a business from scratch—and probably have a good feel for what you have to do to make your business take off. But maybe you'd be better off to buy a business that is already operating. How do you know which might be a better deal? Tradeoffs (particular advantages and disadvantages inherent to each approach) will be discussed here. And you've heard about franchise riches—and ruin—as well. What about franchises? Some of the things you possibly haven't heard about are cooperative deals, syndicates, and joint ventures. You'll learn more about these in this chapter.

So far, we haven't really focused on the spectrum of opportunities available. We'll do so now, with a broad sweep of service, retail, wholesale, manufacturing, and construction, and finally, the way-out approaches the entrepreneurs—the risk-takers in the business world—follow to make a buck.

This chapter will provide answers to these questions:

1. What are the tradeoffs of buying vs. starting from scratch?
2. How can I evaluate a business that's for sale?
3. What are the tradeoffs in buying a money-maker vs. a bargain?
4. How can I negotiate to make money even before I buy a business?
5. What are the secrets of negotiating successful business deals?
6. Shall I consider a franchise?

7. What other "tie-in" deals can I explore?
8. What lines of business can I get into, and what are their characteristics?
9. Are there other business entry options?

START OR BUY?

A fundamental part of business evaluation is an examination of the financial statements. These include the *income statement* and the *balance sheet*. The income statement is based on the formula you encountered in Chapter 1:

Income = Sales − Cost of Goods Sold − Expenses

The term *income* rather than *profit* is commonly used in accounting and financial papers. The income statement covers a period of time, usually a year, and shows the profit a business has earned.

The balance sheet is based on the formula:

Assets = Liabilities + Owner's Equity

The balance sheet relates to a specific point in time—a date—and shows the net worth (owner's equity) of the business, which is what you own (assets) minus what you owe (liabilities). Financial statements are treated in detail in Chapter 7, but the elementary understanding presented here is essential for evaluating a business.

Why Buy?

Buying a business may have advantages over starting from scratch—if you make a good buy. Consider this situation:

Tim Thompson started his business from scratch with $1,000 cash, $4,000 in inventory, and $1,000 in fixtures. He lost $300 a month for the first three months and he lost $2,000 over the next nine months. In his second year, he made a profit of $3,000. His financial statements are shown in Figure 3-1. What is the minimum amount he could have paid for a going business with equivalent fixtures and inventory that made a consistent profit of $6,000 a year, and still have the same equity (net worth) at the end of the second year?

This example is included to show costs in lost profits that you may have to pay if you start your business from scratch. It will also show you why you can pay more for a profitable going business. If Tim Thompson had bought the business, he would have had a $12,000 profit during the first two years of ownership. The business he started lost $2,900 the first year and made $3,000

FIGURE 3-1

(A) Income statements

Jan. 1, 19X1 - Dec. 31, 19X1

Sales	$15,000
Cost of goods sold	9,000
Gross Income	$ 6,000
Expenses	8,900
Net income	($ 2,900)[1]

Jan. 1, 19X2 - Dec. 31, 19X2

Sales	$25,000
Cost of goods sold	15,000
Gross income	$10,000
Expenses	7,000
Net Income	$ 3,000

(B) Balance sheets

Jan. 1, 19X1

Assets		Liabilities	0
Cash	$1,000		
Inventory	4,000	Owner's equity	$6,000
Fixtures	1,000		
	$6,000		$6,000

Jan. 1, 19X2

Assets		Liabilities	
Cash	$ 600	Notes payable	$3,300[3]
Inventory	4,900		
Fixtures	900[2]	Owner's Equity	3,100[4]
	$6,400		$6,400

Jan. 1, 19X3

Assets		Liabilities	
Cash	$1,000	Notes payable	$1,700
Inventory	6,000		
Fixtures	800	Owner's Equity	6,100
	$7,800		$7,800

[1] Parentheses denote loss.
[2] Fixtures depreciated $100 a year.
[3] He borrowed $3,300 to meet cash requirements.
[4] Owner's equity at end of year is beginning of year equity plus profit (minus loss).

the second year, a total net profit of $100 for two years of operation. Here's the analysis:

Purchased profit	$12,000 (2 years at $6,000 a year)
Inventory	$ 5,000
Fixtures	$ 1,000
	$18,000
Profit actually made	– 100
Equivalent price	$17,900

So, Tim Thompson could have paid a minimum of $17,900 to purchase the other business and still been even. It would have cost him $11,900 more (the amount of extra profit he bought) to start. Since he may not reach the $6,000 a year level of profit in his business during the third and possibly the fourth year, he could have paid more to buy and still would have been ahead.

Now, let's take a look at Tim Thompson's return on equity in the business he started.

First year:

$$\text{Return on Equity} = \frac{\text{Profit}}{\text{Equity}} = \frac{(\$2{,}900)}{\$6{,}000} = (48.3\%)$$

(The parentheses denote a loss.)

Second year:

$$\text{Return on Equity} = \frac{\$100}{\$6{,}000} = 1.7\%$$

If he had bought at $17,900:

$$\text{Return on Equity} = \frac{\$6{,}000}{\$17{,}900} = 33.5\%$$

POINT 3-1: Rate of return on equity is one year's profit divided by the equity (sometimes called net worth, equity is what you own less what you owe).

Of course, Tim Thompson didn't know that his business would be unprofitable for so long. You never do know what will happen when you start a new venture. But if your planning is good and if you work your business well, you can reach profitability in a shorter time. We suspect that Tim did not know as much about business as he should have, and that he made some wrong assumptions in his planning.

If you go through a planning process such as the program of Chapter 2 or the SBA business plan and make realistic surveys and assumptions, you may be forewarned of low profitability or loss. In this case, you may want to attempt to buy.

The ideal situation is to purchase a business that is operating profitably with an established clientele. In this case, you start to make money immediately. You don't have separate start-up costs, and you don't have to dole out money in segmented purchases to establish your business. Of course, you'll have to pay more for "good will" (the business's prospects for continuing sales and profit) than you'd have to pay for a loser.

POINT 3-2: You can afford to pay for future profits if you buy a going business. Buying a going business cuts start-up time and headaches. But be sure the profit is there and is likely to continue.

A business is generally for sale for one of the following reasons:

1. Owner's age
2. Owner's health
3. Owner's disinterest
4. Owner's family situation
5. Lack of profitability
6. Loss of location
7. Bad habits
8. Failure or bankruptcy

If you pay a bargain price for a business that is going poorly or that has been forced to relocate, you can sometimes sell some of the assets to pull immediate cash. Some buyers have recouped several times what they paid for businesses in such situations. If you purchase a successful going business, there's still a possibility that you can pull cash by selling off excess assets not needed in the business. Hence, you can end up with a smaller investment than the original price and still have a going business.

POINT 3-3: You can sometimes recoup all or a major part of your investment in a going or ailing business by selling off some of the assets.

The decision to buy is an easy one if a bargain in a going business is presented to you. And it sometimes does happen just that way. But usually you'll have to search aggressively to find good situations.

Money-Maker or Bargain?

A business with substantial profitability sells for more than book value or replacement cost. (*Book value* is the net worth of a business, but it usually understates the replacement value of the business because assets have been depreciated and because inflation has increased replacement cost of assets.) Replacement cost is inadequate because it doesn't account for the cost of set-up and the profitability that is for sale. A profitable business is sometimes valued by capitalizing the profits. Suppose a business has made an average annual profit of \$10,000 a year over the last three years (over and beyond the owner's salary), and a 20 percent rate of return on investment (remember, rate of return on an equity is one year's profit divided by equity) is applied.

$$\text{Value} = \frac{\text{Income}}{\text{Rate of Return}} = \frac{\$10{,}000}{0.2} = \$50{,}000$$

This capitalization method is nebulous since value is so drastically affected by the rate of return used. If a 10 percent rate had been used in this example, the value would have been $100,000. While 10 percent is a reasonable return on a lower-risk investment, a return of 20 percent is not an unreasonable expectation for a small retail business.

There's another approach to valuation that is a hybrid of the capitalization and replacement approach. Business brokers take a more practical rule-of-thumb approach to valuing a business, and the rules vary from business to business. We'll get into these approaches in a succeeding topic. Nevertheless, the capitalization method shows worth in terms of your desired rate of return and does have merit as a tool for quick comparison and analysis. It is used extensively in appraising income-producing real estate.

POINT 3-4: You'll pay more than replacement value for a profitable business unless you stumble onto a very unusual situation.

What about a business that is not very profitable? If you capitalize the profits, the value will probably be less than the replacement value of the assets. For example, if you capitalize a business with annual profit of $1,000 at 20 percent, the value is $5,000. (Divide $1,000 profit by .20, the expected rate of return, to get the capitalized value.) Yet the replacement value of the assets may be $10,000. Unfortunately for the owner, it is unlikely that he'll be able to sell the assets quickly and reap replacement cost. This brings up a new term—*liquidation value*. The liquidation value is what you can net by selling off the assets fast. It's time and trouble to sell them off piecemeal. The time and trouble is worth money. So, to get out quickly, the seller may take $5,000 cash (or less) for a $10,000 replacement value and head for Las Vegas. The emotional state of the seller of a marginal business is such that he's usually willing to take his lumps. Furthermore, he may have book value in the back of his mind, and in this case, it might be only $3,000. So $5,000 looks good to him.

POINT 3-5: The emotional state of the seller plays a big part in creating bargains or overpriced deals. Size up the seller early in your investigation.

Even when a business is marginal, buying it is often better than starting from scratch because you have a business base. A good businessperson can turn one of these bargains around and develop a highly profitable operation.

There are possible pitfalls in buying bargains. The business may have little or no good will. The performance of the business may not be reversible for a number of reasons, including obsolete inventory, poor location, or obsolete fixtures. If the business can't be turned around readily, you may have a real liability on your hands if you buy.

So take your buyer's choice. Buy profit or buy a bargain. But if you buy a bargain, make sure that the business has the potential of being revitalized. Analyze it thoroughly.

Search

How do you find businesses for sale? The first and easiest source of leads is the newspaper want-ad section in a town of any size. You'll usually find businesses listed under a "Business Opportunities" classification. Experience shows that there are many more junk offerings than worthwhile ones in the want ads. But if you want to find the gold, you have to pan the dirt. Some newspapers do simplify the job with classification by type of business. You'll find businesses advertised for sale in other periodicals such as the *Wall Street Journal* or trade specialty magazines.

The next sources of leads are business brokers. Since a broker will generally list anything he can, you won't find his business offerings sorted as to quality either. Look under "Business Brokers" and "Business Consultants" in the Yellow Pages.

At this point you'll have gleaned all the leads that are easy to come by. Your next level of search will be to query wholesalers and distributors. Business-people often let their suppliers know that they're thinking of selling in hopes of uncovering a buyer.

Bankers, accountants, and lawyers can sometimes furnish leads. Commercial loan officers in banks may know of businesses that are for sale either because loans are in default or because owners have spread the word hoping the banker will know of potential buyers. Prospective sellers often spread the word to their accountants and lawyers. Lawyers know of businesses for sale because they're involved in estate settlements. Bank trust officers may have leads on businesses for sale in the course of their activities. Chambers of commerce and officers of civic clubs and fraternal organizations may also have some leads.

Finally, you can canvass business owners directly by asking them if they'd like to sell their business. Most businesspeople are willing to sell, but not anxious to sell. Planting the seed with the "Would you sell?" question and showing a more than casual interest in buying the business may arouse that person's interest in selling and eventually make him anxious to sell.

> POINT 3-6: You can locate businesses for sale in want ads; through brokers; through leads from bankers, accountants, and lawyers; or by canvassing business owners.

What do you do with your leads after you get them? Try telephone calls on the ads for starters. This will enable you to eliminate some. When you have culled your list of businesses to those you want to investigate further, set up appointments and look them over. Brokers will generally want to show you the business and usually don't identify a business over the phone.

Investigation and Analysis

Many sellers look for fools rather than buyers. This is particularly true about sellers of businesses. And the buyers are more often fools than not. Investigate and analyze the business in detail. Don't let your optimism cause you to buy before your investigation and analysis is complete. Verify—don't assume the seller to be a paragon of virtue and honesty.

First, apply this checklist:

1. What's the reason for selling? Is it plausible? Verify.
2. How long has the person owned the business? If less than five years, who owned it before and why did he sell? If it has changed hands three times or more in five years, perhaps you should pass.
3. Is it well located? Would you consider it as a location for a new start? What about the neighborhood? Parking?
4. Are fixtures and equipment adequate and appropriate? Watch out for worn-out, obsolete, and unnecessary equipment.
5. Is the inventory clean, fresh, and currently salable? Is it heavy on slow-moving items and short on fast sellers?
6. Is the store or plant in good repair? Does it need painting? New floor covering? Better lighting? Air conditioning? Does the roof leak? How's the plumbing?
7. Is the lease favorable? Does it have a favorable renewal clause? Watch out for percentage leases[1] and leases about to expire without firm renewal terms.
8. What about the equipment, fixtures, and inventory? Are any of these assets pledged (as debt collateral[2])? Is any of the equipment leased?
9. Do existing agreements limit freedom of operation? Look for franchise agreements, contracts to supply goods or services at disadvantageous prices, and contracts to buy goods and services including Yellow-Page advertising commitments.
10. Are the employees courteous and efficient? How long have they worked there? Will they stay if the business is sold?
11. Is the business so complex and technical that you'd have a problem running it?
12. Does the business depend on the contacts and following of the owner

[1] A percentage lease obligates to the renter (lessee) to pay the owner (lessor) a percentage of his sales. The lease may be (but rarely is) a percentage only, a fixed rental plus percentage, or a percentage with a fixed minimum.

[2] When an asset is pledged as collateral, the borrower cannot transfer clear title to it. However, you can (preferably with the lender's permission) assume the debt. This is one way to obtain debt capital quickly and easily. When you pay off the debt, you have clear title to the asset.

to such an extent that his departure will reduce sales? Is he willing to sign a covenant not to compete? Is he planning to go to work for a competitor?

13. Check the reputation of the business and the businessperson with his banker, the chamber of commerce, his customers, and his competitors.
14. Check the income statements and the owner's income tax returns for the last three to five years. Be sure they match. Look for growth in sales and profits and watch out for rapidly rising expenses. Apply the ratio techniques you'll learn in the chapter on finance and check them against the medians for like businesses.
15. Check the balance sheet in detail. Look for debt items. Run the ratios and compare to like business medians. Check the working capital requirements. How much cash will you need in addition to the purchase price or down payment?
16. Will the owner sell the business on terms? If so, what's the down payment? What's the debt service? How much cash will you have left from each month's operations after you make your payment to him?

POINT 3-7: If you buy a business, you may be stuck with a bad deal. Investigate it thoroughly before you buy. Use the sixteen-point checklist presented above. Above all, take your time.

That's just the beginning. Don't get into full detail and verification on the first visit. Do items 1 through 6 and examine the latest income statement and balance sheet on the first visit. Most of these steps only require observation and don't take long. If you're still interested, ask the owner for copies of the latest income statement and balance sheet. If he'll allow you, take them home to perform your analysis.

If your analysis of the financial statements is favorable, call the owner back in three to five days, and tell him you're interested and want to investigate further. Meanwhile, perform steps 13 and 15. On your second visit, cover items 7 through 12, 14, and 16. *But don't start to negotiate*! If it still looks like a good deal, you're ready to analyze the owner's price.

We'll introduce the hybrid approach first:

Let Adjusted Value	=	Appraised value of tangible assets if available; otherwise use
Adjusted Value	=	Owner's Equity – Cash
Let Adjusted Earnings	=	3 (Profit – Earning Power)
Where Earning Power	=	Your Annual Salary + (Rate of Return X Adjusted Value)
Then Price	=	Adjusted Value + Adjusted Earnings

This formula compensates profit for your personal earning power and the earning power of your investment on the adjusted value. In some of our previous computations the owner's salary was compensated separately before stating owner's profit. Since the income statement of a proprietorship includes the owner's salary (draw) in the profit, it doesn't show up as a salary on the statement. Now, to whittle this down to a short, quick formula, let's assume rate of return at 10 percent. The quick easy formula is:

$$\text{Price} = \text{Adjusted Value} + 3\,(\text{Profit} - \text{Salary} - 0.1\ \text{Adjusted Value})$$

Thus if adjusted value is \$50,000, profit \$25,000, and your salary \$12,000,

$$\begin{aligned}\text{Price} &= \$50{,}000 + 3(\$25{,}000 - 12{,}000 - 0.1 \times 50{,}000)\\ &= \$50{,}000 + 3(\$8{,}000) = \$74{,}000\end{aligned}$$

If the business is more than ten years old and has shown consistent good growth, you can change the 3 in the adjusted earnings formula to 4 or even 5. Why? Earnings have magnitude–it's so many dollars this year. They also have quality. If they've been consistently good for many years, they have high quality, are more likely to continue, and are worth more.

Business brokers have rules of thumb which they apply to businesses. The rules are different for different businesses. For example, drugstores generally sell for a price based on fair market value for fixture and equipment; inventory at cost; accounts-receivable at 90 percent of face value; and 75 percent of the average annual profit for the last three years for good will. Florists sell for fair market value of equipment and inventory plus 25 percent of the annual gross for the best of the last five years.[3]

If, after you've valued the business, the computed value is within 20 percent of the asking price, you can move ahead. At this point it's a good idea to get your accountant into the act. Show him what you've done and let him look the deal over. He should visit the owner with you and check the books. This simply applies expert knowledge that may uncover discrepancies and weaknesses that you didn't notice. If it passes the accountant's review, get verbal negotiations started.

Negotiation

Here's where you make or give away money. Negotiation is one of the most important arts in the business world. Consider this an important tool that you can use in buying or selling anything. The example here, of a business purchase negotiation, should point the way for any kind of negotiation.

First, review the seller's motives, character, and personality mentally. How

[3] James M. Hansen, *Guide To Buying or Selling a Business* (Englewood Cliffs, N.J.: Prentice-Hall, Inc., 1975).

badly does he want out? What will he do when he's out? Does he need cash? Will he sell on terms? You should be able to build a pretty good profile of him from your series of discussions with him.

Next, consider price. Suppose your evaluation showed the business to be worth $40,000 and he wants $50,000. Offer him $40,000 or less.

Suppose he only asked $40,000 and your evaluation showed the business to be worth $50,000. Offer him $35,000. There's a good chance he'll take it. If he does, you've made $5,000 in a very short time. If he doesn't, you may still get if for less then $40,000.

Suppose your evaluation of the business and his price matched at $50,000. Offer him $40,000. He may take it. If he doesn't you'll probably negotiate to some number under $50,000. Don't press him for a decision. Let him think it over.

POINT 3-8: Never offer as much as the price you're willing to pay when you start a negotiation. You may buy for less!

If you want to buy on terms, go in with the lowest down payment you think he could possibly accept. Set a low interest rate (say 6 percent) and offer amortizing payments over a five-year to ten-year term. (Bankers, mortgage lenders, title insurance companies, and real estate brokers have amortization tables available. Title insurance companies often have them imprinted and may give you a copy if you drop in and ask for them.)

You'll have several things that the seller may argue about–the low interest, low price, and low down payment. That's great. You want to start him talking. When that happens, negotiations have begun.

POINT 3-9: Try to get seller financing for high-cost assets. Strive for low interest and long term.

If the seller says he wants all cash, point out the income tax consequences of a cash sale to him. (You'll learn more about taxes later.) If he takes it all in cash this year, it moves him up several tax brackets, and Uncle Sam may get a bunch of it. He needs to make an installment sale to avoid this. If he sells for $40,000 with $10,000 down, and the rest over five to ten years, he'll cut the tax bite way down. Once you win this point, he'll hit the interest. He wants 9 percent. Give a little. Try to reach a compromise at 7 percent to 8 percent. Once you have his second concession, you can be reasonably sure he wants to make a deal.

POINT 3-10: Be ready to show that the terms you propose provide benefits to the other party in a negotiation.

Next, he'll hit the price. He's firm at $50,000 and he won't budge. Try this. "Anything I pay you over $40,000 is a capital gain to you. That's taxed at a lower rate. Here's what I'll do. I'll pay $10,000 down, give you a note for $35,000 at 5 percent on a five-year amortized payout. You're getting $45,000 that way, and I'll be giving you a monthly payment of $660.49.[4] If you sold to me for $40,000 with the same down payment and 8 percent on the note, you'd only get $608.29 a month and you'd be taxed at a higher rate because interest is ordinary income."

Show this to him on paper as you say it. There's a good chance he'll accept this deal. Your objective is to keep your monthly payments as low as possible for a given loan term. If you have some difficulty following this, don't be alarmed. Go back over it and check an amortization table to learn how to come up with monthly payment values.

Tax advantages to the seller give you bargaining advantages as a buyer. If the seller has some doubt about what you're telling him, suggest he discuss it with his CPA.

Once the terms are settled, there's one more thing. That's transition assistance. You want him to work with you for a given period of time, say a week or two and thereafter four hours a week for a month or so till you have everything under your belt. If he likes the terms, this shouldn't usually be hard to get agreement on. After all, if you don't succeed, he won't get his payments!

You're ready to get your lawyer in on the deal to draft the contract (or check it if the seller's lawyer prepares it), to check title, and possibly to join you at the closing. Before you know it, you'll own a business.

POINT 3-11: If you intend to buy a business, try to get transition assistance from the seller. Get your lawyer's help on drafting or checking the formal contract when you decide to buy.

REVIEW EXERCISES 3-A

1. List the reasons for selling a business.
2. Discuss the tradeoffs in buying a money-maker or a bargain business.
3. A business has an annual profit of $25,000. The owner draws $12,000.

[4] The monthly payment was found by using an amortization table. Banks, savings and loan associations, and mortgage companies usually have them. Some mortgage companies and title insurance companies will give you one on request. Some electronic calculators, particularly the kind designated as "financial calculators," can be used to quickly find the amount of payment without the use of a table. This value can also be calculated on some scientific calculators.

So the business has a realistic profit of $13,000. What is its value capitalized at 20 percent?

4. The book value of a fifteen-year-old business is $10,000. Is fair market value of the owner's equity probably more or less than $10,000? Liquidation value? Explain your reasoning.
5. What part does emotion play in getting a good buy on a business? Discuss the emotions of the seller and the buyer.
6. Discuss precautions that you can take to protect yourself from being taken in by a fraudulent business seller.
7. The appraised value of the tangible assets of a business is $20,000. The business shows an average profit of $18,000 for the five years it's been in operation. You earn $14,000 a year. Money can be invested at 8 percent. What is the price that the business is worth?

COOPERATIVE ARRANGEMENTS, FRANCHISES, AND INVESTMENT

There are other ways to start a business. Franchising enables you to start a business without really having to start from scratch, since established reputable franchisors have developed start-up and operating methods, and they provide you with many of the benefits of buying a going business. Franchising began as a cooperative system between either a manufacturer or a wholesaler and a group of retailers. Later the franchise merchandisers entered the picture.

There are a number of cooperative approaches to business. They include pooling of purchasing power, advertising, investment and location, to name only a few. These subjects will be discussed in this section.

Cooperative Arrangements

Cooperative arrangements can be made for almost any aspect of business operation. The arrangement to cooperate may be initiated by a manufacturer or a wholesaler, or by a group of businesses. The manufacturer is motivated to cooperative effort because he knows his wholesalers and/or retailers must sell in order to keep buying from him. Wholesalers are motivated to cooperate for the same reason. National product advertising was probably the first cooperative move in that the manufacturer paid the relatively large ad cost that was reflected in very little additional product cost. The dealers thus benefited from advertising they could not have afforded to take on independently. Automobile and oil companies extended the cooperation movement by establishing dealers and giving them extra training and other benefits in addition to national advertising. This approach turned into a franchise system soon followed by other industries. A *franchised dealer* is authorized by the manufacturer to sell trademarked products or services and to identify himself to the public as a franchised or authorized dealer as long as he adheres to his agreement with the manufacturer. There is usually no initial fee to the dealer in this arrangement, but there may be a requirement for investment in facilities and inventory.

Franchises

The previous subsection defined franchises and introduced you to the earliest and still largest group of franchise arrangements, the dealer franchise. The dealer franchise rarely requires a front-end fee and the franchisor merely benefits from sales to his dealers. A dealer may sometimes have more than one franchise.

In recent decades, franchising has developed new twists. You can get a franchise for an entire store (Ben Franklin, Radio Shack, Western Auto, etc.), a motel (Holiday Inn, Quality Courts, etc.), specialized fast foods (McDonald's, Kentucky Fried Chicken, Taco Bell, etc.), and numerous highly specialized services, to mention only a few of the possibilities.

One of the twists that has developed is a fixed front-end franchise fee (in addition to other fees) for many of the franchises introduced during the last two or three decades. Another is the highly promotional nature of many of the franchises. Finally, there have been many abuses and many failures in franchising. Consider this story:

Buster Bronson decided to go into business for himself after taking a small-business course. He had $50, and decided the best he could do was start a bean sandwich business. So he built a cart, equipped it with a propane range, painted "Buster's Bean Sandwiches–The Newest Treat" on the side, and pushed it through the downtown area. In the first week he made $100. He wanted to make more, so he started working the areas around theaters at night. He made $150 in the second week. Buster decided he could do better, so he built two more carts, hired two people to work them, and he made $500 in the third week. He built two more carts and made $800 in the fourth week.

Buster was no slouch. "If I can make this kind of money in this business, so can other people. I'll show them how to do it, and the franchise fees they pay me will make even more money for me with a lot less effort."

So Buster hired a promoter and they put a franchise package together. For $10,000 and 3 percent of the franchisee's profit, Buster provided ten carts (his cost–$100 each), his secret recipes, one week of "headquarters training" (his cost–$100 per person), and other assistance such as manuals (his cost–$25), a weekly newsletter (his cost–about 50 cents per copy), and the right to use the name "Buster's Bean Sandwiches" and other trademarks he registered. Of course, his plush headquarters and staff are expensive, but Buster's doing fine.

Buster sold 1,000 franchises. About 400 of his franchises make $200 a week, about 100 make $300 to $500 a week, 50 make more than $500 a week and 450 of his franchises were out of business within a year.

This story is fiction, but it should stimulate your thinking. Before you read further, analyze the story. What are the points?

A franchisor generally offers "know-how," trademarks, training, assistance, and in some cases buying power and mass advertising. In return for this he often charges a fixed fee and possibly a percentage of the profits or a profit on the equipment, ingredients, or packaging he sells you. You take all the risks, and you often have to risk more than the mere cost of the franchise.

Now, back to Buster. First of all, why could Buster go into business with $50 and succeed, while others paid $10,000 to go into the same business? And why did 50 do exceedingly well, 100 moderately well, 400 merely make low wages, and 450 fail?

Apparently Buster was different from the rest. He was an entrepreneur and decided to find out for himself how to do it. He only had $50 to start with. His 1,000 franchisees were looking for a proven success formula. They either didn't realize that you can go into some businesses with very little money, were afraid to risk $50 to try something on their own, or lacked other entrepreneurial traits and business knowledge. So the 1,000 people either plunked out $10,000 they had or went into hock for all or part of it. Not one of them was a "Buster." This accounts for the high failure rate and the high number of mediocre performers. The 150 who did moderately to very well were people who could follow specific instructions and were willing to work hard to succeed.

As we see it, these are some of the points on these merchandized franchises:

POINT 3-12: A given type of business can be started from scratch less expensively than it can be started with a franchise. The risk of an independent start is greater, but *you have less risk.*

POINT 3-13: A franchise enhances the chance of success for a person who has limited business knowledge, doesn't want to try something all on his own, but is willing to work hard according to the franchisor's method at something he considers a sure thing.

Many franchisors have high franchisee success scores. Some rate with Buster or below on success scores. And quite a few have failed dismally. If you talk to a franchisee who has succeeded outstandingly, he'll tell you it's the only way to go. If you talk to a franchisee who lost his life savings in a failed franchise, you'll want to cry. But, noting the general success of franchising, it's obvious that there are big opportunities. Each situation is unique with respect to the franchisor, the franchisee, the kind of business, the community, the location, and other variables.

Franchise costs vary over a wide spectrum. Some personal service type franchises require only a few hundred dollars. Others require investments in the $100,000 range (not all to the franchisor).

How to Investigate Franchises

Information on franchises changes rapidly, and the investigation of franchises requires detailed, lengthy explanation. For these reasons, we'll forego further discussion and point you toward sources of information. Bear in mind that information in these sources relating to specific franchisors, fees, and specific details may have changed since some of this material has been published.

1. For an excellent general discussion of franchising, see Clifford M. Baumback, Kenneth Lawyer, and Pearce C. Kelley, *How to Organize and Operate a Small Business,* 5th ed. (Englewood Cliffs, N.J.: Prentice-Hall, Inc., 1973), pp. 116-134.
2. For a thorough and systematic approach to franchise evaluation, see C. R. Stigelman, *Franchise Index/Profile*, Small Business Management Series 35 (Washington, D.C.: Small Business Administration, 1973).
3. For an in-depth, though dated, treatment of franchising, see Harry Kursh, *The Franchise Boom* (Englewood Cliffs, N.J.: Prentice-Hall, Inc., 1968).
4. For current data on franchising opportunities, see *Directory of Franchising Organizations* (New York, N.Y.: Pilot Industries). This directory is published annually.
5. *Franchising Around the World Magazine* is published by Sutton Place Publications, 13132 W. Dixie Highway, Miami, Florida 33161.

Investment and Appreciation

When you go into business for yourself, your first emphasis is usually on profits. There's another factor to consider, and that's growth. As your business grows, so does its value; it *appreciates*. If you buy stock in someone else's company, you may buy it for *income* (dividends) and/or *growth* (appreciation in stock value).

Some entrepreneurs don't put their money into businesses that must be operated. Instead, they "invest" in assets that do not require much management. They may be looking for income along the way, appreciation, or both. Typical investments include securities (stocks and bonds), real estate, oil and gas, movies, plays, and animals (race horses, cattle, etc.).

Another aspect of investment involves the tax laws. Investment incentives in the tax laws include among others:

1. *Investment credit*—a credit on your tax bill proportional to investment in new equipment.
2. *Accelerated depreciation*—depreciation is the charge-off of equipment cost over its life; accelerated depreciation charges a larger portion of the value off in the earlier years of life.

3. *Capital gains*–earned or ordinary income is taxed according to basic tax schedules. Gains resulting from the sale of certain kinds of property held more than a specified holding period (presently it is one year) are subject to a 50 percent capital gains deduction before tax is computed.

There are other aspects of the tax law that a knowledgeable investor or businessperson should understand. Taxes are covered in greater detail in a later chapter. Understanding them will help you increase your earnings after taxes (which is what you really keep, after all is said and done).

We've brought this matter up because you may be able to get a person with high ordinary income (which means he's in a high tax bracket) to invest in your business for *tax shelter* purposes in early years (when you have high depreciation and possible losses), and for appreciation in the future. The tax shelter arises from the fact that your equipment depreciation, start-up expenses, and the lower level of business expected in early years may make your business show a loss. Your investor can deduct his (or her) portion of the loss from his income if you form a partnership or a Subchapter S Corporation; this reduces the amount of tax he has to pay. Hence, the loss has sheltered some of his other income.

While this may not seem like sound business, you can rest assured that it is. In future years as your business grows and makes money, your investor's income grows, and the value of his investment grows. He can then sell his part of the business to you or someone else, and he pays capital gains rather than ordinary income tax. You'll pay more to own your business 100 percent than if you had invested all of the money in the first place. But, if you have no other way to raise the money, this method certainly is prudent.

POINT 3-14: Investments provide *income* (earnings), *growth* (appreciation), and *tax advantages*. If you can't raise enough money to start your business from savings and by borrowing, consider investment by others as a source of capital.

When you take in a partner or sell stock, you're diluting your equity; you don't own your business 100 percent. This is called *equity financing*. When you borrow money to finance your business, it's called *debt financing*. You'll learn more about this in subsequent chapters.

REVIEW EXERCISES 3-B

1. List and discuss ways in which small retail and service businesses can co-operate with each other.

2. Discuss cooperative arrangements manufacturers or wholesalers might make with retail and service businesses.
3. Discuss dealer franchises and merchandised franchises.
4. Does a franchise guarantee success? Why?
5. What do we mean by *appreciation*?
6. Define debt and equity financing.

THE SPECTRUM OF BUSINESS OPPORTUNITIES

The types and kinds of activities that you can go into to make money are almost infinite. Our thrust in this book is on operating businesses, but the principles are equally applicable to investments. Operating businesses can be generally classified as

1. Service
2. Retail
3. Wholesale
4. Manufacturing and construction

Within these general categories there are thousands of variations. The exploration of the spectrum in this section can merely skim the surface and attempt to give you some ideas.

Service Businesses

Most small businesses started by individuals begin as service businesses because specialized skills form natural bases for service businesses. The major inventory of many service businesses is skill and the time application of the skill. Hence, a service business often can be started with very little capital. A repair service business usually has smaller inventory investment and fewer overhead workers (workers whose services cannot be sold directly).

Service output in the United States has grown at a faster rate than manufacturing output since the fifties. Over the past twenty-five years, service expenditures have increased about seven times, while manufacturing sales have increased only about five times.[5] Services are expected to continue to grow at a faster rate than manufacturing in the years ahead. Growing complexity and increased use of mechanical and electrical devices will require greater repair expenditures. Increasing complexity of government regulations and laws are increasing the need for more and new services of all kinds.

Services may be broadly categorized as

[5] *Statistical Abstract Of The United States* (Washington, D.C.: U.S. Department of Commerce, 1975), pp. 731 and 770.

Personal services
Business services
Repair services
Amusements and recreation services
Hotel and lodging services
Professional services

Personal services include laundry and dry cleaning stores, beauty shops, barber shops, photography, shoe repair stores, funeral homes, etc.

Business services include advertising, janitor, extermination, lawn care, and other services to buildings; business consulting services, computer services, credit bureaus, steno services, news syndicates, employment agencies, research and development laboratories, testing laboratories, detective agencies, security and protective services, equipment rental and leasing services, temporary help services, sign shops, and telephone answering services.

Repair services include auto, motorcycle, bike, TV, air-conditioning and refrigeration, appliance, reupholstery, watch, welding, motor rewinding, lawn-mower, furniture, plumbing, electrical, house, and numerous other services.

Amusement and recreation services include entertainers, orchestras, theatrical agencies, bowling alleys, billiard halls, dance halls, nightclubs, public golf courses, skating rinks, theaters, drive-ins, coin-operated arcades, carnivals, etc.

Hotel and lodging services include hotels, motels, trailer parks, dude ranches, and other recreational camps.

Professional services include medical, legal, accounting, architectural, and engineering services.

There are many additional services that can be listed under each of these categories. These partial listings were provided as a reminder of the breadth of activities that service businesses cover.

POINT 3-15: A service business enables you to capitalize on special skills, allows you to work closely with people, provides a variety of working experiences and challenges. Many service businesses may be started with relatively small capital.

Retail Businesses

More than $500 billion is spent annually in some 2 million retail stores which employ about 12 million people. While this includes a number of large chain stores and discount houses, there's still plenty of room for small one-person businesses. There are over 600,000 one-person retail businesses and they do more than $20 billion in sales a year.[6]

It's a little more difficult to get started in retailing than in some service businesses. Factors that make a retail start more difficult are

[6] *Statistical Abstract*, p. 771.

Location requirement
Requirements for fixtures
Large initial inventory requirement
A more competitive environment

Unless you have a large amount of starting capital, you'll probably do best by specializing. Of course, some specialty stores require unusually large investments.

Here are some retail business possibilities: building materials and supplies; heating and air-conditioning equipment; plumbing supplies; paint, glass, and wallpaper; electrical supplies and fixtures; hardware; groceries; meat and/or seafood; fruit and/or vegetables; candy stores; bakeries; tires, batteries and auto accessories; automotive parts; specialized apparel and clothing; furs; leather goods and luggage; furniture; appliances; TV; music; food (restaurants); drink (cocktail lounges and bars); drugs; liquor (stores); antiques; sporting goods; jewelry; fuel; flowers; tobacco; books; cameras; and numerous others.

Wholesaling, Brokerage, and Agency

There are middlemen who function between the manufacturer and the retailer. They are variously called wholesalers, distributors, jobbers, brokers, agents, and manufacturer's representatives.

The primary distinction is based on the ownership of goods in the transaction process. A *merchant middleman* takes title to the goods he handles and resells them. Wholesalers, jobbers, and distributors fall into this category. *Functional middlemen* do not take title to the goods they sell. Brokers, agents, and manufacturer's representatives are functional middlemen. They bring the sellers' goods to the attention of the buyer and negotiate for transfer of title directly from seller to buyer. The goods are usually shipped from buyer to seller. Functional middlemen generally work on commission.

A merchant middleman has substantial investment in inventory. He requires sufficient warehouse space for his inventory, sufficient personnel to handle incoming and outgoing merchandise, and he may need automotive equipment for delivery service. The functional middleman, on the other hand, has a small investment and low overhead. A manufacturer's rep needs only a car, a desk at home, a telephone, and several product lines. The product lines don't cost a thing other than the cost of postage and phone calls to find and get the lines.

If you like to sell, like people, and want to deal in larger-volume sales than you'll experience in a retail business, a middleman business may be just the thing for you.

> POINT 3-16: A retail or wholesale business usually requires more starting capital than a service business. However, a functional middleman operation can be started on minimum capital and has considerable potential.

Manufacturing and Construction

There are more than 300,000 manufacturing plants in the United States, shipping about $1 trillion worth of goods annually. They process food and drink, tobacco, textile mill products, apparel and related clothing products, lumber and wood products, furniture and fixtures, paper and allied products, printed and published matter, chemicals and allied products, petroleum and coal products, rubber and plastic products, stone and glass products, metals, fabricated metal products, machinery, electrical and electronic equipment, transportation equipment, instruments, jewelry, musical instruments, toys and sporting goods, and many more products.[7]

Small businesspeople may enter the manufacturing field either with a proprietory product; an innovative method for producing a standard product; as job shop operators producing parts, subassemblies, or final products under contract to other manufacturers; or as custom manufacturers or fabricators. Sheet-metal workers, machinists, foundry men, electronic technicians or engineers, chemists, printers, and fashion designers often start manufacturing companies to which they can apply their special skills.

A manufacturing company of any size requires a substantial investment. However, many small manufacturing companies have started with the owner-operator as the only employee, with a minimal investment in equipment, and often in a garage or shed. But this is a slow growth approach. Generally, any manufacturing operation with less than twenty-five employees is considered *very* small. But some companies make profits of several hundred thousand dollars a year with twenty-five or fewer employees.

Many large manufacturers have evolved from one-person garage operations in spite of the effort a small start requires. Hewlett-Packard (a multimillion-dollar test instrument and calculator manufacturer), conducted environmental tests on its first signal generator (an electronic instrument) in a kitchen stove. Charles Kaman started Kaman Aircraft Corporation in the basement of his mother's home with a $4,000 investment. Mattel, Inc. (Barbie Dolls and other toys) began when the founder, who operated a "moonlight" picture framing business, visualized his scraps converted into doll furniture.

If you have a special skill, have a special product idea, and know something about machinery and manual skills, manufacturing may be your cup of tea.

We have grouped construction with manufacturing because there are similarities. A construction business is in essence a portable custom manufacturing company. It moves its personnel and equipment to the construction site to manufacture its product, which might be a garage, a house, an apartment house, an office building, a warehouse, a road, a bridge, or any number of other manufactured improvements.

Many people get into the general contracting business by starting with re-

[7] *Statistical Abstract*, pp. 732, 733.

modeling and then building up to larger projects. Sometimes a construction company maintains all the capabilities (concrete work, glass, bricklaying, framing, plumbing, electrical, heat and air, sheetrocking, floor covering, painting etc.) within its own work force. But the approach of subcontracting many or most of these activities is more common. So there are many opportunities for companies that specialize in each of these fields. Some general contractors maintain only management and supervisory capabilities and subcontract all the actual construction. Firms of this kind are often formed by a construction specialist and an accountant partner.

You can get a start in construction with very little money if you'll start with home improvement work or a subcontract specialty and take your time growing. The required capital grows as the size of the projects you want to tackle increases.

> POINT 3-17: Manufacturing and construction businesses generally require more starting capital than other kinds of businesses, but there are possibilities for modest starts. Capital requirements can be kept low by starting with small products or projects and by specializing.

Entrepreneurial Approaches

An entrepreneur organizes and manages an enterprise and is generally long on initiative, willingness to work, and willingness to take risks. As a small businessperson, you're an entrepreneur. But entrepreneurs often find ways to make money outside the conventional business areas that we've defined. Imagination and innovative approaches provide unusual opportunities and often lead to whole new industries. Don't constrain your thinking to conventional approaches. Look for new ideas and new ways to make, market, buy, and use things.

REVIEW EXERCISES 3-C

1. Discuss the business possibilities in (a) service, (b) retail, (c) wholesale, (d) manufacturing and construction businesses.
2. Why would you expect a greater starting capital requirement in most kinds of manufacturing businesses?
3. Discuss ways in which your basic skills and experience might qualify you for a business in each of the four categories of business cited.
4. Describe two different ways a manufacturing company can operate. Do you think a manufacturer could take both routes? If so, what advantages might accrue?

SUMMARY

You can go into business by starting from scratch or by buying a going business. You can save a lot of start-up headaches and begin realizing profits immediately by buying. If you buy, conduct an intensive search and investigate the deal thoroughly. You can get leads through want ads, brokers, bankers, lawyers, accountants, and others. You can even approach an owner about selling directly.

You can buy a money-maker or a bargain. You will have to pay proportionately more for more profitable businesses, but run-down businesses can often be bought at bargain prices, sometimes at considerably less than inventory or book value. A resourceful entrepreneur can usually recoup a major portion of his or her investment by selling off some of the assets, and still have a business left. But you can buy a dud, so be cautious.

Negotiation ability is an important business skill. Specify a broad array of terms and conditions so that you can yield on several without losing what you really want. Never offer the price you're willing to pay as a first offer; always go lower. Try to get seller financing on big-ticket items such as real estate or a business. Don't hurry, particularly if the seller is in a hurry.

Cooperative arrangements can contribute to increased sales, reduced cost of goods sold, and reductions in other expenses. Cooperative arrangements can also be made to finance a business venture and reduce individual risk. A joint venture is cooperative financing of a new business or venture by two or more entities. A syndicate is a group of several investors sharing the risks and possible gain of an investment or venture.

Franchises authorize the franchisee to use the trademark of the franchisor and to sell the franchisor's products for a specified or an unspecified period of time provided the franchisee abides by the terms and conditions of the contract. The oldest (and least expensive) franchises are *authorized dealer franchises*, which usually do not have fees associated with them. Over the past several decades franchising plans based on promotion, merchandising, and management have been developed. These plans usually call for a front-end fee and a percentage of profits, but in some cases the fees are included in equipment costs and the percentage of profits is included in merchandise and supply costs. You can go into business independently for much less money than you can as a franchisee under this kind of program. Investigate franchises thoroughly before committing.

An investment can earn income and undergo value growth (appreciation). In addition, it may provide tax benefits. One or more of these factors may enable you to find investors for your business. But remember, you'll be selling equity and you won't retain ownership of all of the business.

There's a broad spectrum of business descriptions and formats. Most businesses fit into the general categories of service, retail, wholesale, and manufacturing and construction.

KEY TERMS

Appreciation
Asset
Balance sheet
Book value
Capital gains
Cooperative arrangement
Debt financing
Depreciation
Equity financing
Franchise
Good will
Income statement
Investment
Investment credit
Liability
Liquidation value
Owner's equity
Return on equity
Tax shelter

QUESTIONS AND PROBLEMS

1. Discuss the pros and cons of starting from scratch and buying a business.
2. You can buy a business for $30,000. It makes an annual profit of $6,000. What is the return on equity?
3. (a) Can you be sure that the business of number 2 above will continue to make a profit after you buy it? (b) What could cause a profit decline?
4. If you expect a 15 percent rate of return on your investment, how much could you afford to pay for a business that makes $6,000 a year? (Use the simple value capitalization formula.)
5. If the assets of a business are appraised at $60,000, your income is $10,000 a year, the business profit is $15,000 per year, and you expect a 10 percent return, compute the value by the hybrid method.
6. List a set of rules to follow in negotiating to buy.
7. What are some of the tricks an unscrupulous seller can employ to take a sucker?
8. (a) Why should you use the services of an accountant and a lawyer in buying a business? (b) When in the proceedings should they be put to work? (c) What services would you expect each to perform?
9. Joan Arnold decided to start an advertising agency. She reasoned that she'd have more business if it was located close to clients. Discuss some of the possible approaches she can take with respect to location, mode of operation, and profitable activities. (Hint: cooperation can play a part in this.)
10. If an item of merchandise costs $100 singly, $90 in 10s, and $80 in 100s, and merchants X, Y, and Z pool their purchasing power to take 30, 35, and 35, respectively, every two months, how much does each save a month over (a) the single price, and (b) the 10s price (which is probably what each would order if they weren't pooling)? (c) Translate the answers to (b) into annual savings.
11. A wholesaling company can be purchased for $100,000. It makes a profit of $20,000 annually. Four merchants who jointly buy $60,000 worth

of merchandise a year from the company decide to buy it. (a) What is the rate of return on the investment? (b) If each of the cooperators has $30,000 invested in his or her own retail business and is realizing a 15 percent rate of return, what will the rate of return on each person's combined investments be?

12. How might Buster Bronson have operated his franchise business to enhance the chances of success of his franchises?
13. Do you think a "bean sandwich" business of the type described might be successful? Discuss.
14. Barbara Watley went into business with $20,000. She made $5,000 after her draws the first year, $10,000 the next year, and $50,000 the third year. What is the business worth at the end of the third year? (Everyone may not come up with the same answer.)
15. Classify each of the following as ordinary or capital gains income:
    (a) $10,000 on sale of rental building owned for three years
    (b) $10,000 profit from operation of business
    (c) $6,000 rent collected from tenants
    (d) $500 made on sale of truck owned for four months
    (e) $8,000 in salary from employer
16. Discuss the future of services with respect to manufacturing.
17. There are needs for highly specialized repair services. To expand your thinking on the possibilities, scan the lists of *non*repair service businesses under the services subsection in this chapter and list all the kinds of equipment that require repair that come to mind.
18. There are two fundamental kinds of manufacturing. Describe and discuss each. (Construction is not one to be considered in this question.)
19. Estimate the cost of starting a home remodeling business. Assume a one-person operation without rented office or warehouse. (Hint: What equipment is required? Estimate the costs. Not everyone will get the same answer.)

FIELD INVESTIGATION AND PROJECTS

*1. Check the classified section in a city newspaper and pick five businesses for sale that look attractive to you. Call them and get as many details over the phone as you can. Classify them as profit-makers, bargain buys, and duds. Call on two of them personally, preferably a money-maker and a bargain. Analyze them by the methods discussed in this chapter. Write a report. Would you buy either? At what price?

**2. Contact three franchisees and discuss their franchise experiences. Have a set of prepared questions to avoid wasting time. Report.

3. Select a business in each of the four general categories and visit it. (I suggest an advance phone call for an appointment.) Prepare questions. Write or present a verbal report. (This can be handled as a class field trip.)

*4. Call distributors for a brand-name central air-conditioning line and a brand-name home electrical-appliance line for information on becoming an authorized dealer. Ask for copies of their contracts. Report.

Marketing and Sales

The most immediate problem of any new business is to achieve substantial sales. The sales figure is the top line on the income statement; the bigger it is, other things being equal, the bigger the profit on the bottom line. In order to achieve substantial sales, you must identify your target market and develop the proper marketing mix. These steps involve research and the development of strategy. Next comes the action, the actual selling. This chapter introduces the principles of marketing and personal selling. Chapter 5 deals with other key parts of the marketing process, advertising, and promotion, as well as public relations.

As you study this chapter, look for answers to these questions:

1. What is marketing?
2. What is marketing research? Can I afford it in a mini business?
3. How can I get an idea about how much I can sell?
4. What are some of the different ways sales are made?
5. What is a bid? A proposal?
6. Are there secrets to selling? If so, what are they?
7. What are the steps in a sales presentation?
8. What should I do if the customer raises an objection (reason for not buying)?

MARKETING

Before World War II marketing generally was regarded as consisting of personal selling, advertising, and promotion. The modern concept of marketing in big business is that it is a key management function sharing in profit responsibility and the decision-making processes. Thus, in retail concerns, buying is an integral part of marketing. In this section, we'll try to reduce big company marketing principles to mini-business size.

What Marketing Is All About

Marketing is the conduct of *functions* that make goods and services flow from *producers* to *consumers* and *users.*

The key *functions* in a small business include marketing research, advertising, sales promotion, sales, buying, and customer service. (The term "buying" as used here refers to the totality of deciding what to buy and determining what to sell, not simply to the mechanics of purchasing.) The modern marketing concept places the marketing function squarely from the front end of the production or buying cycle all the way through to the consumer or user.[1] Thus market research in a manufacturing company provides inputs that strongly influence the decision to make a product, its design, its price, and how it is to be sold. Similarly, a buyer in a retail company determines what the company will sell; he or she is working at the front end.

The importance of the marketing function in big business is further indicated by large marketing budgets, high salaries for marketing managers, and the high visibility of the marketing department in the company organization. Marketing is an integral part of top management in large, successful companies. Intelligent marketing will increase your profits and make your mini business grow big.

The ultimate goal of your marketing effort is the development and implementation of marketing strategy and tactics. There are two steps in this process:

1. Identification of *target market(s)*
2. Development of a *marketing mix:*
   (a) Product
   (b) Price
   (c) Place
   (d) Promotion

The *target market* idea stems from the approach of *market segmentation,* dividing a larger market with differing demands into smaller markets (segments),

[1] William T. Ryan, *Programmed Learning Aid for Principles of Marketing* (Homewood, Ill.: Learning Systems Company, 1971), p. 1. For further study, see Edward W. Cundiff, Edward R. Still, and Norman Govani, *Fundamentals of Modern Marketing* (Englewood Cliffs, N.J.: Prentice-Hall, Inc., 1973).

Mini customer surveys can be conducted by questioning and polling your customers and passers-by. Mini competition surveys can be made by occasional visits to competitors' stores and through discussions with competitors and with suppliers' salespeople.

Don't overlook the use of "secondary data," information that is already compiled and published, simply waiting for you to extract what you want to know. The *Statistical Abstract of the United States,* the *Survey of Current Business,* and the *Census of Business,* all government publications available from the U.S. Government Printing Office or its stores, provide vast arrays of data that are easy to tap and are useful in marketing research. *Sales Management* (633 Third Ave., New York, N.Y. 10017) publishes an *Annual Survey of Buying Power* every summer.[3] Sales are broken down as far as county-city data. This is a powerful source of marketing information. Trade association publications are also very useful and provide specific data.

POINT 4-3: Collect your marketing data with mini surveys, observation, and secondary research. Don't overdo market research to the extent of neglecting the operating facets of your business.

Market Forecasting

Market forecasting attempts to answer the question, *"How much can I sell?"* The market forecast is the basic input for all business budgets and plans. A good sales forecast should be a realistic estimate of the market; but sales forecasting is difficult, and forecasts often fall short on their estimates. A second purpose for making a forecast is to stimulate your thinking for developing your strategy and tactics.

The most common forecasting approach is to assume that sales will grow according to past history at a given percentage, or that they will grow in proportion to GNP (*gross national product,* the value of all goods and services produced in a year). This approach assumes a level economy without ups and downs, neglects the effects of a previous year's new product failure or success, and doesn't take into account new products or increased and improved advertising and promotion activity. In short, a fixed percentage growth estimate *can be part of the forecast,* but it is inadequate as a total forecast. Furthermore, if you're just starting a business, you don't have a past history to work with![4]

A more sophisticated approach, *series analysis,* is based on the use of indi-

[3] The date of issue of the *Annual Survey of Buying Power* varies.

[4] For further information on forecasting see William F. Butler, Robert A. Kavesh, and Robert B. Platt, *Methods and Techniques of Business Forecasting* (Englewood Cliffs, N.J.: Prentice-Hall, Inc., 1974).

cators to determine swings in the economy (the "ups" and "downs" of the *business cycle*). You'll learn more about this in a later chapter. But this approach is also just part of the data for a sales forecast.

A more direct approach, but one subject to human estimating optimism, is to consolidate the estimates of segments of your sales activity. If you have outside salespeople, each one will prepare a forecast for his or her territory on a regular basis, and you consolidate them. If you're a retailer, you analyze sales in each general product area, consider events that may increase or decrease sales in each area, consider the projected trend in the economy, changes in advertising, promotion, and selling strategies, and then consolidate the data. Again, if you're starting from scratch, this approach won't work in the first few years.

So, you have to start from scratch the first year. The approach presented in the market survey subsection in Chapter 2 (p. 42) is one way to assess the *total market in your area.* Market share estimations are just that—estimates. They are not extremely reliable and should be regarded in that light.

Where do you get the numbers? Consult the publications cited at the end of the preceding subsection on marketing research. A good college or larger city library should have all these publications.

In the computation of share of market in Chapter 2, we assumed equal shares. But the objective of your marketing strategy is to make the situation unequal in your favor. This factor should be considered in your forecasting.

POINT 4-4: The objective of marketing planning and strategy is to develop a superior approach that will enable you to acquire a sizable share of the market.

Summing up, an approach to making a marketing forecast for a starting business should consider

1. Your equal share of the market
2. Factors about your product or service, sales methods, advertising and promotion that will tend to increase (or decrease) your share of the market
3. Factors associated with external events such as the position of the economy in the business cycle that will influence this year's performance with respect to the date period your initial data relates to

For example, suppose you find that \$500,000 is spent on your line of goods in your county and that with your business, there will be a total of five competitors:

$$\frac{\text{Sales}}{\text{Store}} = \frac{\$500{,}000}{5} = \$100{,}000$$

This would be your equal share of the market. However, you're new, and each of the four competitors, if they shared the market equally before you came along, had $125,000 as a share. Facing this situation realistically, you'll have to concede that you'll do well to hit $100,000 in sales your first year no matter how outstanding your approaches to marketing strategy are. So assume this factor to be 1 (representing an equal share of the market).

The business cycle is on the upswing, and you estimate that business in your line will be up 20% this year. This gives you a factor of 1.2. So you bravely (and probably optimistically) forecast

$$\$100{,}000 \times 1 \times 1.2 = \$120{,}000$$

as your share of the market.

Marketing Strategy and Tactics

Let's review the marketing process briefly. Marketing performs its functions by developing *a sales forecast* based on marketing data, *strategy* (broad plans), and *tactics* (details) for moving products into the hands of consumers and users. Strategy focuses on the target market and proper blend or *market mix* of strategies concerning *product, place, promotion,* and *pricing* (the four Ps). Thus, you consider the *product* itself, its design, and the product image (social status, user age group, and product classification). You consider *pricing* in terms of costs, competition, and the market. You consider *promotion* in terms of advertising, personal selling, and sales promotion. You consider the *place* in terms of the market location, channels and middleman functions. Tactics are the individual techniques and details incorporated in the strategy.

A large part of the marketing planning effort focuses on the consumer or user. Here are some of the questions for which answers are sought. What is the geographic distribution of the market? How big is the market? What are the consumer trends in specific market areas? What are the ethnic and racial characteristics of the market area? What are the age groups? What are the income ranges of the consumers in a given market? What are the buying patterns? Answers to these questions are used to develop market profiles. Markets are segmented (broken up into different characteristics) according to these differences, and most marketing plans are developed for maximum impact on given segments (usually the predominant ones) of the market.

> POINT 4-5: Know your customers. Then aim your advertising, promotion, and sales efforts toward them.

Now, examine your own mini business. First of all, your marketing function is not limited to personal salesmanship, advertising, and promotion. Your marketing function begins when you start to select the kind of business you're going into—manufacturing, retail, wholesale, or service—and when you start to decide what kind of products or services you're going to provide. In other words, you *ought to be wearing a marketing hat even before you start your business!*

Next, as you get into the details of starting, your choice of location, store layout, methods of operation, selection of employees, and budgeting should take marketing into account. Here are some of the questions you should ask:

1. Which location will provide the most sales-per-dollar cost?
2. Will the location attract customers that match my merchandise or services? (A plush, high-priced apparel store won't fare well in a lower-income neighborhood, but a discount store probably will.)
3. Is my mode of operation geared to my clientele? (If you're selling to stable customers, you can expect reasonable payment on credit sales. If you're dealing principally with transients, your collections will probably be poor.)
4. Is product and technical knowledge more important than personal sales ability in hiring sales clerks? (If you're a wholesaler, it usually is. If you're a retailer, it may or may not be.)
5. How should my salespeople dress?
6. Should my operation be primarily self-service, or should my sales clerks sell one-on-one? (This answer influences layout.)
7. What media and promotions must I use to reach my target market?
8. How much advertising and promotion shall I budget?
9. What are the quality and other characteristics of goods and services that I must provide for my target market?
10. Who are the suppliers who can provide the kind of goods I need, render fast service, and give me competitive prices?

These questions are by no means all-inclusive, but they should stimulate your thinking on how to use marketing know-how in your business.

Specialization and Diversification

Specialization of your business differentiates it from other businesses. A business can appeal to a broad spectrum of customers with a special line of products or services, or a less specialized business can appeal to a specialized kind of customer. Thus, a business specializing in selling typewriters would sell to many different kinds of customers; a business specializing in sales to law enforcement agencies might sell everything from firearms, sirens, and uniforms to very ordinary office supplies.

The *advantage of customer specialization* is that you focus on a definite market and enter a somewhat restricted competition. The *disadvantages* are that you miss business for your product lines that are outside of your selected market, and you can suffer if the industry you service falls on hard times.

The advantages of *product specialization in a broad market* are differentiation and reduction in competition. But the period between repeat sales is usually longer if your main stock in trade consists of durable goods.

Specialization may introduce an element of instability. For example, specialization may make your business highly seasonal. Air conditioning sales and service is a typical example. Most air-conditioning companies diversify with heating sales and service as well. You can diversify to fill a seasonal void and add stability to your business by adding products and services that enjoy sales activity in the off-season of your primary specialty. Thus a boat dealer might attain seasonal diversification by selling snowmobiles in the fall and winter season.

You can also diversify by increasing your clientele. For example, a hardware dealer who sold principally to builders suffered whenever building slumped. He added kitchenware and promoted it aggressively. He soon had a booming kitchenware business, but he also became the "do-it-yourself" consultant and hardware supplier to everyone in town. His previously cyclical business is now quite stable.

Repair services flourish in bad times because consumers try to make goods last. Repair service business usually isn't as good in good times because many consumers decide to buy new rather than repair the old. Some service firms diversify by adding new product sales.

Diversification requires additional investment and expansion of working capital. A business should be well-established before a costly diversification is attempted. Many large companies have diversified, lost money in the new field, and have retrenched to their original lines of business. You can diversify and still maintain a specialist image. If you choose your secondary line wisely, you merely extend in your area of specialization.

Some Terms and Definitions

Goods are classified as consumer goods and industrial goods. *Consumer goods* are goods that will ultimately be used up for the *satisfaction* of the end buyer, the *consumer. Industrial goods* are those that are used in the *production* of other goods or in performing a service—in this case the end buyer is identified as a *user.*

Consumer goods are further classified as *convenience goods*—those generally bought without regard to price, usually small items frequently needed, not worth a shopping effort. *Shopping goods* as those worth shopping for, usually high-priced; quality, brand, and price are compared by the buyer. *Specialty goods* are specific items the buyer is looking for; he is not too concerned about price, and doesn't want substitutes. *Unsought goods* are those which creative sales and promotion efforts or new developments put before the buyer although he didn't feel a need or want for them initially.

POINT 4-6: Industrial goods are goods to be used in further production. Consumer goods are goods that are ultimately used up to satisfy the end user. Consumer goods include convenience goods, shopping goods, specialty goods, and unsought goods.

The *distribution channel* is the chain, including *middlemen* from producer to consumer or user. *The channel for consumer goods is generally manufacturer to wholesaler to retailer to consumer. The channel for industrial goods is often manufacturer through agent to user.* Middlemen who take title to goods are *merchant middlemen.* Middlemen who do not take title are *functional* or *agent middlemen.* The intermediate merchant middleman is usually called a *wholesaler,* but the terms *distributor* and *jobber* are commonly used. An agent may be a *manufacturer's representative* ("rep") representing one or more manufacturers, working on a commission in a specified territory; a *broker* who deals in specific commodity lines and gets buyers and sellers together, often on a one-shot basis; or a *selling agent* who functions as a marketing department for the entire output of his or her principals. See Figure 4-2.

FIGURE 4-2 Channels

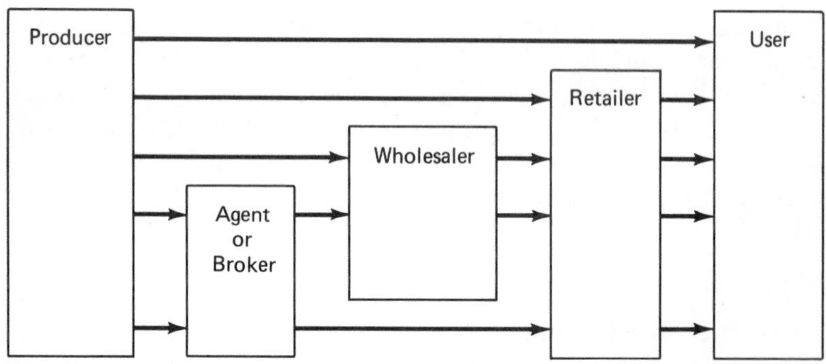

There are some *special-function* middlemen such as *factors* who are wholesalers of credit. They buy accounts-receivable and charge fees of up to about 20 percent for their service. *Field warehousemen* provide a means for segregating merchandise pledged as security for a loan on the manufacturer's premises. A field warehouse is an "on manufacturer's premises" extension service of a public warehouse.

The *retail function* is often performed by a retailer who does not maintain a retail store. The retailer *door-to-door salesperson* who sells Fuller Brushes or Avon Cosmetics, the *route salesperson* who sells from a truck, and the operator of a *mail-order business* are typical examples.

The functions of middlemen include buying, selling, transporting, grading, storing, risk-taking, financing, and providing marketing information.

REVIEW EXERCISES 4-A

1. Discuss the modern marketing concept.
2. List and describe the characteristics of the different classes of consumer goods.
3. What are the four factors in market mix? Discuss.
4. At what point in getting your business going should you begin thinking about marketing? Why?
5. How can you assess your market and your competition?
6. What are some of the publications you can consult to obtain market data?

SELLING: PRIMARY KEY TO BUSINESS SUCCESS

Selling is the primary key to your business success. Sales are the top item on the income statement. For a given margin, increased sales drive gross profits up to the point where you can cover more expenses and still realize greater net profits. Because sales are so vital to business success, salespersons are often the highest-paid people in a company. If successful selling merits such large rewards, isn't it logical that you should go all out to improve your ability to sell and to increase the "sell" aspect of your business?

As a salesperson you provide a service. You provide needed and wanted benefits for people, and show people how a product or service fills a need or a want. In the process you create markets to gobble up the output of American industry. This makes it possible for business and industry to function.

Selling in a small business embraces more than personal selling. Your selling ability surfaces in your advertising, promotion, store appearance and housekeeping, signs, displays, clerk-customer relationships, and sales policies.

POINT 4-7: Sales are vital to the success of a business. The owner-manager of a small business should have excellent sales skills, and he or she needs clerks, salespersons, and service people who can sell, too.

These are the approaches that usually come up in a discussion of what it takes to become a good salesperson:

1. Study personal selling, advertising techniques, success science,[5] and speaking

[5] The term "success science" refers to inspirational literature intended to turn you on and make you use your capabilities to their full potential. The books in the category are often grouped under *self-improvement, inspirational,* and *salesmanship* classifications.

2. Acquire experience and practice by selling for someone else before you start your own business
3. Build your self-confidence
4. Develop enthusiasm for selling and for your products
5. Use common sense in prospecting, organizing your sales itinerary, making presentations, and dealing with people
6. Develop a systematic approach to self-organization, your sales strategy, and the development of your presentations: develop answers to every objection that might be raised
7. Put a reasonable effort into your selling each day; don't start late, take a long lunch, and quit early!

This list is slanted toward the salesperson who leaves his place of business to sell, but it applies equally well to selling by phone and in your place of business. Furthermore, if business is slow in your store, why not go out and sell?

Nothing can take the place of actual selling practice. Your first presentations may seem a bit artificial. You'll say some of the wrong things. But if you'll review and analyze the attempts you made at the end of each day, you'll improve rapidly.

You're just about as good as you think you are and try to be. That sums up the story of self-confidence. If you have reservations about your ability, you probably won't be capable. If you feel that you're held back by the way you look or talk, you may be. But it's usually only because you've made up your mind that you're deficient! Salesmanship requires realistic optimism. Go into a sales presentation convinced that you'll sell, and you probably will. The opposite is true too.

Develop enthusiasm for selling and for your product. If you can hardly wait for the next selling day to come, you're bound to be successful. If you're sold on your product, you'll be able to sell it to others. Use your imagination to add impact to your presentations. To develop enthusiasm for your product, study and know it. Learn its advantages and disadvantages. Know its benefits and special features. Here are some product characteristics that you can use to build selling points based on *product knowledge:*

Style
Design
Kind of material
Finish
Construction
Uniqueness
Comfort
Beauty
Utility

Convert this product knowledge into customer benefits and appeals. For example, "You'll save money and avoid inconvenience because the rugged welded construction will make it last a lifetime."

POINT 4-8: Enthusiasm and self-confidence are key factors in successful selling. Develop these by knowing your product, talking about it and developing "sales pitches."

The Selling Process

The selling process can be subdivided into the following elements:

Prospecting
Pre-approach
Approach
Presentation
Overcoming objections
Closing the sale
Suggestion selling
Recording the sale

Prospecting is the process of finding people who are able and likely to buy. A *prospect* is a person who is able to buy (has the *money or credit capability* to buy and in the case of a commercial account, has the *authority* to buy as well) and who has the use for the product or service that you want to sell. The salesperson who calls on customers depends heavily on prospecting in his or her work. As the owner of a retail store or service shop, you can employ prospecting to make some of your pre-approach efforts more effective.

The *pre-approach* is the totality of things done to influence customers before they are met by the salesclerks in your store, or before a salesperson calls on a prospect. The factors in the pre-approach include

1. *Store advertising,* including newspaper, radio, TV, circulars (handbills), calendars, catalogs, sales letters, word of mouth, etc.
2. *Displays,* including window and interior displays
3. *Store exterior and interior,* including parking, outside signs, storefront appearance, interior appearance, neatness, and layout
4. *Previous customer experience with the business,* including service, clerk attitudes and customer treatment, satisfaction with purchased merchandise, and other good will factors that tend to bring a customer back to the store

The pre-approach factors influence the customer's confidence in the store and his or her purpose for being there.

The *approach* factors include the salesperson's appearance and actions (behavior). A neat, well-groomed salesperson with a pleasant disposition, one who greets the customer with genuine enthusiasm and courtesy, can outsell the sloppy, fumbling, unenthusiastic, discourteous salesperson every time. From an action standpoint, the proper approach consists of more than words; it's a reflection of the salesperson's willing attitude and interest in the customer's needs and desires. A cheerful "Good morning, Mr. Jones" (if you know the customer's name)—"Is someone helping you?", or "Aren't those towel designs attractive?" will help to launch the approach.

The *presentation* is the introduction of the merchandise to the customer. Remember—you're not selling your presentation; your presentation is supposed to sell the merchandise. You can show, tell about, and (depending on the merchandise) let the customer operate, feel, or smell the merchandise. Emphasize the *benefits* of owning, using, and enjoying the merchandise throughout your presentation. The customer buys to please and satisfy himself, not you. The next section will address this and the succeeding steps in the selling process in greater detail.

Overcoming (handling) *objections* consists of the art of canceling a reason not to buy in the buyer's mind and optimally, to convert the objection into a reason to buy.

Closing the sale is the culmination of the sales effort in an order, contract, or otherwise completed transaction for the merchandise presented initially or a suitable substitute.

Next in the selling process is *suggestion selling.* Suggestion is the process of increasing the total sale by selling additional merchandise or services. Thus, if you sell an air conditioner, you could make the next logical suggestion: "The guarantee covers parts and labor for a year and replacement of the compressor up to five years. Would you like the protection of a service contract on the entire unit for five years?" Or, if you sell a camera: "How many rolls of film would you like?" Follow that with, "And how many flash cubes?"

Recording the sale is simply writing it up. But this process is often handled poorly in mini businesses. Recording the sale gives you an opportunity to get the customer's name (so you can address him by name) and address (so you can mail advertising to him), and a series of sales tickets showing his purchases indicates what he's buying from you. Recording the sale on numbered sales tickets reduces the opportunity for employee dishonesty. Recording also minimizes errors that are more apt to occur with mental computations. Finally, recording sales provides basic business records needed for knowledgeable management and compliance with tax laws.

POINT 4-9: The selling process includes prospecting, pre-approach, approach, presentation, overcoming objections, closing, suggestion selling, and recording the sale.

Prospecting

How do you find people to sell? Learn the art of *prospecting*. A prospect is a person authorized and able to buy with a use for the product. Space precludes extensive treatment here, but a few ideas are in order. If you sell commercial accounts, try our old friend, the Yellow Pages, or chamber of commerce directories. Bridal salons watch engagement announcements in the newspapers for prospects. Many businesspeople check local utilities for new connections (indicating who has moved into town). Of course, there's nothing like a personal referral by a satisfied customer, but this is a slow build-up process for a new business. Prospecting is sometimes tedious, but it pays off.

Successful insurance salespeople are usually outstanding prospectors. They watch the newspapers for weddings, births, job promotions, college graduations, new business formations, and other notices of events or accomplishments that might create an insurance need or indicate a capability to buy insurance. Milk and bread route sales personnel watch for "sold" signs on houses on their routes for new prospects.

Retailers can employ prospecting profitably even if they don't have outside salespeople. Pre-approaches by mail or phone can be made. Pre-approaches to prospects can also be made through social, club, church, and other contacts, but exercise good taste in making them. The businessperson who consistently attempts to exploit social and organizational contacts is generally resented. Direct indications by prospects and names of friends who are prospects furnished by satisfied customers are sources of excellent prospects.

POINT 4-10: Prospect for new customers by watching newspapers and other indicators of need for your product or of the identity of possible prospects. A bona fide prospect has a use for your product and the ability and the authority to buy.

How to Put "Sell" in Your Business

The appearance of your place of business, your signs, your displays, and your housekeeping all can add or detract from your ability to sell. These are some key components of your pre-approach. Neat, visible, eye-catching signs can increase your store traffic significantly. Window displays work the same way. Once the customer is inside, he or she is more likely to buy if merchandise is easy to see, is neatly displayed, and if your store is clean and attractive.

Next, neat and courteous clerks who know something about personal selling, who know your products and who can help the prospect learn how to use the products, further enhance your chances of making sales.

Extra service and assurances such as guarantees, service available in event of malfunction, credit, delivery, or trade-in allowance add further to your sales.

Analyze your store to determine what kind of "sell" it has. Have some friends make this same analysis and get their reactions. Start where the passer-by may first notice your store—on the outside (see Figure 4-3). Make a visual appraisal. Then enter the store and make a visual appraisal of the interior. Eavesdrop on some of your clerks' dealings with customers. Are they practicing good personal selling? Are they courteous and knowledgeable about products?

Perk up your clerks with sales and product training. You can get some help from your suppliers. The supplier salespeople will generally be glad to conduct product briefings, show sales approaches and techniques, and provide catalogs, data sheets, and brochures. Suppliers often conduct sales meetings and sales

FIGURE 4-3 "Sell" analysis of store. Points to look for: (1) *Exterior*—visible sign both ways and from front, attractive display windows, clean plate glass, appealing view of interior, and clean sidewalk; (2) *Interior*—attractive, dust free displays, visible from entrance, strategically placed clerk (or clerks) to help customers, convenient counter for completing transactions, and most commonly purchased merchandise from middle to back of store so customer sees other items as he goes for merchandise he wants; (3) *Clerk's sales presentations and customer relations*—should assist buyer but not harass him, should make suggestions and demonstrate promotion products of the week, and should be courteous and kind, but not solicitous.

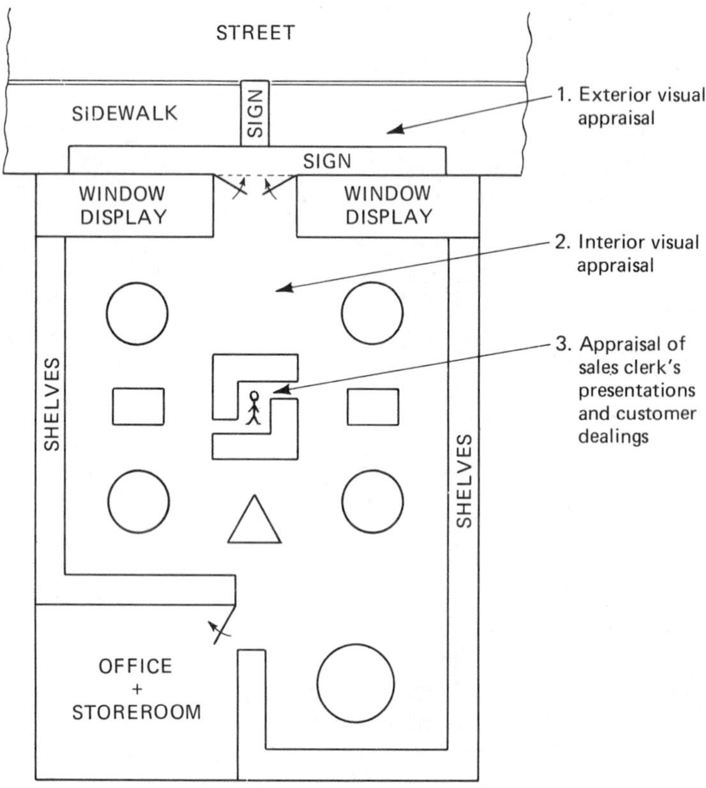

clinics for all of their dealers. They're often aided by factory representatives. Send your salespeople to these clinics whenever possible.

Always have at least one item that is to be promoted. Let's say it's a vacuum cleaner. Before the promotion begins, assemble your staff, demonstrate it, show all the benefits and superior features. There needn't be a price reduction or a premium involved in the promotion. The idea is that every customer who enters your store that week gets the demonstration unless he or she objects. You (or your clerk) will minimize objections if you get the demonstration underway quickly. You can start with, "Mrs. Jones, have you seen our new power cleaner?" (You switch it on.) "Here," (turn the handle toward the customer) "see how easy it is to push?" By this time she's involved. You have a good chance for a sale or referral.

A customer should never leave your store without your polite "Thank you. Please come again." Always proceed on the premise that the customer is right; replace unsatisfactory merchandise cheerfully. Stuff brochures on other merchandise in the bag with the customer's purchase. Set up "point-of-sale" impulse displays.

POINT 4-11: Optimize your pre-approach. Put "sell" in your entire business with eye-catching signs, attractive exterior and interior appearance, courteous customer treatment, extra service, and continuing advertising and promotion.

Steps to Surer Sales

The approach, presentation, and close used by big-ticket salespeople often follows this outline:[6]

Step 1: Break the prospect's preoccupation. Catch his attention!
Step 2: Appeal to his emotions with customer benefits that make his desire grow.
Step 3: Build the value. Show him that the value is far in excess of the investment (price).
Step 4: Ask committing questions that make the customer participate in selling himself.
Step 5: Present proof that builds the customer's confidence and influences his judgment.
Step 6: Close. Show the customer why he should buy today; be ready with clinchers.

Now, let's examine each of these steps in more detail.

[6] There are a host of good books on salesmanship written by practical professionals in print. Check under *salesmanship* in your library subject index.

Step 1: Catch Prospect's Attention. If you catch a prospect when he's preoccupied with his hobby, a conversation, a family problem, or some other attention-holder, you'll do well to arrange to see him at another time. The great interrupter is not a great salesperson. But often when a person is busy, he's involved in work that can be accomplished at any time. In this case, you're not interrupting "a labor of love" or "attention to a crisis." If the prospect is available, and if you must compete against such routine for his time, you must attract his attention.

How do you attract attention? How do you break the prospect's preoccupation?

Get to the point. Don't ever ask a person if he has time. You have a head start if you get right to the point. Try something like, "Mr. Smith, this Elliot bending machine will save you $10,000 a year," or "this Gibson air conditioner will cut utility costs 10 percent."

Step 2: Appeal to Emotions. We have emotions which, if appealed to, motivate us to respond with attention. If these emotions are excited, our desire grows and we can be motivated to action.

These emotions include the following:

1. The desire for recognition, prestige, publicity, and other forms of attention. Emotional response to these results from appeal to the ego.
2. The desire for safety, health, well-being, and shelter. The stimulation of this response by arousing fear of consequences is a secondary approach to this emotion.
3. The desire for wealth, an improved standard of living, and increased money savings as a result of purchase is sometimes called the "material," "acquisition," or "profit" emotion. "What's in it for me?" is the question that an appeal to this emotion answers.
4. The romantic emotion is a world apart from the others because it involves the desire to do things that are out of the ordinary for the individual prospect. Typical key words in appealing to this emotion are "Imagine yourself ________," or "Wouldn't it be wonderful to ________?"
5. The sex emotion involves desire to be attractive to the opposite sex and to establish a home and family. Cosmetic and clothing salespersons commonly appeal to this emotion.[7]

Step 3: Build the Value. Everybody likes a bargain. Build the value. Tell your prospect you're giving him a bargain. *You don't have to reduce the price or resort to expensive premiums.* You don't have to cheapen your image to give your prospect a bargain that will result in a sale. Build up the value!

Here are several phrases to build the value of a product:

> "Saves you $100 a year—costs only $29.95."
> "Buy this car for $4,795—before prices go up."
> "Thousands have paid $300 for this stereo—our price is $199.95."

[7] For further information on behavior and motivation, see Chapters 13 and 14.

Step 4: Ask Committing Questions. Your sale is easier to close if your prospect has gotten into the habit of saying "yes" as you approach the close. This is one reason for asking committing questions. When a customer answers your questions he is participating in making the sale. He is less likely to feel that he is being sold, and more likely to feel that he is buying. Another reason is that the customer logically constructs reasons in his mind for buying as he answers committing questions.

Step 5: Proof. Sometimes you can move right to the close from Step 4. But sometimes you'll have to present proof first. The proof may take many forms. User testimonials, financial statements, magazine articles, guarantees, or other documentation provide the proof used to convince the buyer that his judgment is good; that he's doing what other intelligent people are doing. Another form of proof might be a comparison chart or a demonstration. The most effective proof, though, is an endorsement by someone whom the prospect knows and respects.

Here are some proof and confidence-building phrases:

Testimonials: "Mr. Jones says . . . ," "Mr. Jones endorses . . . "
Approval statements: "Approved by Underwriters Laboratories"
List of famous customers
Test results: "20 percent fewer cavities"
Expert testimony: "Dr. Jones, recognized authority says . . . "
Statistics: "Four out of five auto accident deaths can be avoided with seat belts"
Guarantee: "Money-back guarantee," "Three-year warranty"

Step 6: Close. When you've taken the customer through the five steps leading to the close, you've built his interest from some relatively lower level to a higher level. Build interest till you feel that it is high enough to cause the prospect to buy, then go after the close.

A choice-type question is often effective. An example of a diplomatic close is, "Please check whether you want the blue or the black," as you pass the pencil. After the customer has checked the blank, he'll usually sign the line that you've singled out with a big X without another word. If he doesn't, ask, "Did I mark your signature line?" or—getting more direct—"Please check the order as I've written it and if it's correct, please sign it." "Do you prefer to pay cash or to budget the payments?" leads to the close, and "Shall I write this up for the twelve-month plan or the eighteen-month plan?" gets right to the point.

There are plenty of ways to close the sale, and there are plenty of ways to lose it. When you've closed the sale, leave. Even after you've closed it, you may lose it if you hang around.

You may have to be ready with a "clincher" to make a close. You work the customer toward the close. He's nearly ready to buy, but he needs an additional inducement. A premium for "buying now" is the usual inducement. The customer may state a condition to the sale. Your response should be, "I'm not sure that we can do it, but I've written it up your way. If you'll sign this order subject to approval, I'll try to get it through." The sale will usually be made.

Some of this may sound just a little like the "hard sell," and it is if you don't handle it properly. Remember, you're trying to perform a service for your prospect. And you want him or her as a long-term customer. So present a deal that will provide benefits, and proceed naturally with the six points just covered in mind.

POINT 4-12: Get attention, appeal to emotions with benefits, build value, ask committing questions, present proof, and close your sale.

Selling Pointers—Handling Objections

Correct techniques and adherence to basic rules are useful in any successful selling effort. Here are some pointers that the pros follow.

1. Single out the person or persons authorized to buy or those who influence buying decisions and make your presentation to him (or them).
2. Don't start talking about the weather and other diverting subjects.
3. Translate the benefits of the purchase into the prospect's terms and interests. Remember, he'll only buy if there are *benefits for him* in buying!
4. If the prospect's attention starts to slip, snap him back in with a question or by using his name.
5. Appeal to as many senses and functions as possible. Show samples, pictures, charts, etc.
6. Dress and look like a businessperson. Conservative dress in good taste and a clean, neat, well-groomed appearance help on sales calls. In your own small retail store or service business, less formal dress is normal.
7. Never argue with your prospect or show discourtesy.
8. Always pick up from an interruption such as a phone call with a quick review such as, "We were talking about the headline, Mr. Jones."

A good salesperson fields objections gracefully and tries to turn them into reasons for buying. An objection is a reason not to buy. Usually an objection is a signal that the prospect has some interest in buying. Here are some typical objections (O), and responses (R) that may counter them:

1. O: "Business is bad."
   R: "With this program you'll make your business get better."
2. O: "Business is good."
   R: "Isn't that a good reason to work to make it better so you'll have a firmer base when times get worse?"

or

R: "That means it will cost you less now, since your income tax is higher. It's a deductible business expense."

3. O: "But, I don't need it now."
   R. "Yes, but by working with it now, you'll be ready to use it when you need it,"

   or

   R. "Prices are going up. You'll save by buying it now."
4. O: "It costs too much."
   R: "Let me show you how it will pay for itself three to five times over in the first year."
5. O: "I don't like the color."
   R: "Do you prefer brown, red, or gray? I have those colors too."
6. O: "It's too big."
   R: "You'd rather have a ruggedly built quality product than a flimsy one, wouldn't you?"
7. O: "I don't have time to get into that."
   R: "But it will save you time—may I call again tomorrow?"

POINT 4-13: Counter an objection with a sensible reason to buy or a sensible question that reverses the emphasis or point. Develop all the possible objections that might be raised, and prepare answers in advance.

Suggestion Selling

Suggestion selling builds the dollar size of the sale. You can build the size of the sale *by selling a higher-priced* item of merchandise than that originally sought. The unethical and illegal practice of advertising a low-priced item of merchandise, then knocking it or not having it when the customer comes in, and luring him to a similar but higher-priced merchandise item, is termed *bait and switch.* A sincere effort to point out features and advantages of better merchandise without disparaging the lower-priced product should not be confused with bait and switch.

Another way to increase the size of the sale is to *suggest larger quantities*—for example, "Would you like several so you won't run out?" Or you can *suggest related merchandise* such as the film with the camera cited earlier. You can *suggest new merchandise* (which has just been introduced to the market or is new to your store), or you can *suggest a special* that the customer may not know about. You can *suggest new uses* for merchandise—"This corn popper can also be used to warm food"; and you can *suggest holiday or special occasion merchandise*—"Do you need some candy for the Hallowe'en 'trick or treaters'?"

Finally, don't forget that you can sell services with merchandise, merchandise with services, and expensive merchandise in place of less expensive repair services.

POINT 4-14: Increase the size of the sale with suggestion selling toward higher-priced, related, new or special-priced merchandise, special uses, and holiday or special-occasion uses.

Proposals and Bids

In some lines of business there isn't a set price on the goods and services sold. They are purchased instead by *competitive bidding*. In some instances the *award of contract* to supply or build will be made to the lowest bidder. This is usually the case when the item procured is fairly standard or when detailed specifications can be provided by the buyer. In other instances, the award may *not* be made purely on the basis of price. Technical approach, capability of the bidder, and other factors may be considered as well. In this case, bidders are asked to submit written proposals as well as bids.

Bids and/or proposals are generally required by federal, state, and municipal governments for larger purchases of special equipment and for construction projects. Industrial firms also follow this procurement route for larger purchases, special equipment, and construction projects.

POINT 4-15: Major procurements, construction projects, and specialized products or services are usually bought under contract awarded on the basis of competitive bids.

How Do You Prepare a Bid? First of all, let's assume a lowest-bidder competition for fifty refrigerators for a school district (for home economics classes). You're an appliance retailer and you determine that a refrigerator in your line can meet the specifications. There are five other dealers bidding who handle other brands but can meet the specs. The first thing you do when you receive the RFQ (request for quote) or RFP (request for proposal) is call your distributor (wholesaler) and tell him you want some help from him and the factory (on a low, low price) to bid this school job. (It's very important to the manufacturer, distributor, and you to get those refrigerators in the school home economics kitchens because this will give you promotional exposure to about 2,000 future refrigerator buyers every year. This kind of deal involves a *promotional* bid, hence the request for factory help.)

The refrigerator retails for $500 and ordinarily costs you $350. Delivery from the distributor to the several specified school locations will cost $25 a unit. If you had to buy at your regular cost and were to bid $375 a unit, you'd bid with no profit, and yet you'd probably lose the bid.

Your distributor comes back with a price of $230 a unit from the factory.

You decide you need to take a $25 a unit profit. The $230 unit cost plus $25 unit delivery plus $25 unit profit is $280. That times fifty is $14,000. So you bid $14,000. You may or may not win, because other dealers will employ the same strategy.

Next, let's assume you're a manufacturer and you're bidding on 5,000 subassemblies to a prime contractor.

You meet with the various department people in your factory who'll be involved in the work, show them the specification, and give them a *statement of work* which tells them (a) what each department performs in the process and (b) what to estimate on. The purchasing department usually makes raw-material quotes and the other departments make direct man-hour labor quotes. You usually have a meeting with the estimators from each department after their quotes are in to "knock some of the fat out" of the estimates. Then you have them costed, apply overheads and profit, and submit your bid.

We will discuss pricing in a later chapter. A quote or proposal is a marketing effort, and competitive bidding is an important way of doing business in government and industry.

POINT 4-16: To prepare a bid, get estimates of all costs, consolidate the costs, and add overheads and profit.

REVIEW EXERCISES 4-B

1. Discuss the statement, "A customer buys benefits, not products or services."
2. How can you improve your ability to sell? Do you think rehearsing a sales presentation in front of a mirror or on a tape recorder would help?
3. Discuss the six steps in making a sale.
4. What is an objection? What are the principles of answering objections?
5. List and discuss ways to put "sell" in your business.
6. What are some of the ways an automotive repair service operator can put more "sell" in his business?

CASE: MARKETING AND SELLING

(One or more cases will be presented at the conclusion of this and each ensuing chapter. These cases will provide practical insights to actual business problems and help you build your business and problem-solving ability. The cases may be discussed in detail, present problem and solution only (leaving computations and details to you), or be left open-ended for your solution. A set of review exercises follows each case or set of cases to guide your study).

John Cody completed a two-year course in woodworking and cabinet making. He made beautiful, original pieces of furniture and enjoyed showing his work and talking about it. He decided to open his own shop and picked a low-rent location in a warehouse district to keep his overhead down. He bought the best equipment available and used up most of his capital before he opened the doors for business. He decided that word-of-mouth advertising and some business cards were all he needed to get business. He spent a week visiting and passing cards. The cards read "John Cody, Custom Furniture Builder" with the address and phone number. His wife tended the phone and the shop while he was out.

On the third day the first call came from a Mrs. Rockell, and John made an appointment to see her. Mrs. Rockell, it developed, wanted to have her kitchen cabinets reworked.

"I don't do that kind of work, Mrs. Rockell, but I'll build you a beautiful set of original, custom cabinets that will be the envy of your friends," John told her.

"But I want these reworked and I want the trims and finish changed from this early American to a Mediterranean decor," Mrs. Rockell said.

"Oh, you don't want Mediterranean. I specialize in contemporary, and I could really fix you up for $1,500," John replied. He thought to himself, "Material will cost $1,000 and I'll get $500 for a week's labor."

Mrs. Rockell breathed heavily and said, "I'll think about it."

When John left she looked in the Yellow Pages and found "Joe Taylor—Custom Furniture Rebuilder and Refinisher." She called him, he came to her house, listened to her request, agreed continually with her reasoning, complimented her on her choices, showed her samples of trim and finishes, suggested hardware and locks, and left her house with a $1,500 contract to redo her cabinets. His new materials would cost $300, he reasoned, and he'd have $1,200 for three days' work.

When he delivered and installed the cabinets a week later, Joe Taylor brought along a color photo of a custom sewing machine cabinet he had made for another customer. Mrs. Rockell asked him to build one for her the following week.

REVIEW EXERCISES 4-C

1. Prepare a report on this case. A suitable report would contain a brief summary of the case, an analysis (including computations if pertinent), a statement of the problem(s), your recommendations, and the rationale for your recommendations. (In some of these cases, the actions have been taken and

your report might note actions you would have taken which would have altered the conclusion.)

2. This case contains a contrast. Discuss the two businessmen and their concepts of business, particularly as they apply to marketing policy and strategy and selling.
3. Did either of the businessmen use suggestion selling? Explain.
4. Prepare a list of rules to guide you in your practice of marketing and selling in your business.

SUMMARY

Sales are vital to business success. You can increase your sales by taking a sound approach to marketing management. Marketing is a key management function that is active from the inception of a business. Marketing plays a key role in everything from product design in a manufacturing business or line selection and buying in a retail business through sale and delivery to the customer. Marketing includes the functions of marketing research, advertising, sales promotion, sales, and customer service.

Goods are classified as industrial or consumer goods, and consumer goods are further classified as convenience, shopping, specialty, and "unsought" goods. Marketing moves these goods through *channels* (from middlemen to consumer or user).

In performing your marketing function you develop a sales forecast, marketing strategy, and marketing tactics. Strategy focuses on identification of the target market; the market mix of *products; place, promotion,* and *pricing* (the four Ps). Marketing research plays a key role in these developments. As a mini-business starter and owner you can't afford detailed and exhaustive research as practiced by big business, but you can apply the basic principles on a simplified basis. Examine your product or service, your market, your method of selling, your present and potential customers, and your advertising and promotion. Forecasting should be based on analysis of historic data, the business cycle, intelligence developed by salespeople, your surveys, and statistical information available from secondary sources. The goal of market planning and strategy is to make the market situation unequal in your favor.

Personal sales ability is a major function of marketing in the small company. You enhance your prospects of success by putting a "sell" emphasis in all your business activities. A clean, well-kept store with attractive displays will help your sales.

A good salesperson sells benefits, not mere products or services. Show the customer how the product will benefit him and the extra service that he will get by buying from you. Practice courtesy and sincerity in making your sales presentations. Be ready to *handle objections* and don't forget that the target is to *close* the sale. Try to increase the size of the sale with suggestion selling.

KEY TERMS

Appeal
Approach
Benefits
Bid
Broker
Business cycle
Closing
Consumer goods
Convenience goods
Distribution channel
Industrial goods
Marketing
Marketing research
Market mix
Middleman
Objections
Pre-approach
Presentation
Product knowledge
Promotion
Proposal
Prospecting
Selling agent
Series analysis
Shopping goods
Target market
Unsought goods

QUESTIONS AND PROBLEMS

1. We discussed classes of goods. How can knowing about classes of goods and the motives and methods of buying them help you develop better marketing plans?
2. List as many retail and service businesses as possible that can be operated without a store or shop. Be relatively general in your classifications or the list will get cumbersome.
3. Why should you make a market forecast? How should you use a market forecast?
4. Why should your market forecast account for a number of variables? List the variables you deem important and your reasons for feeling so.
5. For each of the following locations, list three kinds of businesses that might prosper by locating there and three kinds of businesses that would probably fail. Why? (a) A shopping strip in a low-income area, (b) a shopping strip in a medium income area, (c) a downtown store in an active business and industrial city with 500,000 population, (d) a store in a deteriorating area of a large city, (e) a medium-size shopping center in an affluent suburban area.
6. Describe the key function of marketing in larger companies. Translate this to a mini company.
7. How can you conduct marketing research in a small business without diverting too much time to the function?

8. Develop answers to these sales objections: (a) "This refrigerator costs too much." (b) "I don't like blue dresses." (c) "I'd like to have that calculator, but I can't afford it." (d) "Twenty dollars for a service call on my dishwasher! That's too much! I'd better not get it fixed." (e) "That lawnmower is too complicated for me."
9. Develop a short sales presentation for a high-quality dining room suite. Assume any product qualities you wish.
10. What are some of the approaches you can use to work toward a close other than those presented in the text?
11. Discuss methods for putting "sell" in your entire business operation.
12. How can you help and inspire your employees to become better salespeople?
13. When a small retailer has an opportunity to bid on a large procurement, what steps can he take to make his bid most competitive?
14. You want to start a general automotive repair shop. Data you have available shows that there are 75,000 such shops in the U.S., with annual sales of $3.6 billion. The U.S. population at this date was 210 million, and there were 120 million motor vehicles licensed, of which 12 million were less than a year old. There are 10,000 motor vehicles in your suburban community with three existing garages and no auto dealerships. You have no other data. Prepare your market forecast showing your computations and your reasons. (Not everyone will come up with the same forecast, yet they may all be reasonable.)

FIELD INVESTIGATION AND PROJECTS

*1. Obtain a copy of SBA's Small Marketers Aids No. 156, *Marketing Checklist for Small Retailers.* Fill it in for the retail business that you want to start or are presently engaged in.

2. Sales and Marketing Executives International (SME-I), 380 Lexington Ave., New York, N.Y. 10017 has clubs in most major cities. The membership is the elite in the marketing field. If you're located in a relatively large city, check the phone directory or make other inquiries to determine if SME is represented in your city. If so, call in, describe your student status, and ask if arrangements can be made for you to visit one of the meetings. Chances are that you can as a guest of the club or as a guest of one of the members–or you might visit and pay your own way. There's usually an inspiring speaker, a host of interesting sales managers and sales representatives, and a lot of new, creative ideas. Report to the class on your visit. Relate the ideas you obtained to small business.

**3. Defense contractors and subcontractors live by competitive bidding. So do building contractors. Identify and arrange to visit one of these in your locality. Be prepared with questions. Ask to see some of their proposals–successful and unsuccessful. Prepare a report.

Advertising, Promotion, and Public Relations

5

A business has to make sales before it can earn profit. To make sales you have to get people to call or come to your shop or store. To get people to call or come in, you have to let them know that you're in business, what services or products you offer, where you're located, and why they will benefit by buying from you. You can accomplish these ends through advertising, other promotion, and publicity. Advertising is promotion, a part of the marketing mix. It is mass selling, a prelude to individual sales.

Your public relations activity is aimed at building images of your business in the minds of the public. The word "images" rather than "image" is used because you will be different things to different people.

As you read this chapter, look for answers to these questions:

1. What kinds of ads are most likely to get results?
2. What are the principles and techniques for writing a good ad?
3. Are classified ads any good?
4. How can I measure ad effectiveness?
5. How can I run effective, low-cost promotions?
6. What is meant by "daily promotion"?
7. How can I get free publicity?
8. How is "public relations" different from "publicity" and "advertising"?
9. What is "image"?

ADVERTISING

Media, Costs, and Results

A big cut of the Gross National Product (about $26 billion in 1974, for example) is spent on advertising each year.[1] Some of this expenditure brings customers with twenty-dollar bills in their hands, ready to buy. Some of these ads bring in big mail orders, recruit droves of profit-making salespeople, get bona fide buyers on catalog mailing lists, and build formidable business images that inspire confidence and increase patronage.

And some of these advertising dollars don't do a thing. They're dollars that might just as well be thrown to the four winds.

Why failure? Because the advertiser is merely buying space or time. He isn't filling that space or time with

A headline or lead that attracts attention
Appeals and benefits that convert readers and listeners into hot prospects
An offer that converts prospects into customers
A compelling reason to buy now

Put these things into your ads, and you'll sell. Your advertising results will skyrocket. Remember, your advertising costs are the same for a given space or time regardless of the pull of the copy. Bad ad copy costs just as much to print or broadcast as productive copy.

POINT 5-1: Good ad copy is essential. You pay the same amount for an ad of given size whether it gets results or fails.

The available media are extensive—they include newspapers, magazines, radio, TV, direct mail, circulars (handbills), phone and other directories, to mention only a few. A mini business generally cannot afford magazines or TV, except on a participating basis. High postage rates are making direct mail too expensive for a mini business to use except on a selective basis. Radio time is still affordable in some of the less populous parts of the country. But by and large the mini business advertises through the telephone Yellow Pages, display ads in local papers, and classified ads in local and metropolitan papers and circulars. The best kind of advertising is customer word of mouth, and it doesn't cost anything (directly, that is). But a starting business which relies on word-of-mouth advertising exclusively is unlikely to stay around long enough to be talked about.

Telephone directory Yellow Pages rates vary with the circulation of the directory. In a smaller town of under 100,000 population with its own direc-

[1] *Statistical Abstract of The United States* (Washington, D.C.: U.S. Department of Commerce, 1975), p. 790.

tory, you can get a respectable-size Yellow Pages display ad for about $50 a month. You can get a Yellow Pages *listing* in regular type or boldface for just a few dollars a month. If you offer several products and services, you can take a listing or ad under several suitable classifications. But proceed with caution. You can very quickly place more advertising than your business can afford.

Yellow-Page advertising is most effective for special products, services, and repair shops. When people want a service and don't know where to get it, they usually consult the Yellow Pages. The same applies to retail specialty businesses. Yellow-Page listings only may be adequate for small wholesalers. To get information on Yellow-Page advertising, call your local phone company and ask for a Yellow-Pages representative. That person will be able to guide you on copy and use of cuts, and will have a layout prepared to your satisfaction. He'll also try to sell you as much space as he can, so be careful.

Display ads in local papers are within the budget of minibusinesses if they're used discreetly in towns with paper circulation of 50,000 or less. Display space rates go up with circulation. Rates are quoted on a column-inch basis. The rate goes down with increased frequency of use or increasing column-inch placement. Always try to get a proof and check it thoroughly for errors. Contact the display advertising department for details and rates. The paper's display advertising representative will generally be helpful on ad layout. Newspapers subscribe to services that provide them with thousands of illustrations that can be used to provide the art requirements for your ads.

You can get some idea of the effectiveness of display advertising by talking to some of the businesspeople who advertise in the local paper. You may inquire about what kind of ad offer gets the best results. The effectiveness of newspapers varies with the locality and the type of business. Inquire about the days that are most effective, too. For some businesses in some localities, a Monday ad is a loser and for others it's a winner. The same can be said for other days of the week.

Classified ads in local and metropolitan papers are much less expensive than display ads. The use of classifieds in metropolitan papers enables you to extend your trade area considerably if you have something unusual to offer. Since classified ads are inexpensive, you can afford some experimentation to see what they'll do for you.

Circulars (handbills) have lost some of their former attractiveness with increased printing and distribution costs and local ordinances, which may place some limitation on the way you can distribute them. The advent of offset and instant printing has simplified the preparation of circulars in small quantities. You can prepare a circular master with a felt-tip pen, a typewriter, and some artwork that you can cut out of a newspaper, magazine, or material furnished by your suppliers. Doing your own layout and paste-up will save quite a bit of expense.

Radio spots are effective and affordable for mini businesses in some localities. I suggest some inquiry with local small businesses that use them to get an estimate of effectiveness. You can get details on rates from the radio station.

Some manufacturers have *cooperative advertising programs.* They'll pay a portion of your advertising expenditures devoted directly to their product. The arrangements vary, but 50 percent cooperation is common. The maximum amount of co-op a manufacturer will do is sometimes tied to your purchases of his product. Manufacturers occasionally run special promotions or special co-op participation programs. A common example is a series of TV spots for a product with a listing of local dealers. Each dealer pays a small amount or buys a required quantity of merchandise to participate; the manufacturer foots the rest of the bill. Co-op advertising arrangements are generally made through the distributor.

Distributors and other suppliers can provide *additional advertising aids.* These include store and window display material, signs of various kinds, brochures and circulars, and demonstration materials. Some of these are free and others are available at low cost. Your suppliers may provide other services such as providing your storefront sign or paying for a portion of it, getting your truck sign painted, temporary window painting for special promotions, sales assistance in the store, and contributions to the expense of your formal opening. Explore the possibilities with distributors when you're selecting lines to handle.

There are a number of ways to advertise that are free or very inexpensive. One of these is free media publicity, which we cover in a subsequent section. Another is the placement of cards or circulars on public bulletin boards at places such as laundromats, clubs and other organizations, schools, factories, and shopping centers. Some of these may not allow business postings, and in some cases you'll have to make arrangements or secure permission.

Repair shops do well to have stickers that can be attached to appliances (that are serviced) or to telephone directories. The appliance owner can find your name, address, and phone number easily even if he has forgotten it. Business cards will sometimes get you business and referrals, but most mini-business owners have more faith than they should in the possible results. More expensive items such as ballpoint pens are of limited value in getting business. Calendars may pay off. But they're expensive, and the investment may not pay off as well as some other available advertising investments. Assess this aspect in terms of your type of business, the customs in your locality, and the visibility you'll get. If you get your calendars in a number of public places, such as barber shops and beauty shops, they may pay off handsomely.

Beware of the advertising salesperson who tries to sell you a place on a sign that supposedly will be distributed to participating advertisers, an ad in a directory to be distributed by participating businesses, and similar gimmicks. The salesperson will sometimes indicate that your banker or some other solid citizen in the community is participating or is recommending the service. Call the person named; he or she will probably deny a recommendation and indicate that they were given a free ad. That's another clue to bow out–in case the salesperson didn't bolt to the door when you picked the phone up.

Billboards are generally out of the reach of a starting mini business. However, depending on your local and personal situation you may be able to arrange for off-premises signs (painted at your expense) at relatively low rental rates. You can sometimes swap merchandise for the privilege of putting a sign on the owner's property.

POINT 5-2: There are many methods of advertising open to you. The more expensive ones aren't always the best. Results should determine where you put your money. If an approach does not produce results, try something else.

The Principles of Ad Writing

These are the four things that you can do in an ad:

- Make your company famous and well-known.
- Make your company well-known for its products, its quality, and other characteristics on which you wish to found a reputation.
- Make people come to your store or write or call for further information such as a catalog or brochures.
- Sell immediately! You can make an ad bring people into your store to buy a specific product, or you can cause them to place an order by phone or mail.

Your purpose should be to sell immediately.

Headlines attract readership. So make the headlines good. Get attention. Arouse curiosity. Attract the right kind of readers—actual prospects—by addressing the desired audience. If your product has a famous name, use it in the headline. It will help you sell. Motivate the buyer to read further than the headline.

Headlines and copy that are specific outsell generalizations. Discover specific things to say about a product. Use numbers, and add individuality to your product. Pin down the product, the offer, and the reader. Once you have the reader's attention, you have to hold his interest. Do it by showing him benefits that appeal to him. Stack benefit upon benefit till he feels that he must have your product (see Figure 5-1). Note that the headline and the copy stress benefits. Keep your advertising truthful. But *stress what it will do for the customer!* That's what he's interested in. *Benefits will outsell drab product and factory information.*

Everybody likes a bargain. Build the value of what you're offering without reducing the price. Build value without making your offer sound cheap.

Win the reader's trust and confidence. Make your copy sincere and believable. Establish *empathy.*[2] Use references, testimonials, statistics, guarantees,

[2] Empathy: understanding and experiencing the feelings, thoughts, and attitudes of others; getting in tune with the customer's feelings.

FIGURE 5-1 This ad stresses a specific benefit in the headline, employs an illustration, stresses benefits, and builds confidence in the copy. Note the use of boldface type within the copy. Where and how to buy information is detailed and a coupon is provided for requesting further information.

BE WARMER AT WORK!

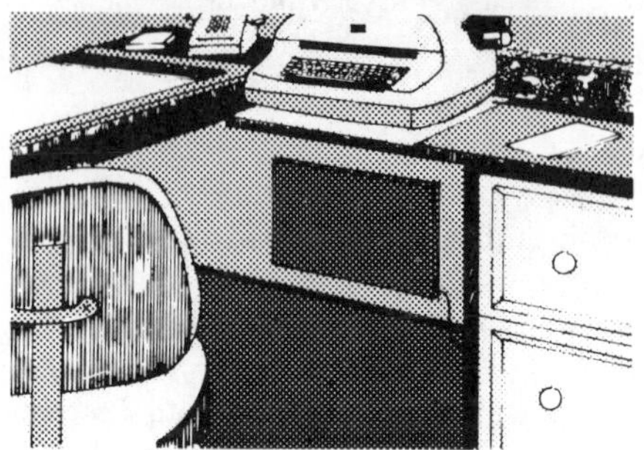

An **Aztec** Radiant Desk Heater will give you the most **comfortable** heat since the Sun. **Safe, Simple, Economical.** It's a smaller version of the 500 watt radiant picture heater manufactured by Aztech for home/office cold spots as seen in **Sears** Fall '76 **General Catalog** (page 1021) and in selected department stores. An **Aztec** Radiant Desk Heater uses 1/6th the energy of other electric portable heaters. Quiet, clean, gentle heat. No air movement. Fits upright against the modesty panel under a desk or stands on feet. Why heat a building to warm one person? 200 watts. 1.7 amps. 110 V. 15" x 24" x 1." Solid Dark Brown. One year limited warranty. **$34.95** each plus **$3.00** ship/handling. 10% discount 6 or more. Optional portable thermostat **$17.95** plus **$1.00** ship/handling. **30-day full money-back guarantee.**

Aztech International, Ltd.
3434 Girard N.E.
Albuquerque, N.M. 87107
(505) 345-5631

Name ______________________

Address ______________________

State ______________________ Zip ______

Send info ☐ on Radiant Picture Heaters; ☐ on ceiling panels for primary/supplemental heat; ☐ on nearest engineering rep.

(Courtesy: Aztech International, Ltd.)

comparisons, and other data to win trust. Then, make it easy for the reader to buy. Show address and phone number, a map, say "downtown," or "near (landmark)." State store hours. Include a coupon in a mail-order offer.

Don't let the reader cool off after you've converted him into a hot prospect. Inspire him to immediate action. Give him a reason to buy now. Offer a special reward for prompt action. Limit the time length of the offer and show that he can avoid a loss by acting now.

Here are some other thoughts. Reward the reader for reading your ad. Tell him a story. Give him food for thought. Give him free information or a free lesson. Give him something that he can cut out and keep, such as a picture, a recipe, or a special checklist. Make him feel rewarded and grateful.

POINT 5-3: The major thrust of your advertising copy should be to sell a specific product or service *immediately.*

Headlines That Attract Readers

The headline is the master key to advertising results. The headline is the hook that causes the reader to

1. Look deeper into your ad, or
2. To skip on to something else

There are a number of words that have been used over the years that are proven attention-catchers. Although they may sound trite from overuse, they still attract attention consistently. You'll find that they're used again and again in headlines and in book titles. Whenever a word loses its power as an attention-puller, you'll find that the ad headline writers and the book publishers quickly abandon them. Here are some of the proven attention-catching words and phrases that draw the reader to read the full headline:

New, Latest, New Discovery, Amazing, Remarkable, Magic, Miracle, How To, Easy, Free, Guaranteed, Special Offer, Introducing, The Real Truth About, Reward.

The words "new" and "free" are the best attention-getters. Note the use of the word new in the headline and in two subheads in Figure 5-2.

There is another group of attention-getting words. They're valuable, and their power lies in the fact that they can attract specific kinds of readers. Here are some frequently used words that are good for attracting specific audiences:

Men, Women, Ladies, Boys, Girls, Housewives, Mothers, Executives, Professional Men, Homeowners, Young Couples, Young Families, Mature Men.

FIGURE 5-2 This ad uses the proven words "new," "improved," and "introductory" in the headlines, backed by an eye-catching picture of the merchandise. The copy features benefits and product information that build the value. The ad makes the recorder easy to buy with a coupon that includes suggestion selling of accessories.

(Courtesy: Contemporary Marketing, Inc.)

It helps when the address compliments the reader. Such a technique sells a lot of "executive homes" to nonexecutives. Any adult male reader is quick to identify himself as a "mature man." The "boys" address may sound corny—but it makes boys read the ad.

A curiosity-arousing headline can hook your reader into reading the copy. Typical examples are:

We're Only Second
Where Will You Be—10 Years From Tonite?
This New Scientific Discovery Will Give You Goose Pimples
30,000 Energy Builders In One Square Inch
How A Fool Stunt Saved $200

The ad copy often follows through with a story that leads into the product and the offer. The curiosity-arouser makes the reader wonder what it's all about—causes him to dig in and learn more. Figure 5-3 is a typical curiosity-arousing ad.

FIGURE 5-3 This ad gets your attention with a specific question and an illustration that causes you to read further in spite of its small size.

How long must you keep important papers?
Write for free booklet, RECORD RETENTION TIMETABLE, describing Retention Periods as allowed by government authorities, and how to dispose of them safely without loss or worry!
On your business letterhead, please.
Electric Wastebasket Corp., 145 W. 45th St., N.Y. 10036
"The MOST in Paper Shredders"

(Courtesy: Electric Wastebasket Corporation)

A headline will attract attention and sell harder if it contains a promise of reward. By making the promise specific, you make it sell much better. Now, let's get specific about being specific.

Don't Say:	*Say:*
Earn big money	Earn $12,000 a year or more
Fast service	4 hour service
This product	Frost-free freezer
Reduced prices	$85 suits now only $49
Fine gun	Precision 22 rifle
Borrow from us	You can borrow $300 today
What would become of her if something happened to you?	Life insurance that pays her $475 a month—if she needs it
Enjoy luxurious travel at low cost	Europe—$471 for 14 days

Note that it's usually better to take the big number when you are talking about reward and the lower number when you are talking about cost. Talk about a year's salary (rather than a month's) to salaried people. Talk about 50¢ a day instead of $15 a month as the cost of a product. Numbers strengthen a headline. Figure 5-4 uses a specific headline to address a specific audience. The subhead cites numbers. Note the use of the word "free."

There are numerous ways to involve the reader. Again, the headline is the hook. It grabs the reader and makes him participate in the body copy. Here are a few classical "involver" headlines:

Take This Simple Test
Do You Make These Mistakes In English?
What Would You Do In This Situation?
Can You Improve This Recipe?
Always A Bridesmaid–Never A Bride (followed by story)
Can you Meet These Tough Requirements? (recruiting ad)
Win $10,000 By Naming This New Automobile
Solve This Brain Twister

You can make your company famous by using the name in the headline repeatedly. You can also project an image relating to your company name in the logotype at the bottom of the ad. But don't count on the logotype at the bottom of the page to build fame and reputation. Many readers don't see it! If you want to increase the reader's chance of seeing it, make it at least as large as the headline type (see Figure 5-4).

FIGURE 5-4 This ad addresses a specific audience, uses numbers, the proven word "free," and the confidence-building "10 day wear trial" in bold type. An attractive illustration and judicious use of type in the headlines and logo make the ad catch the reader's eye. Note the code (Dept. 2445) in the address for measuring pulling power of the ad.

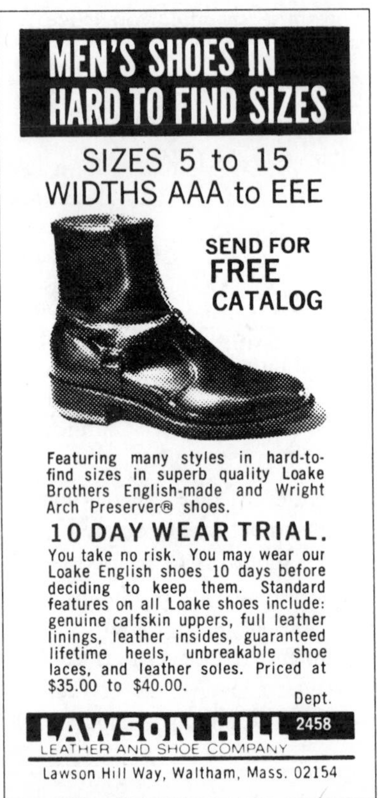

(Courtesy: Lawson Hill Leather and Shoe Co.)

POINT 5-4: The headline has to be good to get the reader to read further. Apply the principles of this section to make your headline pull.

Ad-Writing Suggestions

Make your copy exciting by using short sentences. Use action verbs. Minimize the use of general, colorless adjectives. Use bright, exciting, and specific adjectives. These rules will clarify your ideas and hold attention:

Use simple words, sentences, and paragraphs
Keep the majority of your sentences short
Use a variety of words
Eliminate "excess-baggage" words
Put action into your verbs
Capitalize on reader's background
Add sparkle; use devices and variety
Paint verbal pictures
Write the way you talk
Break complex subjects into simple parts
Express; don't try to impress
Amplify with graphics and photos

People want to be served, so make it easy to buy. People are easily diverted by the numerous competing activities in life. If you make it easy to buy, you enhance your chance to sell with your ad, because you are extending extra service, and because you minimize the possibility of diversion. Here are ways to make it easy to buy:

Tell where to buy it
Tell how to get there ("Downtown at . . . ," or show a map)
Tell how to place phone or mail orders
Tell how to specify size and color, etc.
Include mail-order coupon in ad (see Figure 5-2)
Offer easy payment plan
Off free trial (see Figure 5-4)
Offer a brochure or sample (see Figure 5-1 and 5-3)
Offer to have a salesperson call
Offer free delivery

These devices and others that you can use in writing your ad copy will help you to write advertising that sells.

POINT 5-5: Make your copy clear; make your product easy to buy; inspire action now; build confidence.

Layout, Position, and Size

Your layout can help your ad command attention. If the layout is poor, it can allow your ad to pass unnoticed. There are three basic types of ads and countless variations:

Headline plus dominant solid body copy
Headline plus subheads dividing body copy
Headline plus dominant picture over short copy

The headline-solid body copy approach places a heavy burden on the headline; it has to be a real "grabber." In addition, the first sentence and the first paragraph must have tremendous reader involvement and reader identification power. The challenge to the copywriter is a big one.

This approach can be strengthened with a respected name by-line. The copy then takes on the appearance of a feature article. The approach may be further strengthened by setting the headline and the copy in the type ordinarily used by the publication in which the ad appears. (It still has to be labeled "advertisement.") The headline-solid body copy approach is difficult to handle. You'll do better to try other approaches first.

Headline with subhead dividing or several headlines are more effective than headline plus solid body copy because the reader is more likely to scan beyond the headlines and subheads. See Figure 5-5 for some conservatively-worded small ads that attract and hold attention.

The third extreme in layout features a headline, dominant picture, your logo, and short copy. Automobile manufacturer's ads are typical examples. Clothing ads generally follow this format too.

A picture adds to the reader pulling power of any ad. Note the use of pictures in Figures 5-1 thru 5 4. If color adds to the excitement and appeal of the product, it strengthens the ad further. Automobiles, food, and clothing are typical examples. Use a picture if the space and budget permit it. A picture adds most "sell" if it shows a person enjoying the benefits of the product offered. A small product might get lost in the reduction process with a person in the picture. But don't overlook the fact that you can use as small a part of a person as his face, his hand, or his eye. This may limit the action, but it can produce exciting effects.

Photos are excellent for illustration. They're inexpensive, attractive, and they're available in a hurry. Some product pictures pull better in art form than they do as photos. Women's shoes are a case in point. Art adds glamor and excitement to women's shoes.

A series of ads for an office supply company pushed typewriters. The ad copy appeared in the newspapers as reprints of actual letters typed on the machines that were advertised. This campaign sold a lot of typewriters, made the business better known, and almost doubled the size of the business over a short period of

FIGURE 5-5 (A) This very small ad uses bold type, limited availability, and low price to catch attention. Body copy is factual and concise. (B) This small ad with headlines dividing text promotes three properties. Copy is crisp; the descriptions promote desirable features.

(A)

LOTS FOR SALE
Close to Country Club Road and Miller Road. Paved streets, city water, electrical, and sewer available.
ONLY 6 LEFT!
Own it now-ONLY $900
Total cash price each
(also corner lot $1100)
STAFFORD
Jim and Associates
475-1500 271-2601

(B)

NORTH
QUIET COUNTRY LIVING, 3 bedroom, 2 baths, 2 car rear entry garage with formal dining room and 22 foot long garage with ample turning space for boat.
ALL IN ONE
Under $22,500. 3 bedroom brick, 1½ bath, 2 car garage with gas central air.
ENGLISH ESTATES
3 bedroom, 2 bath, 2 car garage, built-in gas oven/range, dishwasher, freshly painted. Total price $27,500.
OVER A DECADE OF SERVICE - WE CARE -
TRY US
MLS
JIM STAFFORD and Associates
475-1500 271-2601

time. The ads were run in a small local paper at an approximate space cost of $40 per insertion; they were run only once or twice a week.

A combination format is the easiest and most effective one to use. Figures 5-1, 5-2, and 5-4 use combination formats. By using subheads, you increase your chances of hooking the reader. By using a picture, you increase the total attention-catching appeal of the ad. These things pull the reader into the body copy. You give him full exposure to your proposition through the body copy.

You can give portions of your copy standout characteristics that help to strengthen the ad in much the same way that subheads do. You can do these things:

- Underline
- Indent
- Italicize
- Use capital letters
- Capitalize first letters of words
- Change type style or size
- Use a different ink color

What you can use depends on the medium involved, the reproduction process, and your budget. All these techniques are productive in sales letters.

Learn the ground rules of position and size. While you don't always have control over position, there are some things that you can do about forcing position and dominating a page. A 3-column-by-12-inch newspaper ad, for example, will stand out on a page because it cannot be clobbered by an across-the-page, half-page ad. Some papers have rules that don't permit this kind of ad. Check with your paper on ad dimension rules to be sure.

POINT 5-6: You can increase the effectiveness of your ads with good layout and preferred positioning. An ad doesn't necessarily have to be big to be effective.

Classifieds

You can buy circulation of a million for a few cents a classified word. You can reach a large number of readers at low cost if you can frame your ad in a few words. Classifieds must be direct and to the point for lowest costs and best results. Since the reader usually scans classifieds on a shopping basis, he's looking for your ad. Hence long copy and large space are not essential for catching readers.

A good lead sentence or phrase is the best attention-catcher you can use. Use numbers in it. If you're recruiting personnel, stress salary in dollars. If you're selling a product, stress bargain value. Audience address is useful. But make it more specific than the classification heading. Don't waste your words repeating the classification heading.

Economy of words is essential in classifieds. Use only a phone number if the advertising is local and your follow-up is to be a mailing or a sales call. If the desired reader action is a visit to your store, give the store name and address. But don't go overboard on word economy either. If you do, you may get a lot of inquiries that are not qualified. The more specific you get, the more qualified will be the responses you get. More qualified responses save you time, trouble, and money. The classification you choose for your ad is important too—it can make a difference of several hundred percent in the long run.

Classifieds placed in metropolitan papers can pull city business out to small towns. A small music store located in a very small town about fifteen miles out of Dallas advertises in the Dallas paper classifieds and sells a lot of pianos by advertising "low country overhead." A furniture store located in another small town does a substantial business with the same format.

POINT 5-7: Classified ads are inexpensive. Classified readers are usually looking for a specific service. Classifieds offer an excellent advertising vehicle for a mini business.

Result Measurement

You'll have to develop a method of measuring results for your advertising expenditures so you can place your future ad budget more effectively. Mail-order houses measure results by *keying*—using codes (such as "Dept. A3") to identify ad copy and the publication. A local mini business can use equally effective methods.

Response to a specific offer appearing in only one publication can be measured by the difference in sales during the offer period and normal sales of the product offered. Mail and phone orders on a specific offer can be tallied. You can test one publication against another by making a different offer in each publication for a week. Then after two weeks of rest on these offers, switch each offer into the other publication and run for a week. You can get a measure of each paper's effectiveness by comparing the results for each ad.

You'll be able to get the most out of your advertising expenditures if you measure results, analyze them, and put your advertising dollars into the offers, publications, and copy that produce the best results. It takes a little bit of effort to keep the records, but it will pay off.

POINT 5-8: Measure and analyze ad results to get the most from your advertising dollar.

If you're in a quandary about advertising budget size, check on percentage income statements for your line of business. Simply multiply annual sales times the advertising expense percentage to get an idea of what other similar businesses are doing on an annual basis; divide by 12 for the monthly budget. You'll still need to make adjustments for your specific locality, but it's a good starting point.

REVIEW EXERCISES 5-A

1. Discuss the methods of advertising that a mini business can afford.
2. Why are classified ads attractive for a small business?
3. What kind of advertising help can you get from suppliers?
4. What are the four things you can do with an ad? Which should be your objective?
5. Why are headlines so important?
6. What are the attention-getting headline words?
7. How can you "make it easy to buy" through your ad?
8. What can you do to a display-ad layout to make the ad stand out?
9. What does a picture do for an ad?
10. List and discuss several methods you can use to measure ad results. Why is it important to measure ad results?

PROMOTION

Sales promotion focuses your advertising and publicity on strategies, events, and offers that give sales a shot in the arm. Promotion is a long-term part of the marketing mix and includes advertising. This section addresses other facets of promotion. A promotion is a short effort, but you always hope that it will make some long-term gains too. We start here with a specific promotion, with the slant toward the retail or service business.

Events Suitable for Promotions

Events that can be used as promotion themes are

- Grand openings
- Holidays and seasons
- Store remodeling and expansion
- Store anniversaries
- Special purchases
- Fashion shows
- The presence (in the store) of a celebrity to autograph, chat, or demonstrate

You can create an event for a promotion almost any time you want to. Most people call a promotion a "sale." The promotion usually involves a price-saving reduction, but it must not necessarily do so.

A promotion can be as small an effort as a money-saving coupon, a group of merchandise offered at a reduced price, a free checkup on a customer's air conditioner, car, or appliance, or a drawing for prizes. Or it may be a well-publicized grand opening with storewide price reductions, refreshments, prize drawings, free favors, entertainment, and visiting celebrities. The grand opening is usually the most grandiose of all promotions. The mini-business starter usually has budget limitations.

> POINT 5-9: A promotion is a short, concentrated sales effort. You can build a promotion around something as simple as a special offer or as large as a grand opening.

How to Make Promotions Successful

How do you set up and run a grand-opening promotion on a shoestring budget? First, consider the steps for your first promotion—putting a grand opening together:

1. Plan the event
2. Plan publicity and advertising
3. Make event arrangements
4. Activate publicity and advertising
5. Tend to event details
6. Stage the event

The first step, planning, involves determining the event strategy. What will the theme be? In this case, it's a grand opening–let's say it's an air-conditioning and heating sales and service business. The opening has been timed for June, near the beginning of the air-conditioning season. The weather is already warm. So theme possibilities are–"A cool day in the Torrid Zone," "A lovely way to spend a summer," and so forth. Let's assume the first is chosen. A good way to start is to work with your primary distributor. Get his concurrence on a theme. You may want distributor people and several demonstration units present. Your distributor will usually go along with this. He'll also furnish display material, imprinted brochures, and back-up selling material. He'll help with the window and store displays.

You want some plants to add to the atmosphere, so you can call several florists, morticians, and the city park department. You can probably borrow them and trade off some air-conditioning service for the use. You also decide that fans all over the store blowing some crinkled white crepe paper will create more illusion of coolness.

What about demonstrations? How about a heated booth with a working air conditioner in it? The visitor goes into the booth, the thermometer reads 85 degrees, you turn the air conditioner on, and in 30 seconds the temperature is 68 degrees. The distributor may agree to pay for the materials for the booth if you'll build it. Maybe he has one already that you can use without any expenditure of effort. What other demonstrations does he have? He'll probably have one or two that you can use.

What about the window display? Some potted palms, a fan blowing the white crepe tassels, and what else? How about a sound system with an outside speaker and a repeating taped message? What about some people in bathing suits taking turns in the window under the luscious air? That ought to take care of the display windows.

The refreshments? How about fruit punch and cookies? Giveaways? How about balloons with an advertising message for the kids and a little do-it-yourself set of instructions on how to care for your heat and air system (which costs you less than a nickel a copy to produce) for the adults?

Put anything on sale? Maybe. Perhaps a 10 percent discount on equipment for jobs contracted during the sale. Or maybe the manufacturer will make a special deal that still gives you full profit. Explore all avenues.

Prize drawing? Yes. Print entry coupons in the local paper and have them in the store too. Coupons must go in the box during the opening and the first six days thereafter, with the drawing the seventh day. Offer one grand prize–say a window unit air conditioner–and three intermediate prizes worth about $50 retail each, and about ten prizes of, say, a free air-conditioning and heating system cleanup and inspection. You might try to get some help from the utility system that furnishes power for your area too.

There are other details to work out, but you can throw them in place after you're farther along. What about advertising and publicity? Newspaper ads and possibly some radio spots promoting the event starting one to two weeks in advance of the opening. Cover the store windows with wrapping paper that conveys the opening message. This also keeps folks from seeing in while you're setting up and makes them wonder what's behind the paper. A circular campaign to augment the newspaper and radio spots might help in some localities.

If you belong to the chamber of commerce, invite the membership to the opening. The same with clubs you belong to. Get your grand-opening circulars on public bulletin boards. Perhaps the manufacturer or the distributor whose line you're handling will help with a mailing too. They might go along with a mailing to homeowners in developments where the houses are six to ten years old in hopes of selling replacement air-conditioning systems. Get your ads and circulars laid out well in advance, and make arrangements for timely publication and distribution.

This gets you to event arrangements. Some of these will already have been made during the event planning process. But you'll still have plenty to do. You'll have to arrange to get the window and store displays set up, install demonstrations, get personnel to host and staff the grand opening. Generally between the distributor, the power company, your one or two employees, and your family and friends, you can assemble an adequate crew. You'll need to brief these people. You may have costume arrangements to make, and you'll have to arrange refreshments, prizes, and prize-drawing details.

Next, you'll activate the advertising, tend to more details, and work toward the big day. When it arrives, you should be ready. You may want to use a guest register, but you'll have the names and addresses on the stubs for the door-prize drawing, so a register isn't really necessary.

Be sure to invite the local press to the event and have your own photographer snapping pictures too. Get out press releases after the event. Also, have the press and your own photographer catch pictures of the drawing winners when prize presentations are made. Opening photos may make good window-display material for a week or two. Ditto on pictures of the prize presentations. Keep on pulling benefits from the event even after it's over.

POINT 5-10: It takes a lot of work and planning to pull off maximum benefit from a promotion with minimal cost. Plan, organize, staff, direct, and control the event.[3]

What might this grand opening cost? Anywhere from $300 to $2,500 depending on the locality, the business opening size, the amount of help supplied by the

[3] Plan, organize, staff, direct, and control: these are the five major classical functions of management. They're treated in detail in Chapter 13.

distributor, other suppliers, family and friends, and the downright ingenuity of the owner. In most towns of 100,000 people or less, an ingenious owner can pull that kind of opening off for about $400 to $600.

Special Services

Special services differentiate a retail or service business from its competitors. There are several large stores that are noted for the unusual services or the breadth of services they perform; among them, Harrod's of London and Neiman-Marcus of Dallas. A small business can distinguish itself as well with an unusual service. An enterprising New England moonlighter started a mobile tax service by carrying his calculator, forms, and manuals in his car. He advertised in the classifieds "Tax return prepared in your home," and he got more business than he could handle. He performed a special service. Of course, his overhead was low too.

Sewing-machine sales and service businesses often operate the same way. They advertise home service in the classifieds and repair the machine in the home. While the repair person is there he usually manages to demonstrate a new machine and often makes the sale. If he has to take the customer's machine to the shop, he leaves the new one while it's in and encourages the customer to use it. This sells plenty of sewing machines. Home demonstrations are expensive if they're not tied in to a service call unless you have salespeople working on a straight commission.

Home delivery is pretty well gone in larger towns except for large items. This is another special service that you can offer customers.

Free instructions and low-cost courses can be used effectively to sell cameras, typewriters, sewing machines, cooking equipment, sporting goods, arts and crafts supplies, fabrics, woodworking shop tools, decorating items, upholstery material, automotive analyzers and tools, or just about anything that has a "do-it-yourself" connotation. A sewing center ran sewing courses at $30 a course. Most of the customers took two, and some three, of the different courses, averaging $75 a course per student in fabric and notion purchases, and the store sold new sewing machines to about three out of ten of the students.

Some paying special services that a retailer or service shop can offer along with other wares are scissor and cutlery sharpening, key making, and jewelry monogramming. These services don't make a lot of money because the volume usually isn't great enough, but they more than pay their way and they bring extra traffic to the store or shop.

Service shops can build business by offering a special checkup and minor adjustment service for a small fee. These special service calls can be promoted in off-seasons to provide business to fill the gap. An air-conditioner checkup in March or April or a TV set checkup in July or August will usually get immediate business and build good will for later business.

Automotive inspections bring business into garages and service station repair shops in states where these businesses conduct official automotive inspections. If you start an automotive repair service, it's advantageous to be designated as an official inspection station.

These are just a few of the special service ideas that you can put to work in your business. Put your thinking cap on, and you'll come up with many more.

POINT 5-11: Customers buy from you because they want your service. Offer special services on a regular and on a promotional basis to build your business.

Ten Sales Promotion Ideas

1. **"Believe It Or Not" Window Display.** Feature a "Believe It Or Not" sign in your display window or in the store surrounded by products. Tie a sign to each of the products with eyebrow-raising facts such as this: "The cotton in this dress came from a plantation in the Mississippi Delta. More than $50,000 worth of machinery was used to plant, cultivate, protect, and pick it. It took thirty-seven people to convert the raw cotton into this beautiful dress. Yet you can buy it for only $12.98! Believe It Or Not!"

2. **Work a Car Tie-in.** Give three gallons of gas–free–for the purchase of a given product. Make a deal with a service station owner to give you the gas at reduced price. The advantage to him is that it will send new prospects to his filling station. He'll usually sell a fill-up. *Note to filling station operators*–work this deal with retailers to build your business.

3. **Ticket Marking Sales.** Send out numbered tickets with a letter explaining that a given number of lucky tickets have been attached to various pieces of merchandise. The recipient is invited to the store on a certain day (pick a slow sales day) to try to match his ticket. If he finds a matching number he gets the product free.

4. **Free Talks.** Arrange for free talks in a self-improvement subject related to a product you sell to be given in your store at certain times of the day. Publicize them. Typical subjects and associated products are:

"How to Dress Better"	Clothes
"How to Set a Regal Table"	Silverware, table cloths, dining room furniture
"How to Decorate Like a Pro"	Furniture, bric-a-brac, paint, curtains, etc.
"Yard and Garden Care"	Sand, fertilizer, and other garden supplies

5. **Hourly Specials.** Advertise a leader on sale for a one-hour period during a slow part of the day. You can promote a different product every hour of the day.

6. Hold an "After-Hours" Sale. Hold an "after-hours" or "pajama" sale. Run from, say, 8 P.M. to midnight. Dress clerks in pajamas and robes.

7. Hold an Auction. Gather up odds and ends, slow-moving merchandise, and accumulated samples. Add a few "excitement" items. Run an auction. Use a professional auctioneer, radio announcer, or some other lively personality to keep things moving. Publicize before and after.

8. Teenage Sale. Run a teenage sale after regular store hours–6 to 10 Friday night is a good time. Decorate store with phonograph records, tapes, pictures of favorite teenage performers and entertainers, and signs with teenage slang phrases. Offer discount on all merchandise equal to youngsters' age–for example, 14-year-old gets 14 percent discount. Hire a teenage combo (they're usually very inexpensive) to play in front of the store. Promote beforehand in newspapers. Exploit the event afterward through newspaper, radio, and TV publicity.

9. Feature "Off-Day" Sale. Feature an "off-day" sale on the business weekday that is the poorest. In your advertising, call it an "off-day" sale and tie low prices to the fact that business is usually poor that day.

10. Surprise Giveaway Sale. Give away a surprise package with each purchase during a "Giveaway" sale. Giveaways should equal 5 to 10 percent of the sale in retail value. Use 10-cent items for purchases of $1.99 or less, 25-cent items for $2 to $4.99, and so forth. Variety is important.

REVIEW EXERCISES 5-B

1. Expand the list of possible promotion themes listed in this section.
2. If you were opening a grocery store, what kind of help might you expect or request from the distributors and manufacturers of the products you'd sell?
3. What are the steps in planning and staging a successful promotion?
4. Develop a list of special services not listed in this chapter that a small retail or service business might offer.

PUBLIC RELATIONS AND PUBLICITY

Public relations (PR) is an oft-used term. So is *publicity.* They mean the same thing to most people, but they really aren't the same. This section will clear up confusion regarding PR, publicity, and image. It will show you how to employ these concepts to build your sales, growth, and business leadership position.

Definitions

Public relations is the art of creating impressions in the minds of people that cause them to hold an activity or organization (in this case your business) in high esteem. In other words, public relations is the practice of principles that build the *image* of your company in people's minds. *Actions* give the direction and mold the image.

Image is the concept of your company that people hold in their minds. Your image is different for different people. You have different publics.

Your publics include your customers, your employees, your suppliers, the community at large, and, if you're incorporated, your shareholders. When your company becomes larger, your number of publics will increase to include the financial community and others.

Image is dynamic—that is, it is constantly changing. Your public relations strategy should be aimed toward improving the quality and quantity of image that the people in your public hold. Quality deals with opinion—do they think you're good, fair, or lousy? Quantity deals with how strongly they feel about you—do they feel strongly enough to talk to others about you, to comment when your name is brought up, or not enough to comment about you at all? You obviously would like to build a high-quality and high-quantity image in the minds of everyone.

Publicity is the principal means for projecting your image to the public. Publicity is the "shouting of the word" by word of mouth, the printed and spoken word in media press releases, articles, programs, ads, and news.

Image is the result of the action or inaction of your business. Publicity and your daily dealings with your publics provide the means for projecting image.

Image

What kind of image do you want your customer public to hold in their minds about your business?

The best, all the way around, of course. But your thrust should be more specific. Here are some of the themes that you can build on. You ought to select two or three for major emphasis and work some of the others (which don't conflict) into your publicity and advertising from time to time:

Service or product quality
Technical expertise
Efficient service
Quick service
Full or special service
Old-fashioned dealing and service
Progressiveness
Competitive pricing
Guaranteed satisfaction

Note that these themes emphasize service. Service is what your customer pays more or less for. You can emphasize more or better product and service and get more for your product or service. Or you can emphasize price, sell for less, and base your strategy on volume. A mini business will usually do best to take the former position. This still leaves you with choices for your basic themes. But your image-building thrust should be geared to differentiating your business from less attractive ones and building image similar to that of businesses that have attractive public appeal. The really strong universal image appeals are guaranteed satisfaction and quality. The two go hand in hand. Guaranteed satisfaction backs up the concept of "the customer is always right," and while it occasionally will cost you something, the business and free publicity it inspires will outweigh the costs. Quality minimizes the need for customer adjustments and exchanges.

As your company grows, other publics will evolve—suppliers, employees, the financial community, and others. The image that you'll want to project to each of these publics differs because different things are important to each public. Your image with your suppliers, for example, should be one of progressive growth and impeccable credit. Your employee public is more interested in fair treatment and potential for growth.

POINT 5-12: Choose the image you wish to project to your customer public. Choose themes and develop policy, standards, and procedures that will reflect that image in dealing with your customer public. Employ these themes in advertising and publicity.

Publicity

Publicity can inform, explain, stimulate sales, strengthen employee-employer relationships, strengthen stockholder-management relationships, affect the price of company stock, strengthen employee recruiting, build a company image, and make a company famous. We'll limit our discussion to sales stimulation and image building. Publicity is generally free, or at any rate, you don't often pay for it on a line, inch, minute, or other direct basis.

You can get free publicity through news stories in your local paper, national magazines, trade newspapers, trade magazines, house organs, radio, and TV. A mini business generally uses local media. There are plenty of things you can make into news and ways in which you can make news out of an accomplishment or event. You don't even need a specific event. Here are some of the possibilities for a retail or service mini business:

Grand opening
Remodeling or expansion

Management changes
New employees
Outstanding outside accomplishment or honor earned by employee
Attendance at trade conventions
Acquisition of a new product line
Human interest stories about employees
Business anniversaries
Public service activities

Your chances of placing free publicity in your local paper will depend on the editorial policy and the size of the paper. You'll usually be able to get more free publicity in small-town papers. Some papers do tie free publicity to the amount of advertising you buy, although most papers deny this.

If your mini business manufactures a product (or products) there's another free publicity avenue open to you. You can get product publicity through new-product and literature announcements and "circle the number bingo cards" in the "new products" columns of trade periodicals. A "bingo" card is a postage-paid card to the periodical on which the reader circles numbers corresponding to new-product announcements and free literature offers he'd like to receive. The reader can get ten or twenty replies by sending only one card. He circles the numbers, sends the card to the magazine, and the magazine in turn pulls the numbers from the card. The manufacturer receives the list of names requesting his literature from the magazine and sends out the literature. Usually these new-product announcements are free or call for a very small fee.

Don't underestimate this medium. These specialized (almost always free to the reader) trade papers have circulations of 10,000 or more. Most average 20,000; a copy usually has several readers. An editor of one of these magazines told me that on one offering, they received about 3,000 replies. That's a nice field of prospects for a free listing!

Your best approach to receiving free publicity is to write up your own press release ready to use. If possible, include a photo that relates to the story. Supply the release and photo to the publications you feel might publish it. Watch for publication. When it appears in print, get several copies and build a small display for your store window around it. (You can also build window displays around cutout copies of your ads.) It's a good idea to file copies of printed publicity and advertising, too. They may be useful in future business anniversary publicity and displays.

When you hit the jackpot with a really good publicity story, it's a good idea to get reprints and distribute them. Whenever you get into print, most people feel that your business has gained a plus, so play it up.

If you furnish a paper with releases repeatedly and it doesn't use any of them, cross the paper off your list. If it prints as many as one out of five, keep the releases flowing.

POINT 5-13: You can get free publicity for your business. Furnish written releases with a photo.

Daily Relations

Your daily relations with your customers do much for building the image of your business. Spoil your customers with service, patience, understanding, and courtesy, and their opinion of you will grow in a positive way. Customers should always get a cheerful greeting when they enter your store, courteous treatment while they're in the store, and a pleasant "thank you, please come again," whether they buy or not. If they don't buy, it's "thanks for visiting with us," or "for coming to our store."

Courteous treatment calls for showing customers where things are, answering their questions, providing technical know-how that they may want, and in general, making them feel welcome and wanted as valued store customers. But don't annoy them by hovering when they just want to look around.

If you're operating a service repair business that takes you and your employees into your customers' homes, small courtesies and considerations like being sure you're not dragging mud or snow onto the customer's carpet, special care in moving furniture to get at an appliance for service, and cleaning up the mess after you're finished will pay off handsomely. Proper telephone courtesy is another practice that should be part of your daily customer and public relations policy.

These points may seem trivial. But lack of courtesy and tact in retail and service situations are so common that you, as an owner-manager, will save yourself embarrassment and lost business by emphasizing them. Periodic employee meetings and training sessions can help to improve the situation.

Pass your business cards freely. Pass them out to the people you meet and invite them to your store without giving them a hard-sell sales pitch. Let friends in organizations you belong to know that you've started your own business. Do the same with your friends at your previous places of employment. Your spouse can pass your cards around for you too. Although many businesspeople overestimate the results of card passing, the practice does have merit and it will get you some business.

POINT 5-14: Build your image by providing prompt, courteous, and tactful service on a daily basis. Be sure that your employees carry out this policy in their daily contacts.

Public Service and Community Relations

Your public service activity and your involvement in your community will have an effect on your business. Local folks like businesspeople who support the community. You can overdo it and get so involved in community service that you neglect your business. This should be avoided, but a reasonable amount of community involvement and support of community service will help your business image.

Don't be greedy with your windows. If a school, church, scout, or civic group wants to put an occasional poster in your window, go along with it—cheerfully.

Participate in community improvement programs as best you can. If you can't go along with them, don't voice opposition and put yourself in the position of being labeled "an enemy of progress," "a radical," or "a non-cooperator."

Pick a pet project or two for the betterment of your community and become involved in it. Membership in your chamber of commerce and a civic club will provide plenty of options to serve. Your church affiliation provides additional opportunities for public service. All of your affiliations, although made for other purposes, will have an effect on your business.

POINT 5-15: Support community purposes, projects, and organizations as fully as you can without neglecting your business.

REVIEW EXERCISES 5-C

1. What is the difference between public relations and publicity?
2. Discuss the statement, "Image is a result of the public relations of a business."
3. What kind of actions by a business or its employees can lead to poor public relations? How can they be avoided?
4. Why should you try to write publicity releases in ready-to-use form?
5. Why are daily relations the real key to the image of a business?
6. Why does community involvement and leadership contribute to the image of your business?

CASE: ADVERTISING AND PROMOTION

Ann Hudson decided to go into the interior decorating business. She arranged financing, found a location, and opened her shop. She placed classified ads in the Dallas newspapers and display ads in the paper in the suburban community where her shop was located. Most of her calls came from Dallas, and she discontinued her advertising in the local paper because she didn't feel it was effective.

REVIEW EXERCISES 5-D

1. Did Ann reach a rational and correct conclusion in deciding the local paper didn't pull? What about copy, layout, and position?
2. How could Ann have confirmed the pulling power of the local paper?
3. Should she have considered classified ads in the local paper?
4. What else can Ann do to promote and advertise her interior decorating business?

SUMMARY

You pay the same for an ad whether it produces results or fails totally, so it's mandatory that you have an appealing, well-laid-out, and well-placed ad to get the optimum payoff from your advertising. A good headline or illustration (preferably both) creates interest and draws your reader to read further. If the body copy is good, it should create immediate sales and make your business well-known. The guidelines in the first section of the chapter will help you write successful ads.

Classified ads provide an inexpensive means of reaching many qualified buyers. Display ads are more expensive, but they command attention of a large cross-section of readership. Telephone Yellow Pages are excellent for service and repair businesses and for specialized retail businesses. Radio is within the reach of small businesses in some localities.

Explore the possibilities of cooperative advertising and participation advertising with your distributors. Your suppliers can also help you stage promotions, provide store display materials, and imprint brochures and signs.

Your images are the way your publics regard you. Image is a function of action. You increase your projection of image through your advertising and publicity. Develop image themes that you want to measure up to, and base your actions, advertising, and publicity on the chosen blueprint. Courtesy, interest, regard, and attention, as expressed by the actions of you and your employees on a daily basis, go a long way toward projecting your image.

A grand-opening promotion helps a business gain impulse and sales momentum and signals its arrival on the business scene. Promotions can be created for almost any occasion or sales push. A promotion gives a business a temporary shot in the arm and has some lasting benefits.

KEY TERMS

Classified ad
Community relations
Copy
Display ad
Empathy
Headline
Image
Layout
Media
Position
Publicity
Public relations
Publics
Public service
Result measurement
Service

QUESTIONS AND PROBLEMS

1. What media can you use to advertise in your town? What are the rates for (a) newspaper display ads, (b) classified ads, (c) radio spots, (d) Yellow Pages?
2. What are some of the techniques you can utilize to make your headlines attract attention?
3. Examine the ads in a copy of your newspaper. (a) What are the dominant characteristics of the headlines? (b) What are the dominant characteristics of the ads that make you read further?
4. Look through the editorial copy in a newspaper. Try to spot publicity plants and make a note of them. Discuss with the class.
5. How can you get an estimate of the ad budget for your small business?
6. Develop a list of points that you think a small business should incorporate in its public relations policy.
7. Why is a guaranteed satisfaction policy a good image-builder? What are the advantages and disadvantages of this policy for a mini business?

FIELD INVESTIGATION AND PROJECTS

1. Take a trip to your library and check the card catalog under the subject index for advertising, publicity, and public relations. Develop a bibliography. Scan the books listed in your bibliography and make notes on new ideas you pick up. List the three books that seem most useful to you and state your reasons for choosing them.

*2. Visit the advertising department of your local newspaper. Get their rates, look over their available artwork, and observe the preparation of advertising copy. Have a prepared list of questions on any aspects of newspaper advertising that you find puzzling.

3. Prepare a set of ads and publicity releases for the grand-opening example in this chapter, limiting yourself to an advertising budget of $600 ($300 yours and $300 furnished by distributor) based on your local media rates. Indicate number of insertions for each ad and show detailed layout for each ad. Develop an overall plan for advertising and publicity. If you can afford radio and want to, use it.

*4. Do project 3 above for the business you intend to start, using the budget you feel you can afford.

Accounting, Credit, and Collections

6

You have to keep business records and accounts to know how your business is performing. (Are your marketing efforts successful? And are you making a profit or losing?) You also need to know who owes you money and how much, and you need to know what you owe others. Your records and accounts give you clues to ways of improving your business, and they help you detect losing activity, waste, and dishonesty. You're required to keep records for regulatory and tax purposes anyway, so make them serve as working tools for business success.

This chapter will focus on simplifying double-entry bookkeeping so that you will know how to start and use records in your business. You should master the contents of this chapter even if you intend to have someone else keep your books. A knowledge of bookkeeping and accounting will improve your success potential as a business owner and manager.

Finally, if you sell on credit and don't collect, you're in trouble. This chapter addresses these questions:

1. How do you start a set of books for a business?
2. What record forms do you use to assemble business data?
3. What accounts do you need for a mini business?
4. What are debits and credits?

5. What are journals and ledgers and how do you make entries?
6. What are the steps in preparing financial statements?
7. How can you protect yourself against mistakes and dishonesty that bleed cash out of a business?
8. What is a cash-drawer reconciliation?
9. What is a bank-statement reconciliation?
10. What is an accounting work sheet?

DOUBLE-ENTRY BOOKKEEPING SIMPLIFIED

Double-entry bookkeeping is not the complicated process some would have us believe it is. But you'll probably have to spend more time on this chapter than on any other in the book. It will pay off handsomely for you. Your accounts will provide the information that you need to exercise control and point your business toward maximum profits.

The Elements of the System

Figure 6-1 shows the double-entry bookkeeping process simplified. Level 1 is a diagram of the transaction flow, and Level 2 shows the accounts.

All sales and cash receipts enter the system from the left and flow toward the checking account (cash) in the center.

All cash outlays and bills prod the system at the right and move toward the checking account (cash) at the center.

At the left we've lumped cash sales and credit sales in the sales ticket. A sales ticket (Figure 6-2) is prepared for all sales. The ticket is checked or marked as a "cash" or "charge" (credit) sale. At the end of the day you take a total on cash sales and a total on credit sales. The cash sales are entered on the deposit slip.

A formalized system for a large business or a corporation would employ the "accrual basis" of accounting. The accrual method accounts for profit based on all sales (cash and charge) and all expense items (paid and unpaid), inventory changes, and accumulated depreciation. Accountants call this "assigning revenues to the period in which they're earned and expenses to the period in which they're incurred." Hence profit is figured without regard to when cash is received or disbursed in accrual accounting.

The "cash basis" of accounting assumes revenues earned when they're collected in cash and expenses incurred when they're paid in cash. Hence profit is the difference between cash received and cash disbursed during the accounting period in a pure cash-basis system. A cash-basis system of accounting is simpler to use than an accrual-basis system. Most mini businesses use a cash-basis system, and this is the essential nature of the system described in this chapter. In an accrual system you'd enter charge sales in accounts-receivable. In our simplified cash system, we hold charge sales tickets in an "accounts-receivable memo file."

FIGURE 6-1 Double-entry bookkeeping simplified

Level 1 - Diagram

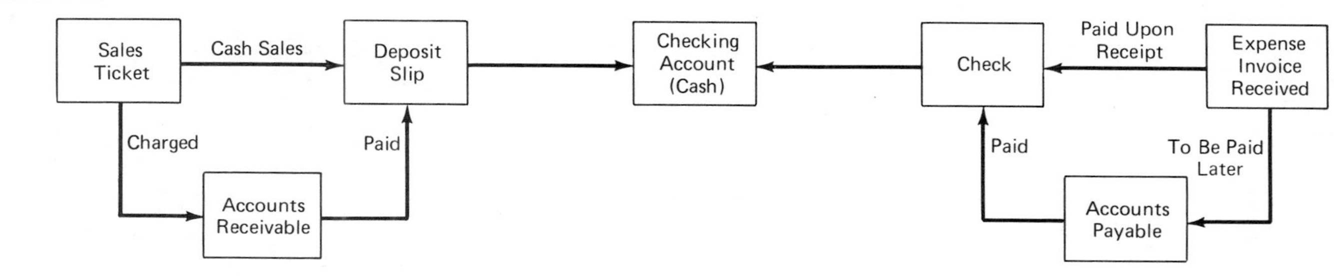

Level 2 - T Accounts

Level 3 - Transactions

1. $100 cash sale made
2. $35 charge account sale made
3. $25 charge account payment received
4. $50 paid on receipt of expense invoice
5. $30 expense invoice received but not paid
6. $20 payment made on account owed for expense item

FIGURE 6-2 Sales ticket form

149151

Customer's Order No. ______ DATE ______ 19__

SOLD TO *William Fischer*

ADDRESS *Coldspring, N.Y.*

SOLD BY	CASH	CHARGE	C O D	PAID OUT	RETD MDSE	RECD ON ACCT	TERMS

QUAN.	DESCRIPTION	PRICE	AMOUNT

ALL Claims and Returned Goods MUST Be Accompanied By This Bill

SIGNATURE ______

FORM K58-AP-3

FIGURE 6-3 Deposit slip form

DEPOSITED WITH

GARLAND BANK & TRUST CO.
GARLAND, TEXAS

THIS DEPOSIT WILL BE CREDITED TO THE ACCOUNT OF THE NAME SHOWN ON THIS DEPOSIT TICKET AND IS ACCEPTED BY THE BANK SUBJECT TO ALL APPLICABLE PROVISIONS OF THE STATE BANKING CODE.

DATE ______ 19__

MR. OR MRS. FORREST H. FRANTZ, SR.

FORM D-4

DEPOSIT TICKET — CHECKING ACCOUNT

	DOLLARS	CENTS
CURRENCY		
COIN		
CHECKS		
CHECKS AS LISTED ON REVERSE SIDE OR ATTACHED TAPE.		
TOTAL DEPOSIT		

⑈119 702 U⑈

RECORD OF CHECKS FOR DEPOSIT

CHECKS LIST SINGLY OR ATTACH LIST	DOLLARS	CENTS
SUB-TOTAL—THIS SIDE		

IMPORTANT: SHOW AMOUNT OF ABOVE CHECKS IN SPACE PROVIDED ON FRONT

FIGURE 6-4 Purchase order form

FIRST NATIONAL BANK IN GARLAND

Purchase Order

This order number must appear on all packing lists and invoices.

Date

Purchase Order No. 215

Vendor

Charge

If freight or postage is charged, please prepay and add to invoice.

Quantity	Description	Unit Cost	Total Cost

Invoice to
First National Bank in Garland
P. O. Box 401228
Garland, Texas 75040

Ship to
☐ First National Bank in Garland
700 W. Avenue A
Garland, Texas 75040

Ship to
☐

First National Bank in Garland
Garland, Texas

Authorized Signature

7341-21-2 FORM #20026

ORIGINAL

(Courtesy: First National Bank, Garland, Texas)

Payments on accounts-receivable are added to cash sales on the deposit slip (Figure 6-3), and hence all money into the business goes into the checking account to add to its size.

Transactions that call money out of the business are initiated with a purchase order, Figure 6-4. This kind of transaction enters the system on the right side of Figure 6-1 in the form of an invoice or bill (Figure 6-6).[1] Expense bills paid immediately are paid by check, (Figure 6-5) and enter the right side of the checking account to reduce its size. Bills for expenses not immediately paid are entered in an "accounts-payable memo file." When you pay an account, you pay by check, and reduce the size of the checking account.

In double-entry bookkeeping there are two sides to each account. The left side is the debit side. The cash account is the key to remembering what goes where. A transaction that *increases the size of the cash account* is debited

[1]Transactions that take money out of the business are usually initiated with a purchase order (Figure 6-4), which is simply used to keep track of orders. The purchase order does not provide an input to a simple small-business accounting system.

FIGURE 6-5 (A) General-purpose business check and stub form

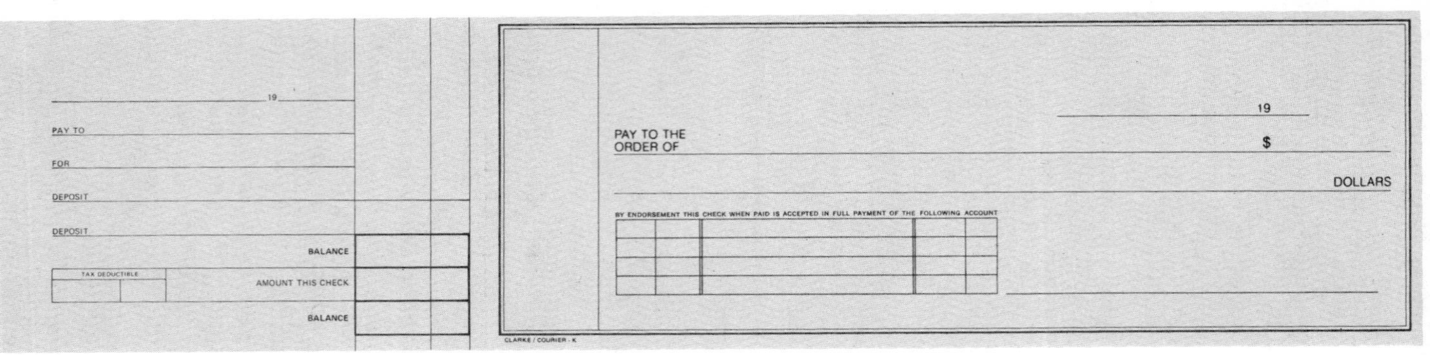

19
PAY TO
FOR
DEPOSIT
DEPOSIT
BALANCE
TAX DEDUCTIBLE
AMOUNT THIS CHECK
BALANCE

19
PAY TO THE ORDER OF
$
DOLLARS
BY ENDORSEMENT THIS CHECK WHEN PAID IS ACCEPTED IN FULL PAYMENT OF THE FOLLOWING ACCOUNT
CLARKE / COURIER - K

(B) Payroll check and stub with extra stub for employee

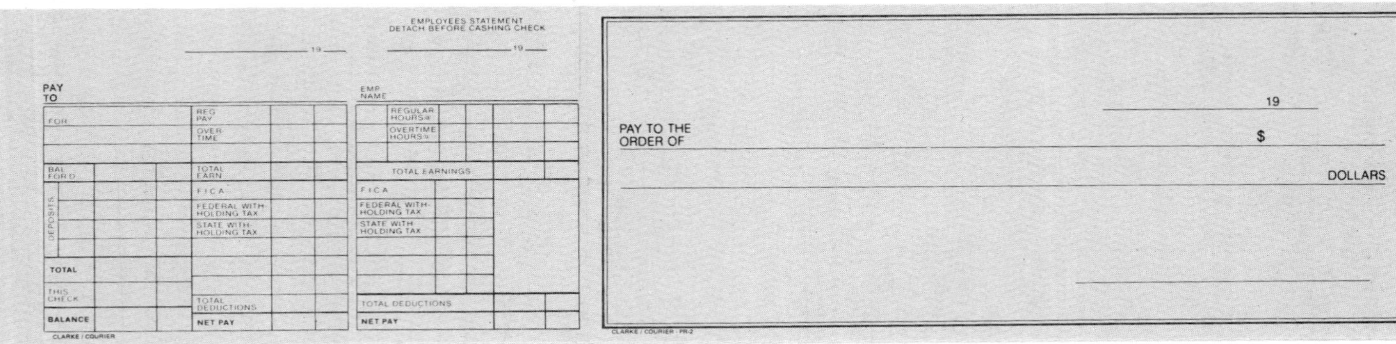

19
PAY TO
FOR
REG PAY
OVER-TIME
BAL FOR'D
TOTAL EARN
DEPOSITS
F.I.C.A.
FEDERAL WITH-HOLDING TAX
STATE WITH-HOLDING TAX
TOTAL
THIS CHECK
TOTAL DEDUCTIONS
BALANCE
NET PAY
CLARKE / COURIER

EMPLOYEES STATEMENT
DETACH BEFORE CASHING CHECK
19
EMP NAME
REGULAR HOURS @
OVERTIME HOURS @
TOTAL EARNINGS
F.I.C.A.
FEDERAL WITH-HOLDING TAX
STATE WITH-HOLDING TAX
TOTAL DEDUCTIONS
NET PAY

19
PAY TO THE ORDER OF
$
DOLLARS
CLARKE / COURIER - PR-2

(Courtesy: Clarke/Courier, Dallas, Texas)

FIGURE 6-6 Invoice form

INVOICE

INVOICE NUMBER ______

C W D MAINTENANCE COMPANY
P. O. Box 54
Garland, Texas 75040
272-8015

SOLD TO ______

SHIPPED TO ______

CUST'S. ORDER NO.	OUR ORDER NO.	INVOICE DATE	TERMS	SHIPPED VIA	DATE SHIPPED	SOLD BY

QUANTITY	DESCRIPTION	UNIT PRICE	AMOUNT

Thank You

(left side), and a transaction that *decreases the size of the cash account is credited* (right side). For teaching purposes we use a "T" account. The left side is debit and right is credit. The "T" accounts are shown at level 2 Figure 6-1 and the numbers in the "T" account represent a series of numbered transactions shown at level 3.

POINT 6-1: When cash flows into the business, debit cash; when cash flows out, credit cash.

Cash Sales

Transaction number 1 is a $100 cash sale. First, you write a sales ticket and mark it paid. The $100 cash or check received goes into your deposit slip and consequently the "cash" account. Cash grows so you debit cash (entry 1b). In double-entry bookkeeping, each entry must be balanced by another entry. Since the cash came from sales, you credit sales (entry 1a).

POINT 6-2: In double-entry bookkeeping, each debit to one account must be balanced by a credit to another account; similarly, each credit must be balanced by a debit.

Now, we've established what to do *if we make a sale. We credit sales* and *debit something else*. For a cash sale, the debit to something else is a debit to cash.

Charge Sales

Next, transaction 2 is a $35 charge-account sale. You write a charge sales slip. If you were keeping an accrual set of books, you would credit sales $35 (entry 2a) and debit accounts-receivable $35 (entry 2b).

In actual practice, using our cash-basis system, we will not make a formal entry to sales or to accounts-receivable. We will simply record the charge sale by date, customer name, and amount charged on an informal ledger sheet at the front of an alphabetical accounts-receivable file, and we'll file the charge sales slip alphabetically. Thus, we have made a durable but informal record of the transaction.

Payment Received on Account

Next, transaction 3 is a $25 payment on account. In an accrual system you would credit accounts-receivable $25 (entry 3a) and debit cash $25 (entry 3b).

In our cash system, you enter the date, customer's name, and the amount of the payment on the informal accounts-receivable ledger sheet and if the amount paid corresponds to the amount of the customer's charge sales slip in the file, you simply mark it "paid" and put it in with the cash sales for the day. Hence, it goes into the formal books as a cash sale. If a partial amount is paid, write a cash sales slip for the amount "paid on account" and reference the original sales ticket number. This amount goes into the formal books as a cash sale. Also note the payment (with reference to the number of the "paid on account" sales slip) and the balance on the original charge slip.

Expense Paid

All expenses are lumped into one account for learning purposes in Figure 6-1. Transaction 4 is a $50 payment upon receipt of an expense invoice. You write a check for $50, so you decrease cash. That means you credit cash (entry 4b) and the balancing entry is a debit to expense (entry 4a).

Expense Invoice Received, Not Paid

Transaction 5 is receipt of a $30 expense invoice that you don't pay immediately. In the accrual system you debit expense $30 (entry 5a) and credit accounts-payable $30 (entry 5b).

In our cash-basis system, you enter the date, vendor's name, amount, and due date on an informal accounts-payable ledger sheet at the front of an alphabetical accounts-payable file, and file the invoice. The formal books do not show a record of the billing.

Accounts-Payable Disbursement

Transaction 6 is a payment of $20 on accounts-payable. You write a check for $20 which decreases cash and decreases accounts-payable. In the accrual-basis system, you credit cash $20 (entry 6b) and debit accounts-payable $20 (entry 6a).

In our cash-basis system you enter the payment date, vendor's name, and check number on the informal accounts-payable file, place it with your paid bills, and credit cash and debit expense. Now that you've written a check, the transaction is recognized on your formal books.

REVIEW EXERCISES 6-A

1. The following transactions have been made: On 1/6/19X8, Joe's garage had a $170 cash sale, a $60 charge sale, and a $50 charge sale. A customer paid $30 on a previously charged sale. A cash purchase of $25 in parts was made (purchase expense) and a light bill for $60 (utility expense) was received but not paid. Payments of $10 and $100 were made to parts suppliers for bills owed on previous purchases.
   (a) Set up the necessary "T" accounts and make the necessary entries on the accrual basis. Number and letter the entries as shown in Figure 6-1 for ease of identification.
   (b) What was the amount of the day's deposit?
   (c) What is the total amount of checks written for the day?
   (d) What is the net balance of each account?
2. On 1/8/19X8, Joe's Garage made cash sales of $50, $25, $90, and $180 and credit sales of $100 and $60. Invoices received and paid the same day were $55 parts, $40 parts, and $30 office supplies. Bills received and not paid were $75 advertising and $20 cleaning rags. Payments of $67 and $53 were made on bills received on 1/1/19X8.

   You may work this as a continuation of Exercise 1 or as a separate problem. Perform steps (a), (b), (c), and (d) as called for in Exercise 1.

3. List the expense-account classifications essential in a mini-business bookkeeping system.
4. You were introduced to the accounting equation–assets equal liabilities plus owner's equity–in an earlier chapter. Can you reach any conclusions about the effect of the position of an account (with respect to the equal sign) on whether you debit or credit an increase in the account? *Hint*: Recall the various asset and liability headings on the balance sheet and substitute them in the accounting equation. Also, recall the income statement format. Does it develop a contribution to the balance sheet?

EXPANDING THE SYSTEM

The simplified approach of the previous section has given us a general idea of the double-entry process. Now, we'll expand and clarify the system–but just as far as we need it for a small business. This chapter will not compete with accounting textbooks running to 500 pages or more; for you as a small businessperson accounting is a tool, not a career. And that's as far as we'll go.[2]

The Accounting Equation

The tough part of learning accounting is getting straight on when to debit and credit on account. Most businesspeople who aren't trained accountants use the two simple principles of points 1 and 2 in the previous section–namely, deciding what to do with cash and knowing that for each entry there's a balancing or offsetting entry.

The detailed form of the accounting equation for a mini-business is developed from the basic equation in Figure 6-7. Accounts-receivable and accounts-payable have been left out of this development since you will not use them in your cash-basis system. Notice that all terms have plus signs in equation 8. To increase any account on the left-hand side of the equal sign in equation 8, you debit the account; to increase any account on the right-hand side of the equal sign, you credit the account.

POINT 6-3: To show an increase in an account (a) debit asset, expense, and owner's draw accounts; (b) credit liability, capital, sales, discounts earned, and accumulated depreciation accounts.

Required Accounts

Now we can construct a chart of accounts, which is a table of contents of the accounts in the system. Numbers are assigned to the accounts to simplify referencing. I'll explain each account and why it's needed.

[2] For further study of accounting, see Glen L. Johnson and James A. Gentry, *Finney and Miller's Principles of Accounting, Introductory*, 7th ed. (Englewood Cliffs, N.J.: Prentice-Hall, Inc., 1970).

MINI BUSINESS
CHART OF ACCOUNTS

Asset accounts (100-199)

101	Cash
102	Petty cash
103	Inventory—merchandise*
110	Equipment*
110-1	Accumulated depreciation—equipment*
120	Utility deposits*

Liability accounts (200-299)

202	Federal income taxes (FIT) withheld
203	Social security taxes (FICA) withheld
204	Sales taxes collected
210	Notes-payable*

Capital accounts (300-399)

301	Capital*
302	Owner's draw
303	Profit*

Revenue accounts (400-499)

401	Sales
402	Discounts earned*
410	Gain from sale of assets*

Expense accounts (500-599)

501	Purchases—merchandise
502	Freight-in
510	Salaries
511	Rent*
512	Utilities
513	Advertising
514	Freight-out*
515	Office
516	Automotive
517	Insurance*
518	Professional fees*
519	Depreciation*
520	Cash over and short
530	Property taxes*
531	Employment taxes*
540	Interest*

*Designates accounts that are usually least active in a small retail or service business.

The skips in the numbering serve several purposes. The hundreds separations segregate accounts by type. The interior separations segregate items within the account. For example, liability and asset accounts carry current items in

FIGURE 6-7 The accounting equation for a cash-basis proprietorship

1. Assets = Liabilities + Owner's Equity
2. Assets = Cash + Inventory + (Equipment – Accumulated Depreciation)
3. Owner's Equity = Capital – Owner's Draw + Profit
4. Profit* = Sales – Expenses + Discounts earned
5. Owner's Equity = Capital – Owner's Draw + Sales – Expenses + Discounts Earned
6. Eq. 2 = Liabilities + Eq. 5 (This is Eq. 1 restated.)
   Cash + Inventory + Equipment – Accumulated Depreciation = Liabilities + Capital – Owner's Draw + Sales – Expenses + Discounts Earned
7. Move minus terms on right to left, and minus terms on left to right. This makes all signs plus.
8. Cash + Inventory + Equipment + Owner's Draw + Expenses = Liabilities + Capital + Sales + Discounts Earned + Accumulated Depreciation
9. To increase accounts on the *left* of the equal sign, *debit* the account. To increase accounts to the *right* of the equal sign, *credit* the account.

*Cost of goods sold was assumed to equal purchase expenses to simplify this development.

accounts 0-9 and long-term items in 10-19. The expense items are separated with expenses directly related to cost of sales in 501-509, indirect expenses in 510-539, and expenses related to financing in 540. The numbering system you follow is up to you. There's no established standard.

Now, let's examine each of the account titles and find out why we need the account in a mini business.

101 Cash: The cash account is your business checking account. You deposit all the money you receive in business transactions in your checking account and you make all disbursements by check. Very small items are an exception, and they're paid with petty cash, which we'll discuss later.

POINT 6-4: The business checking account is the *cash account*. All business transactions, and only business transactions, should flow through this account. This is the business entity principle.

102 Petty Cash: This account is used to set up currency and change for small cash payments and for starting change in the cash drawer. You write and cash a check for the starting amount, and you credit cash and debit petty cash. You'll get more details on this later in the chapter.

103 Inventory–Merchandise: This account keeps track of inventory. You make entries only when you take a physical inventory and close the books. If you're in a retail or service business, you'll use the merchandise designation.

If you're in a manufacturing business, you'll have three inventory accounts; namely, raw materials, goods in process, and finished goods. There are several approaches to valuing inventory of which LIFO (last in, first out) and FIFO (first in, first out) are best known.

110 Equipment: This account is given a new level number because it is a fixed-asset account. You need this account to keep track of your equipment. Since equipment wears out over a period of time and is charged off as depreciation expense, the decrease in equipment value must be reflected on the balance sheet. So, you need an *accumulated depreciation account*, which is shown as 110-1. When you debit depreciation expense, you credit accumulated depreciation as the balancing entry.

If you own the land and building in which your business is situated, you'll need a fixed-asset account, which can be labeled "store property" or "plant," and corresponding accumulated depreciation account.

120 Utility Deposits: This account includes deposits for electricity, water, gas, phone, and trash removal. You credit cash and debit this account when you pay a deposit.

202 Federal Income Taxes (FIT) Withheld: When you write a payroll check for an employee, you're required to withhold income tax for the Internal Revenue Service (IRS). You owe the amount withheld to the IRS and will have to pay it. Therefore, you must show it as a liability, and you do it in this account. You credit this account for the amount withheld (balancing a debit to salary expense) and, when you pay IRS, you debit this account and credit cash.

203 Social Security Taxes (FICA) Withheld: Your employee is required to contribute 5.85 percent (this is subject to change) on earnings up to $15,300 (also subject to change). You collect the contribution and owe it to IRS. You debit salary expense for the amount of the contribution and credit this account. When you pay the government, you debit this account and credit cash. (You'll match the FICA with employment tax payments. See Account 531.)

204 Sales Tax Collected: All but a few states have a state sales tax. You collect the tax whenever you make a sale, and you're liable to the state for the amount collected (usually less a small discount for the collection service). Labor and some other items may not be subject to sales tax in your state. You can record the taxes from your sales tickets or use an approved formula to compute tax on day's sales. *Avoid recording sales tax collected as part of sales!*

Sales tax collected is credited to this account and debited to cash. When you pay the state, you debit this account and credit cash. If the state allows a discount for the collection service, only the amount paid to the state is entered as a credit to cash, and the discount allowed is credited to discounts earned (Account 402).

210 Notes-Payable: This account is given the 210 level number because of its financial nature (as opposed to the operating nature of the other liability accounts). When you borrow money you credit this account for the amount borrowed and debit cash. When you repay the loan, you debit this account and credit cash. Since you will also pay interest, you credit cash for the amount of the interest and debit interest expense (Account 540).

301 Capital: When you start your business you'll invest cash and possibly some other assets in your business. (The capital account is owner's equity.) To record these, you'll credit this account and debit cash or the other asset account in which the contribution of owner's equity is made.

302 Owner's Draw: Whenever you draw money out of a proprietorship or a partnership, you decrease cash. So, you debit this account and credit cash. Since the draw transaction decreases owner's equity, you reflect this when you close the books by crediting this account and debiting capital.

303 Profit: Owner's equity grows with profit. When you close your books at the end of an accounting period, you enter the profit shown on the income statement as a debit to this account and balance it with a credit to capital (Account 301). If you had a loss, the opposite set of entries would be made.

401 Sales and **402 Discounts Earned:** These should be quite clear by now, except for a point concerning discounts. The discount-earned account is set up to handle sales-tax discounts granted by the state for your service in collecting them. Don't use this account for prompt payment discounts on trade accounts. It is much easier to enter the net amount paid after taking the discount as the actual purchase expense.

If you are in a business that sells items or services that are exempt from sales taxes (e.g., labor in a service business), it's a good idea to have two accounts for sales: Sales–Taxable and Sales–Exempt.

410 Gain from Sale of Assets: When you sell an asset, you get cash and therefore debit cash. The cash that you get plus the accumulated depreciation on the asset must equal the original cost plus the gain from sale-of-assets entry. In other words, this kind of transaction usually requires a total of four entries. As an example, a piece of equipment that cost $1,000 with $800 accumulated depreciation is sold for $350. Your entries are:

	Debit	Credit
Cash	$350	
Accumulated depreciation	$800	
Gain from sale of assets		$150
Equipment		$1,000

So, you debit cash $350, debit accumulated depreciation $800, credit sale of asset $150, and credit equipment $1,000.

If you had sold this asset for $100 you would have had a loss. The entries would have been:

Cash	$100	
Accumulated depreciation	$800	
Gain from sale of assets	$100	
Equipment		$1,000

500-599 The Expense Accounts: All of these accounts are handled in the same way. A few deserve special mention.

Whenever you pay an expense, you credit cash and debit the expense account. Purchases and freight-in are placed in the 501-509 category because they contribute directly to cost of goods sold. If you were in a manufacturing business, you would have a "Purchases–Raw Materials" instead of "Purchases–Merchandise" and a direct labor account in this group, because they contribute directly to cost of goods manufactured.

Accounts 510 through 518 are ordinary indirect expenses. Since you'll operate on a cash basis, the handling is very straightforward. Debit the expense, credit cash. Account 518, Professional Fees, includes fees to lawyers and accountants.

519 Depreciation Expense: This expense account is different from the others in that you pay a large amount in year 1 for a piece of equipment and then deduct a portion of its cost for a series of succeeding years without paying any cash during those years. Under the straight-line depreciation method, you simply divide the cost by the years of anticipated life to get annual depreciation expense. The first year's depreciation is the fraction of the year the asset is owned times the annual depreciation. You debit Depreciation Expense and credit Accumulated Depreciation (Account 110-1).

520 Cash Over and Short: This will be covered under cash-drawer reconciliation.

530 Property Tax Expense: You'll pay personal property tax on equipment and inventory, so you need an account for this expense. You'll also pay real property taxes if you own your building. Set real property taxes up in a separate account.

531 Employment Taxes: You'll have to pay an FICA tax of 5.85 percent (subject to change) on salary and wages paid to employees. You make this payment when you submit FIT and FICA withheld from employees. (You'll also be paying "unemployment" taxes which you'll include in this account.)

Your contribution will be equal in amount to the employee's FICA contribution. When you pay, debit employment tax expense and credit cash. (FICA stands for Federal Insurance Contributions Act, more commonly referred to as "social security taxes.")

540 Interest: This expense has been discussed in connection with notes-payable.

The Accounting Cycle

You already know quite a bit about some of the components of the accounting cycle. But we haven't mentioned some of the steps in the process. Now, we'll introduce the process, and fill in the areas not previously covered. The steps in the accounting cycle are:

1. *Data collection*, which includes preparation and collection of sales tickets, bills received, deposit slips, and check stubs
2. *Recording*, which is original entry of the data into the journals
3. *Classifying*, which is posting of entries to the ledger
4. *Summarizing*, which includes totaling the net balance of each account, and taking a trial balance
5. *Adjusting* to make accounts current
6. *Financial statement preparation*

The data-collection step should be pretty clear at this point. Next, the collected data is recorded in "books of original entry" called *journals.* The journals provide a *chronological record* of business activity. The simplest practical journal system for a mini business is to make all entries in a single journal. A journal set-up page is shown in Figure 6-8.

Classifying by posting from the journal to the general ledger (simply called "ledger" hereafter) is straightforward. You simply enter the data from the journal in the appropriate ledger account and column. Journal entries can be made daily. Ledger entries can be made as often as you wish. Monthly entries are recommended. The ledger postings for accounts with separate columns in the journal then are the monthly totals of the journal columns. The less frequently used accounts (indicated by an asterisk on the chart of accounts) are entered in the "general ledger" column of the journal and are posted item by item to the ledger accounts. Use a check mark in the journal to indicate when you've posted an account.

The last three steps in the accounting cycle–summarizing, adjusting, and financial statement preparation–are end-of-period operations. The normal accounting period is one year. You close the books at the end of the year; summarize on a work sheet; and adjust the accumulated depreciation, depreciation expense, and inventory accounts to reflect end-of-year status; and derive the information for the financial statements.

FIGURE 6-8 Journal page format

JOURNAL

DATE	DESCRIPTION	CHECK NO.	CASH		PETTY CASH		SALES	GENERAL LEDGER	
			DR.	CR.	DR.	CR.	CR.	DR.	CR.

SALES TAX COLLECTED CR.	PURCHASES DR.	FREIGHT IN DR.	SALARIES DR.	F.I.T. WITHHELD CR.	F.I.C.A. WITHHELD CR.	UTILITIES DR.	ADVERTISING DR.	OFFICE DR.	AUTOMOTIVE DR.	CASH OVER & SHORT DR.

It's recommended that you prepare an interim income statement every month. Since you won't be taking inventory or recording depreciation on a monthly basis, you estimate cost of goods sold based on gross margin and sales; you estimate depreciation by taking 1/12 of previous year's depreciation. You don't close the books, and these estimates are not entered in the formal books.

A monthly income statement should show all of the normal income statement items with a column for the current month and a column for the year to date. The monthly income statement provides a good overview of operations and increases your ability to control your business. It is a tool for expense and profit control.

POINT 6-5: Make journal entries daily; post to ledger monthly; close the books and prepare formal financial statements annually. Prepare interim income statements monthly.

The "Books"

The "books" can actually be retained in one binder if you wish. A separate binder for the journal and a separate binder for the ledger will serve you well. You'll need a large number of columns in the journal. Wilson Jones form 30-24 or an equivalent has space for date, item description, check number, and ten account columns on the left page (back of sheet) and fourteen columns on the right page (front of sheet). Thus, with the journal open, you have twenty-four account columns across the open journal. Make your journal entries in pencil for easier handling, correction, neatness and speed. Figure 6-8 shows typical column headings for a mini business based on the previously listed chart of accounts. The less frequently used accounts (indicated by asterisks on the chart of accounts) do not have separate journal columns; you enter these items in the columns marked "general ledger."

You can set up the ledger most conveniently by using two different forms. Since you can post monthly totals on the accounts with separate columns in the journal, you have twelve entries a year to each of these accounts. So, you can use a multi-columnar form for these accounts in the ledger. Thus one ledger page can contain all entries for these accounts. You can use the same form for the ledger on these accounts that you use for your journal. However, the accounts that are entered under the "general ledger" heading in the journal will not have equal numbers of entries in a period and a separate sheet for each account is desirable. So, smaller ledger sheets with the Wilson Jones form N2-D or equivalent for the accounts requiring a separate ledger sheet and the Wilson Jones form 10-24 or equivalent for accounts that can be grouped in the ledger are recommended. (The form 10-24 can be used for the journal instead of the 30-24. However, the 10-24 is smaller and "crowds" journal information.)

Starting Entries

Assume you're starting your business with

(a) $5,000 of your own cash capital
(b) $1,000 of your own equipment
(c) $3,000 borrowed from First National Bank

How do you start the books?

First, you set up your journal and ledger using the guidelines of the previous subsections. You deposit your $8,000 cash in the bank. Next, you make these entries in the journal:

March 1, 197X John Jones, starting capital		
Cash	$8,000	
Equipment	1,000	
John Jones, Capital		$6,000
Notes-Payable, First National Bank		3,000

This representation of entries contains the descriptive entry on the first line. The next lines show the account and amount. The left and right positions indicate debit and credit, respectively. You enter this in the journal physically (see Figure 6-9) by entering date and description in the appropriate columns on the first line; you enter $8,000 in the cash debit column on the first line. You write "equipment" in the description column on the second line and write $1,000 in the "general ledger" debit column second line; write "John Jones, capital" in the third line description column, and enter $6,000 in the "general ledger" credit column third line; write "Note–First National Bank" in the descriptive column on the fourth line and enter $3,000 in the fourth line under the "general ledger" credit column.

That's all that's necessary in the way of entries to start a business. You follow the same approach in making operating transaction entries.

Operating Transaction Entries

Now, having set up your books, assume you made the following transactions the next day:

(d) Purchased $500 equipment, check 101, to Tom Jones Co.
(e) Purchased $1,000 merchandise, check 102, to Acme Distributors
(f) Sold $200 merchandise for cash which you deposited in the bank
(g) Bought $50 office supplies, check 103, from Rawlins Office Supply

(The entries are shown in Figure 6-9.)

FIGURE 6-9 Typical journal entries

JOURNAL

DATE	DESCRIPTION	CHECK NO.	CASH		SALES CR.	GENERAL LEDGER		PURCHASES DR.	OFFICE DR.	
			DR.	CR.		DR.	CR.			
197X 3/1	John Jones, Starting Capital		8000			Equipment 1000	Capital 6000			
	Note Payable, INB						3000			
3/2	(d) Equipment	101		500		500				
3/2	(e)	102		1000				1000		
3/2	(f)		200		200					
3/2	(g)	103		50					50	

At the end of the month, you total the columns. All of the column totals except the "general ledger" total are posted to the appropriate ledger account.

POINT 6-6: The simplest journal system employs one journal with multi-column sheets. The most frequently used accounts have their own columns. Less frequently used accounts are entered under the "general ledger" columns.

The Work Sheet

A *work sheet* is used to strike a trial balance, adjust accounts, and summarize the data for the income statement (which shows how much profit you made *during a period* of time), and the balance sheet (which shows your worth *at a given point* in time). A work sheet is shown in Figure 6-10.

The trial-balance column data is the net total of each of the accounts in the ledger. The total debits must equal the total credits on the work sheet. (If they're not equal, you've made an error and need to correct it. You can minimize the chance of an error at year-end by taking a trial balance each month.)

Since we're operating on a cash accounting basis, the only adjustments that must be made are to enter depreciation expense and accumulated depreciation. The adjusted trial balance then differs from the trial balance only for these two items.

Next, we enter those items that are pertinent to the income statement and those pertinent to the balance sheet under the appropriate columns. The income statement column totals provide the profit result. The data in these columns is used to prepare the financial statements shown in Figure 6-11. Another financial statement that won't be covered here is the statement of changes in financial position or *funds statement.*[3]

This brief treatment of the work sheet places the burden of going through it and trying to understand it on you. It isn't easy to understand on first encounter and most students need some help. If you take on the job of doing your own books, I suggest you enlist the services of a CPA or a tax service in preparing your tax return at least the first year. Call on this assistance to help you master the complexities of the work sheet and the preparation of your end-of-year financial statements.

REVIEW EXERCISES 6-B

1. Indicate whether you debit or credit each of the following accounts for a *decrease* in account size: (a) cash; (b) expense; (c) capital; (d) notes-payable; (e) purchases; (f) accumulated depreciation; (g) equipment; (h) sales.

[3] See Charles T. Horngren, *Accounting for Management Control, An Introduction,* 3rd ed. (Englewood Cliffs, N.J.: Prentice-Hall, Inc., 1974), pp. 106-110.

FIGURE 6-10 Worksheet (year ended 19X2)

WORKSHEET (Year Ended 19x2)

ACCOUNT TITLES	TRIAL BALANCE		ADJUSTMENTS		ADJUSTED TRIAL BALANCE		INCOME STATEMENT		BALANCE SHEET	
	DR.	CR.	DR.	CR.	DR.	CR.	DR.	CR.	DR.	CR.
Cash	2000				2000				2000	
Inventory	5000				5000		5000	5800[2a]	5800[2b]	
Equipment	2000				2000				2000	
Accumulated Depreciation		500		400[1a]		900				900
Capital		7000				7000				7000
Notes Payable		500				500				500
Sales		40000				40000		40000		
Purchases	22000				22000		22000			
Salaries	10000				10000		10000			
Rent	3000				3000		3000			
Utilities	3000				3000		3000			
Advertising	1000				1000		1000			
Depreciation			400[1b]		400		400			
	48000	48000	400	400	48400	48400	44400	45800	9800	8400
Profit (also called "Net Income")							1400			1400
							45800	45800	9800	9800

FIGURE 6-11 (A) Income statement (year ended 19X2)

Sales			$40,000
Cost of goods sold			
Inventory, Jan. 1, 19X2	$ 5,000		
Purchases	22,000		
Goods available for sale		27,000	
Inventory Dec. 31, 19X2		5,800	
Cost of goods sold			21,200
Gross profit			29,800
Operating expenses			
Salaries	$10,000		
Rent	3,000		
Utilities	3,000		
Advertising	1,000		
Depreciation	400		
Operating expenses			17,400
Net income			1,400

(B) Balance sheet (Dec. 31, 19X2)

Assets		
Current assets		
Cash	$ 2,000	
Inventory	5,800	
	7,800	
Fixed assets		
Equipment	$ 2,000	
Less accumulated depreciation	900	
	$ 1,100	
Total assets	$ 8,900	
Liabilities and owner's equity		
Liabilities		
Notes payable		$ 500
Owner's equity		
As of Jan. 1, 19X2 $7,000		
Profit for period 1,400		
Owner's equity		$ 8,400
Liabilities and owner's equity		$ 8,900

2. Classify each of the accounts in Exercise 1 as asset, liability, capital, revenue, or expense.
3. Why do you depreciate equipment instead of expensing the full cost immediately?
4. Why are "taxes withheld" liabilities?
5. What are the steps in the accounting cycle?
6. Set up "T" accounts and make the appropriate entries for the transactions shown in Figure 6-9.
7. What is the purpose of the work sheet?

INTERNAL CONTROL

You, as the owner-manager of a one-person mini business have full control insofar as you exercise it. You handle all the cash, make all purchases and payments, and are the sole custodian and user of the assets of your business. When your business grows and you acquire employees, you will lose this direct contact with the activities and the assets in your business. Others will have access to your cash drawer, inventory, equipment, purchasing, billing, and possibly your checking account. A system of internal control is needed to discourage and reveal dishonesty, errors, and shoddy operations. A system of internal control consists of policy, procedures, and organizational assignments that foster asset protection, accurate accounting inputs, and efficient business operation.

Internal Control Policy

Internal control policy generally includes the following points:

1. Clearly define responsibilities so that if assets are lost, errors are made, or something else goes wrong, the source of the problem can be pinpointed and corrective action can be taken.
2. Maintain adequate records to be able to trace transactions and detect error or dishonesty.
3. Separate record-keeping and custodial responsibilities. The record keeping, and the collecting, depositing, and disbursements of your money should not be left to the same person. This means that one person cannot readily steal or misappropriate funds without the help of another.
4. Divide responsibility for related transactions so that the work of one person serves as a check on another.
5. Rotate job assignments from time to time. An employee is less apt to steal or do careless work when he knows he's subject to exposure on rotation.
6. Screen employees carefully and resort to protective measures such as polygraph checks, bonding, and insurance.
7. Establish procedures for cash handling, cash-drawer reconciliation, bank-balance reconciliation, petty cash account, and other items that are vulnerable to dishonesty or error.
8. Have all records serially numbered—sales tickets, cash receipts, checks, and so forth.

You can use mechanical equipment to strengthen the internal control system. A cash register with a locked-in record tape provides cash protection. A check protector guards against check alteration. A time clock keeps people honest about their time.

POINT 6-7: Internal control safeguards assets by detecting and discouraging dishonesty, error, and shoddy operations.

Bank-Balance Reconciliation

Your checking account monthly bank statement should be reconciled to prove the accuracy of the bank's and your own records. The reconciliation process is best shown by example.

Your bank statement shows your balance as $2,532.25. According to your accounting records, your balance is $2,424.52. Your checks no. 176 for $100, no. 178 for $207, and no. 179 for $36.73 did not clear the bank and are not shown on the bank statement. A $210 deposit made the previous day wasn't made on time to be included in the bank's statement. A $20 check written by Harry Blake bounced (NSF-not sufficient funds). The bank charged your account $6 for checks you ordered.

The reconciliation is set up as follows:

Your record cash balance		$2,424.52
Deduct:		
NSF check Harry Blake	$ 20.00	
Charge for book of checks	6.00	26.00
Reconciled balance		$2,398.52
Bank statement balance		$2,532.25
Add:		
Deposit not recorded		210.00
		$2,742.25
Deduct:		
Checks outstanding no. 176	$100.00	
178	207.00	
179	36.73	343.73
Reconciled balance		$2,398.52

The reconciled balances must be equal, or there's an error in your books or in the bank's statement. Now, you have to make entries to correct your books:

Charge for NSF check received,		
Sales	$20.00	
Cash		$20.00
Bank charge for book of checks,		
Office expense	$ 6.00	
Cash		$ 6.00

This process should be performed each month upon receipt of the bank statement.

Cash-Drawer Reconciliation

A reconciliation of the cash in the cash drawer at the end of the day with sales slips totals is essential to correct errors in change making and to detect theft. Many small businesses do not maintain a separate petty cash drawer and pay small items out of the cash drawer. But the cash drawer contains the petty cash account. In this case, a receipt is obtained for the disbursement and the receipt is left in the cash drawer. Assume you're using this system and you have $496.42 in cash at the end of the day and you started your cash drawer with $50.00 in cash or equivalent. You paid out $0.50 for faucet washers and $1.25 for pencils for which you have receipts in the drawer. Your sales tickets for the day total $450.10. Proceed as follows:

Sales		$450.10
End-of-day cash	$496.42	
Less start petty cash	50.00	
	$446.42	
Plus petty cash expended	1.75	
		$448.17
Cash Over and Short		$ 1.93 short

Your journal entries are $1.75 credit to petty cash, $1.93 debit to cash over and short, and $448.27 debit to cash, $450.10 credit to sales. You start cash the next day with $50.00 minus $1.93 or $48.07. The sum of the cash plus petty cash receipts must equal the amount of the original petty cash. When petty cash gets low, you write a petty cash check equal to the receipts on hand and enter these amounts in the appropriate accounts. This differs slightly from the method commonly taught, which we'll describe now.

POINT 6-8: Reconcile your cash drawer daily; reconcile your bank statement monthly.

Petty Cash

Larger businesses set up a petty cash drawer separate from the cash drawer. A check for a small amount, say $25, is written and cashed to place this amount in petty cash. As payments are made from petty cash, receipts (or petty cash vouchers) are placed in petty cash. The total of cash plus receipts in petty cash should always equal the original amount of petty cash.

When the cash in the petty cash account gets low, another check equal to the total of the receipts for disbursement is written, and the receipt amounts are entered in the appropriate accounts. A petty cash record is usually kept by the custodian for quick checking.

I prefer the petty cash method described earlier for a very small business, because it simplifies petty cash disbursements and record keeping and provides a daily signal on what's happening to all petty cash.

Other Precautionary Measures

Dishonest employee practices milk millions out of businesses. One common trick is to destroy the business's copy of a sales slip or a receipt and pocket the money. Serially numbered sales slips help to signal this practice. Check the bottom numbers in salesbooks and receipt books periodically to be sure slips aren't being removed from the back.

Another source of loss is theft of merchandise or supplies. Keep office supply reserves locked up. Display merchandise so employees have a good view of the store and can spot customer theft. Keep customers out of stockrooms and shop areas.

Check hand tools and equipment (used by employees out of the store or shop) to the employees and have them sign for receipt. Check with an inventory of the employee's tools every six months and whenever an employee leaves.

Fake receipts are sometimes turned in for cash disbursements or receipts obtained for personal purchases. Receipts for gas are common, and you can guard against this by having a charge account with a specific service station that has a roster of your vehicles, and requiring all your vehicles to get gas there.

Do not issue keys for your store or shop to employees indiscriminately. Whenever an employee who had a key leaves your employ, have the lock rekeyed.

To protect yourself against burglary, light your store at least partially at night. Be sure you have deadbolt door locks and barred rear windows. A burglar-alarm system will provide added protection.

REVIEW EXERCISES 6-C

1. What are the primary functions of internal control?
2. What are the points that internal control policy should cover?
3. Your bank statement shows a balance of $3,276; your books show a balance of $3,061. The bank statement contains a $5 charge for your safety deposit box, and checks written for a total of $210 have not cleared the bank. Reconcile this. What entries should you make in your journal?
4. At close of business today your cash drawer contained $347; you opened with $25. Sales slip total is $327. You paid $3 for freight-in and $1.50 for office supplies. Reconcile the cash drawer and list appropriate journal entries.
5. Develop a list of precautionary measures that you can implement to protect your business. Do not limit yourself to those listed in this chapter.

CREDIT AND COLLECTIONS

Credit is a sales tool, and if you sell on credit but don't collect, you're worse off than if you didn't sell at all. It's important that you don't forget this. You take preventative measures to avoid "getting stuck" by developing and implementing a credit policy. This determines your standards for granting credit. You take remedial action to collect from those to whom you've granted credit who are slow to pay or who resist payment by developing and implementing a collection procedure.

Credit—A Sales Tool

Credit is a sales tool because you can make sales on credit which you might miss if you didn't grant credit. A consumer would have to forego the purchase of a $7,000 car or a $500 dishwasher if cash were required and he didn't have the cash. Or the consumer might have the cash but prefer to hold it for possible future emergencies or investment opportunities. In either case, you cannot make the sale for cash, but can make it if credit is available.

Credit can also be a convenience to the buyer. For example, your own business's charge account at an office supply store consolidates small purchases into a monthly total billing. Retail store credit is a convenience because the shopper does not have to carry cash. The convenience motive brings business to the credit seller that the cash seller cannot get.

> POINT 6-9: Credit is a sales tool because it enables you to make sales you would otherwise miss. Credit does this by providing convenience and providing immediate purchasing power to those who cannot pay now.

Credit can be classified in many ways. Classified by *user,* there is consumer, business and industrial, and government credit. Classified by *time,* there is short-term (less than a year), intermediate-term and long-term credit. Classified by *use,* there is purchase and loan credit. *The focus in this subsection is on consumer and business credit of short-term to intermediate-term duration for purchase purposes.* We will deal with the *charge, open,* or *trade* account, *installment sales,* and *variations* that enable you to extend credit to your customers.

The *open account,* also known as a charge account or a trade account, generally extends credit to the customer for a period of about thirty days. The customer merely signs the sales ticket when he buys; his purchases are accumulated till the billing date when a summary statement is prepared and mailed to him. The billing date is often the twenty-fifth of the month with full payment due on the tenth of the following month. Charge accounts are generally employed for buying lower-priced merchandise. There is no interest charge if the account is settled on time.

Installment sales involve higher-priced merchandise. An installment sale is written up on a *conditional sales contract* (title does not pass to the buyer till the merchant is paid) or on a secured contract (the purchased merchandise is pledged as collateral to the merchant or a lender such as a finance company or commercial bank used by the merchant for financing sales). The Uniform Commercial Code Retail Installment Contract is shown in Figure 6-12. Installment sales involve a specific contract for each sales transaction, and interest is usually charged. Payments are made periodically (usually monthly) and usually in equal amounts.

Variations are numerous. The most common is the *revolving charge account,* which generally gives the buyer the option to pay his account in full within a given time of the billing date (usually twenty-five days) without an interest charge. Or he may pay a specified percentage of the total amount, and an interest charge on the unpaid balance is added to the following month's statement.

Credit cards operate in much the same way as a revolving charge account as far as the customer is concerned. However, there is a difference for the seller. The seller does not have to use his own funds to finance credit-card sales. But there is a charge for the service which varies but usually falls in the 3 to 6 percent range. Hence, if your bank credit-card contract calls for a 4 percent charge, you get only $9.60 for a $10.00 sale, but you get cash (in reality a credit to your checking account). The collection burden is on the credit-card company. Two national credit cards usually available through local banks are BankAmericard and Master Charge. To be able to accept and collect on credit-card sales, you have to make arrangements at a bank franchised for the particular credit card. The bank usually requires that you maintain a checking account, and there is a minor initial fee. The bank will supply you with charge tickets and deposit forms as you need them.

POINT 6-10: Credit sales in small businesses usually are on open account, installment sales contract, or credit card. Installment sales contracts may involve merchant or outside financing.

Credit Policy and Evaluation

If you're going to grant credit, you should establish a policy for determining

1. To whom you should grant credit
2. How much credit you should allow
3. The terms and conditions that apply to credit sales

How will you define *who* gets credit? You'll meet the 5 C's of credit here and again in Chapter 8. They're the *Character* of the borrower, the *Capacity* of the

FIGURE 6-12 Retail installment contract form, front page. The back page of this form contains further buyer agreements, remedies in the event of default, and provision for assigning the contract to a third party.

340 – RETAIL INSTALLMENT CONTRACT—General Form

TEXAS STANDARD FORM

CONSUMER GOODS, EQUIPMENT AND GENERAL PERSONAL PROPERTY

RETAIL INSTALLMENT CONTRACT, SECURITY AGREEMENT AND NOTE

(Consecutive and Substantially Equal Monthly Installments)

____________________, hereinafter called Seller,
of __________ (Address) __________ (City, State & Zip Code)
and ____________________, hereinafter called Buyer,
of __________ (Address) __________ (City, State & Zip Code)
have entered into the following agreement:

Subject to the terms and conditions of this agreement, Seller hereby sells and Buyer hereby purchases the following described personal property, hereinafter called "Collateral:"

No.	Year Model	Appliance, Furniture or Equipment (Make) (Kind)	New or Used	Model Number	Serial Number	Cash Price
1						
2						
3						
4						
5						

TRADE IN INFORMATION (if applicable):

Buyer agrees to maintain property insurance covering Vehicle in the amounts shown below.

NOTICE: BUYER MAY FURNISH REQUIRED INSURANCE THROUGH VALID EXISTING COVERAGE OR THROUGH ANY COMPANY OF BUYER'S CHOICE AUTHORIZED TO DO BUSINESS IN THIS STATE.

Required insurance coverage is to be furnished by:
☐ Buyer
☐ Seller

If required insurance is to be furnished by Seller, premiums for _____ months are:

Fire and extended coverage $ ______

Other: ______ ______

Total Property Insurance Premium $ ______

CREDIT LIFE AND DISABILITY INSURANCE is not required to obtain this credit. No charge is made for credit insurance and no credit insurance is provided unless the borrower signs the appropriate statement below. The cost of these coverages for the term of the credit will be:

Credit Life Insurance only $ ______

Credit Life and Disability Insurance $ ______

1. Cash Price (including sales tax of $ ______) $ ______
2. Down Payment:
   - Cash $ ______
   - Trade In Allowance $ ______
   - Balance Owed ______
   - Net Trade In ______
   - Total Down Payment ______
3. Unpaid balance of Cash Price (1 less 2) $ ______
4. Other charges to be financed:
   - a. Official Fees (Filing, etc.) $ ______
   - b. Property Insurance Premium ______
   - c. Credit Life and/or Disability Premium ______
   - d. Other: ______ ______
   - Total other charges ______
5. Amount Financed (3 plus 4) $ ______
6. **FINANCE CHARGE** ______
7. **ANNUAL PERCENTAGE RATE:** ______%
8. Total of Payments $ ______

I desire Credit Life Insurance only	I desire Credit Life and Disability Insurance	I DO NOT want Credit Life or Disability Insurance
______ (Date) ______ (Signature)	______ (Date) ______ (Signature)	______ (Date) ______ (Signature)

BUYER WARRANTS AND COVENANTS TO SELLER AS FOLLOWS:

1. Buyer's residence is
   ( ) At the address shown above ( ) At ______ (Street Number) ______ (City) ______ (State)
2. The Collateral will be kept at:
   ( ) Buyer's residence as shown above ( ) At ______ (Street Number) ______ (City) ______ (State)
3. Buyer's chief place of business or employment is
   ( ) At the address shown above ( ) At ______ (Street Number) ______ (City) ______ (State)
4. The Collateral is to be used primarily for:
   ( ) Personal family or household purposes ( ) Farming operations ( ) Business other than farming operations
5. If Collateral is to become fixtures attached to real property:
   Description of land is: ______
   Record owner of land is: ______

Buyer hereby acknowledges delivery and acceptance of Collateral in its present condition, and grants to Seller a security interest in the Collateral, together with all additions, accessories and substitutions thereto or therefor, and all similar after acquired property, to secure the payment of Total of Payments set forth in item No. 8 above, and any renewals and extensions thereof and substitutions therefor, and all existing and future liabilities, of whatever type, of Buyer to Seller.

Buyer promises to pay to the order of Seller, at the address of Seller stated above, said Total of Payments in ____ monthly installments of $ ______ each, and

one final installment of $______, the first installment being due and payable on the ____ day of ______, 19____, and the remaining installments being due and payable on the same day of each successive month thereafter until fully paid. Proceeds of Collateral are also covered but Seller by this does not impliedly consent to any sale of such Collateral. Failure to pay any installment of this note when due or failure to carry out any of the terms, covenants and conditions securing this note shall authorize the holder of this note to declare the whole of this note due and payable and to exercise any and all rights granted to holder. Buyer agrees to pay additional interest for default at the rate of five cents for each one dollar of any scheduled installment payment when any portion of said installment continues unpaid for ten days or more and deferment interest equal to the difference between the refund which would be required for prepayment in full as of the date of deferment and the refund which would be required for prepayment in full as of one month prior to such date multiplied by the number of months in the deferment period. Buyer shall have the right at any time during regular business hours to prepay this note in full or any one or more installments

thereof. Any unearned finance charge will be refunded based upon the Rule of 78's or ______.
Each of the undersigned hereby waives presentation hereof for payment, notice of non-payment, protest and notice of protest, diligence in collection, or in bringing suit against any party hereto. If this note is collected through judicial proceedings, then each of the undersigned promises to pay the amounts actually incurred by holder as court cost and attorney's fees assessed by a court.

Notice to the BUYER — Do not sign this Contract before you read it or if it contains any blank spaces. You are entitled to a copy of the Contract you sign. Under the law you have the right to pay off in advance the full amount due and under certain conditions may obtain a partial refund of the FINANCE CHARGE. Keep this Contract to protect your legal rights.

NOTICE: See other side for important information. The warranties, covenants, terms, and agreements on the reverse side are incorporated herein and made a part hereof for all intents and purposes. SELLER and BUYER, as used in this contract, include the heirs, executors, and administrators, successors, or assigns of those parties.

BUYER hereby acknowledges that this combined Retail Installment Contract, Security Agreement and Note was completed as to all essential provisions and disclosures before it was signed by BUYER and a copy thereof was delivered to BUYER at the time this Contract was signed.

EXECUTED this ____ day of ______, 19____.

______ SELLER ______ BUYER

By ______ ______ BUYER

ORIGINAL

The Odee Company, Publishers, Dallas, Texas 75201

borrower to repay, the *Collateral* pledged to secure the loan, the borrower's *Capital* or worth, and business *Conditions.* All of these play a part in determining whether you'll get paid and should provide measurements for deciding whether to extend credit to an individual or a company. (And incidentally, if the term "borrower" strikes you as inappropriate, remember that you're lending the money to the credit buyer to make his or her purchase.)

In order to assess character (you're more interested in whether or not people pay debts on time than in their churchgoing), you need credit references—bank loans, other stores where the customer has charge accounts, home mortgage, etc.

In order to assess capacity, you need to know his (or her) place of employment, salary, how long he (or she) has worked there, other income, whether the spouse works, and if so what the spouse earns. You'll also want to know about the person's cash outflow—that is, monthly living expenses and payments on loans. A $2,000 a month income with a $2,200 outflow doesn't indicate capacity!

Your assessment of the collateral is pretty straightforward since it's the merchandise you sold the customer. But it's weak collateral unless it's pledged, and even then, its value after a day of use is likely to be much less than the amount owed.

In order to assess capital, you need to know the customer's approximate net worth. How much does he or she have in savings and checking accounts, home equity, furniture, and autos? What are his or her debt obligations?

Business conditions require judgment on your part. If business is good or improving or has gotten about as bad as you think it can get, they're generally favorable for extending credit. If business is near the peak in a boom or has started slowing down, your buyer's ability to pay when due may erode.

You ask for all of the information cited above on a credit or loan application blank, Figure 6-13. You can get those used by the banks and finance companies that finance your sales, or you can design your own.

Next, investigate the applicant either by getting a credit bureau report (if you belong to your local credit bureau) or by contacting the sources of information on his or her credit application, or both. The results of this investigation should enable you to determine whether to extend credit, and if so, how much. This is your evaluation in terms of your policy.

POINT 6-11: Collect data on your potential credit customer by requiring him or her to fill in an application. Evaluate the customer's credit-worthiness by verifying and investigating. Then grant or decline credit based on your credit policy.

What is your credit policy? If it's so tight that you'll suffer *no credit losses,* you'll miss sales because you'll reject many applicants who would pay! If it's so loose that you write off 30 percent of your credit sales as uncollectible, you'll

FIGURE 6-13 Loan application form

GARLAND BANK & TRUST

LOAN APPLICATION

Date ________ 19 __

Loan Requested $ __________ No. of Months ____ Purpose of Loan ______________________

Security For This Loan ______________________

Mr. Mrs. Miss — Please Print Your Full Name	Age	Marital Status: Married ☐ Single ☐ Divorced ☐ Separated ☐ Widow ☐ Widower ☐	No. Dependents	How Long In City

Residence Address	City	State	Zip Code	How Long	Home Phone	Business Phone
Mailing Address (If Other Than Above)	City	State	Zip Code	Previous Address		How Long

Employed By	How Long	Address	Position	Salary or Income $ ☐ Week ☐ Month ☐ Year

Spouse's First Name	Spouse's Employer	How Long	Address	Phone No.	Salary or Income $ ☐ Week ☐ Month

Your Former Employer	How Long	Position	Other Income $	Source of Other Income

How Much Life Insurance $	Beneficiary	Cash Value $	Amount Borrowed Against Insurance	If You Rent - Show Amount You Pay Per Month $

Address and Description of Real Estate Owned	Purchase Price	Balance Owing	Monthly Pmt.	To Whom Payable
Address and Description of Real Estate Owned	Purchase Price	Balance Owing	Monthly Pmt.	To Whom Payable

Automobiles Owned — Year, Make and Model	Year, Make and Model	Year, Make and Model

Other Assets — List Stocks — Bonds — Notes — Boats — Livestock, etc.

Name of Nearest Relative Not Living With You	Relationship	Street Address	City	State	Phone No.
Name of Spouse's Nearest Relative Not Living With You	Relationship	Street Address	City	State	Phone No.
Personal Reference	Occupation	Street Address	City	State	Phone No.

List Other Obligations — Include Banks, Finance Co.'s, Credit Unions, Doctor Bills, Open Accts & All Installment Obligations

To Whom Owed	Original Amount	Balance Owing	Mo. Pmt.	Security

Your Bank — Checking Bal $ — Savings Bal $	Name of Your Savings and Loan — Savings Bal $	Soc. Sec. No.	Drivers License No.

Are You Comaker, Endorser or Guarantor on any Note or Account? Where? Amount $	Have You Ever Been Bankrupt or Had Any Judgements or Legal Proceedings Against You? ☐ Yes ☐ No	The above statement is tendered for the purpose of obtaining the loan indicated hereon and you are authorized to obtain such additional information as may be considered necessary. It is agreed that you may retain this statement for your files. SIGNATURE X

Note Number	Orig. Amt.	Mo. Pmt.	Security	Net P.O.	Rec.

History — CBS

Insurance From

Credit Acct __________ $ ______

Draft From __________ $ ______

CC# ______ To __________ $ ______

Other $

New Money Disb $ ______

Renewals # ______ # ______ # ______ $ ______

Cash Ad.ance $ ______

Credit Life ______

____ Day A & H ______

Total Insurance $ ______

Filing Fees $ ______

Total Advance $ ______

Interest (Finance Charge) $ ______

Amount of Loan $

Note Number

Date of Note

First Due Date

Final Due Date

Payments @

Final Payment

Int. Rt. | Annual % Rate

Charge Account: CK | Sav

Lending Officer & Committee Approval

LD-425 (Rev.)

(Courtesy: Garland Bank & Trust, Garland, Texas)

go broke. So, what's the happy medium? Unfortunately, there's no clear-cut answer. Be relatively conservative at the outset. A reasonable rule of thumb might be to loosen up if your collection losses are less than 2 percent of credit sales; if they are over 5 percent, tighten up.

Your policy criteria for charge accounts and installment sales will not necessarily be the same. You might make an installment sale to a person to whom you wouldn't grant a charge-account privilege. Why? Because you get a down payment of 10 to 20 percent on an installment sale and because you have a written contract with a collateral pledge. This of course is part of the matter of terms and conditions of credit sales policy. Another focuses on whether you give discounts such as 2/10 net 30 (2 percent discount if paid in ten days; net price if paid in thirty days), and what kind of penalties you assess on late payments. A "late charge" will usually improve collections and late charges collected will help defray the costs of money tied up in delinquent accounts.

Collections

So you establish a pretty fair credit policy, evaluate your credit applicants, and at the end of your second month in business, some of your customers haven't paid. What do you do? The longer an account overdue goes unpaid, the more likely the chance of the debtor moving, dying, getting further into debt, or otherwise further losing his ability to pay. Furthermore, with no collection on your part, he may just decide he can beat you out of it. And, if you continue to extend credit to a loser or a deadbeat, he'll eventually decide he has as much as he can get, and he'll conveniently disappear and go to work on the next sucker.

Your first move on a past-due account is to call and ask for payment. Next, you can cut off credit to minimize possible loss and encourage payment. Next, you should pursue collection. First, use telephone calls to try to work an amicable settlement. Next, send a certified letter to establish legal notice preparatory to court action. Finally, court action. You can use mail reminders ("Your account is overdue") along the way, but if they are disregarded and you don't take the action just prescribed, kiss your money goodbye. The value of using a collection agency is questionable; it can't usually collect if you can't. An agency charges a high percentage on any collection it makes, and it usually sends intimidating letters that create further ill will. Go after it yourself, and quick. You'll still lose some.

You can sue for collection in small-claims courts for amounts under a few hundred dollars in most states. You do not need an attorney in these courts. Investigate this locally. The certified letter or a witnessed delivery of notice and intent to sue for collection is usually required.

Repossession of merchandise can sometimes be affected on amicable terms. Still, you're usually in for a loss. If the customer resists repossession, you're probably in for a headache and a greater loss.

REVIEW EXERCISES 6-D

1. Why is credit an important sales tool?
2. Does it cost a merchant anything to grant credit? Discuss.

3. Specify whether each of the following items might be more likely to be sold on open account, an installment sales contract, or possibly either: (a) $25 worth of hardware, (b) a $50 air-conditioning repair bill, (c) a $500 refrigerator, (d) an $8,000 car.
4. Discuss the advantages and disadvantages of bank credit cards for the merchant.
5. Discuss credit policy and why it is important.
6. What are the possible approaches to collecting overdue accounts?

OTHER APPROACHES TO MINI-BUSINESS ACCOUNTING

There are packaged simplified bookkeeping systems available. Some of these systems are geared to specific businesses. The simplified systems are generally single-entry systems. They're not bad for a one-person business, but with any kind of growth, you'll need a double-entry system tailored to your specific needs. The packaged systems often are more costly for what they provide than your own double-entry system. Unless you intend to keep your business small, I recommend that you set up your own double-entry system. Most office supply stores stock packaged accounting systems.

After your business grows, you may find that you can improve your system and reduce the amount of work required by adopting a peg system. With a peg system, you can write a check and make a book entry in one writing. National Cash Register Company (NCR) has "Peg-n-Post" systems to fit most business needs. They reduce labor substantially. For details, call your local NCR office.

CASE: A RETAIL AND SERVICE BUSINESS MISADVENTURE

The Apex Appliance Sales and Service Company was founded by Mr. Apex in 1972 when he purchased and merged two smaller businesses at a cost of $10,000. Mr. Apex managed the business himself for two years and in the process acquired two part-time employees. His financial statements for 1974 are shown in Figure 6-14. In early 1975 his son came into the business as manager, which allowed Mr. Apex to devote time to his other business interests. The son was to have the opportunity to buy the business after a few years.

Initially all went well. After two months, the son decided he wanted the business as his own, and he convinced Mr. Apex to sell it to him on credit. Mr. Apex became involved in his other activities and didn't set foot in the business for several months. When he did, he found the housekeeping poor, with dust on merchandise, dirty floors, and some lights burned out. He discussed the matter with his son, who indicated that he didn't have time to tend to all those things. The records were poorly kept and after considerable interpretation, showed sales behind those of the previous year. But because the records were so poor, it was hard to get an accurate picture of how bad things were. Further attempts by Mr.

Apex to advise his son were cut off. Mr. Apex went to the store the following Saturday afternoon and found the store closed. The son had cut Saturday hours, which had been 9-5, to 9-12.

FIGURE 6-14 Apex Appliance Sales and Service Co. *Balance sheet, Jan. 1, 1975*

Assets		*Liabilities*	
Cash	$ 2,000	Accounts payable	$ 400
Accounts receivable	1,000	Bank loan	600
Inventory	13,000		1,000
	$16,000	Owner's equity	17,000
Fixtures & equipment	2,000		$18,000
	$18,000		

Income statement, Jan. 1, 1974-Dec. 31, 1975

Sales	$50,000	
Cost of goods sold	22,000	
Gross income		$28,000
Wages and salaries	$16,000*	
Rent	2,400	
Other expenses	3,000	
		$21,400
Net profit		$ 6,600

*Includes owner's salary of $10,000.

When Mr. Apex visited the shop a month later, he found the appliance inventory considerably reduced, and the space thus freed was filled with the son's woodcarvings and carving kits. His son was engrossed in conversation with a woodcarving hobbyist and it was 45 minutes before Mr. Apex could talk to him. The son insisted that the appliance business was slowing down and the woodcarving diversification would take up the slack. Mr. Apex asked his son to show him sales records that confirmed this. The son said he had stopped keeping records. Mr. Apex tried to advise the son, expressed his dismay at the proceedings, and the conversation became heated.

In June 1976 the son missed his payment; he missed the following ones as well. In December 1976, after several conversations, Mr. Apex decided the son should get out of the business before he had depleted all the assets. The son landed a job in industry in October 1977 at a substantial salary and Mr. Apex proceeded to try to sell the business. He eventually did, at a considerable loss. The sales level had not increased during the son's two years of operation and was falling; the inventory had been cut in half.

REVIEW EXERCISES 6-E

1. What would Apex, Jr. have learned about the business and his operations if he had continued to maintain proper business records?
2. What marketing and sales lessons does this case contain?
3. Easy credit from his father enabled Apex, Jr. to run a sloppy operation that eventually cost both father and son a substantial amount of money. Why can easy credit make a business owner complacent while his business base is eroding?

SUMMARY

Business accounting records show you how your business is doing, provide a monitoring tool for the control function, and provide data and back-up for income tax returns.

The accounting process (accounting cycle) begins with data collection on sales tickets, bills from vendors, check stubs, and deposit slips. These are recorded in the books of original entry, the journal, usually on a daily basis. The accounts are classified in the third step by being posted to the ledgers, usually monthly. An interim income statement should be prepared each month, using estimated cost of goods sold and estimated depreciation. The last three steps—summarizing, adjusting, and financial statement preparation—require preparation of a work sheet. These steps are normally performed once a year. The income statement shows the financial position of the business at the end of the period.

You can operate your accounting system on an accrual basis or a cash basis. An accrual-basis system matches revenues and expenses to the period in which they are incurred. A cash-basis system handles transactions as completed when cash is received or disbursed. A cash-basis system is simpler and requires fewer formal entries than an accrual-basis system. A cash-basis system is recommended for mini businesses.

In double-entry bookkeeping there are two sides to each account—debit (left) and credit (right). *An increase in asset, expense, and owner's draw accounts is debited; an increase in liability, capital, revenue and accumulated depreciation accounts is credited.*

A chart of accounts lists the accounts utilized in the books. Accounts can be generally categorized as asset, liability, capital, revenue, and expense accounts. The asset account known as "cash" is in reality your bank checking account. Three of the liability accounts in a small business result from the fact that the owner is an interim collector of sales taxes, withheld income, and Social Security taxes.

Simplest and most practical accounting systems for small businesses utilize a single journal with multi-column sheets. The most frequently used accounts have their own columns, and less frequently used accounts are entered under the "general ledger" columns.

A work sheet is used to strike a trial balance, adjust accounts, and summarize data for the financial statements. The only work-sheet adjustments for a cash-basis accounting system are depreciated expense, accumulated depreciation, and inventory.

You can keep your finger on anything you choose to in a one-person business. As the business grows you lose close contact and have to resort to methods of internal control. These include responsibility, definition, adequate record keeping, separation of record keeping and custody, maintenance of divided responsibility in a chain of related transactions, possible utilization of employee bonding and insurance, establishment of procedures of cash handling and reconciliations, and using serially numbered forms. Mechanical equipment strengthens internal control and is worthwhile after a business grows adequately.

Bank-balance and cash-drawer reconciliations detect errors, permit account adjustment, and signal irregularities. Petty cash disbursements may be made from the cash drawer or from a separate petty cash drawer or "purse." Use one system or the other; avoid using both.

Credit and collections should be considered an integral part of your marketing activity because credit is a sales tool and because your sale is no good if you don't collect for the goods or service sold. If you're going to grant credit, you should develop a credit policy, evaluate credit applicants, and establish collection procedures.

KEY TERMS

Accounting equation
Accounts-payable
Accounts-receivable
Accrual basis
Adjusting
Asset
Balance sheet
Bank-balance reconciliation
Capital account
Cash
Cash basis
Charge account
Chart of accounts
Classifying
Collection
Cost of goods sold
Credit policy
Debit credit

Expense
5 C's of credit
Fixed assets
Income statement
Installment sales
Internal control
Inventory
Journal
Ledger
Liability
Petty cash
Recording
Transaction
Work sheet

QUESTIONS AND PROBLEMS

1. How do you handle a credit sale and its eventual payment if your books are kept on a cash basis?
2. What is the difference between the accrual- and cash-basis method of accounting?
3. Show debits and credits to the appropriate "T" accounts for each of the following transactions:
   (a) Cash sale $20, nontaxable
   (b) Cash sale $25 plus sales tax of $1.25 collected
   (c) Cash purchase of merchandise of $50
   (d) Investment of $500 in business by owner
   (e) Owner's draw of $100
   (f) Profit of $6,000 indicated on work sheet
4. What is a chart of accounts, and what purpose does it serve?
5. What is the principal reason an annual inventory must be taken? Can you think of any other reasons?
6. What is the purpose of the accumulated depreciation account?
7. Explain how straight-line depreciation expense is computed and how it differs from other expenses.
8. List all the accounts that are affected when you write a payroll check. What entries must you make?
9. You sell a truck that cost you $6,000 and has accumulated depreciation of $4,000 for $1,000 cash. Show your entries using "T" accounts.
10. List and discuss the steps in the accounting cycle.
11. Why is a single journal with many columns most convenient for a mini business? How does it save your time?
12. How do you arrive at cost of goods sold for use in an interim income statement? Depreciation expense?
13. Why isn't it necessarily productive to prepare a monthly balance sheet?
14. List the key points of internal control policy.
15. Your cash drawer contains $672 at close of business and had $100 when you opened. Sales slips total $574. You paid out $2 for freight-in and

$1.75 for postage. Reconcile the cash drawer and show the appropriate book entries with "T" accounts.

16. Your bank statement shows a balance of $1,000; your books show a balance of $1,265. The bank has collected a $100 note for you and charged you a $2 collection fee. Checks totaling $87 have not cleared, and you made a $450 deposit too late for posting to the bank statement. Reconcile and post proper entries to "T" accounts.
17. A couple asks for a charge account in your plant and gift shop. Both are employed, they have a joint income of $30,000, have five charge accounts (all current), two bank loans (both current) and a loan on their house (payments current). After they pay all living expenses and their bills, they save $200 a month. (a) Would you grant them charge-account credit in your store? Why? (b) Would you grant charge-account credit if she were pregnant? Why? (c) Would you grant charge-account credit if he were on a new job with a new employer at $17,000 a year while his previous job paid only $12,000? Why?
18. A man enters your TV shop, says he wants a color set on credit, and has $50 cash for a down payment. He earns $8,000 a year, has a wife, and three children under 12 years of age. Would you sell him on a charge account, an installment sales contract, or refuse to sell on credit in each of these cases: (a) his payment record is good and he's been with his present employer five years; (b) his payment record is good, but he's just switched from a salaried job as a bookkeeper at $8,000 a year to a commission insurance salesman's job; (c) his payment record is poor, but he says he's going to inherit $10,000 from his parents' estate? (d) he's been slow to pay, but he's always paid up eventually. State reasons for your decisions.

FIELD INVESTIGATION AND PROJECTS

*1. Visit several office supply stores and investigate available accounting systems, binders, and forms. Look over packaged systems for various kinds of businesses and make comparisons. Summarize your investigation and report your conclusions about the kind of system you intend to use.

2. Obtain an introductory accounting textbook from your library. Scan it and relate what you've learned in this chapter to the accounting textbook presentation. (This will take several hours of effort.) Then go through some of the examples of transactions and entries. Strive for understanding. Finally, go through the chapter that covers the use of the work sheet and preparation of financial statements.

**3. There are quite a few differences in the accounts for a manufacturing company from those for a service or retail business presented in this chapter. Study the sections on manufacturing concerns in an introductory accounting textbook and attempt to solve some of the problems presented.

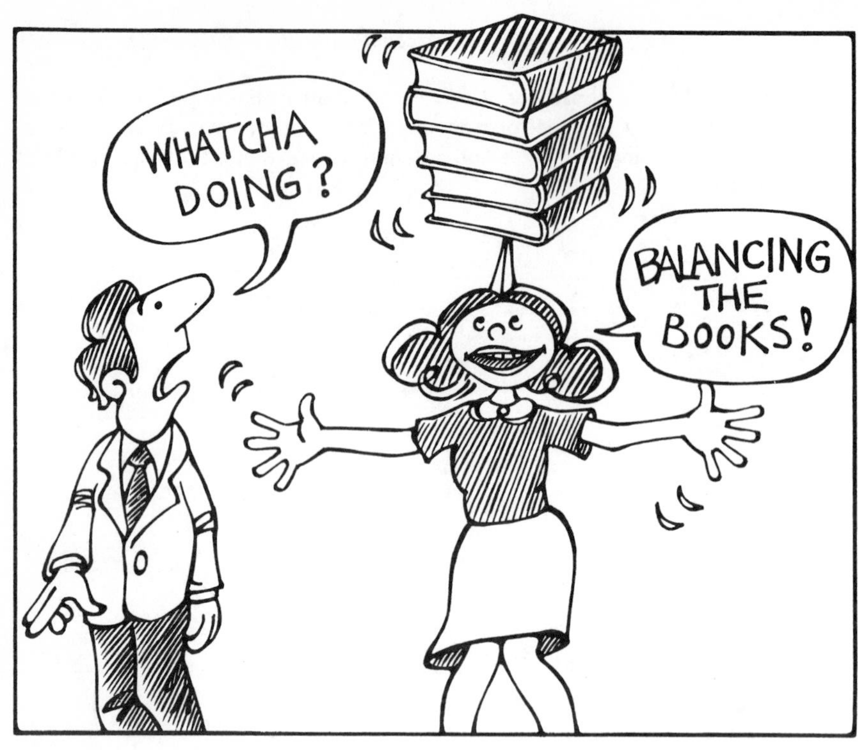

Financial Analysis and Management

7

Financial knowledge is of utmost importance in determining the start-up needs of a business, in evaluating a going business, and in keeping a business alive and healthy. A basic knowledge of finance as it applies to a mini business will help you stave off the bleeding of cash from too small a supply and the cancerous growth of debt that kills so many mini businesses early in life.

In this chapter you'll build on the accounting knowledge you acquired in the preceding chapter. You'll learn more about financial statements (income statements and balance sheets), and how to use them; you'll study financial ratios (measures of profitability, liquidity, turnover, and leverage) and the basic principles of sound financial management. The presentation is made with practical illustrations that you'll find easy to learn and apply.[1]

You should know the answers to these questions after you've completed your study of this chapter:

1. How can you determine the equity (net worth) of a business or an individual?

[1] For further study of financial analysis and management, see Louis K. Brandt, *Analysis For Financial Management* (Englewood Cliffs, N.J.: Prentice-Hall, Inc., 1972), or J. Fred Weston and Eugene F. Brigham, *Essentials of Managerial Finance* (New York: Holt, Rinehart and Winston, Inc., 1968).

2. What elements must be considered in calculating the profit of a business?
3. What is an asset? A liability?
4. How does a banker determine whether your business deserves a loan on the basis of its profitability and worth?
5. What are ratios of profitability, liquidity, turnover, and leverage? What do they tell? How do they help you in starting, buying, and operating a business?
6. What is working capital?

PROFIT AND WORTH

Two things concern you more than anything else when you evaluate a business. They're

1. Profitability
2. Owner's equity (net worth)

Profitability (or loss) is shown on the *income statement.*

Owner's equity, frequently called net worth, is shown on the *balance sheet.*

The data on the income statement and balance sheet can be reduced to ratios of profitability, liquidity, turnover, and leverage. These enable you to compare one business to another quickly and easily.

Profitability is easy to measure when it can be based on historical numbers (an income statement on previous operations). But profitability is not a fixed quantity. A business can show a large profit one year and a large loss the following year. For example, a business may have placed half of its sales with one customer in 1976 and lost that customer in 1977. Or, the people responsible for good management of a business in one year may have left in the next, possibly taking some of the future sales with them (business is frequently done with "people" instead of "a company"); or business can decline because the new management is inferior. The point is that the income statement applies only to the period it covers. Now, let's learn more about the income statement.

THE INCOME STATEMENT

The income statement shows the sales, cost of goods sold, gross profit, expenses, and net profit of a business. You'll recall from the first chapter that *sales less cost of goods sold is gross profit; gross profit minus expenses is net profit. An income statement covers a period of time, usually a year.* But it's a good idea to develop an interim income statement each month to see what you've done and how you can improve operations.

Developing the Income Statement

If the year's figures are totaled, you'll have all sales that have been paid for, all purchases that have been paid, and all expenses that have been paid as indicated in the previous chapter. These are numbers you'll need to develop the income statement. (You'll also have accounts-receivable and accounts-payable totals, which you'll use to develop the balance sheet.)

Now, let's examine the income statement of Able Hardware, developed in just the way we described. (We'll use rounded numbers in our examples to focus on principles.) This is a summarized or abbreviated income statement since it doesn't show details of development of cost of goods sold and expenses. We'll expand it shortly.

ABLE HARDWARE COMPANY

Income Statement for Year Ended December 31, 19X3

Sales	$80,000
Cost of goods sold	50,000
Gross profit	$30,000
Expenses	20,000
Net profit	$10,000

> POINT 7-1: The income statement shows (*for a given period of time*) sales, cost of goods sold, gross profit, expenses, and net profit.

Gross Profit

You know how the sales were tabulated. What about the cost of goods sold—how was this computed? You're probably way ahead of the text at this point, but let's review it anyway. You take *inventory* periodically—at least once a year. You count the goods for sale and determine the total value of what's on your shelves. If you hadn't bought anything during the year, the cost of goods sold would simply be:

$$\begin{aligned}\text{Cost of Goods Sold} &= \text{Beginning Inventory} - \text{Ending Inventory}\\ &= \$70{,}000 - \$20{,}000\\ &= \$50{,}000\end{aligned}$$

if beginning and ending inventories were $70,000 and $20,000, respectively.

That of course is absurd. You couldn't afford a $70,000 starting inventory to do $80,000 in sales. If, for some odd-ball reason, you could and it was required, then the $20,000 inventory at the end of the year would be catastrophically small! Actually, the starting and ending inventories will be in the ballpark of $20,000 for this example. But you'll be purchasing merchandise in lumps of various sizes all during the year. Now if you'll think of the total of purchases for the year as adding to initial inventory, you have the whole concept for arriving at cost of goods sold.

Cost of Goods Sold = Beginning Inventory
+ Period Purchases – Ending Inventory

or in this example (assuming $21,000 starting and $20,000 ending inventory with purchases of $49,000),

Cost of Goods Sold = $21,000 + $49,000 – $20,000
= $50,000

We can incorporate this in the Able Hardware income statement as follows:

Sales		$80,000
Beginning inventory	$21,000	
Purchases	49,000	
Available for sale	$70,000	
Ending inventory	20,000	
Cost of goods sold		50,000
Gross profit		$30,000
Expenses		20,000
Net profit		$10,000

Remember, this is profit before taxes. This book deals with profit before taxes unless otherwise noted. The point is made to remind you that you don't have all of the profit left because you'll have to pay some of it in income taxes.

Expenses

So, we've filled in the blanks up to gross profit. What about expenses? What are the expenses associated with running your business? Some of your expenses can be attributed to making sales. Some of your expenses can be attributed to the management and administrative costs of running your business. You could separate these expenses, but it would not serve a significant purpose for mini-retail businesses. Therefore, all expenses will be included under the general heading of expense. Expenses are classified in categories. These are typical for a small business: *salaries, rent, utilities, phone, advertising, freight-out and delivery, freight-in, supplies, interest, insurance, fees, miscellaneous expenses* and *depre-*

ciation. You can detail expenses further, but there's no point in doing it unless it serves a useful purpose.

POINT 7-2: Expenses should be broken down into as many categories as necessary to understand operations and control expenses.

This is Able Hardware Company's income statement with detailed expenses:

ABLE HARDWARE COMPANY
(Corporate Equivalent)

Income Statement for Year Ended December 31, 19X3

Sales		$80,000
Beginning inventory	$21,000	
Purchases	49,000	
Available for sale	$70,000	
Ending inventory	20,000	
Cost of goods sold		50,000
Gross profit		$30,000
Expenses		
Salaries	$11,800	
Rent	3,000	
Utilities and phone	1,500	
Advertising	1,400	
Freight-in and delivery	300	
Supplies	500	
Insurance	300	
Accountant fees	400	
Depreciation	800	
Total expenses		20,000
Net profit – LS*		$10,000

*Less salary.

The classifications cited are self-explanatory for the most part. If the term *depreciation* is vague in meaning to you, it's simply an allowance for wearing-out of fixtures and equipment. If you buy a set of gauges for your air-conditioning business at a cost of $50, you do not charge all of the cost off in the current year. If the gauges will last five years, you depreciate (charge off to depreciation expense) one-fifth of the cost or $10 per year for five years. Of course, you don't really know how long an asset will last, but for accounting and income tax purposes most equipment and fixtures will have a three- to ten-year life. If they don't wear out in that period of time, they may become obsolete. If you use an asset (a resource that you own) for a longer period than the projected life, it doesn't matter. When you've charged off total depreciation equal to the cost, you simply stop depreciating the asset.

POINT 7-3: Fixed assets (long life plant and equipment) are not expensed. An amount corresponding to the fractional life used is charged off as depreciation expense each year. The value of the asset is reduced accordingly.

Net Profit

Net profit is the reward for investment and risk. It's what's left after the cost of goods and all expenses are subtracted. Is Able Hardware earning a fair return for the owner? He's making a profit of $10,000 a year. What's included in that profit?

In the real accounting world, it includes his wages, his return on capital, and his reward for enterprise, because he functions as a proprietorship. If Able Hardware were a corporation his wages and his managerial reward would be charged off as an expense.

This poses a problem in getting ideas across and in making comparisons. So, let's resolve it here and now. Whenever we're working with figures involving financial analysis and judgments, we'll assume that even in a proprietorship, the owner's salary is an expense, and we'll note the fact with the letters "LS" (for "less salary") after the profit.

We've done this on the final Able Hardware income statement. So Mr. Able's accounting income statement has been altered to a "corporate equivalent" statement. His own salary is shown lumped into the $11,800 salary expense, and the profit on a corporate equivalent basis is $10,000.

POINT 7-4: In accounting, a proprietorship or partnership profit has owner salaries lumped into it. For financial analysis purposes in this text, we'll examine these forms of entity as though they were corporations (owner's salary an expense). When a statement has owner's salary thus placed it will be headed "corporate equivalent" in the text and the letters "LS" will appear in the profit line.

Able Hardware is indeed profitable. It would be attractive to you as a business to buy if you felt that the business was growing and that this wasn't a flash-in-the-pan year when maybe Able's brother bought $40,000 worth of hardware. You can allay your fears by examining Able's comparative income statement for the past three years.

Comparative income statements usually show the results for the current and the previous year–however, they may show results for a number of years. The abbreviated comparative income statement for Able Hardware for three years is:

	19X3	19X2	19X1
Sales	$80,000	$60,000	$30,000
Cost of Goods Sold	50,000	38,000	19,000
Gross Profit	30,000	22,000	11,000
Expenses	20,000	15,000	12,000
Net Profit (Loss)	$10,000	$ 7,000	($ 1,000)

This shows that net profits and sales have grown each year since 19X1. From all appearances Able Hardware is growing. If Able's sales and profits had been decreasing since 19X1, the decrease would signal problems. Thus, the comparative income statement tells a fuller story.

POINT 7-5: A comparative income statement shows sales, expenses, and profits over several periods. It is useful in assessing trends in the operations of the business.

REVIEW EXERCISES 7-A

1. Why is a single year's income statement an inadequate basis for a decision to buy a business?
2. Would bank deposits for a period indicate sales accurately? Discuss.
3. A company's sales are $50,000, cost of goods sold is $40,000, expenses are $6,000. What is gross profit? Net profit?
4. A company's net profit is $20,000, gross profit is $40,000, and cost of goods sold is $80,000. What are sales? Expenses?
5. Joe Smith had sales of $62,000, starting inventory of $20,000, purchases of $31,000, and ending inventory of $16,000. His expenses were: rent $4,000; utilities $1,500; interest $500; freight-in $200; part-time help $2,000; gas, oil and repairs $1,000. He has $3,000 worth of capital equipment on which he's taking ten-year straight-line depreciation. Prepare his detailed income statement.

MEASURES OF PROFITABILITY

If you compared the income statement of Able Hardware to the income statement of another company, the differences in sales, cost of goods sold, and expenses wouldn't reveal relative performance at a glance. You can make quantitative measures that are easy to compare by taking ratios.

There are ratios of *profitability*, *liquidity*, *turnover*, and *leverage*. The profitability ratios derive principally from income statement data; the liquidity and leverage ratios are from the balance sheet. The turnover ratios hinge equally on balance sheet and income statement.

POINT 7-6: Ratios provide a means for comparing financial statements at a glance.

Net Profit Margin

The first important profitability ratio is *net profit margin.* Net profit margin is the ratio of net profit to sales. In the case of Able Hardware Company,

$$\text{Net Profit Margin} = \frac{\text{Net Profit}}{\text{Sales}} = \frac{\$10{,}000}{\$80{,}000} = 0.125$$

If Prudent Hardware has a net profit margin of 0.2, it is making more money on each dollar of sales than Able. Able is making 12.5 cents net for each dollar of sales; Prudent is making 20 cents on each dollar of sales. This tells you that Prudent is doing a better job of pricing, buying, or controlling expense, or a combination of these.

Return on Equity

Another measure of profitability is the return on equity, the ratio of net profit to owner's equity. Owner's equity, you will recall, is the net worth of the business. If Able's net worth is $20,000,

$$\text{Return on Equity} = \frac{\text{Net Profit}}{\text{Owner's Equity}} = \frac{\$10{,}000}{\$20{,}000} = 0.500$$

This is a very high return on equity, probably resulting because Mr. Able figured a small salary for himself, thus leaving more of his income in profit.

If Prudent's abbreviated income statement is

Sales	$70,000
Cost of goods sold	36,000
Gross profit	$34,000
Expenses	20,000
Net profit	$14,000

and the owner's equity is $20,000,

$$\text{Return on Equity} = \frac{\text{Net Profit}}{\text{Owner's Equity}} = \frac{\$14{,}000}{\$20{,}000} = 0.700$$

Prudent is realizing a better return on equity than Able.

Gross Margin

Finally, compute the *gross margins* (introduced in Chapter 1):
For Able,

$$\text{Gross Margin} = \frac{\text{Gross Profit}}{\text{Sales}} = \frac{\$30{,}000}{\$80{,}000} = 0.375$$

For Prudent,

$$\text{Gross Margin} = \frac{\text{Gross Profit}}{\text{Sales}} = \frac{\$34{,}000}{\$70{,}000} = 0.486$$

This shows that Prudent is realizing a better gross margin than Able. Margins are frequently expressed in percentages, and Prudent's 48.6 percent is 11.1 percent greater than Able's 37.5 percent. This tells you that Prudent is doing a better job of pricing or buying (or both) than Able. This is the key to Prudent's success. Prudent has smaller total sales than Able, has the same total dollar expenses, but Prudent's net margin is 20 percent compared to Able's 12.5 percent. The edge accrues from the superior gross margin. Since net worth is the same for Able and Prudent, it follows that return on equity is greater for Prudent.

This points up to the fact that total sales are meaningless if gross margins are inadequate and/or if expenses are excessive.

Percentage Income Statements

A percentage income statement is useful for comparison of different income statements. Let's start with expense as a percentage of sales.
For Able,

$$\%\ \text{Expense} = \frac{\$20{,}000}{\$80{,}000} = 25.0\%$$

For Prudent,

$$\%\ \text{Expense} = \frac{\$20{,}000}{\$70{,}000} = 28.6\%$$

Although Able kept percentage expense lower than Prudent, the difference wasn't great enough to make up for Prudent's superior gross margin.

Gross margin and net margin are the percentage of gross profit to sales and net profit to sales respectively. Thus

Gross Margin – % Expense = Net Margin

Able: 37.5% – 25% = 12.5%

Prudent: 48.6% – 28.6% = 20.0%

Able's abbreviated statement with percentage of sales shown is

Sales	$80,000	100%
Cost of goods sold	50,000	62.5%
Gross profit	$30,000	37.5%
Expenses	20,000	25.0%
Net profit	$10,000	12.5%

You can break down the percentages on the details of the statement if you want to compare percentage for specific items.

REVIEW EXERCISES 7-B

1. Sales are $50,000, cost of goods sold is $40,000. What is gross profit margin?
2. Gross profit margin is 40 percent. Cost of goods sold is $36,000. What are sales (in dollars)? What is gross profit?
3. Better Boot Shoe Store has a gross profit of $30,000 and expenses of $10,000 for 19XX. Owner's equity is $8,000. Compute (a) net profit and (b) return on equity.
4. Using the data given in question 3, if sales were $65,000, compute (a) gross margin, (b) net profit margin, (c) percentage expense.
5. Using the data of problem 5, from Review Exercises 3-A, prepare a detailed percentage income statement.

THE BALANCE SHEET

The analysis of the income statement gives part of the picture of a business. In order to introduce the profitability measure of return on owner's equity, we had to go elsewhere to find *owner's equity*. The source of this data is the *balance sheet*. The balance sheet shows *assets, liabilities,* and *owner's equity*. The balance sheet provides the data for liquidity and leverage ratios.

The income statement says, "Here's how the business is doing." The balance sheet says, "Here's what the business has to work with."

POINT 7-7: The balance sheet is simply a tabular form of the equation: Assets = Liabilities + Owner's Equity.

Thus, if you have $1,000 as your total assets and your only liability is a bill for $100, your owner's equity is $900. Owner's equity is sometimes called *net worth.*

Assets

The balance sheet expands assets and liabilities into detailed classifications. It also groups them by liquidity and maturity. *Current assets* are assets that exist in the form of cash or that can be readily converted into cash or consumed within a year. Current assets include *cash* (on hand and in banks), *accounts-receivable* (money owed to you on sales you've made), *notes-receivable* maturing within a year, and *inventory* (goods for sale or for direct use in a manufactured product).

Fixed assets have a life or maturity of more than a year. They include *store* or *plant* (if owned); *manufacturing, office, store,* and *automotive equipment;* and *notes-receivable* with maturity in excess of one year.

Liabilities

Current liabilities include *accounts-payable, notes-payable* (due within a year), *wages-payable, interest-payable,* and others.

Long-term liabilities include *long-term debt* (more than a year maturity). The term "notes" when used on the balance sheet usually refers to notes with maturities of less than one year. The phrase "long-term debt" is usually used in connection with notes with maturities greater than a year.

Owner's Equity

Owner's equity indicates the worth of the business. Owner's equity consists of the amount you invested in the business minus withdrawals plus retained earnings. Retained earnings are merely profits left in the business. If you invested $10,000 when you started your business, made a profit of $8,000, and withdrew $12,000, your net worth at the beginning of the next year would be only $6,000! A common reason for business failure is withdrawing more from the business than it earns, thereby invading the starting capital. A business cannot continue for long when this happens.

> POINT 7-8: Owner's equity is the net owner's investment in the business plus retained earnings (retained profits).

Now, let's look at Able Hardware Company's balance sheet.

Current Assets		
Cash	$ 5,000	
Accounts-receivable	300	
Inventory	20,000	
Total current assets		$25,300
Fixed assets		
Equipment and fixtures	4,000	
Delivery truck	2,000	
Total fixed assets		6,000
Total assets		$31,300
Current liabilities		
Accounts-payable	$ 3,300	
Notes-payable	1,800	
Total current liabilities		$ 5,100
Long-term debt		6,200
Total liabilities		$11,300
Owner's equity		20,000
Total liabilities and owner's equity		$31,300

What does the balance sheet indicate about the worth of the business? It shows the owner's equity or net worth to be $20,000. What else does it show? It shows that there's almost enough cash to pay off the total current liabilities. That's a good cash position. The receivables are very low, indicating that most sales are for cash. The owner's equity is almost twice the debt, an excellent equity position.

Ratios simplify the evaluation of the balance sheet in comparison to others, just as ratios simplified the analysis of the income statement.

REVIEW EXERCISES 7-C

1. What is the basic accounting equation relating assets, liabilities, and owner's equity?
2. What distinguishes fixed assets from current assets?
3. If you have $1,000 worth of equipment, $2,000 in cash, and $500 in accounts and notes-payable when you start your plumbing service business, what is your owner's equity?
4. You've been in business three months. You have $1,000 in the bank, $850 in accounts-receivable, $250 in notes-receivable, $500 in inventory, $400 in accounts-payable, $1,000 in long-term debt, and $1,000 in equipment. Set up your balance sheet. What is your owner's equity?
5. Set up a percentage balance sheet for Able Hardware, using total assets as reference (100 percent).

MEASURES OF FINANCIAL POSITION AND ACTIVITY

Measures of financial position deal with liquidity and leverage. The balance sheet contains the data required to compute them. Liquidity measurements focus on *current* assets and liabilities. Leverage measurements focus on *total* debt, total assets, and equity.

Activity (turnover) ratios give an indication of how a business uses its assets.

Liquidity

The liquidity of an asset is the ease with which it can be converted to cash without loss. A business is considered to be liquid if it can pay its bills as they come due.

There are two commonly used liquidity measurements. They are the *current* ratio and the *quick* ratio (also called the *acid test* ratio).

$$\text{Current Ratio} = \frac{\text{Current Assets}}{\text{Current Liabilities}}$$

The bigger the current ratio (to a point), the better. For Able Hardware,

$$\text{Current Ratio} = \frac{25{,}300}{5{,}100} = 4.96$$

This indicates an unusually liquid situation. However, Able has $20,000 in inventory. Inventory is not as liquid as cash or receivables. (If you don't believe that, ask anyone who has tried to sell out in a hurry!)

The quick ratio remedies the situation and focuses squarely on short-term liquidity.

$$\text{Quick Ratio} = \frac{\text{Current Assets} - \text{Inventory}}{\text{Current Liabilities}}$$

The bigger the quick ratio (to a point), the better. In the case of Able,

$$\text{Quick Ratio} = \frac{25{,}300 - 20{,}000}{5{,}100} = \frac{5{,}300}{5{,}100} = 1.04$$

This is a respectable quick ratio and is excellent for a small retail hardware store. This indicates that Able has excellent liquidity even under these stringent measurement terms. Since current assets minus inventory equals cash plus receivables, the quick ratio may also be stated as

$$\text{Quick Ratio} = \frac{\text{Cash + Receivables}}{\text{Current Liabilities}}$$

There is another measure that is important in analyzing a company. This measure is the definition of a very important financial concept. The concept is *net working capital.* Inadequate working capital can strangle a business quickly. Inadequate working capital situations often forewarn of business failure. A company usually ends up in an inadequate working-capital predicament as a result of poor financial management.[2]

$$\text{Net Working Capital} = \text{Current Assets} - \text{Current Liabilities}$$

In the case of Able Hardware,

$$\text{Net Working Capital} = \$25{,}300 - \$5{,}100 = \$20{,}200$$

Notice that Able's working capital exceeds its net worth by $200. Another company might have a net worth of $50,000 but only have working capital of $5,000. The secret to maintaining adequate working capital lies in the ability to finance current assets out of equity and long-term debt sources. Hence, a company with substantial owner's equity, heavy on fixed assets, and too low on long-term debt *can* be short on working capital. Here's the condensed balance sheet for a company in this pickle:

Current assets	$ 30,000
Fixed assets	70,000
Total assets	$100,000
Current liabilities	$ 25,000
Long-term debt	25,000
Total liabilities	$ 50,000
Owner's equity	50,000
Total liabilities and owner's equity	$100,000

Note that if $20,000 of the current liabilities were converted into long-term debt, working capital would zoom to $25,000! You merely borrowed long-term to pay off a major portion of the short-term debt. Note that the current and quick ratios would zoom too!

The most frequent excuse you hear from business failures who were short on business savvy in the first place is, "I didn't have enough working capital." They may not have, but it's more likely that they simply didn't know what working

[2] For further study of working capital, see Dileep R. Mehta, *Working Capital Management* (Englewood Cliffs, N.J.: 1974).

capital is and how to manage it. I'll have more to say on this subject in a later chapter.

> POINT 7-9: A business needs working capital to finance current asset needs. Working capital needs tend to grow with the business.

Leverage

Leverage is the use of a high proportion of debt to equity. Thus, commercial building investments often consist of 10 to 20 percent equity and the balance in debt. This is an example of a highly leveraged investment. If a business is highly leveraged, the financial position of the business is weakened. The risk position of the business increases, and when small reverses occur, it cannot pay its debts. On the other hand, if a company is not highly leveraged, it has sufficient reserve assets to borrow in time of need. Total debt to total assets defines leverage. For Able,

$$\frac{\text{Total Debt}}{\text{Total Assets}} = \frac{\$11,300}{\$31,300} = 0.36$$

This is low for small hardware stores, indicating low leverage and a stronger financial position than most hardware stores. The lower the ratio is, the better the company's financial position.

Debt-to-equity ratio is another measure of financial leverage.

$$\frac{\text{Total Debt}}{\text{Equity}} = \frac{\$11,300}{\$20,000} = 0.57$$

Again, the smaller the ratio, the better the financial position of the business. A 1.0 ratio for a small hardware store is more normal. Able Hardware's leverage is very low, indicating conservatism in its financing. In other words, although a very low leverage position indicates financial strength, if it is too low, it's an indication that a business is inefficient in its use of capital. This will be reflected in the return the business gets on equity. If you can earn $10,000 with $50,000 in capital, your return on equity is 20 percent if all of the capital is equity:

$$\text{Return on Equity} = \frac{\$10,000}{\$50,000} = 20\%$$

If only $25,000 of the capital is owner's equity and the balance is long-term debt, the return on equity is 40%:

$$\text{Return on Equity} = \frac{\$10,000}{\$25,000} = 40\%$$

This is called "trading on the equity."

Activity

Thus far, you've learned how to use ratios to assess profitability, and financial position. There's another parameter of business that requires assessment. This is the efficiency of the mobilization of assets. This leads to activity ratios and the return on assets ratio.

$$\text{Inventory Turnover} = \frac{\text{Cost of Goods Sold}}{\text{Average Inventory at Cost}} \quad \text{or}$$

$$\frac{\text{Sales at Retail}}{\text{Average Inventory at Retail}}$$

$$\text{Days' Supply in Inventory} = \frac{365}{\text{Inventory Turnover}}$$

In the case of Able Hardware,

$$\text{Inventory Turnover} = \frac{50,000}{1/2\ (21,000 + 20,000)} = \frac{50,000}{20,500} = 2.44$$

$$\text{Days' Supply in Inventory} = \frac{365}{2.44} = 150 \text{ days}$$

This doesn't indicate a very high rate of turnover, but it's reasonable for a hardware store.

(This brings up the question of, "Where can I find out how a ratio for a given type of business can be compared with average ratios for that industry?" The answer will be forthcoming. Let's concentrate on the mechanics right now.)

Another activity ratio is:

$$\text{Receivables Turnover} = \frac{\text{Credit Sales}}{\text{Average Receivables}}$$

and then you can compute:

$$\text{Age of Receivables} = \frac{365}{\text{Receivables Turnover}}$$

If Able Hardware did credit sales of $1800 a year and average receivables were $300,

$$\text{Receivables Turnover} = \frac{1800}{300} = 6$$

$$\text{Age of Receivables} = \frac{365}{6} = 61 \text{ days}$$

Return on Assets

Finally, let's look at return on assets. This is a broad measure of the efficiency of utilization of all assets.

$$\text{Return on Assets} = \frac{\text{Net Profit}}{\text{Total Assets}}$$

In the case of Able Hardware,

$$\text{Return on Assets} = \frac{10{,}000}{31{,}300} = 0.32$$

This is a very respectable return on assets.

REVIEW EXERCISES 7-D

1. A company has current assets of $1,000 cash, $2,000 accounts receivable, and $10,000 inventory. Current liabilities include $3,000 accounts payable and $2,000 in current notes payable. Compute working capital, current ratio, and quick ratio.
2. A company's current ratio is 0.7. If current assets are $2,000, what are the current liabilities? Working capital?
3. A company has a mortgage loan of $10,000 on its store building, a $25,000 SBA five-year loan, and accounts-payable of $10,000. It has total assets of $55,000. What is the debt-to-asset ratio? The debt-to-equity ratio?
4. Is the business of question 1 in a good or bad liquidity position? Discuss.
5. Is the business of problem 3 highly leveraged, average, or overly conservative in its use of debt? What are the possible consequences of its position if business gets very poor? Gets very good?
6. A company's cost of goods sold is $100,000 for 19X1. Beginning inventory was $20,000 and ending inventory was $30,000. What is the turnover? What is the amount of the days' sales?
7. A business has an average of $4,000 in accounts-receivable and did $32,000 in credit sales in 19X1. What is the turnover of receivables? Age of receivables?

CASE: THE RETAIL FORECLOSURE

Joan Toms invested $45,000 in a Merit Jewelry franchise. The major portion of her investment bought merchandise. The merchandise included jewelry, luggage, gift items, small appliances, stereos, and CBs. Merit published a slick catalog which franchisees mailed to prospective customers. Joan located her business in a light industrial park fronting on a heavy, fast-traffic street. She had an attractive showroom and was staffed for business. She opened in September and by January had sales of $80,000 with a net of $20,000. Joan decided to expand the business and borrowed $40,000 from Northern Bank to increase inventory and expand facilities. She leased additional available space on the back of her building and expanded her showroom.

During the next eight months, Joan did only $50,000 in sales, at a loss of $30,000. She was unable to make her payments to the bank and the bank began to pressure her. Business from September to December amounted to sales of $100,000 with a net of $25,000. Joan caught up on her payments to the bank in December, but her cash and inventory were severely depleted. She was unable to make payments from January through April, and the bank foreclosed. The company's assets were sold at public auction, and a $10,000 deficiency judgment against Joan Toms was entered in favor of Northern Bank.

REVIEW EXERCISES 7-E

1. Do you think that Joan Toms might have conducted her business differently if she had read this chapter? Explain your position.
2. What fundamental rule of finance did Joan violate?
3. Does this case drive home any lessons about the seasonal nature of some businesses? What are they?
4. How could Joan have avoided failure?
5. Discuss Joan's choice of business location. What kind of location would you have chosen?

COMPARISONS

Now you know how to compute the ratios and they're second nature to you—aren't they? Probably they're not. You may be confused. What you should know is

1. What the ratios mean
2. Where to find them in the text

3. And, you should know these as "second-nature" tools:

(a) Net Profit Margin $= \frac{\text{Net Profit}}{\text{Sales}}$

(b) Return on Equity $= \frac{\text{Net Profit}}{\text{Owner's Equity}}$

(c) Current Ratio $= \frac{\text{Current Assets}}{\text{Current Liabilities}}$

(d) Quick Ratio $= \frac{\text{Current Assets} - \text{Inventory}}{\text{Current Liabilities}}$

(e) Working Capital = Current Assets – Current Liabilities

You have plenty of time to learn the ratios we didn't put on the "second-nature" list. But those on the list shouldn't be mere memorizations. You should know how to apply them to the financial statements of a business and you should be able to analyze and interpret the results. It's easy to compare one business to another and reach conclusions concerning the relative financial and performance quality of the two businesses. But what about the quality of the company relative to a standard? What do you measure against?

Since there's considerable difference between a manufacturing and a retail business, and since there's considerable difference between two different retail businesses (e.g., a shoe store and a drug store), it's impossible to have a universal standard. So, you use a different standard for each type of business. But even in the same kind of business, there are substantial differences in size. You'd hardly have a good measure comparing a business with $100,000 annual sales to one with $10 million annual sales.

Standard ratios for various kinds of businesses are compiled by a number ot organizations. Dun & Bradstreet compiles ratios for many kinds of businesses, and Robert Morris Associates (the National Association of Bank Loan Officers and Credit Men) publishes data on several hundred kinds of businesses in *Annual Statement Studies.* You can probably locate a copy of the *Annual Statement Studies* at your bank or at your nearest Small Business Administration Field Office.

Now, let's compare some of Able Hardware's ratios to median ratios for retail hardware stores doing less than $250,000 a year in sales.

Able's current ratio is 4.96 compared to a 2.4 median; the quick ratio is 1.04 compared to a 0.6 median. We must conclude that Able is very liquid in contrast to most others in the industry.

Able's total debt to equity is 0.57 compared to a 1.0 median. Able is *not* highly leveraged, and is conservative. Able has sufficient worth and low enough debt to weather rough financial times. It does not have high fixed-interest expense to whittle away at profits, and it has enough assets and worth to borrow money if it's needed.

Able's inventory turnover is 2.44 against an industry median of 2.7. Able is not turning inventory quite as fast as most hardware companies. Days' supply is 150 for Able and the median is 133.

Able's return on equity is 50 percent, as contrasted to a median of 12.7 percent. However, it appears that he's paying himself a very low salary. If his salary were raised (reducing his profit on the corporate equivalent basis), this ratio would decrease. The same thing would happen to his net profit margin.

SUMMARY

In this chapter, you've learned financial principles and techniques related to income statements, balance sheets, measures of profitability, measures of financial position, and activity ratios.

The income statement shows the performance of a business for a given period of time, usually a year. It's a good idea to complete an interim income statement each month to see how you are performing. An income statement shows sales, cost of goods sold, gross profit, expenses, and net profit.

$$\text{Net Profit} = \text{Sales} - \text{Cost of Goods Sold} - \text{Expenses; or}$$
$$= \text{Gross Profit} - \text{Expenses}$$

The measures of profitability are:

$$\text{Net Profit Margin} = \frac{\text{Net Profit}}{\text{Sales}}$$

$$\text{Return on Equity} = \frac{\text{Net Profit}}{\text{Owner's Equity}}$$

$$\text{Gross Margin} = \frac{\text{Gross Profit}}{\text{Sales}}$$

$$\%\ \text{Expense} = \frac{\text{Expense}}{\text{Sales}} \times 100\ \%$$

You measure worth and financial position with balance sheet data. The balance sheet shows a business's assets, liabilities, and owner's equity (net worth) on a specific date. The balance sheet separates current items (to be collected or paid in a year) and fixed or long term items (with a life, payment time, or collection time of more than one year). The basic equation for the balance sheet is:

$$\text{Assets} = \text{Liabilities} + \text{Owner's Equity}$$

Current assets include cash (on hand and in banks), accounts receivable, notes receivable, and inventory. Current liabilities include accounts payable, notes payable, wages payable, interest payable and others. The difference between current assets and current liabilities is net working capital:

$$\text{Net Working Capital} = \text{Current Assets} - \text{Current Liabilities}$$

Long-term assets are long-lived things such as a plant, fixtures, and equipment. Long-term liabilities include long-term debt. Owner's equity is the owner's investment and retained earnings in the business, sometimes called net worth or book value.

Measures of liquidity include net working capital, current ratio, and the quick (acid test) ratio:

$$\text{Current Ratio} = \frac{\text{Current Assets}}{\text{Current Liabilities}}$$

$$\text{Quick Ratio} = \frac{\text{Current Assets} - \text{Inventory}}{\text{Current Liabilities}}$$

Poor management of working capital is a frequent cause of business failure. Working capital dissipation usually signals business failure.

The leverage ratios are total debt to total assets and total debt to owner's equity. The higher these ratios are, the greater the leverage and the risk. When these ratios are low, risk is low.

Activity ratios enable you to measure turnover and days' supply or age. They include:

$$\text{Inventory Turnover} = \frac{\text{Cost of Goods Sold}}{\text{Average Inventory}}$$

$$\text{Days' Supply In Inventory} = \frac{365}{\text{Inventory Turnover}}$$

$$\text{Receivables Turnover} = \frac{\text{Credit Sales}}{\text{Average Receivables}}$$

$$\text{Age of Receivables} = \frac{365}{\text{Receivables Turnover}}$$

A useful ratio for measuring the efficiency of asset utilization is:

$$\text{Return on Assets} = \frac{\text{Net Profit}}{\text{Total Assets}}$$

KEY TERMS

Balance sheet
Current assets
Current liabilities
Current ratio
Depreciation
Fixed assets

Gross margin
Gross profit
Income statement
Inventory turnover
Leverage
Liquidity
Long-term liabilities
Net profit
Net profit margin
Profitability
Quick ratio (acid test)
Receivables turnover
Return on assets
Return on equity
Turnover

QUESTIONS AND PROBLEMS

1. Does the amount of your daily bank deposit equal your sales for the day, every day? Why?
2. If you want to prepare an income statement every month, is it necessary to take a physical inventory count each month? If not, how do you determine cost of goods sold?
3. You buy a machine for $3,000. It has a three-year life with a scrap value of $500. How much will it depreciate each year?
4. Depreciation is an expense that you don't have to pay out in cash. Explain why this is so.
5. If you were going to buy Able Hardware, how much would you estimate it is worth? Discuss your reasoning.
6. Company A has sales of $100,000 a year. Company B has sales of $400,000 a year. If they're both in the same line of business, would you expect A's working-capital requirements to be the same, less, or more than B's? Explain the reasons for your conclusion.
7. High Voltage Electrical Contractor has the following assets and liabilities, cash $2,000, accounts-receivable $4,500, notes-receivable $1,000, equipment $6,000, accounts-payable $1,000, debt on building $20,000, building $30,000. (a) Set up the balance sheet. (b) Compute the current ratio. (c) Compute the quick ratio. (d) Compute working capital.
8. High Voltage's purchases in 19X8 were $40,000. Starting inventory was $5,000 and ending inventory was $7,000. (a) Compute inventory turnover. (b) Compute days' supply in inventory.
9. High Voltage's credit sales in 19X8 were $30,000. Average receivables were $4,000. (a) Compute receivables turnover. (b) Compute age of receivables.
10. High Voltage's gross margin is 45 percent. Expenses were $20,000. Use the other data of problems 8 and 9. Develop High Voltage's income statement,
11. You were shown in the chapter how the income statement was developed from daily records. Assume you have the balance sheet for 19X5 and the income statement for 19X6. How would you develop the balance sheet of 19X6?

FIELD INVESTIGATION AND PROJECTS

1. Obtain the annual report of a local corporation by calling or writing the public relations department of the corporation. Compute the financial ratios using the income statement and balance-sheet data in the report. (Bonds and debentures are long-term debt.)

*2. Call on your banker and discuss the use of ratios in evaluating business loans. Go prepared with questions like the following:
(a) Do you use ratios to evaluate business-loan applications?
(b) Which ratios carry the most weight in your evaluation?
(c) The inventory turnover ratio is misleading in that some inventory turns twenty times a year and large portions of an inventory may turn once or less a year. How can you justify its merit as a measuring tool?
(While you're visiting with your banker, ask if you may have a look at a copy of the Robert Morris Associates *Annual Statement Studies.*)

*3. Prepare your personal financial statement. *Suggestion:* Go to your bank and ask for a "Personal Financial Statement" form. This project is one that you'll have to perform when you borrow substantial amounts from banks. Compute the ratios you've learned in this chapter where possible.

Financing Your Own Business

8

The major question in the mind of a business starter is, "How much money will I need?" A few business starters have enough in savings, but most do not. Other questions are:

1. How can I determine how much money I'll need?
2. Where can I get the money?
3. What must I do to get the money?
4. If I borrow, for how long can I borrow?
5. How can I convince a lender to make a loan?

CAPITAL AND FINANCING

The word "capital" is an oft-used business term. What is capital? Is it money? Is it something else? Are there different kinds of capital?

Capital is any form of wealth employed to produce more wealth. It's the wealth owned and employed in a business. *Net capital* is the ownership interest in a business, and therefore is *assets minus liabilities.* The key, though, is capital's ability to produce more wealth. Capital can exist in any asset form—cash, receivables, inventory, equipment, or plant, to mention just a few.

How Much Will You Need?

This is the key question in the mind of most aspiring business owners. There's no pat answer. The amount needed is a function of the kind of business you're going to start, the size of the business, how lavishly you're going to equip it, the size of inventory required, the geographical range of the business, the location, your own ability, and many other factors.

There are a number of methods for estimating capital needs. They include:

1. Research of available data published by trade associations, banks, SBA, and others. This research will sometimes require the use of other methods listed here;
2. Computations based on financial ratios and percentage financial statements;
3. The construction method, which is simply an item-by-item estimate based on actual equipment, inventory, time to profit, and working capital needs.

The research method can be fastest and most productive if you can find a reliable compilation of data geared to the specific business you're going to start. The Bank of America *Small Business Reporter* series cited in an earlier chapter provides extensive data on approximately thirty specific businesses. The SBA *Small Business Bibliography* series (free) lists trade associations, some of which may provide industry data. The *Statistical Abstract of the United States* provides a broad array of data, but it takes some looking and some computing. Another government source of business data is the U.S. Department of Commerce *Urban Business Profiles* series, available at small cost from the U.S. Government Printing Office. Don't overlook your library as a possible source of business data for determining capital requirements.

Published financial ratios and percentage financial statements are available from Robert Morris Associates and Dun & Bradstreet, as noted earlier. NCR Corporation, Corporate Advertising and Sales Promotion, Dayton, Ohio 45479, publishes *Expenses In Retail Business*, which contains percentage income statements for a large array of retail and service businesses.

Finally, to get inputs geared to your locality, you can gather data that may be helpful by visiting local businesspeople in the line of business you're investigating. This is usually more productive for obtaining general information than for obtaining quantitative data.

Computations based on ratios and percentage financial statements provide reasonable estimates for preliminary analysis and planning. However, because of the generality of published ratios concerning size of company, location, form of entity, and the specific time nature of the ratios (they may pertain to a recession, boom, or normal period), they provide less reliable numbers than the third method. Remember, when you use ratios, they're usually stated on a corporation basis with owner's salary as an expense. Your income is a reasonable salary plus the net profit. We'll use this approach whenever we're using ratios.

The third method is an actual construction of required capital and provides the most reliable figure. It should be used as your refined figure for detailed planning.

Figure 8-1 is a generalized percentage income statement (labeled "Expense Statement") for repair service businesses doing $50,000 to $125,000 a year sales. A range of percentages is shown to allow for variations in size and type of business. Figure 8-2 shows a range of minimum starting capital requirements for a number of different repair service businesses. The ranges are broad, but they'll give you an idea about capital needs for starting a service business.

FIGURE 8-1 Operating expense statement

The following expense statement shows typical ranges of operating ratios for a hypothetical television and appliance repair shop with annual gross sales of between $50,000 and $125,000.

Net sales	100%
Parts	35.0% - 42.0%
Labor	58.0 - 65.0
Cost of sales	57.0%
Parts costs	17.0% - 22.0%
Technicians' wages	35.0 - 40.0
Gross profit	43.0%
Expenses	
Office wages	4.0% - 6.0%
Owner salary	9.0 - 10.0
Employee benefits	2.5 - 2.9
Rent	2.6 - 3.0
Utilities and telephone	1.0 - 1.5
Advertising	1.0 - 1.6
Insurance	1.2 - 1.5
Repairs and maintenance	0.6 - 1.2
Depreciation	2.5 - 3.0
Taxes and licenses	1.5 - 1.8
Bad debts	0.5 - 0.8
Supplies	0.8 - 1.4
Accounting and legal	0.4 - 0.5
Truck and delivery	3.5 - 4.0
Miscellaneous	3.0 - 3.5
Total expenses	37.0% - 40.0%
Net profit	3.0% - 6.0%

Data not additive vertically.
Figures developed by *Small Business Reporter.*

(Reprinted by permission from "Repair Services," Vol. 10, No. 9, *Small Business Reporter*, Bank of America, N.T. & S.A., San Francisco, 1972.)

FIGURE 8-2 Minimum starting capital requirements

Type of Business	*Range*
Furniture repair	$10,000 to $20,000
Auto repair	$15,000 to $40,000
TV/Radio repair	$10,000 to $25,000
Appliance repair	$ 6,000 to $20,000
Clock or watch repair	$ 8,000 to $12,000
Shoe repair	$15,000 to $25,000
Business machines	$ 6,000 to $10,000
Bicycle repair	$ 6,000 to $10,000
Contractors (plumbing, carpentry, electrical, etc.)	$10,000 to $30,000

(Reprinted by permission from "Repair Services," Vol. 10, No. 9, *Small Business Reporter*, Bank of America, N.T. & S.A., San Francisco, 1972.)

Computations

The Problem: An electronics service shop (TV, radio, and stereo repairs) anticipates sales at $150,000 the first year.

(a) How much capital is needed?
(b) What net profit can be anticipated?
(c) What total earnings can the owner anticipate?

Possible Solution: Your research should uncover Bank of America's *Small Business Reporter*, Vol. 13, No. 10, "Consumer Electronic Centers," Dun & Bradstreet's ratios for radio and television stores, and statistics compiled by National Appliance and Radio TV Dealer's Association.

The "Consumer Electronic Centers" profile contains an equipment cost range for an owner-operated five-employee shop doing under $300,000 a year (Figure 8-3), and an operating expense range (percentage income statement) shown in Figure 8-4; it also tells you that inventory turnover is four times a year. This still leaves you with some computing.

Those of you who are electronics technicians will be quick to note that Figure 8-3 calls for more pieces of certain types of equipment than you'd want and leaves out audio generators and some other equipment that is needed for stereo work. But, here's where you have to stop being a technician and start being a businessperson. The amounts cited are broad estimates. The amounts show a range of $15,700 to $27,200 (rounded) for what appears to be a business twice the size of that in our problem. You'll probably be working with an outside person, yourself, some part-time inside employees, and one full-time inside employee. So you need two inside set-ups and one outside set-up. You decide to use the low figures because you can buy some of the equipment used.

FIGURE 8-3 New equipment costs for a hypothetical electronics service shop employing 3 inside and 2 outside technicians *Annual gross sales: Under $300,000*

Shared equipment

	Typical Ranges
Module kits (3 @ $200 to $300)	$ 600 – $ 900
Sweep/mark generator	450 – 450
Lab transistor checker	150 – 165
Substitution box	77 – 77
Signal generator	229 – 229
DC power supplies	175 – 175
Picture tube checker	122 – 400
Capacitor analyst	100 – 200
Television analyst*	350 – 400
Subtotal	$2,253 – $2,996

Equipment for inside technicians

Oscilloscopes (3 @ $190 to $580)	$ 570 – $1,740
TV test jigs (3 @ $200 to $400)	600 – 1,200
High voltage probes (3 @ $35 to $40)	105 – 120
Color bar generators (3 @ $96 to $270)	288 – 810
Tube testers (3 @ $150 to $270)	450 – 810
Solid state digitable multimeters* (3 @ $200)	600 – 600
Subtotal	$2,613 – $5,280

Equipment for outside technicians

	Typical Ranges
Tube caddies (2 @ $500 to $600)	$ 1,000 – $ 1,200
Color bar generators (2 @ $75 to $190)	150 – 380
Transistor checkers (2 @ $160 to $300)	320 – 600
Service mirrors (2 @ $5 to $20)	10 – 40
Simple volt ohm meters* (2 @ $5 to $60)	10 – 120
Sweep circuit analyzer* (2 @ $40)	80 – 80
Miscellaneous hand tools	300 – 500
Trucks (2 half-ton vans @ $4,500 to $8,000)	9,000 – 16,000
Subtotal	$10,870 – $18,920
Total	$15,736 – $27,196

*Optional
Figures compiled by ***Small Business Reporter*** in California.

(Reprinted by permission from "Consumer Electronics Center," Vol. 13, No. 3, ***Small Business Reporter,*** Bank of America, N.T. & S.A., San Francisco, 1975.)

Shared equipment =	$2,253.
Inside = 2/3 X 2,613 =	$1,742.
Outside – 1/2 X 10,870 =	$5,435.
Total	$9,430.

Next, you need to determine inventory needs. Figure 8-4 shows that parts sales are 37 to 42 percent of sales. Taking 40 percent as parts sales times $150,000 sales gives $60,000 retail parts sales. Next, parts cost is 22 – 27 percent of retail parts sales, so taking 25 percent cost times $60,000 retail sales gives $15,000 parts cost. Divide the $15,000 parts cost by the inventory turnover ratio of 4 to get inventory of $3,750.

Next, what do you need in the way of cash for working capital and cushion? The Bank of America profile suggests three times monthly expenses plus a cash reserve which appears to be roughly 1 percent of sales. Figure 8-4 shows ex-

FIGURE 8-4 Operating expense ratio for a hypothetical electronics service shop
Annual gross sales: under $300,000

	Typical Ranges
Sales	100%
Parts	37.0% - 42.0%
Labor	58.0% - 63.0%
Cost of sales	58%
Parts costs	22.0% - 27.0%
Technicians' wages	31.0% - 36.0%
Gross profit	42.0%
Expenses	
Salaries	14.5% - 16.0%
Rent	2.0% - 3.0%
Utilities, telephone	1.2% - 1.9%
Advertising	1.2% - 1.6%
Insurance	1.4% - 1.9%
Depreciation	2.4% - 2.9%
Taxes, licenses	0.9% - 2.0%
Bad debts	0.6% - 0.9%
Professional services	0.3% - 0.5%
Delivery trucks	3.2% - 4.0%
Supplies	1.1% - 1.4%
Miscellaneous	0.4% - 0.9%
Total expenses	29.2% - 37.0%
Net profit	5% - 12.8%

Chart reads horizontally; only expenses are additive vertically.

Figures compiled by *Small Business Reporter* in California.

(Reprinted by permission from "Consumer Electronics Centers," Vol. 13, No. 3, *Small Business Reporter,* Bank of America, N.T. & S.A., San Francisco, 1975.)

penses in the 29.2 to 37 percent range. We select 33 percent and multiply this times sales of $150,000 to get annual expenses of $49,500. One-quarter of that amount of $12,375 represents expenses for three months.

Our reserve cash should be 1 percent of $150,000, or $1,500.

Finally, allow $2,000 for start-up expenses including promotion, and shop for all start-up items.

Now, take the total as follows:

Equipment	$ 9,430
Inventory	3,750
Expense cushion	12,375
Cash reserve	1,500
Start-Up expenses	2,000
Total starting capital	$29,055

Note that this exceeds the upper amount for TV-radio repairs in Figure 8-2 by about $4,000 (as it should, since our problem involves a business doing more than $125,000, the sales corresponding to the $25,000 amount of capital in Figure 8-2).

Next, the answer to part (b) of the problem is the net profit percentage times sales. Figure 8-4 shows a net profit range of 5 to 12.8 percent; let's use 8.5 percent. Then 8.5 percent times $150,000 is $12,750 net profit.

The answer to part (c), the owner's total earnings, are the net profit plus his salary. Total salaries shown in Figure 8-4 range from 14.5 to 16 percent. Using 15 percent times $150,000 sales, we get $22,500 in salaries. (Note that technicians' wages are included in cost of sales.) This $22,500 probably covers a combination bookkeeper-secretary-dispatcher at about $8,000 and a salary of $14,500 for the owner. The owner's total earnings are net profit of $12,750 and a salary of $14,500, or $27,250.

In case you're wondering about the seemingly large amount allocated to technicians' wages, it's common practice in many service businesses, particularly TV repairs and other high-skill businesses, to use part-timers. The moonlighters are top talent and they put your facilities to work at night. This shop is getting about one and a half employee-years of labor from moonlighters. Thus it has the equivalent of 3.5 technician employees.

Another Solution Approach: A quick approach to determining capital needs is simply to use a ratio involving net worth and sales or profits. Thus, using Dun & Bradstreet ratio for radio and TV stores of net sales to net worth of 5.32, you simply divide annual sales of $150,000 by 5.32, which gives $28,195 as needed net worth. This is very close to the amount computed by the first method. Note that this is owner's equity in actuality, and this isn't quite the same as starting capital. Part of starting capital will be in the form of debt. But you can play just a bit loose with the net worth figure for this particular purpose and assume that owner's equity in a business that has been operating for some time has accrued as a result of retained earnings.

Again, we like to emphasize that ratios aren't sacred quantities because of the different kinds of business, different localities, different times, different depreciation factors, and different sizes (to mention only a few) involved in computations.

So, the surer way to go in your final detailed planning is to determine equipment and inventory needs and price them right out of the catalogs. Then determine your monthly expenses based on actual rents and salaries and whatever other expenses and payouts you can pin down. *Don't forget debt service on any capital you borrow*!

POINT 8-1: To estimate starting capital, determine equipment and inventory needs, add three months' expenses, 1 percent of sales, and an amount sufficient to cover start-up expenses. Use ratios and percentage financial statements for rough estimates; construct actual costs and expenses for more precise planning.

Long-Term Financing

Long-term capital is the wealth a business needs to finance long-term assets. Long-term assets are arbitrarily defined as those having a life of more than one year. They're commonly called fixed assets and consist of plant (we use the term to include factory, store, office, warehouse, or other facility, or the aggregate of all buildings used by a company), and equipment (including machines, tools, rolling stock, aircraft, fixtures, or anything else used in the business with a life of more than one year).

A fundamental rule of finance is:

Finance long-term assets with long-term capital, never with short-term capital.[1]

So, the capital for financing plant and equipment must come from long-term capital sources—namely, owner's equity and long-term debt. Don't ever violate this rule. Many large companies violated the rule in the early 1970s by borrowing on a short-term basis from the banks because interest rates were high and they didn't want to get locked in at high interest rates for a long term. They were counting on refunding (selling bonds and using the proceeds to pay off the banks) when interest rates went down. They didn't go down until 1975. As a consequence, some companies went under, and those that didn't went through serious financial stress.

The source of owner's equity for a starting proprietorship or partnership is the wealth of the owner or owners. The source of owner's equity for a starting corporation is the sale of stock. Each share of stock represents a fraction of equity. Of course, after a business gets going, profits contribute to the equity. Whatever profits are not drawn by the owner or owners of a proprietorship or partnership become a part of the owner's equity. Similarly, the part of the after-tax profits of a corporation not paid out to stockholders as dividends are retained earnings which become part of the owner's equity. Thus, owner's equity grows as a business prospers.

The basic forms of long-term debt for a proprietorship or a partnership are real estate mortgage loans, insurance policy loans, and unsecured loans from relatives and friends. The basic forms of long-term debt for a corporation are real estate mortgages, bonds secured by real estate or equipment, and debentures.

There is a form of debt called a "term loan" which matures in a period of more than a year but less than a specified number of years—three, five, or ten—depending on the expert defining it. (The Federal Reserve, which is akin to the divine in these matters, does not place an upper time limit in its definition.) An installment equipment loan is one type of loan in the "term" category that a small business might use. Term loans appear under the long-term liabilities on the balance sheet of the business.

[1] George A. Christy and Peyton Foster Roden, in *Finance Environment and Decisions* (San Francisco: Canfield Press, 1973), p. 10, state it this way: "A second principle is *suitability*, or the preservation of time-balance between assets and liabilities."

POINT 8-2: Sources of long-term financing are owner's equity and long-term debt.

Off-Balance Sheet Financing

There is another approach to meeting long-term capital needs that reduces the amount of immediate cash that has to be allocated to provide long-term assets. It's called "off-balance sheet financing." Although the term is relatively new, business has been using the technique for years.

Off-balance sheet financing is the process of getting the use of an asset without buying it, simply by leasing it. If you don't buy it, it doesn't show up on the balance sheet; it merely shows up on the income statement as an expense. Businesses have been using the technique for years. Instead of buying your building, you lease it. Instead of buying a computer, you lease it. You can also lease machines, automotive equipment, and aircraft to mention only a few of the possibilities.

Most small businesses (and many very large ones) operate in leased buildings. Beyond that, most very small business don't do much leasing. The basic reason is that leasing companies don't want to take chances with very small businesses. They prefer to lease big-ticket items worth $50,000 or more to large companies with excellent credit.

The primary disadvantage of leasing is that over the long run, it costs more than buying. But in most cases the difference is not as great as you might suspect when you take interest and other costs into account. Leasing is particularly attractive when specialized maintenance service is provided in the lease contract.

So, you can reduce your long-term capital needs by leasing.

How else can you reduce your long-term capital requirements? You can cut them quite a bit by buying used or reconditioned equipment and fixtures. If you need $10,000 worth of new equipment, you can often buy it used for $3,000 or so by doing some thorough shopping.

Next, think in terms of reducing the cash requirement for long-term capital equipment by converting assets you already own from personal use to business use. Your car or pick-up, for example, can be used in the business. If you already own tools and equipment needed in the business, you have another cash-need saving. Remember, you can establish owner's equity with cash or any of the physical assets that the business needs.

Once you've pared your long-term capital cash needs down by the methods mentioned, you're ready to start raising the needed cash. Your first sources are your savings accounts, stocks and bonds (don't forget U.S. Savings Bonds), and money deposited in your credit union. If you have a substantial equity in a home, you can sell it to raise cash. When you run out of assets to sell, you're down to borrowing for the required balance.

POINT 8-3: You can reduce capital cash requirements by off-balance sheet financing and conversion of personal assets directly to business use.

Short-Term Financing

Your initial capital requirements include working capital needs. You'll need some cash in the bank, inventory, and as the business grows, sufficient cash to permit you to carry receivables. *Your initial working capital requirements are financed from long-term sources.* The three-month expense cushion discussed earlier is in essence your working capital. After you get the business rolling, your permanent working capital requirements are financed from profits and long-term sources. *Remember that the major part of your working capital needs are permanent.* (Most students find this hard to grasp, and that's why I stress it.) The balance of your working capital requirements fluctuate. In many businesses, they fluctuate with the seasons. This fluctuating working capital requirement is part of your working capital that can be financed with short-term debt.

Short-term debt matures in a period of less than one year. It appears on the balance sheet under current liabilities as accounts-payable and notes-payable. A short-term loan may be geared to a single payment at maturity or to monthly installment payments.

Accounts payable on the balance sheet covers short-term financing provided by suppliers in the form of trade accounts. You buy raw materials or merchandise and the supplier sends you a bill, generally due in thirty days. In some industries, you're given sixty days. Most suppliers grant a cash discount for early payment. The usual terms are2/10/net 30; it costs you what amounts to 36 percent annual interest not to pay in ten days. It's smart to take the discounts, because you can borrow short-term money for considerably less at the bank.

Notes payable covers short-term loans. In some instances, a supplier will take your note for 90 to 180 days at a reasonable rate of interest in lieu of payment. Or, if you buy equipment on the installment plan, you make a down payment and pay the balance with interest over a period of months. This form of financing is sometimes provided by suppliers, but is more commonly placed with banks.

The portion of long-term debt falling due in the current year is realistically a current liability. It is sometimes included in current notes-payable, or it can be shown as "long-term debt maturing in the current period."

POINT 8-4: Short-term debt is debt maturing in less than one year.

Customer "Out-Of-The-Business" Financing

Selling on credit increases sales. If you carry the credit yourself in the form of accounts-receivable, you increase working capital needs.

You can sell merchandise in the $200-per-sale or larger category on terms to the customer without financing the sale yourself. You simply have the sale financed through a bank or a finance company. You get your cash immediately. The procedure is relatively simple. You get copies of the bank or finance company's application and contract form. You get the customer's credit information and fill in the blanks. The customer signs. You deliver the paper to the lender. He looks it over and checks the customer's credit. If the credit check is good and the deal is otherwise in order, he gives you a go-ahead and you make the sale.

Credit cards offer another means of financing customers' sales without becoming involved in the financing yourself. There are national credit-card systems. To learn more about using these plans, consult your banker.

Many of your customers will belong to credit unions. Credit unions will finance purchases of larger items such as major electrical appliances, automobiles, and boats for their members.

Out-of-the-business financing of consumer sales does for working capital what off-balance sheet financing does for long-term capital; it reduces the amount needed. It does so by reducing the amount of money you tie up in accounts-receivable.

POINT 8-5: "Out-of-the-business" customer financing enables you to reduce or or eliminate receivables, and consequently reduces working capital needs.

REVIEW EXERCISES 8-A

1. You want to make a profit of $15,000 in your business. The ratios for this type of business are: net profit margin, 20 percent; return on assets, 30 percent; gross margin 50 percent. How much starting capital will you need? What limits should you set on monthly expenses?
2. You need $5,000 worth of equipment and $4,000 for working capital to start your business. You already own part of the needed equipment valued at $2,000. You have $2,500 in savings, $500 in U.S. Savings Bonds, an insurance policy with a cash value of $2,000, and an equity of $4,000 in your home. Discuss the ways in which you can raise the needed capital and recommend the approach that you consider best.
3. Discuss "off-balance sheet financing." What are the advantages and disadvantages?
4. What is the basic rule for financing long-term capital needs?
5. What is the difference between long-term and short-term debt?
6. What kind of loan (long- or short-term) should be obtained to finance fluctuating business needs? Why?
7. Discuss the ways in which you can give your customers the benefit of installment buying without tying up your own money.

LOAN TERMS AND LENDERS

You need to understand how lending works in order to be able to borrow successfully. In this section you'll learn the various loan collateral mechanisms in common use, how to compare the often confusing terminology associated with interest rates, and how to handle renewals and refinancing.

Collateral

We say a debt is *secured when it is backed by collateral* (an asset that may be liquidated by the lender to obtain payment if the borrower defaults on the debt).

A debt is *unsecured when no collateral is pledged.* Unsecured loans are made based on the net worth, proven earning ability, and payment reputation of the borrower. They aren't often made by professional lenders to an unproven individual to start his or her first business. Relatives and friends do sometimes make unsecured loans.

A *real estate mortgage loan* is a loan secured by real estate.

A *bond* is a debt instrument usually secured by real estate or equipment.

A *debenture* is an unsecured bond.

Loans are sometimes secured by *guarantees.* Thus stockholders in a small corporation may endorse the corporation's loans in order to obtain otherwise unavailable financing. The SBA guarantees loans for small businesses that qualify.

Life insurance policy loans provide a source of long-term financing for proprietorships and partnerships. Most policies provide a loan privilege against the cash value of the policy at low interest for an indefinite term. Consult your insurance agent for details.

Short-term loans to cover needs during current asset demand periods are usually obtained from banks. A short-term loan may be secured in a number of ways. Manufactured inventory may be used as collateral if it is placed in a public warehouse and a warehouse receipt is obtained. The warehouse receipt stays with the bank till the loan is repaid. The merchandise can't be removed from the warehouse without the receipt.

Accounts receivable may be pledged to a bank to secure a short-term loan. Accounts receivable also can be sold to a factor, a firm that buys accounts-receivable at a discount and then collects them. The bank will take the receivables *with recourse*; that is, you remain liable for any of the receivables that go bad. Factors usually take receivables without recourse, but factoring is more costly than bank lending.

It you're a small retailer, you can't logically tie up inventory in a warehouse, and it's possible that you won't do much open-account business. There are other avenues open to you. If you sell merchandise such as TV sets and large appliances – in general, any merchandise of relatively high dollar value that is easily identifiable, preferably with a serial number – you can finance the merchandise by "floor planning." In floor planning, the bank's loan on your eligible merchandise inventory is secured by the merchandise. As you sell the merchandise, you pay the bank an amount based on the merchandise withdrawal. The bank will lend 50 percent or more on your merchandise, depending on how well you're established and the nature and length of your relationship with the bank.

POINT 8-6: Collateral can take the form of real estate, equipment, warehouse receipts, floor-planned merchandise, pledged accounts-receivables, or a guarantee in lieu of collateral.

Interest Rates And Computations

The cost of debt is the annual percentage rate or simple interest that you pay on borrowed money. Thus if you borrow $100 for one year at 8 percent, the interest is $8. This assumes that the $100 plus the $8 interest or $108 is repaid at the end of the year. The cost of capital is 8 percent, the simple interest, or the annual percentage rate (APR).

Now, suppose this transaction is handled as a discounted loan. In this case, the borrower pays the interest in advance by receiving $100 minus the $8 interest, or $92. But he signs a note for $100. The basic interest formula is interest equals rate times principal times the time in years. In this case, the real principal, the money the borrower receives is $92, and he's paying $8 interest for one year. The APR therefore is $8/$92 or 8.7 percent.

Now, let's take the case of a discounted installment loan. In this case, the borrower gets $100 minus $8, or $92 once again. However, he'll repay it in twelve monthly installments equal to $100/12, or $8.33. You might think that he has the use of an average $50 or $46 during the year. Neither is correct. He has the use of $92 the first month, and never has the use of a zero amount, even in the last month. Actually, the way it works out (by the rule of 78's – which is the sum of the digits of the months 1 through 12) is that he has use of an average of

$$\frac{\$92}{12} \times \frac{78}{12} = \frac{\$92}{12} \times 6.5 = \$49.83$$

plus something more. The something more is the larger amounts of interest accruing during the first months, which the borrower is actually getting the use of. That amount is

$$\$8 \times \frac{12}{78} = \frac{\$8}{6.5} = \$1.23$$

Then, the actual average amount available is $49.83 plus $1.23 or, $51.05– therefore,

$$\text{APR} = \frac{\text{Interest}}{\text{Average Amount}} = \frac{\$8}{\$51.05} = 15.67\%$$

The APR is almost double the stated interest! It's easy to see how an uninformed layperson might believe he was paying only 8 percent interest, while he was actually paying almost double that amount. Congress put an end to the confusion with the Truth-in-Lending Act, which among other things requires lenders to spell out APR in loan contracts.

Don't spend a lot of time memorizing how to do this. Even bankers and finance company loan officers use tables to obtain annual percentage rates. But the development is worth seeing to get a grasp of how interest works.

The cost of debt capital then is the annual percentage rate, or APR. Clearly, you want to borrow at the lowest APR possible. From the previous examples, it's easy to see that if you can borrow $1,000 at 10 percent simple interest payable at maturity, you're getting a better rate than you are with an 8 percent installment loan. That is, you're better off if you can utilize the full $1,000 or most of it for the full period of a year. If you set aside one-twelfth of the loan plus interest each month in your non-interest-earning checking account in order to be able to pay the debt off when it matures, you're losing. You are in effect paying a higher APR than you would have paid with the 8 percent installment loan.

The point is that cost of capital has practical meaning only if you put it to work. If you borrow $2,000 at 10 percent simple interest, but need and use only $1,000 of it, the interest you pay based on what you use is in effect 20 percent!

POINT 8-7: Annual percentage rate is the true annual rate (APR) of interest. Discounted notes, installment loans with add-on interest, and other frequently used loan terms state rates lower than the true rate or APR.

Other Terms

Banks often stipulate a compensating balance as a condition for making a loan. The compensating balance can take different forms. The bank may require you to maintain a compensating balance in your checking account. For example, if you borrow $10,000, the bank may require that you keep your checking account above $3,000 at all times. Since you only have the use of $7,000, an interest rate of 10 percent on $10,000 would translate to 14.3 percent on $7,000.

At the time that this book is being written, banks do not pay interest on checking accounts. Consequently, a bank has the use of the compensating balance interest-free. Changes are occurring in the financial industry, and banks may be permitted to pay interest on checking accounts. If this is the case, the interest on checking accounts will be less than interest on savings accounts. Thus, the bank will still have a profit margin in the use of checking-account balances. Other forms that compensating balances may take are balances in savings accounts or investments in certificates of deposit. Again, the bank has a margin of profit in interest differential. (A certificate of deposit is a deposit for a given amount at a prescribed rate of interest and time. If the certificate is cashed before maturity, the interest is reduced or forfeited.)

Other sweetener mechanisms employed by lenders include advance deduction of interest from the loan proceeds and add-on interest. These approaches to interest increase the annual percentage rate, as you learned earlier.

Sources of Debt Capital

Here are some sources and means for obtaining debt capital, some of which may not qualify as classic sources of financing for small business:

1. Suppliers and sellers
2. Commercial banks
3. Insurance companies
4. The government (SBA and others)
5. Thrifts (S & Ls and mutual savings banks)
6. Credit unions
7. Finance companies
8. Factors
9. Pension and trust funds
10. Relatives and friends

First, you can get short-term credit from suppliers—thirty- to sixty-day trade credit as noted earlier – in addition, you may be able to get them to take a note at the end of the account period at a reasonable rate of interest. Another possibility includes seller installment sales, which provide long-term credit. This kind of financing comes to play in the purchase of equipment, a business, or real estate. It may work something like this: Say you're buying a property for $10,000. You can pay $1,000 down. The seller agrees to finance the balance of $9,000 over a period of nine years. Your obligation is to repay $1,000 per year plus the accrued interest. Ordinarily, you can obtain better interest rates from a seller than you can from a financial institution. Thus, the seller might accept an interest rate of 8 percent although the market rate is 10 percent. There's a consequent saving to you and the seller is still earning a greater return than he could in the market.

Commercial banks are your principal source for short-term loans. They generally prefer not to make long-term loans to small new businesses. Bear in mind that banks do make guaranteed long-term loans if you have a substantial relative or friend who'll guarantee your loan (and that's asking quite a bit) or if you can get the SBA to guarantee the loan.

Banks can offer a *line of credit* and will generally do so for an established and proven customer. In essence the bank commits to lend you money any time you need it over a given period of time with a top limit on the amount of loan outstanding. Thus you might establish a line of credit of $5,000 maximum for the next year. The deal is sometimes a verbal one without a commitment charge. A more formal arrangement would be a written commitment from the bank for which you'd pay a small percentage fee on the limit. Thus, for a $5,000 commitment, you might pay 1 percent or $50. The bank charges you interest, of course, on any money you borrow against the line of credit. The interest terms may be expressed in the letter at a fixed rate, or they may be related to the prime rate (the rate banks charge their most credit-worthy customers, a fluctuating rate). If you're granted a fixed rate, you have protection from increased future interest rates caused by increased loan demand. Line of credit is generally good for handling short-term fluctuations in working-capital needs.

Insurance companies don't make small-business loans. However, if you're a policyholder, and your policy has cash value, you can usually get a loan in that amount at an attractive interest rate. They also make loans on apartment houses and office buildings.

Thrifts have traditionally been mortgage lenders. They're extending their role substantially in most parts of the country and some do make other types of loans now.

Credit unions do not make business loans. If you or your spouse belong to a credit union, you can borrow money for a car, truck, or other specific piece of equipment that you might later divert to your business.

Finance companies will make loans on specific identifiable pieces of equipment. The rates are higher than commercial bank rates, but they usually take greater risks.

Factors buy receivables, as noted earlier, and are rather expensive. Pension and trust funds rarely make small-business loans to strangers. Forget them.

Friends and relatives are sometimes sources of long- and short-term loans. These family arrangements can be difficult and traumatic if the lender is meddlesome or if things go wrong and you can't pay off. There are good and bad family deals. Assess your relationship with your relative or friend carefully before you discuss a loan or an investment in your business.

The government is a source of many kinds of financing. When we use the term "government," we mean local, state, and national. Municipalities will frequently build plants to suit and lease them to business at below market rates to provide employment and foster community growth. Most of this activity occurs in the less developed states. Municipalities sometimes become involved in financing low-income housing. State governments sometimes have veterans' loan programs, which although usually not oriented toward business loans, may enable you to make a switch in financing. They're usually geared to housing and farm loans. So, if you're a veteran and if you have a conventional house loan, you may be able to sell, invest the equity in your business, and move into another home with government financing, insurance, or guarantee. An FHA-insured loan or a VA-guaranteed loan for housing is one avenue. A caution here: If you have already used up your VA loan eligibility, you'll have to turn to an FHA loan. If your current home loan carries FHA insurance, you may have to extinguish the loan (sell with new financing rather than by assumption) in order to be eligible for a new loan.

The U.S. government has many loan programs that won't be recounted here. Many are highly specialized and availability and terms fluctuate. Watch for new government loan programs and economic injections when the economy is down, especially in pre-election years.

The Small Business Administration (SBA) has been involved in loans to small business since its inception. SBA loans are made only if you cannot obtain a loan from a bank or other private source. You should apply to a second bank (only one required in a town of less than 200,000 population) if the first bank turns you down. If you're refused on a direct loan, ask if the bank will make the loan under SBA's loan guaranty plan or if it will participate with SBA in a loan. If a bank agrees to either, see SBA.

If you get a flat turn-down, see SBA anyway. It still may be able to work something out. SBA has eighty eight field offices located in major cities. Look under U.S. Government for Small Business Administration in the phone directory.

This is a quick summary of sources of debt financing. You've been exposed to some of these sources in the previous section, and you'll learn more about them in succeeding sections.

> POINT 8-8: Loans don't look for you. You have to find them. Check the sources listed and any others you can think of.

Renewals and Refinancing

Short-term loans are usually made for periods of 90, 180, or 270 days. It is important that you be able to meet your obligations on these loans as they fall due. However, there may be times when you're hard-pressed and you see that you won't be able to pay any or all of a note when it is due. If you're able to pay off part of the loan you're in better shape than if you have to try to extend the entire loan.

In any event, contact the lender when you determine that you are going to be unable to pay off on time. Indicate what the special circumstances are, and what you can do. Ask for an extension or a renewal on what you can't pay. If you have an established lending connection with the lender, he will probably go along with anything you want to do. However, there are some restrictions on commercial banks set by bank regulatory laws. The banker has to live within these ground rules, and the ground rules may be such that there are limitations on the banker's ability to renew your note.

In the event you are unable to renew the note, you will have to find another source of finance to pay the note off. You may be able to obtain a long-term loan from this same banker if you have an unpledged long-term asset to offer as collateral. In this case, you may be able to increase the loan amount, get a longer payout, and increase your overall cash flow.

If you're unable to renew or refund your short-term note at your regular bank, you'll have to go to another lender. When you approach another banker, he may require you to establish a checking account with him. Your chances of getting a loan from him will be improved if you already have an account established. Therefore, it's a good idea to set up a checking account in a second bank as soon as you put your business on its feet.

POINT 8-9: If you see that you can't pay off a note nearing maturity, see your banker about alternate arrangements as early as possible.

REVIEW EXERCISES 8-B

1. Discuss the various forms of collateral that are used to secure short-term loans.
2. Discuss long-term loan collateral.
3. You borrow $15,000 at 9 percent simple interest for 180 days. (Assume a 360-day year.) What is the total amount due in 180 days?
4. A $1,200 note at 11 percent simple interest for a term of a year is discounted for the interest. What APR are you paying?
5. What are the sources of financing open to very small businesses?
6. Why is "seller financing" often more attractive than bank financing?
7. Define "loan refunding."

HOW TO BORROW MONEY

There's an art to borrowing. Your capability to borrow is a function of your resources, your track record, the purpose of the loan, your past credit history, and numerous other factors. We'll discuss these and the techniques that you can use to increase your chances of obtaining loans for business purposes.

The 5 C's of Credit

Lenders generally evaluate borrowers on five basic criteria. They are (1) the *Character* of the borrower, (2) the *Capacity* of the borrower to repay, (3) the *Collateral* that is pledged to secure the loan, (4) the borrower's *Capital*, and (5) business *Conditions*. These are the 5 C's of credit.

The *character* of a borrower is certainly an important factor to consider in deciding whether to grant a person a loan. If you are honest, good-intentioned, hard-working, and responsible, a lender is more likely to grant a loan than if you appear to be unprincipled, insecure, and lazy.

Your *capacity* to repay a loan is another factor the lender considers. In evaluating your capacity as a borrower, he judges the presentation that you make to him, its merit, and the probability that you will be able to repay the loan when it falls due. He'll try to decide whether you're a good businessperson, whether you keep close control of your business, and whether you exhibit a high degree of confidence.

Collateral is the asset you pledge to secure a loan. Loans may be unsecured, but generally a lender wants collateral. The better the collateral, the more secure the loan is. Your proven credit-worthiness is a factor in requiring collateral. If you are required to provide collateral, the lender will want to know about the quality and the saleability of the collateral.

Capital is your net worth. Your net worth is an indication of your capability to repay the loan if your plans go amiss. Should your collateral fail, then your unpledged capital forms a cushion to protect the lender from loss.

"Business *conditions*" refers to the general state of business and the economy. If business conditions are good, your business has a better chance of success. If business is bad, there's a possibility that your business may suffer as a result. Consequently, the lender always considers business conditions.

Loan Request Preplan

When you approach a lender to borrow money, there are several things that he will want to see. One of these things is the balance sheet. Your balance sheet will tell the lender something about your capacity and about your capital. Your track record in your personal finances and in your business will show your banker something about your character, a lot more about your 5 C's of credit, and will provide subjective information that will be helpful in encouraging him to make the loan. The personal financial statement form shown in Figure 8-5 is required for this purpose by most banks. If you have been successful in previous businesses or in managing your personal business, you're more likely to have the capacity to manage a business of your own and to repay the money that you borrow. In presenting your track record, it is a good idea to state your previous work experience as it relates to the business you are about to enter.

The *purpose of the loan* is important to the lender in determining his willingness to make the loan. If the loan is to be used for capital equipment, he will want to know that the equipment will contribute an amount to profit in excess of the amortization of interest and principal. If the loan is being used to finance inventory and is to be paid off with collected receivables, the lender may want to know something about your collection experience over a prior period.

The lender will conduct a credit investigation to determine your credit-worthiness. He'll call other banks in which you have accounts, and suppliers or retailers with whom you have charge accounts. A previous record of prompt payment increases your borrowing ability.

FIGURE 8-5 Personal financial statement form used by most banks

(A) Front

PERSONAL FINANCIAL STATEMENT

Name________ To:________ Bank

Address________ ________ City ________ State

Telephone________

Business or Occupation________

Partner or Officer in any other venture________

Age______ Married______ Single______ No. of Dependent Children______

Are any assets pledged?________

Have you ever made a composition settlement or taken bankruptcy? Explain:________

For the purpose of procuring and maintaining credit from time to time in any form whatsoever with the above named Bank, for claims and demands against the undersigned, the undersigned submits the following as being a true and accurate statement of its financial condition on the following date, and agree that if any change occurs that materially reduces the means or ability of the undersigned to pay all claims or demands against it, the undersigned will immediately and without delay notify the said Bank, and unless the Bank is so notified it may continue to rely upon the statement herein given as a true and accurate statement of the financial condition of the undersigned as of the close of business________, 19____.

ASSETS		LIABILITIES AND NET WORTH	
Cash on Hand and in Banks (Schedule 1)	$	Notes Payable to Banks — Secured (Schedule 1)	$
U. S. Government Securities		Unsecured (Schedule 1)	
Accounts, Loans and Notes Receivable (Schedule 2)		Notes Payable to Relatives	
Cash Surrender Value Life Insurance (Schedule 3)		Accounts and Notes Payable to Others	
Other Stocks and Bonds (Schedule 4)		Rents and Interest Due	
Real Estate (Schedule 5)		Taxes Due (Schedule 5)	
Automobiles — Number ( )		Liens on Real Estate (Schedule 5)	
Other Assets (Itemize)		Other Liabilities (Itemize)	
		TOTAL LIABILITIES	
		NET WORTH	
TOTAL ASSETS	$	TOTAL LIABILITIES AND NET WORTH	$

SOURCE OF INCOME		CONTINGENT LIABILITIES	
Salary	$	As Endorser or Co-Maker	$
Bonus and Commissions		On Leases or Contracts	
Dividends and Interest		Legal Claims	
Real Estate Income		Provision for Federal Income Tax	
		Other Special Debt	
TOTAL INCOME	$		

INSURANCE COVERAGE		COMPARISON OF MONTHLY INCOME AND EXPENSES		
Fire Insurance — Buildings	$	Net Monthly Income		$
Household Effects and Autos		Rent or Home Payment	$	
Liability Insurance — Automobiles		Food and Utilities		
Personal		Incidentals		
General Public		Avg. Amt. Paid on Open Accts.		
Other Insurance		TOTAL EXPENSES		$
		DIFFERENCE BETWEEN INCOME AND EXPENSES		$

(SEE OTHER SIDE)

LD-442

Approaching the Lender

When you approach a lender for a loan, put on your best front. Wear business clothes and try to reflect your enthusiasm for your project in your appearance and facial expressions as well as in the words you have to say. Since it is most

(B) Back

SCHEDULES

No. 1. Banking Relations. (A list of all my bank savings and loan accounts.)

Name and Location	Cash Balance	Amount of Loan	Maturity of Loan	How Endorsed, Guaranteed or Secured
	$	$		

No. 2. Accounts, Loans and Notes Receivable. (A list of the largest amounts owing to me.)

Name and Address of Debtor	Amount Owing	Age of Debt	Description or Nature of Debt	Description of Security Held	Date Payment Expected

No. 3. Life Insurance.

Name of Person Insured	Name of Beneficiary	Name of Insurance Co.	Type of Policy	Face Amount of Policy	Total Cash Surrender Value	Total Loans Against Policy	Amount of Yearly Premium	Is Policy Assigned?

No. 4. Other Stocks and Bonds.

Face Value Bonds No. Stock Shares	Description of Security	Registered in Name of	Cost	Present Market Value	Income Received Last Year	If Pledged State to Whom

No. 5. Real Estate. The legal and equitable title to all the real estate listed in this statement is solely in the name of the undersigned, except as follows:__________

Description or Street No.	Dimensions or Acres	Improvements Consist of	Mortgages or Liens	Due Dates and Amounts of Payments	Assessed Value	Present Market Value	Unpaid Taxes	
							Year	Amount

The undersigned certifies that the information inserted on each side hereof has been carefully read and is true and correct.

Date__________________ Signed__________________

important that you obtain the financing to start your business, you should approach this matter as you would any matter of major importance. You should be armed with a balance sheet and an income statement reflecting your current financial situation. You should have a cash-flow projection for the business that you intend to start or buy. It is also helpful to have a résumé to show your track record in the working and the business world. Finally, make up a *summary sheet* that indicates the *amount you wish to borrow*, the *term of the loan, how you will repay it, what the money is to be used for,* and *the earning potential* of the business or project for which the loan is to be used.

If you go in to see the lender with less preparation than this, you're taking a big chance. First of all, if you don't look neat, the banker may decide that you're disorganized, sloppy, and that you tend to operate your business in a similar fashion. If you can't express yourself clearly and lucidly, the lender may decide that you're a fumbler. Be prepared to discuss your loan requirement intelligently. If you do approach the banker without the income statement, balance sheet, and the other documents he will probably ask you to develop them for him if he decides to pursue the matter any further with you. However, he may decide not to pursue the matter any further with you if he thinks you're inexperienced about loan matters.

The mere act of going to see the banker with the exhibits cited puts you way above most people who walk in for a new business starting loan. It shows the banker some business know-how, and there's evidence of planning. It will go a long way in helping you get any reasonable amount that you request.

Banks and Bankers

Banks are in the business of lending money. They're anxious to lend money when they believe it will be repaid on schedule. So, if you have a sound deal and measure up reasonably on the 5 C's, you'll get the money – unless the bank is actually short on money to lend. The point is, you're not in the position of begging for a loan, because lending is how banks make money. If you have to beg for the loan, you probably don't deserve it.

Various bank loan officers have told me that most of the people who come to them for starting business loans are totally incompetent and sometimes don't even have the vaguest idea about the kind of business they want to get into. The bankers are actually doing them a favor by turning them down. If you're turned down by several banks, re-examine your deal. There must be something wrong with it. Revise it, and see if you can't make it measure up to the 5 C's of credit. Then, try it again – perhaps with some of the same bankers.

Banks provide a broad array of services besides lending. Pick up some of the bank's brochures and learn about these other services. The principal service that you'll use (besides the lending service) is a business checking account. Your bank also has a credit-card activity either of its own or in conjunction with one of the national cards. If you accept credit cards, you have an additional sales tool without having to do charge account business. Banks provide a host of other services. Check into them.

POINT 8-10: Banks are in business to lend money. When you see your bank for a loan, go prepared with *balance sheet, income statement, cash flow statement, résumé,* and a *summary of loan usage.*

REVIEW EXERCISES 8-C

1. Discuss the 5 C's of credit.
2. Why is it important to make a businesslike approach to your banker when you're seeking a loan?
3. What documents should you take along when you go in to request a loan?
4. What services other than lending and providing checking accounts are performed by commercial banks?

CASES: LOANS

Case: The Refusal

Jerry Bates was employed as a dispatcher by Thunderball Delivery Service at a salary of $12,000 a year. His wife worked as a waitress in the Mecca Cafe. Her earnings were $8,000 a year. Jerry decided to start his own delivery service and went to see his local banker for financing. This is the conversation that took place:

Jerry: I want to borrow some money to start a business.
Banker: What kind of business?
Jerry: Oh, a delivery service.
Banker: Why?
Jerry: Because there's money in it.
Banker: What do you know about a delivery service?
Jerry: I've worked for Thunderbolt Delivery Service for four years.
Banker: What do you do?
Jerry: I'm a dispatcher.
Banker: May I see your financial statement?
Jerry: I don't have one. I'm not in business yet. Look, I make $12,000 a year —that means I know my business. My wife works and makes $8,000 a year.

We own a new Cadillac and a nearly new Buick, and we're buying our own home. And with all of that, we have a thousand dollars in the bank! What more do you need?

Banker: A financial statement would help. So would a little more money in the bank, considering your earnings and years of employment. How much money do you want to borrow?

Jerry: Oh, something like $20 or $30 thousand. Just enough to get started.

Banker: I'm afraid we can't accommodate you now. (The banker had more to say. What else do you think he told Jerry?)

Case: Loan Granted

Mary Applewhite was a salesperson at Crown Jewelers. She earned excellent commissions and her total earnings were about $12,000 a year. Her husband was a grade school teacher who earned $10,000 a year. They had saved $6,000 during their three years of marriage. Mary decided to start her own gift shop. She determined that she needed $30,000 (she wanted to borrow $25,000) to start the business and found a suitable location. She prepared a set of financial papers including a *personal balance sheet,* a *personal budget* geared to a reduced standard of living that showed how she and her husband could live on his salary alone, and a cash-flow projection for her first three years in business that showed the orderly repayment of a $25,000 loan. She also prepared a *summary of her sales* for the year at Crown Jewelers, a *list of suppliers* she intended to use, and an *advertising and promotion plan.* She phoned her bank, made an appointment with a loan officer, and met with her. A day later the officer called and told Ms. Applewhite that the loan would be granted.

REVIEW EXERCISES 8-D

1. Why was Jerry Bates' loan request refused? List the reasons as you see them.
2. Why was Mary Applewhite's loan granted? List reasons.
3. If you had been Jerry Bates, what preparations would you have made before seeing the banker?
4. If Jerry had made proper preparations but still only had $1,000 in the bank, do you think he'd have gotten the loan? Explain your reasoning.

SUMMARY

You can estimate the starting capital needed for your business by research, computations with ratios and percentage income statements, or computations that construct actual costs of equipment and inventory and estimate working-capital needs. A combination of approaches is usually used. Sources of data for these computations are cited in the chapter. Remember that ratios aren't sacred, but they provide better estimates than an outright guess.

Finance long-term capital needs with long-term sources of capital—namely, equity and long-term debt. Long-term debt has a maturity of more than one year and includes corporation bonds and debentures. For proprietorships and partnerships, long-term debt includes insurance policy loans, mortgage loans, equipment loans, unsecured loans, and off-balance sheet financing. Off-balance sheet financing consists of leasing a long-term asset rather than buying it. It reduces your capital needs. You can further reduce capital needs by extending credit through credit cards and other outside financing, and you can reduce cash capital needs by employing assets you already own in your business.

You can raise equity capital by converting assets you own into either cash or assets usable in your business. Some of your personal assets can be used as collateral for debt financing.

The major portion of working capital is permanent and grows linearly with sales. A portion of working-capital requirements is fluctuating—often seasonal—and should be financed with short-term debt. Short-term financing can be handled through judicious use of trade credit or bank loans collateralized with warehouse receipts, floor-plan merchandise, equipment, or pledged accounts-receivable.

Simple interest or annual percentage rate (APR) consists of interest computed by multiplying rate times period times principal. If a loan is discounted or interest on an installment loan is figured as add-on interest, the APR is greater than the stated interest. If you borrow more money than you actually need, the effective cost is greater than the stated interest. Lenders sometimes increase effective interest yields by requiring a compensating balance.

Sources of debt capital for mini businesses include suppliers, sellers, commercial banks, insurance companies (on policy loans), the government (including SBA), finance companies, factors, or relatives and friends. Thrifts sometimes finance commercial buildings.

When you approach a lender, have a first-class presentation with financial statements, projections, résumé, and a brief summary concerning the loan. A professional approach improves your chances of borrowing.

KEY TERMS

Annual percentage rate (APR)
Capital
Collateral
Commercial banks
Compensating balance
Credit card
Debt
Equity capital

Factor
Floor planning
Line of credit
Long-term financing
Mortgage
Net capital
Off-balance sheet financing
"Out-of-the-business" financing
Percentage statements
Pledge
Recourse
Refinance
SBA loan
Short-term financing
Thrifts

QUESTIONS AND PROBLEMS

1. What methods can you use to estimate capital needs?
2. Why are ratio methods less accurate than actual construction of capital needs?
3. You read and hear about people going into business on a shoestring. (a) Does this contradict the validity of the methods presented in this chapter? (b) What differences may be involved? (c) Comparing "shoestring" capitalization to that indicated by the methods in this chapter, which is safer? Discuss.
4. Compute the dollar values for all expenses in Figure 8-4 using the left-hand column.
5. (a) What advantages accrue from the use of "moonlighters" in a service business? (b) What are the disadvantages?
6. Differentiate between short-term, term, and long-term loans.
7. Differentiate between owner's equity and debt capital.
8. Why should long-term assets and the major portion of working capital be financed from long-term sources?
9. Discuss off-balance sheet financing.
10. How can you reduce cash capital needs for starting a new business? Don't confine your thinking to approaches covered in this chapter.
11. List and discuss the 5 C's of credit.
12. Discuss the various forms of collateral commonly used to secure (a) long-term loans, and (b) short-term loans.
13. Consignment of merchandise wasn't mentioned in this chapter. You'll have to look elsewhere to find out what it is and how it works. (a) Explain consignment. (b) If merchandise is consigned to you by a supplier, who really owns it? (c) Does consigned merchandise show on your balance sheet?
14. You borrow $10,000 from a relative to start your business at 7 percent simple interest. You are to pay off $2,000 of the principal plus the accrued interest at the end of each year for five years. Compute the total principal and interest for repayment each year.

15. Compensating balances increase the true loan yield for a lender. Does a compensating balance serve any other purposes for the lender? Discuss.
16. What sources of equity capital can you tap to start (a) a proprietorship? (b) a corporation? (c) a partnership?
17. Why is it a good idea to keep your banker informed periodically of your progress with your business?

FIELD INVESTIGATION AND PROJECTS

1. Research the SBA small-business lending programs. Discuss guaranteed, participating, and SBA direct loans; how to apply; the maximum loan amounts; ineligible businesses; and SBA policy on minority-business loans.

*2. Analyze a business you're interested in. Determine the start-up capital requirements by the methods discussed in this chapter, including a detailed construction of equipment and inventory needs using prices in catalogs obtained from equipment suppliers and wholesalers. (*Suggestion:* Have several members of the class analyze the same business, compare results, and discuss differences.)

Reporting, Taxes, and Tax Planning

9

A business is subject to taxation and regulation by the various governments. Taxation and regulation requires you as a small-business owner to keep records that you otherwise might not take the trouble to keep. Some small-business authorities argue that the Internal Revenue Service (IRS) has helped to make businesses successful (that otherwise might have failed) by requiring them to keep adequate records. There is probably a great deal of truth in this. While you should have gained an appreciation for the value of records at this point in your study, you still might be prone to "let down." The pressure of state sales tax, FICA, withholding, tax deposits, worker's compensation (formerly Workman's Compensation) and federal income tax reporting requirements put pressure on you to keep good records.

But there are more important reasons for understanding taxation—expecially the federal income tax. They are:

1. To be able to make business plans that will preserve income by capitalizing on the tax laws
2. To be able to make your investment and financial plans to preserve your earnings and your equity in your investments and personal finances

The use of an experienced accountant is recommended. But you have to know something about the tax laws to use his services most productively. *The specific tax laws, as stated here, change with time.* You need the accountant to stay abreast of the changes and to fill the gap on what cannot be presented here. But what is presented will give you the communicating knowledge you need to work with your accountant and to optimize your profits.

In this chapter you'll learn more about reports and tax collections you must make, taxes you must pay, the federal income tax, and federal income tax planning.

These are some of the questions that this chapter will help you answer:

1. What do I have to do in connection with sales taxes?
2. What forms must I submit for social security (FICA) and income tax withholding on employees?
3. Where can I get federal tax information?
4. How can I minimize my federal income tax liability?
5. What are the mechanics of preparing an income tax return?

TAXES, RECORDS, AND REPORTS

As a small businessperson you collect taxes and keep records for various governments. At this point we'll look at the various taxes you'll collect, the reports you'll have to make and when you have to make them. We'll also discuss the federal income tax laws. It is particularly important that you understand the income tax laws in order to plan for and minimize your tax liability.

Sales Taxes

Most states have sales taxes. Generally, the retailer collects these sales taxes and makes a quarterly report and remittance to the state. The retailer is generally allowed a small discount for the collection service. The reporting form for the State of Texas is shown in Figure 9-1.

How do you get lined up for sales-tax handling? In the State of Texas you contact the state comptroller's office in Austin or one of the field offices located in major Texas cities. If you live in a major city, simply look under your state's name in the telephone directory and call the comptroller (or controller) office listed for information. If you don't get results or if you live in a smaller town, ask one of the merchants with whom you deal who to contact. Call or write for the appropriate forms, fill them in, and you'll receive a sales-tax number and the necessary forms.

The guidelines given in Chapter 6 for record keeping and accounting will provide all of the back-up you need for your sales-tax records. If you are audited by the state, your books and your original sales slips will provide adequate evidence of sales taxes collected.

Many small businesspeople fall into a trap by failing to remember that the taxes they've collected must be remitted to the state. They feel flush because the

FIGURE 9-1 State of Texas sales and use tax return

Form 2A95-2.02

STATE OF TEXAS

COMBINATION STATE - CITY SALES & USE TAX RETURN

TAXPAYER NUMBER
1. 1-00-0000000-1

DO NOT WRITE IN ABOVE SPACE

PERIOD ENDING
2.

3.
TAXPAYER NAME
DRAWER SS
AUSTIN, TX 78775

4. IF YOUR NAME OR MAILING ADDRESS IS INCORRECT AS SHOWN, WRITE THE CORRECTIONS IN SPACE BELOW.
IF AN OWNERSHIP CHANGE, NEW OWNER MUST MAKE APPLICATION FOR A LIMITED SALES TAX PERMIT.

CORPORATION NAME CHANGE MUST FIRST BE FILED WITH THE OFFICE OF THE SECRETARY OF STATE.

T Code 02100 INDICATE ANY CORRECTIONS TO OUTLET INFORMATION NEXT TO THE INCORRECT ITEM.

PART I - 4% STATE TAX ONLY

ROUND TO NEAREST DOLLAR
REPORT WHOLE DOLLARS ONLY

5. OUTLET NO. 00001 — TRADE NAME TAXPAYER NAME — LOCATION 9821 CONGRESS AVE. AUSTIN, TX 78701

7. OUTLET NO. 00002 — TRADE NAME TAXPAYER GIFT SHOP — LOCATION 7778 E. PARK AVE. HOUSTON, TX 77001

9. OUTLET NO. 00003 — TRADE NAME TAXPAYER HARDWARE SALES — LOCATION 30 LAVACA ST. DALLAS, TX 75203

Line	GROSS SALES	GROSS TAXABLE SALES	DEDUCTIONS	Use Tax Purchases	Amount Subject State Tax	%	Method
6.	4032	3247	168	0	3079		
8.	5700	4950	150	0	4800		
10.	4500	4500	0	100	4600		

11. Total amount subject to 4% state tax (Line 6 plus Line 8 plus Line 10)	11.	$ 12479	
12. Total Tax Due (4% of Line 11)	12.	499	16
13. Less prepaid deductions if filed on time $ ______ OR $ ______ Remitted prepayment if filed late	13.		
14. Tax due after prepayment deduction (Line 12 minus Line 13)	14.		
15. Less 1% of Line 14 if return is filed on time	15.	4	99
16. Net tax due (Line 14 minus Line 15)	16.	494	17
17. Less: Prior overpayments (verify any preprinted amounts with your records before deducting)	17.		
18. Tax due after prior overpayments (Line 16 minus Line 17)	18.		
19. Late filing penalty: 1-30 days late - 5% of Line 18; 31-60 days - 10% of Line 18; minimum of 1.00 each tax	19.		
20. Total State Amount Due And Payable (Line 18 plus Line 19)	20.	494	17

FOR COMPTROLLER'S USE ONLY

SAMPLE OF PROPERLY COMPLETED REPORT

T Code 04010

PART II - 1% CITY TAX ONLY

	CITY CODE	CITY NAME	AMOUNT OF 1% CITY TAX DUE	
REPORT TAX ONLY 21.	057011	DALLAS	46	00
(NOT TAXABLE SALES) 22.	101017	HOUSTON	48	00
23.	227016	AUSTIN	30	79

24. Total amount of 1% city tax (Line 21 plus Line 22 plus Line 23)	24.	124	79
25. Prepaid deduction if filed on time $ ______ OR Remitted prepayment if filed late $ ______	25.		
26. Tax due after prepayment deduction (Line 24 minus Line 25)	26.		
27. Less 1% of Line 26 if return is filed on time	27.	1	25
28. Net Tax Due (Line 26 minus Line 27)	28.		
29. Less: Prior overpayments (Verify any preprinted amounts with your records before deducting)	29.		
30. Tax due after prior overpayments (Line 28 minus Line 29)	30.		
31. Late filing penalty: 1-30 days late - 5% of Line 30; 31-60 days - 10% of Line 30; minimum of 1.00 each tax	31.		
32. Total City Amount Due And Payable (Line 30 plus Line 31)	32.	123	54

TOTAL AMOUNT OF CHECK
617. 71

FOR COMPTROLLER'S USE ONLY

PAY ALL AMOUNTS DUE IN FULL FOR EACH TAX. AN OVERPAYMENT OF ONE TAX MAY NOT BE APPLIED AGAINST AN UNDERPAYMENT OF THE OTHER. ANY OVERPAYMENT OF EITHER TAX WILL INITIATE REFUND PROCEDURES WHEN THIS REPORT IS RECEIVED.

REMIT THE TOTAL OF LINE 20 PLUS LINE 32 IN ONE CHECK PAYABLE TO THE STATE TREASURER AND MAIL TO: BOB BULLOCK
COMPTROLLER OF PUBLIC ACCOUNTS
CAPITOL STATION
AUSTIN, TEXAS 78775

I DECLARE, UNDER PENALTIES PRESCRIBED IN CH. 95, GENERAL AND SPECIAL LAWS OF TEXAS (REGULAR SESSION), 1961, THAT THE INFORMATION IN THIS DOCUMENT IS TRUE AND CORRECT

Taxpayer Signature
SIGNATURE OF TAXPAYER OR DULY AUTHORIZED AGENT

Oct. 30, 1976
DATE

bank account is fat going into the third month. Then, at the end of the third month, the tax forms show up and they owe the state a sizable sum of money. Remember, sales taxes, FICA and income tax withheld must be paid, and the bank account may look deceptively fat just before you pay them!

POINT 9-1: Taxes collected and withheld must be remitted. Don't be deceived by the size of your bank account before you pay them.

FICA, Withholding, and Tax Deposits

If you have employees, which you surely will if your business prospers, you'll have to perform a good bit of extra paperwork. Your first chore is to get an employer identification number. Obtain an IRS *Form SS-4* shown in Figure 9-2 from your local Internal Revenue Service (IRS) office, complete it, and submit to IRS. Then IRS will send you an *Employer's Quarterly Federal Tax Return, Form 941* (Figure 9-3) and several copies of *Federal Tax Deposit Form 501* each quarter. In the initial mailing, you'll also receive a copy of *Circular E, Employer's Tax Guide.*

The *Employer's Tax Guide* tells you how to complete the Form 941 and contains tables for determining employee tax and FICA withholding. When you've completed the 941 you submit it to IRS; you deposit the tax due with the Federal Tax Deposit Form 501 at a commercial bank authorized to accept tax deposits. Note that you'll be matching the FICA contributed by your employees! The Form 941 handles this.

Each employee must fill in a form W-4 (Figure 9-4) when he or she is hired and before December 1 when his/her withholding allowance will be different in the next year. The W-4 lists the employee's exemptions.

You must provide each employee with a Form W-2 (Figure 9-5) before January 31 or at the end of his or her employment. The W-2 shows the employee's earnings.

Figure 9-6 is a calendar for your tax and FICA withholding chores. The references to sections pertain to circular E. Circular E provides detailed guidance for the entire process.

POINT 9-2: IRS Circular E, *Employer's Tax Guide* (free) provides step-by-step guidance for handling employee tax and FICA withholding records and filings. The calendar, Figure 9-6, lists everything you have to do.

Incidentally, banks have special checkbooks available for payroll checks. These provide the employee with a stub showing his earnings and withholdings, and provide you with a similar stub. It's easy to pick the information from the stubs when you complete your Form 941.

FIGURE 9-2 IRS form SS-4

D4263 ☆ U. S. GOVERNMENT PRINTING OFFICE: 1972—473-042

FOR CLEAR COPY ON ALL PARTS TYPEWRITE OR PRINT WITH BALL POINT PEN—PRESS FIRMLY
(See Instructions on Reverse)

FORM SS-4 (3-69)
PART 1 U.S. TREASURY DEPARTMENT—INTERNAL REVENUE SERVICE
APPLICATION FOR EMPLOYER IDENTIFICATION NUMBER

1. NAME (*TRUE name as distinguished from TRADE name.*)

2. TRADE NAME, IF ANY (*Enter name under which business is operated, if different from item 1.*)

3. ADDRESS OF PRINCIPAL PLACE OF BUSINESS (*No. and Street, City, State, Zip Code*) | 4. COUNTY OF BUSINESS LOCATION

5. ORGANIZATION Check Type ☐ Individual ☐ Partnership ☐ Corporation ☐ Other (*specify e.g. estate, trust, etc.*) ☐ Governmental (See Instr. 5) ☐ Nonprofit Organization (See Instr. 5) | 6. Ending Month of Accounting year

7. REASON FOR APPLYING (*If "other" specify such as "Corporate structure change," "Acquired by gift or trust," etc.*) ☐ Started new business ☐ Purchased going business ☐ Other | 8. Date you acquired or started business (*Mo., day, year*) | 9. First date you paid or will pay wages (*Mo., day, year*)

10. NATURE OF BUSINESS (*See Instructions*) | 11. NUMBER OF EMPLOYEES → IF "NONE" ENTER "0" | Non-agricultural | Agricultural

12. If nature of business is MANUFACTURING, list in order of their importance the principal products manufactured and the estimated percentage of the total value of all products which each represents. A % B % C %

PLEASE LEAVE BLANK: R | DO | TA | FR | FRC

13. Do you operate more than one place of business? ☐ Yes ☐ No
If "Yes, attach a list showing for each separate establishment: a. Name and address. b. Nature of business c. Number of employees.

14. To whom do you sell most of your products or services? ☐ Business establishments ☐ General public ☐ Other (*Specify*)

PLEASE LEAVE BLANK →	Geo.	Ind.	Class	Size	Reas. for Appl.	Bus. Bir. Date

FORM SS-4 (3-69)
PART 2 DO NOT DETACH ANY PART OF THIS FORM. SEND ALL COPIES TO
INTERNAL REVENUE SERVICE
PLEASE LEAVE BLANK

NAME AND COMPLETE ADDRESS

1. NAME (*TRUE name as distinguished from TRADE name.*)

2. TRADE NAME, IF ANY (*Enter name under which business is operated, if different from item 1.*)

3. ADDRESS OF PRINCIPAL PLACE OF BUSINESS (*No. and Street*)
(*City, State, Zip Code*) | 4. COUNTY OF BUSINESS LOCATION

5. ORGANIZATION Check Type ☐ Individual ☐ Partnership ☐ Corporation ☐ Other (*specify e.g. estate, trust, etc.*) ☐ Governmental (See Instr. 5) ☐ Nonprofit Organization (See Instr. 5) | 6. Ending Month of Accounting year

7. REASON FOR APPLYING (*If "other" specify such as "Corporate structure change," "Acquired by gift or trust," etc.*) ☐ Started new business ☐ Purchased going business ☐ Other | 8. Date you acquired or started business (*Mo., day, year*) | 9. First date you paid or will pay wages (*Mo., day, year*)

10. NATURE OF BUSINESS (*See Instructions*) | 11. NUMBER OF EMPLOYEES → IF "NONE" ENTER "0" | Non-agricultural | Agricultural

12. Have you ever applied for an identification number for this or any other business? ☐ No ☐ Yes
If "Yes," enter name and trade name (if any). Also enter the approximate date, city, and state where you first applied and previous number if known. →

DATE	SIGNATURE	TITLE

FIGURE 9-3 IRS form 941, front side only. Back side contains instructions and space for record of federal tax deposits.

Form **941** (Rev. Oct. 1975) Department of the Treasury Internal Revenue Service

Employer's Quarterly Federal Tax Return

Schedule A—Quarterly Report of Wages Taxable under the Federal Insurance Contributions Act—FOR SOCIAL SECURITY

List for each nonagricultural employee the WAGES taxable under the FICA which were paid during the quarter. If you pay an employee more than $14,100 in a calendar year, report only the first $14,100 of such wages. In the case of "Tip Income," see Instructions on page 4. IF WAGES WERE NOT TAXABLE UNDER THE FICA, MAKE NO ENTRIES IN ITEMS 1 THROUGH 9 AND 14 THROUGH 18.

1. Total pages of this return including this page and any pages of Form 941a ▶
2. Total number of employees listed ▶
3. (First quarter only) Number of employees (except household) employed in the pay period including March 12th ▶

4. EMPLOYEE'S SOCIAL SECURITY NUMBER 000 00 0000	5. NAME OF EMPLOYEE (Please type or print)	6. TAXABLE FICA WAGES Paid to Employee in Quarter (Before deductions) Dollars Cents	7. TAXABLE TIPS REPORTED (See page 4) Dollars Cents

If you need more space for listing employees, use Schedule A continuation sheets, Form 941a.

Totals for this page—Wage total in column 6 and tip total in column 7 ⟶

8. TOTAL WAGES TAXABLE UNDER FICA PAID DURING QUARTER. $ ______
(Total of column 6 on this page and continuation sheets.) Enter here and in item 14 below.

9. TOTAL TAXABLE TIPS REPORTED UNDER FICA DURING QUARTER. $ ______
(Total of column 7 on this page and continuation sheets.) Enter here and in item 15 below. (If no tips reported, write "None.")

YOUR COPY

Name .... **Date Quarter Ended** ....

Address .... **Employer Identification No.** ....

IMPORTANT.—Keep this copy and a copy of each related schedule or statement.

Before filing the return be sure to enter on this copy your name, address, and identification number, and the period for which the return is filed.

10. Total Wages And Tips Subject To Withholding Plus Other Compensation . . . . . . ⟶
11. Amount Of Income Tax Withheld From Wages, Tips, Annuities, etc. (See instructions) . . .
12. Adjustment For Preceding Quarters Of Calendar Year . . . .
13. Adjusted Total Of Income Tax Withheld . . . . ⟶
14. Taxable FICA Wages Paid (Item 8) . . $ .... multiplied by 11.7% = TAX
15. Taxable Tips Reported (Item 9) . . . $ .... multiplied by 5.85% = TAX
16. Total FICA Taxes (Item 14 plus Item 15) . . . . ⟶
17. Adjustment (See instructions) . . . .
18. Adjusted Total Of FICA Taxes . . . . ⟶
19. Total Taxes (Item 13 plus Item 18) . . . .
20. TOTAL DEPOSITS FOR QUARTER (INCLUDING FINAL DEPOSIT MADE FOR QUARTER) AND OVERPAYMENT FROM PREVIOUS QUARTER LISTED IN SCHEDULE B (See instructions on page 4) . . . .
Note: If undeposited taxes at the end of the quarter are $200 or more, the full amount must be deposited with an authorized commercial bank or a Federal Reserve bank. This deposit must be entered in Schedule B and included in item 20.
21. Undeposited Taxes Due (Item 19 Less Item 20—This Should Be Less Than $200). Pay To Internal Revenue Service And Enter Here . . . . ⟶
22. If Item 20 Is More Than Item 19, Enter Excess Here ▶ $ And Check If You Want It ☐ Applied To Next Return, Or ☐ Refunded.
23. If not liable for returns in the future write "**FINAL**" (See instructions) ▶ Date final wages paid ▶

See "Where to File" on Page 2.

FIGURE 9-4 IRS form W-4, front side only. Back side contains tables.

Form W-4 (Revised December 1975)

Employee's Withholding Allowance Certificate

The explanatory material below will help you determine your correct number of withholding allowances, and will assist you in completing the Form W–4 at the bottom of this page.

Avoid Overwithholding or Underwithholding

By claiming the proper number of withholding allowances you are entitled to, you can fit the amount of tax withheld from your wages to your tax liability. In addition to the allowances for personal exemptions to be claimed in items (a) through (g) below, be sure you claim any additional allowances you are entitled to in item (h) "Special withholding allowance," and item (i) "Allowance(s) for itemized deductions." While these allowances may be claimed on Form W–4 for withholding purposes, they are not to be claimed under "Exemptions" on your tax return Form 1040 or Form 1040A.

You may claim the special withholding allowance if you are single with only one employer, or married with only one employer and your spouse is not employed. If you have unusually large itemized deductions, you may claim the allowance(s) for itemized deductions to avoid having too much income tax withheld from your wages. On the other hand, if you and your spouse are both employed or you have more than one employer, you should take steps to assure that enough has been withheld. If you find that you need more withholding, claim fewer exemptions or ask for additional withholding. If you are currently claiming additional withholding allowances based on itemized deductions, check the table on the back to see that you are claiming the proper number of allowances.

How Many Withholding Allowances May You Claim?

Please use the schedule below to determine the number of allowances you may claim for tax withholding purposes. In determining the number, keep in mind these points: If you are single and hold more than one job, you may not claim the same allowances with more than one employer at the same time; or if you are married and both you and your spouse are employed, you may not claim the same allowances with your employers at the same time. A nonresident alien, other than a resident of Canada, Mexico, or Puerto Rico, may claim only one personal allowance.

Figure Your Total Withholding Allowances Below

(a) Allowance for yourself—enter 1 . . . . ______

(b) Allowance for your spouse—enter 1 . . . . ______

(c) Allowance for your age—if 65 or over—enter 1 . . . . ______

(d) Allowance for your spouse's age—if 65 or over—enter 1 . . . . ______

(e) Allowance for blindness (yourself)—enter 1 . . . . ______

(f) Allowance for blindness (spouse's)—enter 1 . . . . ______

(g) Allowance(s) for dependent(s)—you are entitled to claim an allowance for each dependent you will be able to claim on your Federal income tax return. Do not include yourself or your spouse * . . . . ______

(h) Special withholding allowance—if you are single with only one employer, or married with only one employer and your spouse is not employed—enter 1** . . . . ______

(i) Allowance(s) for itemized deductions—if you do plan to itemize deductions on your income tax return, enter the number from the table on back** . . . . ______

(j) Total—add lines (a) through (i) above. Enter here and on line 1, Form W–4 below . . . . ______

* If you are in doubt as to whom you may claim as a dependent, see the instructions which came with your last Federal income tax return or call your local Internal Revenue Service office.

** This allowance is used solely for purposes of figuring your withholding tax, and cannot be claimed when you file your tax return.

See Table on Back if You Plan to Itemize Your Deductions

Completing Form W–4.—If you find that you are entitled to one or more allowances in addition to those which you are now claiming, increase your number of allowances by completing the form below and filing it with your employer. If the number of allowances you previously claimed decreases, you must file a new Form W–4 within 10 days. (Should you expect to owe more tax than will be withheld, you may use the same form to increase your withholding by claiming fewer or "0" allowances on line 1, or by asking for additional withholding on line 2, or both.)

▼ **Give the bottom part of this form to your employer; keep the upper part for your records and information** ▼

Cut along this line

Form **W-4**
(Rev. Dec. 1975)
Department of the Treasury
Internal Revenue Service

Employee's Withholding Allowance Certificate

(This certificate is for income tax withholding purposes only; it will remain in effect until you change it.)

Type or print your full name	Your social security number
Home address (Number and street or rural route)	Marital status ☐ Single ☑ Married (If married but legally separated, or spouse is a nonresident alien, check the single block.)
City or town, State and ZIP code	

1 Total number of allowances you are claiming . . . . ______

2 Additional amount, if any, you want deducted from each pay (if your employer agrees) . . . . $

I certify that to the best of my knowledge and belief, the number of withholding allowances claimed on this certificate does not exceed the number to which I am entitled.

Signature ▶ .... **Date ▶** ...., **19** ......

16—83587-1

FIGURE 9-5 IRS form W-2

For Official Use Only

Wage and Tax Statement 1976

Type or print EMPLOYER'S name, address, ZIP code and Federal identifying number.

Copy A
For Internal Revenue Service Center

Employee's social security number	1 Federal income tax withheld	2 Wages, tips, and other compensation	3 FICA employee tax withheld	4 Total FICA wages

21 ☐

Type or print Employee's name, address, and ZIP code below (Name must aline with arrow)

5 Was employee covered by a qualified pension plan, etc.?	6 *	7 *

Name ▶

* See instructions on back of Copy D.

Form **W-2** See instructions on Form W-3 and back of Copy D Department of the Treasury—Internal Revenue Service

FIGURE 9-6 IRS calendar

Calendar

On or Before January 31 and at End of Employment

Give each employee a completed Form W-2, Wage and Tax Statement. See section 21.

On or Before January 31

For Federal Unemployment Tax.—File Form 940, Employer's Annual Federal Unemployment Tax Return. If you deposited the full amount of tax when due, you are allowed ten additional days to file the return. See sections 2, 4, 14, and 17.

On or Before February 28

For Income Tax Withholding.—File Form W-3, Transmittal of Income and Tax Statements, and include all required Internal Revenue Service copies (Copy A) of Form W-2 furnished employees for the preceding calendar year. See section 22.

On or Before April 30, July 31, October 31, and January 31

Deposit Federal unemployment tax due if more than $100.

File a quarterly return on Form 941 or 941E and pay balance of undeposited taxes. If you deposited the full amount of taxes when due, you are allowed ten additional days to file the return.

Before December 1

For Income Tax Withholding.—Request a new Form W-4 from each employee whose withholding allowances will be different in the next year from those shown on the employee's current Form W-4.

On May 1

Discontinue the exemption from withholding for each employee who has not given you a new Form W-4E. See section 13.

Unemployment Taxes

The federal government and state governments collect unemployment taxes. *Form 940* (Figure 9-7) is the federal return form. Note that you report on contributions made to the state on the federal form, and your state payments influence your federal payments. Each state has its own form and arrangement. The state rates are usually based on the experience rate of each specific business and range from a fraction of a percent to several percent of payroll up to a specified limit of wage per person.

Since there are variations from state to state and since the federal form utilizes state contribution, treatment here is impossible. I suggest you ask your accountant or bookkeeping service either to prepare or show you how to prepare unemployment tax returns.

POINT 9-3: If you have employees, you're subject to federal and state unemployment taxes. The federal return is a Form 940 and is filed annually before January 31. State forms must generally be filed quarterly.

FIGURE 9-7 IRS form 940

Form **940** Department of the Treasury Internal Revenue Service

Employer's Annual Federal Unemployment Tax Return **1975**

Name of State 1	State reporting number as shown on employer's State contribution returns 2	Taxable payroll (As defined in State act) 3	Experience rate period 4 From—	To—	Experience rate 5	Contributions had rate been 2.7% (col. 3 × 2.7%) 6	Contributions payable at experience rate (col. 3 × col. 5) 7	Additional credit (col. 6 minus col. 7) 8	Contributions actually paid to State 9
	Totals ▶								

10 Total tentative credit (Column 8 plus column 9). . . . .

11 Total remuneration (including exempt remuneration) PAID during the calendar year for services of employees

Exempt Remuneration	Approximate number of employees involved	Amount paid
12 Exempt remuneration. (Explain each exemption shown, attaching additional sheet if necessary):		
13 Remuneration in excess of $4,200. (Enter only the excess over the first $4,200 paid to individual employees exclusive of exempt amounts entered on line 12)		

14 Total exempt remuneration . . . .

15 Total taxable wages (line 11 less line 14) . . . .

16 Gross Federal tax (3.2% of line 15) . . . .

17 Enter 2.7% of the amount of wages shown on line 15 . . . .

18 Line 10 or line 17 whichever is smaller . . . .

19 Net Federal tax (line 16 less line 18) . . . .

Record of Federal Tax Deposits for Unemployment Tax (Form 508)

Quarter	Liability by period	Date of deposit	Amount of deposit
First			
Second			
Third			
Fourth			

20 Total Federal tax deposited . . . .

21 Balance due (line 19 less line 20—this should not exceed $100). Pay to "Internal Revenue Service" . . ▶

22 If no longer in business at end of year, write **"FINAL"** here ▶

Under penalties of perjury, I declare that I have examined this return, including accompanying schedules and statements, and to the best of my knowledge and belief it is true, correct, and complete, and that no part of any payment made to a State unemployment fund, which is claimed as a credit on line 18 above, was or is to be deducted from the remuneration of employees.

Date ▶ Signature ▶ Title (Owner, etc.) ▶

T	
FF	
FD	
FP	
I	
T	

(If incorrect make any necessary change.) ▶

Name (as distinguished from trade name)

Trade name, if any

Address and ZIP code

Calendar Year 1975

Employer Identification No.

16—•—1

Form **940** (1975)

Other Taxes

A business is subject to other taxes. These include *personal property* taxes levied on equipment and inventory by cities, school districts, counties, and states; *real property* taxes levied by these same governments; *excise* taxes levied by these governments; and excise taxes levied by the federal government.

Property taxes are imposed on property according to value (*ad valorem*). The assessed value is usually a percentage of the appraised value, and the way that the appraised value and assessed value are developed varies widely. In essence, the taxing government decides how much money it needs and sets the base accordingly. From that point, it becomes a matter of human judgment and your relationship with the people in the various tax assessment offices. The assessed value times the tax rate is the tax liability.

Thus if you own your store with a fair market value of $10,000 and the assessment rate is 60 percent with a tax rate of 20 percent ($20 per $100), the assessed value is $6,000 and your tax liability is $1,200. Personal property taxes are computed in a similar fashion. They're levied on equipment and inventory. The value on the first day of the year is the value generally used. Hence, merchants usually try to reduce inventory before January 1 and defer substantial equipment purchase till after that date.

POINT 9-4: Personal and real property taxes are levied by cities, school districts, counties, and states. The taxes are apportioned according to value (ad valorem).

Real estate and personal property taxes on your business property are an expense of doing business and are entered as a business expense on Schedule C of your Form 1040 income tax return if your business is a proprietorship, or on your Form 1120 if you're incorporated.

Excise taxes are levied on specific commodities and products. Typical items subject to excise taxes are tobacco products, alcoholic beverages, automotive equipment, and gasoline. The state and local level methods of collection and reporting vary, and you should inquire into these yourself. If you manufacture or sell items subject to federal excise tax, you'll have to file a Form 720 and make federal tax deposits. If you sell firearms or liquor, you're subject to an occupational tax. See the *Tax Guide for Small Business, IRS Publication 334,* for full information on these taxes, required forms, reporting, and rates.

And of course, there's the federal income tax that everyone who earns anything much has to pay. This is the subject of the next sections.

POINT 9-5: Some product sales are subject to excise taxes. Check for local government excise taxes. Consult IRS Publication 334 for information on federal excise taxes.

REVIEW EXERCISES 9-A

1. Describe the procedure for establishing the required relationship with the government for handling income tax and FICA withholding.
2. What is the sales-tax rate in your state? What agency of your state government handles this, and how can you get your relationship established?

3. What is the common financial pitfall of beginning small businesses related to sales taxes collected and taxes withheld?
4. Describe the difference in functions of IRS Forms 940 and 941.
5. (a) If an employee earns $600 in January, what amount is withheld for FICA? (Assume a 5.85 percent rate.) (b) If his total earnings for the first quarter are $1,800 how much FICA will you withhold? (c) How much much must you pay out of the business income for FICA relative to 5(b)? (d) What is the total tax deposit you must make for the first quarter, assuming no income tax withheld?
6. Why is it a good idea to use a separate payroll checkbook?

FEDERAL INCOME TAX

The federal income tax laws are complex and few laypersons have more than a vague understanding of them. The complexity is compounded by frequent changes. Yet an understanding of these laws is essential to you as a businessperson because your knowledge of these laws has a direct bearing on your ability to generate business profits. This and the next section will provide a general introduction to the income tax laws important to businesspeople. To facilitate discussion, we will use limits, numbers, and rates in effect at the time of writing. Bear in mind that these limits, numbers, and rates are subject to change.

Filing and Forms

Anyone with more than poverty income must file a tax return. You may file a single, joint, or head of household return depending on your family and dependent status. Most married taxpayers benefit by filing jointly. The individual tax return is Form 1040, Figure 9-8. The Form 1040 contains additional schedules for data and computations concerning the various activities in which individuals engage and special features of the tax laws requiring special treatment. Here is a list of schedules for the Form 1040; you file only the ones needed as a result of your taxable activities.

Schedule A—Itemized deductions
Schedule B—Dividend and interest income
Schedule C—Profit or (loss) from business or profession
Schedule D—Capital gains and losses
Schedule E—Supplemental income schedule
Schedule R—Retirement Income Credit Computation

Schedule C is the one on which you'll report your business operations if you're organized as a proprietorship. If you're organized as a partnership, the partnership files a Form 1065, which is an information return, but you take your income from the partnership and report it on your Form 1040. If you're organized as a corporation, you file a Form 1120. If you're organized as a Subchapter S Corporation, you file an 1120-S. A Subchapter S Corporation report is informational, since income of a Subchapter S Corporation is taxable to the owners just as is the income of a partnership.

POINT 9-6: An individual uses Form 1040 for his or her tax return; Schedule C covers his/her proprietorship. A partnership uses a Form 1065 and a Subchapter S Corporation uses a Form 1120S. Both of these are information returns and the individuals report the income on their 1040s. A corporation files a Form 1120 and pays taxes directly.

Proprietors and partners must pay estimated tax quarterly, since they're not on payroll withholding. You'll have to file a Form 1040 ES, *Declaration of Estimated Tax* for the current year on or before April 15. Generally, you prepare this form and submit it with your 1040 for the previous year. You remit one-quarter of your estimated tax liability for the current year (based on anticipated income and exemptions) with your 1040 ES, and remit like amounts again before June 15, September 15, and January 15.

POINT 9-7: Individuals with their own proprietorships must file a 1040 ES *Declaration of Estimated Tax*, and make quarterly tax deposits before April 15, June 15, September 15, and January 15.

The Basic Tax Formula

Here is the basic tax formula for an individual return (Form 1040):

All income
– Exclusions
= Gross income
– Deductions for adjusted gross income (AGI)
= Adjusted gross income (AGI)
– Deductions (itemized or standard)
– Exemptions
= Taxable income
X Tax Rates
= Gross tax liability
– Tax credits
– Prepayments
= Net tax payable with return

Exclusions include stock dividend income up to $100 for a single taxpayer and special exclusions such as those based on age, armed forces service, and illness. If you're under 65, healthy, don't have a scholarship, aren't in the armed forces, and don't collect stock dividends, you don't have any exclusions.

The "all income" part of the formula enters the return in increments. If you're earning a wage or salary (or your spouse is, and you're filing jointly), it goes directly into the 1040. However, interest (from savings accounts, for example) and stock dividends are entered on Schedule B. Rents, royalties, pensions, and *income from a partnership or Subchapter S Corporation are entered on Schedule E.* If you operate your business as a *proprietorship, you report its income and deductions (expenses) on Schedule C.* The results from these schedules are entered on the 1040, and you arrive at *AGI* or *adjusted gross income.* (Get this term under your belt; we'll use AGI frequently in this chapter.) This is an admitted and intentional simplification. You can bog down in the details very quickly.

You may have deductions for arriving at gross income even if you're not operating a proprietorship and if you or your spouse is an employed wage- or salary-earner. If one of you is salaried or on wages (which you would be if your business is a corporation), you may have deductions beyond those in the schedules for arriving at AGI. Those allowed would be those associated with your work, for which you're not reimbursed.

Income earned in a trade or business from the sale of goods or services is taxed at ordinary income tax rates. However, income earned by selling an asset that is not considered as goods bought for resale, which is held for a required holding period (presently more than twelve months), is considered a *long-term capital gain.* A long-term capital gain is subject to a special deduction. Capital gains and capital gains deductions are entered on Schedule D and the result is channeled onto the 1040.

POINT 9-8: Ordinary income includes wage earnings and earnings from trade or business. Expenses of starting a business are deductible business expenses for arriving at AGI, and that includes this book! Capital gains include profits realized on the sale of capital assets such as securities, real estate, and equipment not used for resale in a trade or business. If the asset is held more than twelve months, the gain is a long-term capital gain subject to a capital gains deduction.

Once you have established AGI, the next step is to make *deductions from AGI.* Note that the deductions to this point were deductions *for* AGI. The deductions *from* AGI may be taken as the so-called *standard deduction* or as itemized on Schedule A. The standard deduction is 16 percent of AGI, but no more than $2,300 for a single taxpayer or $2,600 for married taxpayers filing jointly or $1,300 filing singly. Hence, *to determine whether to itemize deductions, you must go through the itemized computations anyway.* The itemized deductions *from* AGI include:

1. *Medical*—including *part* of medical care insurance premiums, drugs, medicine, doctor, dental, nurses, hospital fees, and so forth.

2. *Taxes*—including real estate taxes on your home; state and local income; gas and sales taxes; and personal property taxes.
3. *Interest expense*—including interest paid on the loan on your home and

FIGURE 9-8 IRS form 1040

(A) Front

Form **1040** Department of the Treasury—Internal Revenue Service **U.S. Individual Income Tax Return** **1976** This space for IRS use only

For the year January 1–December 31, 1976, or other taxable year beginning 1976 ending , 19 .

Please print or type

Name (If joint return, give first names and initials of both) | Last name | Your social security number

Present home address (Number and street, including apartment number, or rural route) | For Privacy Act Notification, see page 5 of Instructions. | Spouse's social security no.

City, town or post office, State and ZIP code | Occupation Yours ▶ Spouse's ▶

Filing Status

1 ☐ Single (Check only ONE box)
2 ☐ Married filing joint return (even if only one had income)
3 ☐ Married filing separately. If spouse is also filing give spouse's social security number in designated space above and enter full name here ▶
4 ☐ Unmarried Head of Household. See page 7 of instructions to see if you qualify ▶
5 ☐ Qualifying widow(er) with dependent child (Year spouse died ▶ 19). See page 7 of Instructions.

Exemptions

6a Regular ☐ Yourself ☐ Spouse Enter number of boxes checked ▶
b First names of your dependent children who lived with you Enter number ▶
c Number of other dependents (from line 7) . ▶
d Total (add lines 6a, b, and c) . . . . ▶
e Age 65 or older. ☐ Yourself ☐ Spouse Enter number of boxes checked ▶
Blind . . . . ☐ Yourself ☐ Spouse
f TOTAL (add lines 6d and e) . . . . ▶

7 Other dependents: (a) Name	(b) Relationship	(c) Months lived in your home. If born or died during year, write B or D.	(d) Did dependent have income of $750 or more?	(e) Amount furnished for dependent's support: By YOU. If 100% write ALL.	By OTHERS including dependent.
				$	$

8 Presidential Election Campaign Fund . . ▶ Do you wish to designate $1 of your taxes for this fund? . . Yes No. If joint return, does your spouse wish to designate $1? . . Yes No. Note: If you check the "Yes" box(es) it will not increase your tax or reduce your refund.

Please attach Copy B of Forms W–2 here

Income

9 Wages, salaries, tips, and other employee compensation (Attach Forms W–2. If unavailable, see page 6 of Instructions.) 9
10a Dividends (See pages 9 and 16 of Instructions) ...., 10b less exclusion ...., Balance ▶ 10c
(If gross dividends and other distributions are over $400, list in Part I of Schedule B.)
11 Interest income. {If $400 or less, enter total without listing in Schedule B / If over $400, enter total and list in Part II of Schedule B} 11
12 Income other than wages, dividends, and interest (from line 37) 12
13 Total (add lines 9, 10c, 11 and 12) 13
14 Adjustments to income (such as moving expense, etc. from line 42) 14
15a Subtract line 14 from line 13 . . . . 15a
b Disability income exclusion (sick pay) (attach Form 2440) 15b
c Adjusted gross income. Subtract line 15b from line 15a, then complete Part III on back. (If less than $8,000, see page 2 of Instructions on "Earned Income Credit.") 15c

Tax, Payments and Credits

16 Tax, check if from: ☐ Tax Table ☐ Schedule G ☐ Tax Rate Schedule X, Y or Z ☐ Form 2555 OR ☐ Schedule D ☐ Form 4726 16
17a Multiply $35.00 by the number of exemptions on line 6d 17a
b Enter 2% of line 47 but not more than $180 ($90 if box 3 is checked) 17b
Enter larger of a or b 17c (If box on line 3 is checked see page 10 of Instructions)
18 Balance. Subtract line 17c from line 16 and enter difference (but not less than zero) . . 18
19 Credits (from line 54) 19
20 Balance. Subtract line 19 from line 18 and enter difference (but not less than zero) . . 20
21 Other taxes (from line 62) 21
22 Total (add lines 20 and 21) 22
23a Total Federal income tax withheld. (attach Forms W–2, or W–2P to front) . . 23a
b 1976 estimated tax payments (include amount allowed as credit from 1975 return) . . 23b
c Earned income credit. (from page 2 of Instructions) 23c
d Amount paid with Form 4868 . . . . 23d
e Other payments (from line 66) 23e
24 TOTAL (add lines 23a through e) . . . . ▶ 24

Pay amount on line 25 in full with this return. Write social security number on check or money order and make payable to Internal Revenue Service.

Please attach Check or Money Order here

Due or Refund

25 If line 22 is larger than line 24, enter BALANCE DUE IRS . . . . ▶ 25
(Check here ▶ ☐, if Form 2210 or Form 2210F is attached. See page 10 of instructions.)
26 If line 24 is larger than line 22, enter amount OVERPAID . . . . ▶ 26
27 Amount of line 26 to be REFUNDED TO YOU . . . . ▶ 27
28 Amount of line 26 to be credited on 1977 estimated tax ▶ 28

Sign here

Under penalties of perjury, I declare that I have examined this return, including accompanying schedules and statements, and to the best of my knowledge and belief it is true, correct, and complete. Declaration of preparer (other than taxpayer) is based on all information of which preparer has any knowledge.

▶ Your signature Date ▶ Preparer's signature (and employer's name, if any) Date

▶ Spouse's signature (if filing jointly, BOTH must sign even if only one had income) ▶ Identifying number (see instructions) Address (and ZIP code)

other loans for personal purposes such as personal auto, furniture, and so forth.

4. *Contributions*—to charity, church, and other eligible causes.
5. *Casualty or theft losses.*

(B) Back

Form 1040 (1976) Page 2

Part I Income other than Wages, Dividends and Interest

29	Business income or (loss) (attach Schedule C)	29	
30a	Net gain or (loss) from sale or exchange of capital assets (attach Schedule D)	30a	
b	50% of capital gain distributions (not reported on Schedule D—see page 10 of Instructions).	30b	
31	Net gain or (loss) from Supplemental Schedule of Gains and Losses (attach Form 4797)	31	
32a	Pensions, annuities, rents, royalties, partnerships, estates or trusts, etc. (attach Schedule E)	32a	
b	Fully taxable pensions and annuities (not reported on Schedule E—see page 10 of Instructions)	32b	
33	Farm income or (loss) (attach Schedule F)	33	
34	State income tax refunds (does not apply if refund is for year in which you took the standard deduction—others see page 10 of Instructions)	34	
35	Alimony received	35	
36	Other (state nature and source—see page 11 of Instructions) ▶	36	
37	Total (add lines 29 through 36). Enter here and on line 12 ▶	37	

Part II Adjustments to Income

38	Moving expense (attach Form 3903)	38	
39	Employee business expense (attach Form 2106)	39	
40a	Payments to an individual retirement arrangement from attached Form 5329, Part III	40a	
b	Payments to a Keogh (H.R. 10) retirement plan	40b	
41	Forfeited interest penalty for premature withdrawal (see page 12 of Instructions)	41	
42	Total (add lines 38 through 41). Enter here and on line 14 ▶	42	

Part III Tax Computation

43	Adjusted gross income (from line 15c). If you have unearned income and can be claimed as a dependent on your parent's return, check here ▶ ☐ and see page 9 of Instructions	43	
44a	If you itemize deductions, check here ▶ ☐, and enter total from Schedule A, line 40, and attach Schedule A		
b	Standard deduction—If you do not itemize deductions, check here ▶ ☐, and: If you checked the box on line: 2 or 5, enter the greater of $2,100 OR 16% of line 43—but not more than $2,800 1 or 4, enter the greater of $1,700 OR 16% of line 43—but not more than $2,400 3, enter the greater of $1,050 OR 16% of line 43—but not more than $1,400	44	
45	Subtract line 44 from line 43 and enter difference (but not less than zero)	45	
46	Multiply total number of exemptions claimed on line 6f by $750	46	
47	Taxable income. Subtract line 46 from line 45 and enter difference (but not less than zero)	47	

- If line 47 is $20,000 or less and you did not average your income on Schedule G, or figure your tax on Form 2555, Exemption of Income Earned Abroad, find your tax in Tax Table. Enter tax on line 16 and check appropriate box.
- If line 47 is more than $20,000, figure your tax on the amount on line 47 by using Tax Rate Schedule X, Y, Z, or if applicable, the alternative tax from Schedule D, income averaging from Schedule G, tax from Form 2555 or maximum tax from Form 4726. Enter tax on line 16 and check appropriate box.

Part IV Credits

48	Credit for the elderly (attach Schedules R & RP)	48	
49	Credit for child care expenses (attach Form 2441)	49	
50	Investment credit (attach Form 3468)	50	
51	Foreign tax credit (attach Form 1116)	51	
52	Contributions to candidates for public office credit (see page 12 of Instructions)	52	
53	Work Incentive (WIN) Credit (attach Form 4874)	53	
54	Total (add lines 48 through 53). Enter here and on line 19 ▶	54	

Part V Other Taxes

55	Tax from recomputing prior-year investment credit (attach Form 4255)	55	
56	Minimum tax. Check here ▶ ☐, and attach Form 4625	56	
57	Tax on premature distributions from attached Form 5329, Part V	57	
58	Self-employment tax (attach Schedule SE)	58	
59	Social security tax on tip income not reported to employer (attach Form 4137)	59	
60	Uncollected employee social security tax on tips (from Forms W-2)	60	
61	Excess contribution tax from attached Form 5329, Part IV	61	
62	Total (add lines 55 through 61). Enter here and on line 21 ▶	62	

Part VI Other Payments

63	Excess FICA, RRTA, or FICA/RRTA tax withheld (two or more employers—see page 13 of Instructions)	63	
64	Credit for Federal tax on special fuels, nonhighway gasoline and lubricating oil (attach Form 4136)	64	
65	Credit from a Regulated Investment Company (attach Form 2439)	65	
66	Total (add lines 63 through 65). Enter here and on line 23e ▶	66	

☆ U.S. GOVERNMENT PRINTING OFFICE : 1976—O-218-393 — 58-040-1110

6. *Miscellaneous items*—including alimony paid, union dues, eligible child and dependent care, tax-return preparation cost, investment expense, and so forth.

> POINT 9-9: To determine whether to file an itemized deduction (Schedule A) on your 1040, complete the Schedule A, and if it exceeds the standard deduction allowed, use. it. Otherwise take the standard deduction and discard the Schedule A.

These deductions, taken from AGI, get you within one step of taxable income. Your next step is to subtract your exemptions. Currently you are allowed a $750 exemption for yourself, your spouse, and each of your dependent children. If you're over 65, you get another exemption, and if you're blind, you're entitled to an additional exemption. The same applies to your spouse. Thus a couple under 65 with no children or other dependents has $1,500 total exemptions; a couple with two children has $3,000 total exemptions; a couple with no dependents, both over 65, one blind, has $3,750 total examptions. Subtraction of your exemptions yields taxable income.

> POINT 9-10: All income minus exclusions, minus deductions (*for* and *from* AGI), minus exemptions equals *taxable income.*

Rates and Schedules

To arrive at your *gross tax liability,* you use the appropriate tax-rate schedule. If you're a single taxpayer, you use Schedule X; if married, use Schedule Y; if single but qualify as head of household (which we will not define here), use Schedule Z. A tax-rate schedule is shown in Figure 9-9. This is a 1975 schedule, chosen because it is more concise than later schedules. It will serve the illustrative purpose of this text; but bear in mind that the schedules may change from year to year. You'll want to use the most current schedule for actual tax computations. Notice that the rates are graduated; that is, you pay only 14 percent on the first $1,000 of taxable income, but after the first $10,000 of taxable income you pay 27 percent on the next $2,000 if single (Schedule X) or 25 percent if married and filing a joint return (Schedule Y). The increasing rate with increasing income is based on the principle of ability to pay.

At this point, you should recognize that the tax laws are complex, but you should also have a better understanding of how to arrive at the bottom line of the tax return. Now you know your gross tax liability. Next, you simply deduct tax credits and prepayments to arrive at net tax payable with return. The *prepayments* you made with the form 1040 ES based on your estimated tax liability. The *tax credits* are special credits allowable under special tax-law provisions. This is very important to you as a businessperson, because some of your equipment is likely to be subject to an *investment credit* of as much as 10 percent of the equipment cost. Since this credit is deducted from *tax liability,* it

FIGURE 9-9 1975 income tax rate schedules

1975 Tax Rate Schedules

If you do not use one of the Tax Tables, figure your tax on the amount on Form 1040, line 47, by using the appropriate Tax Rate Schedule on this page. Enter tax on Form 1040, line 16a.

SCHEDULE X—Single Taxpayers Not Qualifying for Rates in Schedule Y or Z

Use this schedule if you checked the box on Form 1040, line 1—

If the amount on Form 1040, line 47, is: / Enter on Form 1040, line 16a:

Not over $500 . 14% of the amount on line 47.

Over—	But not over—		of the amount over—
$500	$1,000	$70+15%	$500
$1,000	$1,500	$145+16%	$1,000
$1,500	$2,000	$225+17%	$1,500
$2,000	$4,000	$310+19%	$2,000
$4,000	$6,000	$690+21%	$4,000
$6,000	$8,000	$1,110+24%	$6,000
$8,000	$10,000	$1,590+25%	$8,000
$10,000	$12,000	$2,090+27%	$10,000
$12,000	$14,000	$2,630+29%	$12,000
$14,000	$16,000	$3,210+31%	$14,000
$16,000	$18,000	$3,830+34%	$16,000
$18,000	$20,000	$4,510+36%	$18,000
$20,000	$22,000	$5,230+38%	$20,000
$22,000	$26,000	$5,990+40%	$22,000
$26,000	$32,000	$7,590+45%	$26,000
$32,000	$38,000	$10,290+50%	$32,000
$38,000	$44,000	$13,290+55%	$38,000
$44,000	$50,000	$16,590+60%	$44,000
$50,000	$60,000	$20,190+62%	$50,000
$60,000	$70,000	$26,390+64%	$60,000
$70,000	$80,000	$32,790+66%	$70,000
$80,000	$90,000	$39,390+68%	$80,000
$90,000	$100,000	$46,190+69%	$90,000
$100,000	....	$53,090+70%	$100,000

SCHEDULE Y—Married Taxpayers and Qualifying Widows and Widowers

If you are a married person living apart from your spouse, see page 5 of the instructions to see if you can be considered to be "unmarried" for purposes of using Schedule X or Z.

Married Taxpayers Filing Joint Returns and Qualifying Widows and Widowers (See page 5)

Use this schedule if you checked the box on Form 1040, line 2 or 5—

If the amount on Form 1040, line 47, is: / Enter on Form 1040, line 16a:

Not over $1,000 . 14% of the amount on line 47.

Over—	But not over—		of the amount over—
$1,000	$2,000	$140+15%	$1,000
$2,000	$3,000	$290+16%	$2,000
$3,000	$4,000	$450+17%	$3,000
$4,000	$8,000	$620+19%	$4,000
$8,000	$12,000	$1,380+22%	$8,000
$12,000	$16,000	$2,260+25%	$12,000
$16,000	$20,000	$3,260+28%	$16,000
$20,000	$24,000	$4,380+32%	$20,000
$24,000	$28,000	$5,660+36%	$24,000
$28,000	$32,000	$7,100+39%	$28,000
$32,000	$36,000	$8,660+42%	$32,000
$36,000	$40,000	$10,340+45%	$36,000
$40,000	$44,000	$12,140+48%	$40,000
$44,000	$52,000	$14,060+50%	$44,000
$52,000	$64,000	$18,060+53%	$52,000
$64,000	$76,000	$24,420+55%	$64,000
$76,000	$88,000	$31,020+58%	$76,000
$88,000	$100,000	$37,980+60%	$88,000
$100,000	$120,000	$45,180+62%	$100,000
$120,000	$140,000	$57,580+64%	$120,000
$140,000	$160,000	$70,380+66%	$140,000
$160,000	$180,000	$83,580+68%	$160,000
$180,000	$200,000	$97,180+69%	$180,000
$200,000	....	$110,980+70%	$200,000

Married Taxpayers Filing Separate Returns

Use this schedule if you checked the box on Form 1040, line 3—

If the amount on Form 1040, line 47, is: / Enter on Form 1040, line 16a:

Not over $500 . 14% of the amount on line 47.

Over—	But not over—		of the amount over—
$500	$1,000	$70+15%	$500
$1,000	$1,500	$145+16%	$1,000
$1,500	$2,000	$225+17%	$1,500
$2,000	$4,000	$310+19%	$2,000
$4,000	$6,000	$690+22%	$4,000
$6,000	$8,000	$1,130+25%	$6,000
$8,000	$10,000	$1,630+28%	$8,000
$10,000	$12,000	$2,190+32%	$10,000
$12,000	$14,000	$2,830+36%	$12,000
$14,000	$16,000	$3,550+39%	$14,000
$16,000	$18,000	$4,330+42%	$16,000
$18,000	$20,000	$5,170+45%	$18,000
$20,000	$22,000	$6,070+48%	$20,000
$22,000	$26,000	$7,030+50%	$22,000
$26,000	$32,000	$9,030+53%	$26,000
$32,000	$38,000	$12,210+55%	$32,000
$38,000	$44,000	$15,510+58%	$38,000
$44,000	$50,000	$18,990+60%	$44,000
$50,000	$60,000	$22,590+62%	$50,000
$60,000	$70,000	$28,790+64%	$60,000
$70,000	$80,000	$35,190+66%	$70,000
$80,000	$90,000	$41,790+68%	$80,000
$90,000	$100,000	$48,590+69%	$90,000
$100,000	....	$55,490+70%	$100,000

SCHEDULE Z—Unmarried (or legally separated) Taxpayers Who Qualify as Heads of Household (See page 5)

Use this schedule if you checked the box on Form 1040, line 4—

If the amount on Form 1040, line 47, is: / Enter on Form 1040, line 16a:

Not over $1,000 . 14% of the amount on line 47.

Over—	But not over—		of the amount over—
$1,000	$2,000	$140+16%	$1,000
$2,000	$4,000	$300+18%	$2,000
$4,000	$6,000	$660+19%	$4,000
$6,000	$8,000	$1,040+22%	$6,000
$8,000	$10,000	$1,480+23%	$8,000
$10,000	$12,000	$1,940+25%	$10,000
$12,000	$14,000	$2,440+27%	$12,000
$14,000	$16,000	$2,980+28%	$14,000
$16,000	$18,000	$3,540+31%	$16,000
$18,000	$20,000	$4,160+32%	$18,000
$20,000	$22,000	$4,800+35%	$20,000
$22,000	$24,000	$5,500+36%	$22,000
$24,000	$26,000	$6,220+38%	$24,000
$26,000	$28,000	$6,980+41%	$26,000
$28,000	$32,000	$7,800+42%	$28,000
$32,000	$36,000	$9,480+45%	$32,000
$36,000	$38,000	$11,280+48%	$36,000
$38,000	$40,000	$12,240+51%	$38,000
$40,000	$44,000	$13,260+52%	$40,000
$44,000	$50,000	$15,340+55%	$44,000
$50,000	$52,000	$18,640+56%	$50,000
$52,000	$64,000	$19,760+58%	$52,000
$64,000	$70,000	$26,720+59%	$64,000
$70,000	$76,000	$30,260+61%	$70,000
$76,000	$80,000	$33,920+62%	$76,000
$80,000	$88,000	$36,400+63%	$80,000
$88,000	$100,000	$41,440+64%	$88,000
$100,000	$120,000	$49,120+66%	$100,000
$120,000	$140,000	$62,320+67%	$120,000
$140,000	$160,000	$75,720+68%	$140,000
$160,000	$180,000	$89,320+69%	$160,000
$180,000	....	$103,120+70%	$180,000

has an impact of several times that of a mere expense on your tax bill. (You get depreciation expense as well as the investment credit on equipment that qualifies.) This subject will be pursued in the section on income tax planning.

POINT 9-11: Tax liability is derived from the appropriate tax-rate table based on taxable income. Tax liability minus tax credits (such as investment credit) minus prepayments yields net tax payable.

Where to Get Information and Help

There's plenty of free information available from the IRS on tax-return preparation. Call or write your local IRS office for the following publications:

1. *Your Federal Income Tax Return–For Individuals,* IRS Publication 17.
2. *Tax Guide For Small Business,* IRS Publication 334. In addition, IRS will furnish detailed information on a large number of specific subjects and regulations. These are cited by number in the publications listed above and can be obtained as the need arises.

You may be asking yourself, "Shall I prepare my own tax return?" If you have done it in the past, you should be able to do it even with a business of your own thrown in. However, you may miss some of the deductions an experienced bookkeeping and tax service or an accountant would catch. Employ one of these for the first year or two at least.

You may wonder why you're bothering to learn all this if it's prudent to have it done the first year or two. The simple answer is that you're learning this so you can do a better job of tax planning in your business, investment, and personal financial affairs. Your knowledge of tax matters and your ability to preserve income will be improved by this study and by reviews of returns prepared for you by an accountant the first year or two. I strongly recommend professional help, at least at the outset. It takes quite a while to achieve an in-depth understanding of the income tax laws and their impact on your business.

POINT 9-12: Use professional help to prepare your first business tax return, and go over it with the preparer to better understand the implications and procedure. This will help you to do a better job of tax planning.

REVIEW EXERCISES 9-B

1. What do each of the Schedules A, B, C, D, E, and R of the Form 1040 cover?
2. In chart form, show how individual tax liability is developed on the Form 1040 and its schedules.

3. What is the amount of the individual exemption?
4. What is the difference between an exclusion, a deduction, and an exemption?
5. What is the difference between deductions *for* AGI and deductions *from* AGI?
6. What is the difference between ordinary income and a long-term capital gain?
7. You paid $50 interest for a loan on equipment used in your business (a proprietorship) in 19XX. Where would this be deducted in your individual tax return?
8. Define gross income, AGI, tax liability, tax credit, and tax prepayment.

FEDERAL INCOME TAX PLANNING

The simple truth about what you make in your own business is that it's the money you take in, minus your cost of goods, minus your expenses, *minus your income tax liability.* Clearly, you can increase profits by getting better gross margins on goods sold and by cutting expenses. But you don't get to keep all of that profit. Uncle Sam takes part of it in income taxes. If you understand the tax laws and take all the deductions and tax incentives available to you, you reduce your tax liability and *increase the amount of money you really keep after taxes.*

You can increase what you keep (and really make) through income tax planning and management. The first section in this chapter should have unraveled some of the mysteries of the general mechanics of income tax reporting. But the real "goodies" have been reserved for this section. You'll learn more about depreciation, investment credit, capital gains, the graduated tax, and other facets of income tax law. You won't be a tax expert when you're through, but you'll be better able to plan and manage your business for greater tax savings.

Depreciation

A long-term asset such as plant and equipment cannot be expensed at full cost immediately. Instead, you depreciate the asset over a number of years, the estimated life of the asset. You've met *straight-line depreciation* in earlier chapters. By the straight-line method, you assume that each year's wear-out rate of the asset is the same. Thus if the asset costs $1,000, has an estimated life of six years, and zero salvage value, the annual depreciation is one-sixth of $1,000, or $166.67 per year. *If the asset has a salvage value of $100* at the end of six years, the value to be depreciated is only $900. The annual depreciation is one-sixth of $900, or $150.

However, here the tax laws differ from accounting practices. *Code section 167(f) of the IRS permits you to neglect the salvage value up to 10 percent if the asset has a life of three or more years.* So you would depreciate the asset at $166.67 per year for six years, although you can recover $100 at the end of six years.

POINT 9-13: Salvage value of 10 percent or less of asset cost on personal property with a life of three or more years may be neglected in computing depreciation for income tax purposes.

But wait, there is still another bonanza in store. Uncle Sam has a bonus depreciation for you. You may take 20 percent additional first-year bonus depreciation based on cost (regardless of salvage value) on tangible personal property to the extent of $10,000 of cost ($20,000 on a joint return) for $2,000 (or $4,000 joint) depreciation *if the asset has a useful life of six or more years.* Now, assume again a $1,000 asset with a life of six years. The first year's bonus depreciation is 20 percent of $1,000, or $200. This leaves $800 to be depreciated over six years, or $133.37 per year. Thus you depreciate $333.37 the first year and $133.37 for each of the next five years.

Is this necessarily the smart way to compute your tax? If your profits are low in the year you purchase the asset, it's smart *not* to take the bonus depreciation. The reason is that income tax rates are graduated. Refer to Figure 9-8, Schedule X. If taxable income is between $4,000 and $6,000, the incremental rate above $4,000 is 21 percent. But if taxable income is between $12,000 and $14,000, the incremental rate above $12,000 is 29 percent. Clearly, deductions are more valuable in the years in which your income is greatest. Assuming that your income will be less in your first year than in succeeding years, it's wise to take straight-line depreciation only and ignore bonus depreciation in your first year of business.

POINT 9-14: You can take a bonus depreciation of 20 percent the first year (on business assets with a useful life of six or more years) and depreciate the balance by any IRS-approved method over the life of the asset.

POINT 9-15: It isn't necessarily smart to take bonus depreciation or to use the accelerated depreciation methods to be described. Use maximum allowed depreciation on assets bought in good years, but use straight-line on assets bought in low-income years.

There are two methods of computing accelerated depreciation that are allowed by the IRS. Accelerated depreciation is based on the concept that an asset loses more value in the early years than it does in later years. Hence, accelerated methods depreciate more per year than straight-line in the earlier years and less in later years.

The most commonly used accelerated method is *accelerated declining-balance depreciation.*

Thus, if you apply double declining-balance (200 percent declining balance) depreciation to a $1,000 asset with six years life, you would take one-sixth of $1,000 times 2, or $333.33 depreciation the first year.

The second year's beginning balance would be \$1,000 minus \$333.33 or \$666.67. The second year's depreciation is one-sixth times \$666.67 times 2, or \$222.22. The balance at the end of the second year is \$666.67 minus \$222.22, or \$444.45.

The third year's depreciation is one-sixth times \$444.45 times 2, or \$148.15. The balance at the end of the third year is \$296.30. Further computation gives fourth-year depreciation of \$98.77; fifth-year \$65.84; sixth-year \$43.90 with a balance of \$87.79.

Thus, the asset was depreciated \$333.33 the first year and only \$43.90 the last year. Notice also that the declining-balance method leaves a residual value. This can be written off as a loss if the asset is disposed of for zero salvage at the end of the sixth year. Or you can change from the double-declining-balance method to straight-line after the first few years. Thus, if you changed to straight-line at the end of the third year, you would depreciate the balance of \$296.30 times one-third, or \$98.77 per year for each of the three remaining years to wind up with zero salvage value at the end of the sixth year. *Note:* You can change from accelerated to straight-line, but not from straight-line to accelerated method, once you've set up your depreciation plan for a given asset.

The other accelerated depreciation method is the *sum-of-the-years digits* method. First you take the sum-of-the-years digits. That's 1 plus 2 plus 3 plus 4 plus 5 plus 6 for our six-year example.

A short-cut method of getting the sum-of-the-years digits is to square the number of years, add the number of years to that, and divide the resulting number by 2. In formula style, that's

$$\frac{n^2 + n}{2} = \frac{6^2 + 6}{2} = \frac{42}{2} = 21$$

First year's depreciation for our \$1,000 six-year life asset is 6/21 times \$1,000, or \$285.71 with a balance of \$714.89. Second-year depreciation is 5/21 times \$1,000, or \$238.10 with a balance of \$476.19. For years, 3, 4, 5, and 6 you use 4/21, 3/21, 2/21, and 1/21, respectively, and obtain \$190.48, \$142.86, \$95.23, and \$47.62, respectively.

Note that you operate on the total value of the asset with the years' life left divided by the sum-of-the-years digits; you don't use the balance in doing the sum-of-the-years computation.

You can use accelerated depreciation for any tangible property asset with a life of three or more years. Tangible personal property (such as machinery, tools, and fixtures but *not real property*) purchased may be depreciated by either of the three methods up to 200 percent accelerated declining balance, but used personal property may only be depreciated by straight-line or by up to 150 percent accelerated declining balance. A different set of rules applies to real estate, which we won't cover here.

If you acquire a new personal property type asset in a year in which you feel you will have unusually good profits, take the bonus depreciation (if the asset has a life of six or more years) and use an accelerated-depreciation method.

Thus, for a $1,000, six-year life asset, you would depreciate $200 for the bonus and one-sixth times $800 (the balance) times 2, or $266.67 double declining depreciation the first year. Total first year's depreciation would be $466.67! That would leave a balance of $533.33 for depreciation in subsequent years.

POINT 9-16: New tangible personal property may be depreciated by any of the three methods if it has a life of three years or more. If anticipated earnings are low for the year of acquisition, depreciate the asset by the straight-line method; if anticipated earnings for the year of acquisition are high, take bonus depreciation (if applicable) and use accelerated depreciation.

Investment Credit

From time to time an investment incentive known as *investment credit* is activated. In the past the investment credit was at one time 7 percent and later 10 percent on an asset with a life of seven or more years. You'll have to check current tax laws to know if the investment credit is in effect for the year for which you're filing your return. The investment credit, when it has been in force in the past, applied to depreciable tangible personal property used in a trade or business. For an asset with seven or more years of life you were able to take the full 10 percent credit; five to seven years, two-thirds of 10 percent or 6.67 percent; and three to five years, one-third or 3.33 percent.

The investment credit applies directly to your tax bill, and consequently, the 10 percent investment credit saves you much more tax outlay than a 10 percent depreciation deduction.

Let's look at a $1,000 asset with a seven-year life for a taxpayer with $12,000 in taxable income. His investment credit is 10 percent of $1,000, or $100. His tax bill before the credit (Figure 9-8, Schedule X) is $2,630. With the credit, his tax bill is $2,530. In addition to the credit, he can take depreciation. If he takes bonus depreciation and double-declining-balance depreciation ($200 + 1/7 × $1,000 × 2, or a total of $485.71), his taxable income is $12,000 minus $485.71, or $11,514.29. Computing his tax from Figure 9-8, Schedule X, he owes taxes of $2,090 for the first $10,000 and 27 percent of $1,514.29, which is $311.66, or a total of $2,401.66 before the investment credit. When the $100 investment credit is applied, his tax liability is only $2,301.66. Thus, the taxpayer lowered his bill from $2,630 to $2,301.66 by purchasing a $1,000 asset! In effect, he has spent only $1,000 minus his tax saving of $328.34, or $671.66 for the asset in the year of acquisition, and he'll recover some of that in depreciation in subsequent years.

This demonstrates again the prudence of acquiring needed assets in prosperous years, and highlights the added gains in tax liability saving when assets can be acquired in years when investment credit is active.

POINT 9-17: Investment credit is applied directly to tax liability. Plan to acquire assets in years when the investment credit is active to minimize tax liability.

Other Ways to Minimize Tax Liability

You can minimize tax liability by taking the maximum expense deductions allowable under the tax laws. This means that if you keep accurate records that catch every item of expense that you paid out, you'll be taking an excellent first step. Anything that you spend for an expense item other than purchases for inventory or depreciable equipment is directly and immediately deductible. We discussed depreciation in the preceding section. Purchase expense finds its way into tax considerations by way of *cost of goods sold,* which is determined from inventories and purchases.

There are a number of ways in which you can value inventory. Each of the methods derives different values of cost of goods sold and inventory. If the *paper value* of cost of goods sold is high, *paper profits* are lowered, and *you pay less tax.*

The two most commonly used methods of inventory valuation are FIFO (first in, first out) and LIFO (last in, first out).

In inflationary periods, LIFO deflates the value of the inventory and inflates the cost of goods sold, resulting in a decreased paper profit and lower tax liability. The American economy has been inflationary for several decades. Under the LIFO method, you sell the highest-cost units of a given kind first. Thus, if a given product cost you $10 a unit five years ago and costs $15 a unit today, you assume you're selling the $15 units first under the LIFO method. Most companies, large and small, use the LIFO method for the tax benefits that accrue through its use.

POINT 9-18: Use the LIFO method of inventory valuation to minimize tax liability in an inflationary economy.

The methods of minimizing tax liability for the long run in a small business may be summarized as follows:

1. Record and take all possible expense deductions.
2. Make highest-expense deductions fall in anticipated good years and reduce them in anticipated bad years. You can, for example, stock up on office supplies, shop supplies, pay taxes, pay rent in advance, pay expense bills of all kinds (which could be deferred till the next year) just before year-end if your profit for the current year is high.
3. Purchase new capital equipment in years when the investment tax credit is operative.
4. Purchase new capital equipment in high-income years, and take bonus depreciation (if applicable) and use an accelerated depreciation method.
5. Use straight-line depreciation for capital equipment that has to be bought in bad years in the hope that the higher depreciation in later years (over accelerated methods) will fall in good business years.
6. Use the LIFO inventory valuation method to show lowest profits (and save taxes) for any year in an inflating economy. (*Note:* If you pick LIFO,

you're stuck with it. Inflation is more likely than deflation, so it's a safe bet.)

7. Review memberships in associations and clubs, subscriptions to magazines, expenses on automotive equipment, trips, education, interest expense, and other expenditures that you're making from your personal account to see if they don't rightfully and legally constitute a business expense. Consult an accountant on this.
8. There is an additional area of tax liability savings. This area encompases so-called *tax preferences,* which include special treatment to certain endeavors and *capital gains.* Consult an accountant on these.

REVIEW EXERCISES 9-C

1. You have purchased a $5,000 asset classified as new tangible personal property for your business. It has a ten-year life and $250 salvage value. Assuming a 10 percent investment credit operative and no bonus depreciation, compute (a) the investment credit, (b) the straight-line depreciation schedule, (c) the double-declining-balance depreciation schedule, (d) the sum-of-the-years-digits depreciation schedule.
2. Do Exercise 1 above assuming you take the 20 percent bonus depreciation the first year.
3. Do Exercise 1 assuming the salvage value is $1,000 at the end of ten years.
4. You have acquired a used machine for $1,000. It has a life of three years. Compute the first year's depreciation by the method that gives you the largest legal deduction in the first year.
5. You have acquired a machine for $1,000 new. It has a life of three years. Compute the investment credit and the maximum legal first year's depreciation.
6. Discuss the differences between the LIFO and FIFO methods of inventory valuation. Which is preferable and why?
7. Summarize the methods and techniques to reduce income tax liability.

CASE: INCOME TAX PROBLEMS

William Gorman opened a candy store and enjoyed a brisk business. He used a simple cash drawer and didn't write sales tickets. He paid for a lot of small shipments and small-expense items out of the cash drawer and took $15 to $20 out of the drawer every day for lunch, cigarettes, and other personal use. He made no entries of these withdrawals and merely figured sales as the daily change in the level of the cash drawer. His income tax showed sales of $40,000, cost of goods $30,000, other expenses $4,000 and a draw of $6,000. He had no other income. IRS audited him, and in the absence of adequate records reconstructed his operations as follows: Sales $50,000, cost of goods $30,000, expenses $4,000, and draw $21,000. There was discussion of fraud which IRS dropped when William agreed to ante up the deficiency, pay the normal penalty, and keep records of draws and all expenses in the future.

REVIEW EXERCISES 9-D

1. The practice of taking money out of the cash drawer without a record of the draw and reporting only cash left as sales is known as "skimming." It's fraudulent and can land you in prison. William was skimming, possibly unintentionally. Since he did not record small cash-expense disbursements, IRS also attributed these withdrawals to draws.
   (a) How do you suspect IRS decided his sales must have been $50,000? List all indications of sales in excess of $40,000 (if you hadn't known he was skimming).
   (b) What records should William Gorman have kept?
   (c) If he had kept records, at what figure would you estimate Gorman's draws for the year to have shown?
2. What additional liability does William Gorman have to a taxing entity? Explain.
3. Aside from his neglect of records, do you think Gorman is a good businessman? Justify your answer.

SUMMARY

Records are essential in tax and regulatory matters and may affect your ability to prove, under the law, your position in dealings with customers and suppliers. Most states have sales taxes, and you as a businessperson are in effect, a deputized sales tax collector for your state. You're also an FICA (social security) and tax withholding collector for Uncle Sam. The trap most starting businesspeople fall into is that they forget how much they've collected for the state and the IRS, and what seemed a fat bank account is suddenly inadequate to pay taxes due.

IRS Circular E, *Employer's Tax Guide* (free), tells you how to handle FICA and withholding in detail and includes useful time-saving tables. A special payroll checkbook available through your bank will facilitate payroll, FICA, and tax withholding work.

You must pay unemployment tax to state and federal governments, and you must file your own federal income tax return. The individual tax return is IRS Form 1040, and Schedule C covers your proprietorship business. A partnership files a 1065 information return, and a corporation files a Form 1120. If you're in a proprietorship or partnership, you must submit quarterly payments of one-quarter of estimated annual income on a Form 1040 ES.

Ordinary income is income earned as salary, wages, or fees, or from profit on the sale of goods or services in a trade or business. Capital gains income is income earned by selling an asset not considered as goods bought for resale in a trade or business. Typical examples are securities and real estate. A capital gain is a long-term capital gain if the asset was held more than six months, and it is subject to a special deduction of 50 percent of the gain.

Obtain IRS Publications 17 and 334 for further information on income taxes. You'd do well to utilize a tax service or an accountant, at least for your first year's return, after you've gone into your own business.

You're also subject to personal property taxes on equipment and inventory and real property taxes if you own your plant, shop, or store building.

Excise taxes are levied on specific commodities and products. Depending on the type of business you're in, you may find yourself once again in the role of tax collector.

You can reduce your income tax liability through planning. Use maximum expense deductions (bonus and accelerated depreciation and expenses paid in advance) and earn investment credit by buying equipment in highly profitable years when the investment credit is operative. Keep expenses down in low-profit years. The idea is to stay in the lowest possible tax bracket over the long run. (A method known as "income averaging" may be used to reduce tax liability in an exceptionally profitable year. Ask your accountant about this.) Another way to minimize tax liability over the long haul is to value inventory by the LIFO method.

KEY TERMS

Accelerated depreciation
Ad valorem tax
AGI (adjusted gross income)
Assessed rate
Capital gains
Deductions
Depreciation
Excise tax
Exclusions
Fair market value
FICA
FIFO
Form 1040
Form W-4
Form W-2
Investment credit
IRS
LIFO
Ordinary income
Personal property
Real property
Taxable income
Tax deposits
Tax liability
Tax rate
Withholding

QUESTIONS AND PROBLEMS

1. An employee earns $150 a week. Compute her weekly FICA withholding (at 5.85 percent) and estimate her tax withholding (using Figure 9-9) assuming that she is married, her annual taxable income is $5,000, and she

and her husband file jointly. (In practice, you would use the tables in IRS Circular E, *Employer's Tax Guide.* The FICA computation and the table should check if a 5.85 percent rate is the basis for your table. Your computed tax withholding won't check with the withholding taken from the tables in Circular E. Don't be concerned about it. Use Circular E tables in practice.)

2. Your sales for the month of May include $700 in merchandise, $600 in parts, and $2,100 in labor. Assuming a 5 percent sales tax with labor exempt, how much should be set aside to pay sales tax?
3. What is the common trap concerning sales tax and withholding that new business owners usually fall into during the first three to six months in business?
4. List and describe the forms used in connection with employee tax withholding.
5. You buy an asset for $500. It has a life of four years. Can you take investment credit? If so, how much?
6. Do you think you'll need a tax service or an accountant to prepare your first return after you've gone into business for yourself? Discuss the pros and cons of using outside help.
7. What other (than income) taxes will you have to pay as a small-business owner?
8. Which of the following *business expenses* are deductible on a proprietorship's Schedule C: (a) Ad valorem taxes, (b) interest, (c) trade magazines, (d) professional or trade group memberships, (e) asset depreciation, (f) automobile expense, (g) office supplies.
9. The IRS allows you to deduct 15 cents a mile for automobile expense, or you may deduct all actual expenses plus depreciation on the auto. If your truck cost $6,000; has a salvage value of $1,000 at the end of three years; gets 12 miles to the gallon at 80 cents a gallon; and oil, repairs, insurance, and other expenses are $300 a year, which method should you use for maximum tax benefits if you run 10,000 miles a year?
10. Discuss ways to minimize tax liability in a given year by planning: (a) depreciation scheduling and methods, (b) timing of expenses, (c) use of inventory valuation method, (d) investment timing, (e) capital gains timing.

FIELD INVESTIGATION AND PROJECTS

1. Obtain Form 1040, the schedules cited in this chapter, and a copy of IRS Publication 17. Without referring to your tax return for the last year, complete the 1040 based on your last year's income. Then compare it to the return you actually submitted.

*2. Obtain a copy of your state's sales tax return form. Assuming quarter's sales at $5,000 for merchandise, $2,000 for parts, and $10,000 for labor, complete the form in detail, assigning current dates and a fictitious name to the business.

*3. Make a thorough study of Schedule C Form 1040 in IRS Publication 334. Report.

Law, Regulation, Risk, and Insurance

10

An understanding of business law is useful in personal business dealings, and is essential if you operate a business. We can treat the subject only briefly in this text. Further study of business law is recommended.

Regulation by governments is felt in even the smallest businesses. There are business licensing requirements in most localities. Zoning regulations, building regulations, and Occupational Safety and Health Administration (OSHA) regulations affect all businesses. Other laws and regulations affect most businesses, and some kinds of business are subject to special regulation. "Ignorance of the law is no excuse," and you should have some knowledge of these laws and regulations.

Operating a business of your own involves the risk of failure. You reduce the risk of failure by learning and practicing the principles and techniques of good business. This kind of risk is a *speculative risk* because there is a chance of success as well as failure. However, you are exposed to another kind of risk which can only result in loss. This kind of risk is classified as a *pure risk* and includes losses from fire, theft, and accident. An understanding of risk, risk management, and insurance is essential for the small businessperson.

Look for answers to these questions in this chapter:

1. What are the laws pertaining to business transactions?

2. What should I know about the legal aspects of contracts, agency, property, sales, negotiable instruments, and security?
3. What regulation am I subject to as a small businessperson?
4. What kinds of licenses will I need for my business?
5. What kinds of insurance should I buy?
6. How can I avoid insurance? Is it prudent to do so?

BUSINESS LAW

This section will provide a brief summary on business law. We will not make an attempt to include the myriad of laws and acts that apply to big business and specialized activities.

Business law covers these specific subjects:

1. Contracts
2. Agency
3. Form of entity and entities
4. Property
5. Sales
6. Negotiable transactions
7. Security

Each of these subjects involve principles and knowledge that should be a part of your business tool kit. You have been exposed to most of these subjects directly or indirectly in the preceding chapters and you'll have continuing exposure throughout this book. At this point, we'll discuss each of these subjects so you'll have a central reference on business law in this chapter.[1]

Contracts

A contract is an agreement containing an *offer* and an *acceptance.* To be valid, the contract *must be made without duress, both parties must be competent, the contracted matter must be within the law, and a consideration (usually money) must be involved.* A contract may be oral in some states, but a written contract is always desirable. (Real estate contracts must be in writing to be binding in most states.) Contracts made with drunks, the insane, and infants are voidable. A contract that involves breaking the law is illegal. A contract that is unconscionable (unreasonable and unfair in the business sense at the time it was made and obtained by a party with sufficient economic or strategic power) will usually not be enforced by the courts.

The Uniform Commercial Code (U.C.C.) adopted by all of the states covers contracts for the sale of goods. It provides that a contract for the sale of goods of more than $500 value must be in writing to be valid.

[1] For further study of business law, see Robert N. Corley and William J. Robert, *Fundamentals of Business Law* (Englewood Cliffs, N.J.: Prentice-Hall, Inc., 1974).

POINT 10-1: Make all contracts in writing to assure that each party's obligation is understood, and to assure legal compliance when there might be doubt.

Contracts are *valid, unenforceable, voidable,* or *void.* A *valid contract* meets all legal requirements and is enforceable in the courts. An *unenforceable contract* is one that is basically valid, except that specific laws forbid enforcement (such as the written requirement for contracts of more than $500 by U.C.C. cited above). A *voidable contract* is one from which a person may withdraw, for a reason such as proven incompetence. A *void contract* is not really a contract. An example is a contract for performing an illegal act.

POINT 10-2: Contracts are *valid, unenforceable, voidable,* or *void.* The objective in any contractual arrangement is a valid contract.

A contract is of most value when the terms and conditions are clearly listed. These include the time in which the work is to be performed, the quality of materials that will be used or delivered, the performance that shall result from the service, the amount of money to be paid, when and how it is to be paid, provisions for changes in the scope of the contract, and in some instances provisions for terminating, voiding, or canceling the contract. The more complex the offer (work to be done or goods to be delivered) and the greater the cost, the more essential the need for specific and detailed specifications becomes. Thus a defense contract, a building or ship construction contract, or a contract to automate a factory may contain hundreds of pages of specifications. A contract for the purchase of a TV set, on the other hand, is relatively simple.

POINT 10-3: Nail down the terms and conditions of a contract with specific details on performance, time for completion, quality of materials, and other details to be sure to receive what you expect.

Figure 10-1 is a standard city property lease for the State of Texas. This lease form is commonly used for smaller commercial properties. Leases for larger properties commanding, say, $1,000 a month in rent and up are considerably more complex. Note the extent of the detail concerning insurance, taxes, fire losses, signs, and so forth.

POINT 10-4: The detail of specification of terms and conditions in a contract generally increases with the scope of the offer and the magnitude of the consideration.

Agency

An agency relationship is established when a person agrees to act for the benefit and under the control of another person. There are several basic forms of agency. The *employer-employee* relationship is the most common. The *princi-*

FIGURE 10-1 Texas standard city lease

C-248 LEASE CITY PROPERTY

Martin Stationery Co., Dallas, Texas

THE STATE OF TEXAS, } **THIS AGREEMENT OF LEASE:**

COUNTY OF

Made this **day of** **, A. D. 19** **, by and between**

, known herein as LESSOR,

and

, known herein as LESSEE,

(The terms "Lessor" and "Lessee" shall be construed in the singular or plural number according as they respectively represent one or more than one person.)

WITNESSETH, That the said Lessor does by these presents Lease and Demise unto the said Lessee the following described property, to-wit: Lying and being situated in the City of

and County of State of Texas, and being

for the term of beginning the day of

A. D. , and ending the day of , to be occupied as

and not otherwise, Lessee paying

therefor the sum of DOLLARS,

Payable

upon the conditions and covenants following:

1st. That the Lessee shall pay the rent at , Texas, monthly in advance as aforesaid, as the same shall fall due.

2nd. That the Lessee shall take good care of the property and its fixtures, and suffer no waste; and shall, at Lessee's own expense and cost, keep said premises (including plate glass) in good repair; keep the plumbing work, closets, pipes and fixtures belonging thereto in repair; and keep the water pipes and connections free from ice and other obstructions, to the satisfaction of the municipal and police authorities, during the term of this lease, and at the end or other expiration of the term shall deliver up the demised premises in good order and condition, natural deterioration, and damage by fire and the elements only excepted; all alterations, additions, and improvements, except trade fixtures, put in at the expense of Lessee shall be the property of the Lessor and shall remain upon and be surrendered with the premises as a part thereof at the termination of this lease. Lessee agrees to accept possession of the premises in their present condition and to allow for changes in such condition occurring by reasonable deterioration between the date hereof and the date Lessee occupies said premises; that no improvements or alterations shall be made in or to the hereby demised premises without the consent of the Lessor in writing.

That the Lessee shall pay the water tax imposed on the hereby leased premises as the same shall become due during the term of this lease.

3rd. That the Lessee shall promptly execute and fulfill all the ordinances of the city corporation applicable to said premises and all orders and requirements imposed by the Board of Health, Sanitary and Police Departments, for the correction, prevention and abatement of nuisances in or upon or connected with said premises during the said term, at Lessee's expense.

4th. That the Lessee shall not assign this agreement or underlet the premises, or any part thereof (except as may be mentioned herein) or make any alteration in the building (except as may be mentioned herein), without the consent of the Lessor in writing; or occupy or permit or suffer the same to be occupied for any business or purpose deemed extra hazardous on account of fire.

5th. That the Lessee shall, in case of fire, give immediate notice to the Lessor, who shall thereupon cause the damage to be repaired forthwith; but if the premises be by the Lessor deemed so damaged as to be unfit for occupancy, or if the Lessor shall decide to rebuild or remodel the said building, the lease shall cease, and the rent to be paid to the time of the fire.

6th. That in case of default in any of the covenants herein, Lessor may enforce the performance of this lease in any modes provided by law, and this lease may be forfeited at Lessor's discretion if such default continue for a period of ten days after Lessor notifies said Lessee of such default and his intention to declare the lease forfeited, such notice to be sent by the Lessor by mail or otherwise to the demised premises; and thereupon (unless the Lessee shall have completely removed or cured said default) this lease shall cease and come to an end as if that were the day originally fixed herein for the expiration of the term hereof, and Lessor's agent or attorney shall have the right, without further notice or demand, to re-enter and remove all persons and Lessee's property therefrom without being deemed guilty of any manner of trespass, and without prejudice to any remedies for arrears of rent or breach of covenant, or Lessor's agent or attorney may resume possession of the premises and re-let the same for the remainder of the term at the best rent said agent or attorney may obtain, for account of the Lessee, who shall make good any deficiency; and the Lessor shall have a lien as security for the rent aforesaid upon all the goods, wares, chattels, implements, fixtures, furniture, tools and other personal property which are or may be put on the demised premises.

7th. That the Lessor shall not be liable to Lessee or to Lessee's employes, patrons, or visitors, for any damage to person or property, caused by the act of negligence of any other tenant of said demised premises, or due to the building on said premises or any appurtenances thereof being improperly constructed, or being or becoming out of repair, nor for any damages from any defects or want of repair of any part of the building of which the leased premises form a part, but the Lessee accepts such premises as suitable for the purposes for which same are leased and accepts the building and each and every appurtenance thereof, and waives defects therein and agrees to hold the Lessor harmless from all claims for any such damage.

8th. That the Lessee shall not place any signs at, on, or about the premises except as and where first approved by the Lessor; and the Lessor shall have the right to remove any sign or signs in order to paint the building or premises or make any other repairs or alterations.

9th. It is expressly understood that in the event that the Lessor herein shall not be the owner of the premises herein leased, but shall hold a lease of the property of which the demised premises are a part, then this sublease is and shall remain subject to all of the terms and conditions of such existing lease to the Lessor, so far as they shall be applicable to the premises herein leased.

10th. In the event that the Lessee shall become bankrupt or shall make a voluntary assignment for the benefit of creditors, or in the event that a receiver of the Lessee shall be appointed, then, at the option of the Lessor and upon five (5) days' notice to the Lessee of the exercise of such option, this lease shall cease and come to an end.

11th. It is agreed and understood that any holding over by the Lessee of the hereby leased premises after the expiration of this lease shall

operate and be construed as a tenancy from month to month at a rental of $

12th. Lessor agrees to pay to the Real Estate Broker negotiating this lease the customary leasing fee.

IN TESTIMONY WHEREOF, The parties to this agreement have hereunto set their hands in duplicate, the day and year above written.

____

____________________________, LESSOR.

____

____________________________, LESSEE.

pal-agent relationship is the situation in which the agent works for the principal for a fee or commission. The agent is bound to abide by the principal's rules and orders pertaining only to his obligation to the principal. Lawyers, accountants, real estate brokers, and manufacturer's representatives are typical agents in this kind of relationship. A *general agent* has broad authority to act over a specified time period for the principal. A *special agent* is authorized to act on a one-shot or otherwise defined piece of business.

The principal is liable for the acts and representations of his agent. So, be careful in choosing and appointing agents. The agent is bound to loyalty to the principal, confidential handling of the principal's information, and avoidance of conflict of interest. But in spite of this, an inadequate or dishonest agent can cause a lot of grief for the principal.

POINT 10-5: A principal is responsible and liable for the representations and acts of his agents. Choose carefully.

Form of Entity and Entities

This subject was discussed in detail in Chapter 2. Refer to that material for review if it is required.

Property

Ownership of property entails a so-called "bundle of rights," which includes the *right to possess, enjoy, use,* and *dispose of* the property or rights associated with it. *Real property* consists of ground and structures attached to the ground. *Personal property* consists of all other goods or objects that can be owned. *Tangible* goods have physical being and can be personal or real property. Intangible objects such as good will or a patent can be personal property.

The bundle of rights associated with property can be subdivided. Thus, if you own real estate *fee simple,* you have all the rights. But you can create a *leasehold,* which gives the lessee (the person paying rent) the *right to possess, use,* and *enjoy* the property for a determined period of time. You can convey mineral rights to another party while retaining all other rights to the property.

There are several forms of ownership. You can own a property as an *individual* or as a *corporation.* You can own a property by *tenancy-in-common,* which means that ownership of the property is undivided and in the event of death of one of the tenants-in-common his interest passes to his heirs. The property may be subdivided in court upon disagreement of the tenants-in-common.

Joint tenancy provides for undivided ownership. However, the surviving tenant has full ownership on the death of the other. This is a common husband-wife arrangement.

> POINT 10-6: Property ownership implies the full bundle of rights—possession, enjoyment, use, and freedom of disposal. Portions of these rights may be rented or sold at the discretion of the owner.

Sales

The key items in sales matters concern (1) who has title to the goods and (2) when title passes. A contract under the U.C.C. is valid even if the terms are not fully defined. An offer to buy or sell that gives reasonable assurance that it will be held open is not revocable because consideration wasn't received during the time stated, and if a time period was not stated, with a limit of ninety days. The term F.O.B. (free on board) from the seller's place of business means the buyer pays freight. The cost of freight is included in the selling price in a C.F. contract.

Title to the goods sold passes to the buyer when the seller delivers the goods to the carrier in an F.O.B. sale, and upon delivery to the buyer in a C.F. sale. If the goods are sold and delivered without being moved, title passes at the time and place of the sales contract.

The title to goods sold is only as good as the title of the seller. If the seller delivers stolen goods, the original owner may claim the goods upon proving ownership.

Goods are sometimes delivered on consignment, which means the buyer has the right to sell or return the goods. In this case, title to the goods remains with the consignor (usually a manufacturer or wholesaler) till the goods are paid for. However, the consignor must obtain written agreement from the consignee that the consigned goods are collateral for the cost of the goods. Otherwise, if the consignee fails, the other creditors can claim the consigned goods.

> POINT 10-7: Title to goods sold F.O.B. passes to the buyer when the seller delivers goods to the carrier. Title to C.F. goods passes to the buyer when the goods are delivered to the buyer.

A manufacturer of goods has product liability. That is, he is responsible for reasonable quality or fitness for purpose intended and the marketability of the goods. The middlemen dealing in the goods have similar liability to their customers. This applies to all kinds of merchandise, including food and drinks. The liability of the seller reaches beyond the buyer to the final consumer injured by the product, even if he is only a guest of the buyer. In general, the injured person can and does sue the manufacturer in the case of a manufactured product or the food-preparing establishment when food or drink is involved. It's important to have product liability insurance if you run a restaurant or a bar.

POINT 10-8: If you manufacture a product or prepare food, protect yourself with product liability insurance.

Negotiable Transactions

Negotiable instruments are contracts that are readily transferred and are just like money in this respect. They give the person to whom the instrument is assigned (transferred) full right without any defenses. Defenses may be raised in connection with a simple contract. There are no defenses for failing to meet the obligation incurred with a negotiable instrument. (Recent legislation has clouded this issue by giving a borrower the right to refuse to pay off a note given for merchandise that does not perform properly or is otherwise defective.)

Negotiable instruments include drafts, checks, promissory notes, stocks, bonds, bills of lading, warehouse receipts, and certificates of deposit.

A *draft* involves three parties—a *drawer* who orders a *drawee* to pay a certain amount of money to a *payee* either at a future date or upon demand. The drawee ordinarily owes money to the drawer. The drawer employs his credit with the drawee to pay a debt he owes the payee.

A *check* is a specialized draft. The bank is the drawee, the signer is the drawer. The check is made payable to the payee and is payable on demand (whereas a draft may be payable at some future time).

A *promissory note* is a credit instrument in which the *maker* promises to pay a certain amount of money to the payee either on demand or (usually) at a specified time in the future. Interest may or may not be specified.

A *stock* is a certificate showing ownership (equity) of a specific number of shares in a corporation A *bond* is a credit instrument containing a promise by the corporation to pay either the bearer (*bearer bonds* have coupons that are clipped and sent in to collect interest) or the registered owner (interest checks are sent to the *registered owner* as they come due) a specified amount (usually $1,000) on a specified date plus interest at specified intervals.

A *bill of lading* is a negotiable title document. It specifies that the goods it represents are to be delivered to the bearer of the bill of lading or to his order.

A *warehouse receipt* is also a negotiable title document. It specifies that the goods it represents are to be surrendered to the bearer or to his order. This permits inventory to be used as collateral since the borrower can assign the receipt to the lender as security for a loan.

A *certificate of deposit* (CD) acknowledges receipt of money by a commercial bank or a thrift institution and contains a promise to repay the money on a specified date with a specified rate of interest. Large corporations invest idle cash in CDs, commercial paper (corporate promissory notes), and treasury bills, which are all short-term instruments (less than a year) so that temporary excess cash earns some interest, yet is not tied up for long periods of time. If the money is needed in advance of maturity, it can readily be obtained by sale of the instrument at a discount (which is usually just a portion of the interest).

POINT 10-9: Negotiable instruments are contracts that are readily transferred just as cash is. Negotiable instruments include drafts, checks, promissory notes, stocks, bonds, bills of lading, warehouse receipts, and certificates of deposit.

Promissory notes are referred to merely as "notes," and comprise the fundamental instrument in a lending transaction. Warehouse receipts are used to secure loans, as noted earlier. A common method of collection for a shipment of merchandise to a buyer of unknown or poor credit standing is to send the bill of lading attached to a "sight" (due when seen) draft to a commercial bank in the buyer's city. The buyer pays the draft, receives the bill of lading, and can pick up the merchandise.

POINT 10-10: A negotiable instrument must be in writing, signed by the maker or drawer; it must contain an unconditional promise to pay a certain amount of money, be payable either at a definite time in the future or on demand, and must be payable either to the bearer or to order.

Negotiation of an instrument is the *transfer* to another person who becomes the *holder.* A holder is a person who possesses the instrument which *was drawn to him, issued to him, or endorsed to him, to his order, to bearer, or in blank.* Negotiation of an instrument *payable to bearer occurs upon delivery to the intended holder.* An instrument payable to order is negotiated by delivery with the necessary endorsement. An instrument is *endorsed* when the holder signs the instrument. Everyone has enjoyed the experience of endorsing a check.

There are several kinds of endorsements. A *special endorsement* specifies the person to whom or to whose order the instrument is payable. This type of endorsement requires the second person's signature before the instrument can be negotiated further. Postal money orders contain a special endorsement option printed on the back side. A *blank endorsement* exists when the instrument is merely signed by the person to whom it is drawn. In this case, the instrument is negotiated simply by delivery; the instrument can be negotiated by the bearer (e.g., on a check endorsed by the payee). The holder simply provides a second endorsement to negotiate the instrument again. A *restrictive endorsement* prohibits further negotiation of an instrument, the common example being "for deposit only." A *qualified endorsement* disclaims the contractual promises usually made by an endorser. (Each endorser of a negotiable instrument makes himself liable to all subsequent endorsers and holders if the drawer fails to pay unless a qualified endorsement is used.) The qualified endorsement "without recourse" disavows liability.

POINT 10-11: Negotiable instruments may be readily transferred by delivery if payable to bearer or by endorsement if payable to order. An endorsement may be blank, special, restrictive, or qualified.

Security

Most credit transactions and loans are *secured* by transfer of an interest in property owned by a debtor or by the guarantee of a third party. If the debt is not paid, the creditor can sell the property pledged as security or can demand payment from the guarantor.

The creditor attaches collateral by having the debtor sign a written security agreement which describes the collateral and conveys a security interest in the property to the creditor. The creditor can protect himself against sale of the asset by the debtor by *perfecting* his interest, usually by filing and recording a financing statement in the county recorder's or clerk's office or by taking physical possession of the collateral. In the case of consumer goods sold on credit, you can obtain limited perfection by attaching your secured interest to the goods sold.

In the event of default, the goods are sold and the proceeds of the sale cover first the debt and foreclosure costs; any excess must go to the debtor. If the sale of the goods does not provide adequate proceeds to satisfy the debt, the creditor may obtain a *deficiency judgment.* This means the creditor has a further claim against the debtor. Ordinarily a deficiency judgment is hard to collect because if the debtor can't pay you, he probably doesn't have any other unencumbered assets that can be sold to yield cash for you. Ordinarily, you lose if a debtor cannot pay or if he decides not to pay, unless the collateral is adequate to recoup the debt.

POINT 10-12: You can strengthen your chances of debt collection by securing the debt, attaching the collateral, and perfecting your interest in the collateral. The fair market value of the collateral should exceed the amount of debt for maximum protection.

Mortgages are commonly used to obtain a security interest in real property. The key to protecting your interests is to record the note and the mortgage with the county recorder or clerk.

REVIEW EXERCISES 10-A

1. Why should a contract be written rather than oral?
2. Under what conditions is a contract voidable?
3. What liability do you as a principal have for your agent's representation?

4. What are the three forms of business entity?
5. What is the bundle of rights associated with property?
6. Differentiate between real and personal property. Cite examples.
7. Discuss title to goods and identify who has title at what point in an F.O.B. sale, a C.F. sale, and an "on-site" sale.
8. Discuss product liability.
9. List and define as many negotiable instruments as you can.
10. How does a check differ from a draft?
11. Discuss the various kinds of endorsement of negotiable instruments.
12. What is the remedy if a debtor defaults on a secured loan?

REGULATION

Business is subject to regulation under federal, state, and local laws. The extent to which regulation is felt by the businessperson depends on the size of the business and the type of the business.

Federal Regulation

Federal regulation of big business is complex, far-reaching, and thorough. While your mini business is affected by federal regulation, you won't feel most of the effects that larger businesses do. For example, large businesses are open to charges of monopoly and price fixing and discrimination under the Clayton Act of 1914 or the Robinson-Patman Act of 1936. It's unlikely that you'll run afoul of these or that you need to concern yourself with them unless you become a manufacturer and engage in interstate commerce.

If you engage in food, drug, or cosmetic manufacture, you'll be subject to the Pure Food and Drug Act and regulation by the Food and Drug Administration. This agency also has a product safety responsibility under the Child Protection and Toy Safety Act of 1969 and can ban toys it deems unsafe.

If you get into clothing manufacture, you're subject to Federal Trade Commission regulation under the Flammable Fabrics Act. This law prohibits interstate sale of dangerously flammable clothing and requires flammability testing and fire-retarding treatment.

The Occupational Safety and Health Administration (OSHA) develops and promulgates occupational safety and health standards, issues regulations, and makes investigations and inspections to determine compliance. It can issue citations and propose penalties for noncompliance. OSHA has ten regional offices. You can obtain information from any of these or write to Department of Labor, Office of Information, Publications and Reports, Washington, D.C. 20210. You'll feel OSHA's impact most if you're in manufacturing, but they also have jurisdiction over retail and service businesses with employees.

If you engage in interstate commerce, you're subject to minimum wage laws in most businesses. The minimum wage was $1.60 in 1966, $2.25 in 1976, and is continuing upward. Time over forty hours a week must be paid at time and a half rates if you fall in this category.

The Truth-in-Lending law enacted in 1969 requires you to disclose the finance charge in annual percentage rate (APR) and in dollars in writing to your customer before you close an installment-sale deal. The finance charge includes interest and other fees which you tack onto a credit sale over those you'd normally have on a cash sale.

The federal government registers trademarks, grants patents, and issues copyrights. The U.S. Patent and Trademark Office (Washington, D.C. 20231) can provide information on patents and trademarks. For information on obtaining copyrights, write Copyright Office, Library of Congress, Washington, D.C. 20540.

POINT 10-13: The federal government imposes considerable regulation on business. Its impact is principally upon big business, but small business feels it as well. A mini retail or service business gets less attention from big government.

State Regulation

State regulations may affect you most in connection with labor, safety, health, and licensing. Licensing takes time and can produce costly delays. Start on it well in advance of your planned business start. Some states have minimum wages which apply to employers who don't come under the federal minimum wage laws. Your state may have other labor laws that can affect your operations. Learn about them early!

Many states have dropped store licensing since sales-tax laws provide a registry of businesses. Check your local situation to determine requirements.

Some states have safety laws and require inspections of places of business or specific kinds of equipment such as boilers and fire protection equipment. If you're in the restaurant business or manufacture food products, you may be subject to state food and health laws. If you sell liquor, you're subject to state liquor laws in most states. Some states have licensing requirements for some specific professions such as barbering or beauty operators. Of course, you're subject to state motor vehicle and operator laws.

Finally, some states have laws that require businesses to close on Sunday or prevent them from being open both Saturday and Sunday. Check with local authorities.

Local Regulation and Licenses

The principal local regulations that affect all businesses are zoning ordinances, building codes, parking regulations, sign ordinances, and fire regulations. Zoning ordinances separate and position industrial, light industrial, commercial, and retail activities away from residential areas. You can check zoning maps and regulations at your city hall to determine whether areas you're interested in comply with your zoning needs.

Building codes generally won't affect you if you rent an existing building, unless you start to do a remodeling job. If you do, you'll have to get a building permit in most localities. When you do, you may open a Pandora's box if the building is extremely old! For example, the city may require you to bring the plumbing and electrical service up to code. This can become expensive! It's a good idea to check with the city building inspection department before you lease an old building to be sure you won't be hit with a big modernization program. Better yet, ask the owner to do the remodeling and pay him a little more rent.

Parking regulations may affect the access to your intended business site. Check them out before you lease.

Sign ordinances may kill your plans to put up an inexpensive sign yourself. These ordinances may require minimum heights, may outlaw some types of signs, and in some localities require installation by a bonded sign man. Check on your city's sign ordinances before you make decisions about your signs.

Fire regulations usually require well-marked exits, fire extinguishers, and other fire precautions. Some types of fire extinguishers are not recognized as adequate in certain localities. Check into your town's fire regulations before you sign a lease on a building or buy fire extinguishers.

Check your city on licenses required to go into business. There may be special licensing requirements for specific businesses or trades. Securing licenses for plumbers and electricians, for example, usually involves tests and experience. Some cities are requiring appliance and electronic technicians to be licensed if they conduct a service business.

If you get into the restaurant or food business, your city health department will be vitally interested in your proposed layout and equipment. Don't buy any equipment or begin any renovations for a restaurant until you've contacted your local health department. And, they'll inspect you periodically after you open.

POINT 10-14: Check local, state, and federal regulations that may affect your kind of business early in your new-business planning.

REVIEW EXERCISES 10-B

1. Do very small businesses feel a heavy, direct impact of federal government regulation beyond federal income tax laws? Discuss.
2. Discuss state and local laws and licensing regulations that may affect your business.
3. What kinds of small businesses are subject to unusual amounts of regulation?

RISK AND INSURANCE

Previous sections have been concerned with helping you keep as much as possible of what you earn. This section concerns itself with helping you keep what you already have, as well as what you may be capable of earning for the rest of your life. The subject matter is risk, insurance, and liability.[2]

Risk

A *speculative risk* involves a possible favorable or unfavorable outcome. The risk of owning and operating your own business is a speculative risk.

A *pure risk* entails only a possible loss. Fire damage, plate-glass breakage, physical disability, and personal liability fall into this category.

There are four methods to meet risks of this kind. They're *avoidance, prevention, transfer,* and *retention.*

Avoidance is a poor method, because avoidance would preclude most of the activities you want, need, and like to engage in. Thus, you can avoid the danger of a fire loss by not owning a home or a business. But most Americans want to own homes in due time, and many want to go into business.

Prevention is the best solution if the cost of prevention is not excessive. For example, you can reduce the hazard of fire with a fireproof building, a sprinkler system, and fire extinguishers. The cost of a fireproof building may be exhorbitant. Furthermore, prevention isn't always effective. Even so-called "fireproof" buildings have been damaged beyond economical repair by fire and their contents totally destroyed.

Transfer is removal of the risk from yourself to someone else. This is usually accomplished by buying an insurance policy. (There are other methods of risk transfer, such as guaranteeing the price of a commodity for future delivery at a known price through *hedging.* Our concern here is with risks that can be transferred through the purchase of an insurance policy or a bond.)

Retention of risk by a small-business owner is sensible only when the possible loss is small or the risk is insignificantly small. You retain a risk by doing nothing till an unfortunate event occurs. A typical example is not to insure an old automobile with a value of $300 for collision (although you would prudently carry liability insurance, since the possible liability loss is great).

POINT 10-15: A pure risk may be dealt with by avoidance, prevention, transfer, or retention. Insurance is the most common method of risk transfer.

Insurance

There are thousands of insurance companies offering over a hundred different kinds of insurance policies. The insurance idea builds on the probability of an event's future occurrence based on past history. A large number of policyholders

[2] For further study of insurance, see Robert Riegel, Jerome S. Miller, and C. Arthur Williams, Jr., *Insurance Principles and Practices: Property and Liability,* 6th ed. (Englewood Cliffs, N.J.: Prentice-Hall, Inc., 1976).

each pay a small premium, and the total collected will cover the losses of the unfortunate few, pay expenses of insuring, and provide a fair return on investment to the owners of the insurance company (who are the policyholders in the case of a mutual company).

Figure 10-2 is a classification of risks grouped according *to property losses, earning-power losses, future expenses,* and *liability losses.* Note that loss of property can result from damage or destruction of property, and dishonesty or the failure of others. Similarly, other losses can result from several sources or causes. If you bought all of the insurance listed in Figure 10-2 applicable to a small business, you'd go broke buying insurance. So what should you buy? A good and reputable insurance agent who's interested in helping your business grow so that he can do business with you over the long haul will give you sensible direction.

An insurance policy is a contract under which the *insurer,* for a consideration (the *premium* which you pay), assumes a risk of loss for you (the *insured*). Insurance is generally sold through an agent (whose job is to *qualify* you rather than to sell to you). When you call your agent and ask for insurance on a specified property in a specified amount, the property is insured under a *binder* pending writing of a policy. A binder of this kind usually is oral, and you're covered till the policy is written and issued.

A policy specifies the property covered, the location(s) of the property covered, the perils covered, the losses covered, the persons covered, the time period of the coverage, excluded hazards, and the amount of coverage. Much of this is fine print on a standard policy form with standardized attachments for additional coverage.

Coinsurance and Deductibles

Many property-insurance contracts are written with a *coinsurance clause.* Since most property damage claims fall below 20 percent of total property value, there is a temptation to underinsure. If almost everyone insured property for only 20 percent of the value, rates would have to be higher, and the few who wanted full coverage would be unduly penalized. The coinsurance clause prevents this by requiring you to insure at a required level, usually 70 percent to 85 percent of the actual property value, in order to have a full claim on all loss below the required level of insurance. Thus, if a company requires 80 percent insurance under a coinsurance clause, you're required to carry $8,000 in insurance on a $10,000 property. If you carry $8,000 you recover full amount on any loss up to $8,000 and $8,000 on any loss exceeding $8,000. If you insured for only $6,000, you'd collect a percentage of total loss equal to your amount of insurance coverage divided by amount required under the clause in most states. That's $6,000/$8,000, or 75 percent for any loss under $8,000, and $6,000 for any loss in excess of $8,000. Thus, on a $4,000 loss, you'd collect only $3,000. (Some states would recognize a loss of $6,000 as a total loss and require payment of that amount—the face value of the policy.)

FIGURE 10-2 Risks and available insurance (or bonding)

RISKS AND AVAILABLE INSURANCE (OR BONDING)

1. LOSS OF PROPERTY

   A. DESTRUCTION OR DAMAGE

      Commercial Multiperil; Fire; Hail, Earthquake, Tornado, etc.; Glass; Marine; Boiler & Machinery; War Damage; Valuable Papers; Sprinkler Leakage; Water Damage; Riot & Insurrection; Automobile Physical Damage

   B. DISHONESTY

      Commercial Multiperil; Automobile Theft; Burglary, Robbery & Theft; Forgery; Fidelity (Bond)

   C. FAILURE OF OTHERS

      Credit Insurance for Bad Debts; Surety (Bond); Title

2. LOSS OF EARNING POWER

   A. PERSONNEL LOSSES

      Life; Health; Unemployment

   B. PROPERTY LOSSES

      Business Interruption; Profits; Rent; Commercial Multiperil

3. FUTURE EXPENSES

   A. PERSONNEL LOSSES

      Medical Expense

   B. PROPERTY LOSSES

      Extra Expense; Replacement Cost; Leasehold; Commercial Multiperil

4. LEGAL LIABILITY

   A. TO EMPLOYEES

      Worker's Compensation; Employers' Liability

   B. TO THE PUBLIC

      Commercial Multiperil; Owner's Landlord's and Tenant's Liability; Automobile Liability; Boiler and Machinery; Product Liability; Professional Liability

Other common clauses that limit loss recovery are *deductible* clauses such as the common $100 deductible on auto collision and the two-thirds vacancy clause on rental property (since an empty building is a greater hazard than a fully occupied building).

POINT 10-16: Coinsurance clauses require you to insure for a given percentage or more of the appraised value of the property in order to be able to collect full damages suffered for losses below the policy face value.

Policies and Forms

The standard fire insurance policy, which is identical in most states, with slight changes (usually in wording only) in all but a few of the rest of the states, provides for coverage against direct loss by fire and lightning only. A policy generally consists of this basic form plus one or more attachments which fall into three categories: (1) forms describing the property and locations covered, (2) forms covering additional perils, and (3) forms covering additional losses. In some states the basic form may contain extended coverage. Consult your insurance agent if there's any question.

The first category is descriptive. The second category–forms covering additional perils–is something you should know more about now. You can get an *extended-coverage endorsement,* which extends the standard fire policy's coverage to include damage caused by windstorm, hail, explosion, riot and civil commotion, damage by aircraft, damage by vehicle, and some types of smoke damage. Extended coverage endorsement is inexpensive and worthwhile.

Forms in the third category, *additional losses,* include business interruption (losses resulting from inability to do business, *including loss of nominal earnings*), extra expense (incurred by having to temporarily continue business in a more expensive location, leasing equipment, etc., till regular operation can be restored), and *consequential* loss (caused indirectly–for example melted candy at the unburned end of a burned candy store).

Liability insurance protects you against the claims of others. You can be liable by *contract* or by *tort.* A tort is a wrong to another not resulting from a breach of contract. Most tort claims arise from negligence–for example, when someone stumbles on a loose floor tile in your store and is injured. You'll want *comprehensive general liability* to protect yourself, and if you prepare food or manufacture a product, you should have *product liability* insurance as well.

POINT 10-17: Liability protects you against the claims of others. Since liability claims can become extremely large, you should definitely carry general liability insurance.

You can cover your business automobiles under your family automobile insurance policy *if you're organized as a proprietorship,* but your trucks aren't eligible under the family policy. Auto coverage should include *material damage* and *liability.* Material damage coverage is divided into *collision* and *comprehensive* (fire, lightning, theft, windstorm, earthquake, explosion, transportation, hail, and water damage). Auto liability hazards include owned, hired (rented), and nonowned (borrowed) vehicles. You can purchase these coverages separately or under a comprehensive policy. Bodily injury liability, property damage liability, and medical payment coverage is available.

You can protect yourself against the dishonesty of others. Protect yourself against employee dishonesty by requiring employees to have fidelity bonds. If an employee cheats or robs you, the bonding company restores your losses up to the amount of the bond. You also can insure yourself against burglary and theft with a policy. Generally, you can cover these and other perils with *multiple-line coverage* tailored to your specific needs.

You can obtain specialized insurance protection for glass, boilers, and machinery; credit (losses over and beyond normal credit losses), and accounts-receivable (protection against losses resulting from damaged, lost, or destroyed records). Another form of specialized insurance, workers' compensation insurance, was discussed earlier.

Life insurance and health insurance are beyond the scope of this discussion. However, these coverages are vital to the small businessperson, since his or her temporary absence from business can result in loss of business and income; an owner's death could result also in the demise of the business, unless the spouse has sufficient funds to hire adequate management. If you rely heavily on any one of your employees, and his or her replacement would be difficult, it's a good idea to carry insurance on that person. This is sometimes called *key* insurance, and key policies generally provide for payment to the business if the key person's services are lost by any means, including defection to another employer.

REVIEW EXERCISES 10-C

1. What is the difference between pure and speculative risk? Give examples of each.
2. What are the four methods for meeting risk?
3. What is a binder? Why and under what circumstances is a binder used?
4. What are the general descriptions, statements, and specifications included in an insurance policy?
5. A company has a policy with a 75 percent coinsurance clause. A building is insured for $80,000, but its value has increased to $120,000. If a $10,000 fire damage is incurred, how much will the insurance company pay?
6. Same data as Problem 5, but an $80,000 loss is incurred. What does the insurance company pay?
7. List the perils covered by a fire policy with an extended-coverage endorsement.
8. What are the common additional losses a business can suffer as a result of fire beyond the actual direct fire loss?
9. Why should you have comprehensive general liability insurance?

CASES

Business Law

Barry Lattimer leased a building under a standard Texas lease (Figure 10-1) which contains a convenant that "all alterations, additions, and improvements except trade fixtures put in at the expense of Lessee shall be the property of the Lessor and shall remain upon and be surrendered with the premises as a part thereof at the termination of this lease."

Upon termination of the lease, Barry prepared to remove an overhead door that he had installed at the rear of the building, a window-unit air conditioner that he had installed, and a row of display shelves that he had attached to one of the walls. The landlord told Barry that he couldn't remove any of these under the lease covenant that has been cited.

An Insurance Claim

(This case concerns a facet of insurance not discussed in the text. Detailed discussion is provided.)

Mildred Hampton had a restaurant. She owned the building and fixtures. The building was insured for $50,000, the contents for $8,000, and she had coverage for loss of profit up to $1,000 a month for up to four months. There was *no* coinsurance clause in the policy. She had a large fire, called her insurance agent, and he advised the insurance company. An insurance adjuster appeared two days later with a building contractor, and they assessed the damage. The adjuster told Mildred that he could recommend settlement for the building damage at $30,000, contents at $3,000, and loss of profit at $3,000 total. The contractor had bid the building repairs at $35,000. Mildred wasn't satisfied that this was an adequate settlement. The adjuster told her that the $5,000 taken off the building repairs was depreciation. Mildred figured that it would cost $15,000 to replace the contents, which included $1,000 worth of food, and her loss of profit would amount to $2,000 a month for four months until repairs were made and her business was re-established.

Mildred asked her insurance agent what she should do. He told her to get a contractor of her choice to give her a bid on the repairs to the building and to use it in negotiating with the insurance company. He also told her to list all of the contents destroyed with the new replacement cost and the age of each piece of equipment for computing depreciation. He advised that $8,000 was the maximum she could collect on contents. On loss of profit, he advised her to claim the full $4,000 insured, or to insist that partial settlement be made with the balance to be negotiated and settled at the end of four months, based on actual loss of profit–subject, of course, to the maximum set by her coverage.

While she was preparing figures, she mentioned her problem to a businessman who owned some apartment houses. "Shucks, Mildred," he said, "Give it to a public adjuster. He'll get you a good settlement even after his fee comes out. I call one before I call the fire department whenever I have a fire."

Mildred discussed the matter of using a public adjuster with her insurance agent. He advised against it. She followed his recommendation. She got a bid from a local contractor for building repairs. It was $45,000. She compared the bid with that of the contractor used by the adjuster and found some items omitted on the lower bid and some differences in costs. She negotiated a $40,000 settlement on the building, got an $8,000 settlement on the contents, and took a partial settlement of $2,000 on profits; the balance was to be determined four months after the date of the fire.

REVIEW EXERCISES 10-D

1. On what items was Barry's landlord correct? Could there be a question on any of the items? Discuss.
2. Could Larry have tried to delete the covenant cited when he originally negotiated the lease? What notations and initialing procedure would have been required?
3. Does the insurance claim case bring to mind any precautions that should be taken with business records? Discuss. What parts of Mildred's claim negotiations would her business records have simplified?
4. How much money will Mildred have lost on the fire? Are there any steps she can take to restore her building and the contents, and to re-establish her business that will minimize her losses? Discuss them.

SUMMARY

Business law concerns itself with contracts, agency, entities and form of entity, property, sales, negotiable transactions, and security. The Uniform Commercial Code (U.C.C.) has standardized transaction forms and business law in most states.

Federal regulation directly affecting small business includes Food and Drug Administration regulation of food, drug, cosmetic, and toy manufacturers; the Federal Trade Commission with respect to advertising and flammable fabrics; and Occupational Health and Safety Administration (OSHA) for health and safety compliance, to mention only a few. You're also subject to the Truth-in-Lending Law, and if you engage in interstate commerce, to the Minimum Wage Law. The federal government registers trademarks, grants patents, and issues copyrights.

State regulations that affect small businesses include minimum wage and other labor laws, safety and health laws, and specialized licensing requirements. Local regulations that affect small businesses involve zoning ordinances, building codes, parking regulations, sign ordinances, health ordinances, and fire ordinances.

You can meet risk by avoidance, prevention, transfer, or retention. Prevention is the best method if cost is not excessive. Transfer is the most commonly used method of meeting risk, and transfer is generally accomplished through insurance and bonding. Risks covered by insurance may be classified as property loss, earning-power loss, future expense, and liability loss. Adequate insurance is mandatory, but you can overinsure. Find a good agent who will work with you for success over the long haul rather than one who'll try to load you with insurance for quick commissions now.

KEY TERMS

Acceptance
Agency
Agent
Bill of lading
Binder
Blank endorsement
Bond
Bundle of rights
CD (certificate of deposit)
Commercial paper
Contract
Deficiency judgment
Draft
Endorsement
Enforceable
Extended coverage
Fee simple
F.O.B.
Form of entity
Insurance
Joint tenancy
Leasehold
Liability
Negotiable instruments
Offer
OSHA
Personal property
Premium
Principal
Promissory note
Property
Pure risk
Qualified endorsement
Real property
Restrictive endorsement
Risk avoidance
Risk prevention
Risk retention
Risk transfer
Security
Special endorsement
Speculative risk
Stock
Tenancy-in-common
Title
Tort
U.C.C. (uniform commercial code)
Valid
Void
Warehouse receipt

QUESTIONS AND PROBLEMS

1. Discuss the essential contents of a contract, and the conditions under which it is voidable, valid, or unenforceable.
2. Discuss property, real and personal; the bundle of rights; and forms of ownership.
3. What is a negotiable instrument? Discuss the principal types.
4. Discuss negotiable-instrument endorsements.
5. Why is it desirable to have a loan secured? Discuss methods of securing a loan and the various forms of collateral.
6. Discuss the forms of entity and the characteristics of each.
7. List agencies of federal, state, and local government that might have regulatory powers over these businesses: (a) a small retailer of firearms, (b) an electronics service shop, (c) an automotive repair shop, (d) a small meat-packing plant with customers in four states, (e) a clothing manufacturer.
8. How can you deal with employee dishonesty by (a) risk avoidance, (b) risk transfer, (c) risk prevention, (d) retention?
9. Under what conditions would you consider risk retention with regard to an asset?
10. Explain (in your own words) how insurance works.
11. Explain the purpose of coinsurance.
12. What kinds of insurance should a small retail business carry? A service business?
13. Under what conditions would you want boiler insurance?
14. Why is it a smart idea to buy life insurance on key employees?
15 Do you see any reason for subsidizing life insurance policies for employees with their families as beneficiaries?

FIELD INVESTIGATION AND PROJECTS

1. Study a text in business law on any of the seven business-law subjects presented in this chapter. Report.

*2. Research and report on your city's zoning, building, and licensing laws.

*3. Contact a local insurance agent. Get his or her views on the coverage a small businessperson should have and prepare a report.

*4. Research OSHA regulations and prepare a report.

Pricing, Planning, and Budgeting for Profit

11

Profit is essential for the continuing life and growth of a business. The sooner a new business is made profitable, the greater are its chances of growth and survival. If a business loses continually, it eventually consumes its assets and fails. Planning for profit, pricing for profit, and budgeting resources are essential to near and long-term profitability.

These are some of the questions that this chapter will answer for you:

1. What can I do to maximize my profit?
2. What counteracting effects can higher prices produce?
3. How can I find out what parts of my business are profitable or unprofitable?
4. What factors should I consider in determining pricing policy?
5. How do retail, wholesale, service, and manufacturing businesses differ in product-cost makeup?
6. What techniques are available for determining cost and arriving at prices?
7. How can I make my business less dependent on the ups and downs of the economy?
8. How can I plan intelligently for profit?

PROFIT RATIONALE

New small businesses often are losing money even when their owners feel that they're doing well. This occurs because the owners confuse sales volume and cash position with profit while overlooking expenses and liabilities. Another pitfall is the assumption that sales will continue at peak levels throughout the year. In this section, you'll examine profit rationale generally and specifically with respect to three types of businesses—retail, service, and manufacturing.

An Elementary Analysis

The profit equation for any business is simply:

$$\text{Profit} = \text{Sales} - \text{Cost of Goods Sold} - \text{Expenses}$$

You can increase profit by

1. Increasing unit sales prices
2. Increasing sales volume in units
3. Decreasing cost of goods sold
4. Decreasing expenses

The possibility of *increasing unit prices* is limited by the actions of competition. However, there are exceptions. If you have an established reputation and people deal with you for convenience, quality, or some other reason which they value greatly, you can charge more than your competitors. If you sell something that is hard to find, offer special technical service or advice, or provide some other special service which your competitors do not offer, you can command a higher selling price. Usually the extra service will be reflected in higher expenses, but the increased margin can readily exceed the increased expense.

Small parts and materials such as screws, washers, grommets, and solder used in repair service businesses are usually priced five or more times cost. More expensive parts costing the business $1 to $3 are usually billed at two or more times cost, and larger parts are billed at one and a half to two times cost. Specialty houses dealing in plumbing, appliance, electronic, optical, and other specialized parts for the general public often follow these pricing formulas.

Increasing unit sales volume to increase profits can be accomplished in a number of ways. Sales volume can be increased by lowering prices, by building the value of your product or service in the mind of the buyer, by exposing more potential buyers to your product or service (advertising, salespeople, special promotions, and so forth), by concentrating your efforts on fast-moving products or services, or by increasing the customer groups you sell to.

A decision to *decrease cost of goods sold* may be implemented in several ways. Distributors have special promotions from time to time that provide additional discounts on products bought during the promotion. Some lines of goods and parts carry *price breaks*—for example, one to ten units, $1 each; eleven to twenty-four units, $.90 each; twenty-five to a hundred units, $.85 each. The danger of "stocking up" through quantity buying is that you increase inventory costs and tie up cash. However, you may be able to work a *group buying arrangement* whereby you and others in similar businesses in other locations pool your purchases to take advantage of price breaks. Trade discounts should be taken to further reduce cost of goods sold.

Other possibilities for reducing cost of goods sold include surplus and special purchases and purchase of liquidated business inventories. Another method is to buy in bulk and repackage small items for resale. All of the methods mentioned thus far apply to retail, wholesale, service, and manufacturing businesses. Manufacturing businesses can further reduce the cost of goods sold by increasing manufacturing efficiency through better control, more productive workers, segmenting labor so that lower-paid skills can be employed, automating (sometimes offset by equipment cost), and reducing factory overhead expense (which is a part of cost of goods sold).

Decreasing expenses will increase net profits, although some expenses cannot be reduced without reducing sales volume. Earnings of salespeople and advertising expenses are typical examples. Most other expenses aren't directly related to sales, and if you can cut them, you increase net profit. Expense control will be dealt with in the next chapter.

The elements of the profit equation are interrelated. For example, if you increase unit prices, you may decrease sales; if you want to increase volume, you may have to reduce price or increase advertising expenses. If you decrease cost of goods sold by quantity purchase, you may incur interest expense and inventory expense, and deplete operating cash. This may result in loss of trade discounts and sales volume owing to improper inventory mix. Decreasing an expense may result in increasing another expense or in reducing volume. There are additional factors that center on the fact that some costs and expenses are *fixed* and are unrelated to unit volume while others are *variable* and are related to volume. This is the subject of a subsequent section in this chapter.

POINT 11-1: You can increase profit by increasing sales price per unit and/or volume of units sold, decreasing cost of goods sold, or decreasing expenses.

Activity Segregation

The preceding discussion has focused on total profit, sales, costs, and expenses. While a business may be profitable as a whole, portions of a business may not be profitable. For example, consider this case of an office-supply store that has an office-machine sales department (OMS), an office-supplies sales department (OSS), and an office-machine repair department (OMR). Here are the figures:

Profit	=	Sales	–	Cost of Goods Sold	–	Expense
(OMS) $15,000	=	100,000	–	60,000	–	25,000
(OSS) $12,000	=	70,000	–	36,000	–	22,000
(OMR) ($5,000)	=	48,000	–	40,000	–	13,000
Total $22,000	=	218,000	–	136,000	–	60,000

Elimination of the office-machine repair department (OMR) would seem to add $5,000 to profit, raising total profit to $27,000. But wait a minute. Part of the expense is attributable to the floor space occupied by the repair department. It's apparent that you need to look further. Space allocations are as follows:

Dept.	Square Feet	Profit/Square Foot
OMS	1,000	$15
OSS	3,000	$ 4
OMR	500	($10)
Total	4,500	$ 4.89
		(Not additive)

You divide profit of $22,000 by 4,500 square feet to get $4.89. Assume the space is rented at $10/square foot/year, including utilities. Then $5,000 in expense is charged to the service department. This is exactly equal to the loss! If you eliminated the service department and left the space idle, total profit would still be just $22,000.

However, if the space were allocated to office supplies and a $4 per square foot return could be realized, profit would not be $22,000 nor $27,000, but $29,000!

Or, if the space could be utilized for office-machine sales with a return of $15 per square foot, profit would be $7,500, bringing total profit to $34,500. You can't always realize equivalent yield by allocating additional space.

Another approach to activity segregation and the effect on total profit is based on turnover. For example, if you have two items of equal cost and one turns 10 times a year and the other turns 0.5 times a year, you reap 20 times the return on inventory from the first item over the second item. You would obviously want to maintain most of your inventory in fast-moving items. Yet you may have to stock the slower-moving ones in order to be able to service all of your customers. The point is, you should stock heavier on fast-movers, lighter on slow-movers. Thus, if you maintain a $10,000 inventory, try to get a respectable inventory balance, say $5,000 in the 10 times turnover items, $3,000 in the 5 times turnover items, and $2,000 in items with less than 5 times turnover.

You will sometimes latch onto a loser that you can't get rid of conveniently. When this occurs, you may have to take some hard lumps. For example, if you're in manufacturing and one of your product lines is losing \$20,000 a year and you're in debt to the tune of \$100,000 for investment on the equipment on that product line, you may only be able to salvage \$50,000 for the equipment. Thus, you have to take a \$50,000 loss to get out. That's hard to take. But if losses will be \$20,000 a year or more for succeeding years, you're well off to get out, because losses may continue and it may cost you more to get out in the future. Ideally you would want to turn this activity into a profitable activity, and then sell it at a profit. But if doing so will drain your other operations, you're well off to take your lumps and get out.

POINT 11-2: Examine business activities and profits on a segregated basis in order to improve the total profit picture. Eliminate or improve performance of losers. Avoid heavy inventories in slow-moving merchandise.

The Retail and Wholesale Business

For retail and wholesale businesses:

	Sales
–	Cost of goods sold
	Gross profit
–	Sales expenses
–	General and administrative (G&A) expenses
	Net profit

This format used in retail and wholesale businesses separates sales and general overhead, so you readily spot the cost makeup of each kind of expense. You allocate rent and utilities according to the amount of space utilized by each function. Phone, supplies, salaries, depreciation, and other expenses are allocated to the appropriate activity.

The format for a manufacturing business differs from this format, as you'll see shortly.

The retail trade uses special terms applicable to pricing. We don't feel it essential that you learn these terms, but we present them for future reference if needed. These terms and methods are used principally in large retail establishments. The *original sales price* is the price at which the product is first offered for sale to the customer. *The markup* is the margin between sales price and the cost (the gross margin), sometimes called *markon.* An *additional markup* is an increase above original sales price. A *markup cancellation* is a reduction in sales price after an additional markup (as long as the new price is not less than the original sales price). Additional markups less markup cancellations are *net mark-*

ups. A *markdown* is a reduction to below the original sales price. A *markdown cancellation* is an increase in sales price following a markdown. Markdowns less markdown cancellations are *net markdowns.*

Thus, a seasonal product that costs $40 and has an ***original sales price of $60*** has a *markup of $20 or 33.3 percent.* If an ***additional markup of $5*** is added in response to increased demand, selling price is $65. *The net markup now is $25 or 38.5 percent.* When demand subsides, the price might be dropped to $62, a *markup cancellation of $3,* leaving a *net markup* of $22. Then, as the end of the selling season approaches, the price might be reduced to $50, a *markup cancellation of $2 and a markdown of $10.*

The Manufacturing Business

A manufacturing business has three categories of inventory:

1. Raw materials
2. Work in process
3. Finished goods

The *raw-materials inventory* might include bar stock, sheet metal, lumber, fasteners, finishes, and other items purchased but not yet entered in actual product manufacture. The *work in process* includes partially completed assemblies and subassemblies. Note that inventory in this form contains direct labor as well as raw materials. Factory overhead is also allocated into the value of work in process. *Finished goods* include finished products ready to ship and the cost contains raw material, labor, and factory overhead costs.

The income statement for a manufacturing business takes this form:

Sales
– Direct material
– Direct labor
– Manufacturing overhead
Gross profit
– Sales expenses
– General and administrative expenses
Net profit

There are a number of accounting techniques applied to a manufacturing business for budgeting, planning, and control that aren't generally used in retail or wholesale businesses. These techniques are covered in courses in managerial accounting and cost accounting. Some of these techniques will be covered in this chapter.

POINT 11-3: Cost of goods sold in a manufacturing business includes raw-material costs, direct labor, and factory overhead.

The Service Business

A service business has similarities to retail and manufacturing businesses in that direct service labor is part of cost of goods sold, but not all hours paid for are sold. A point to watch in a service business is that labor paid by the hour still ticks up expense, although it may not be productively employed. Thus, if you can only bill thirty hours out of an employee's forty-hour week, and if he earns $6 an hour, he costs you $240 in base salary a week plus one-fiftieth times two weeks vacation pay ($9.60 a week), plus your 5.85 percent contribution to FICA (on $249.60), which is $14.60 for a total of $264.20. In addition you have unemployment insurance, worker's compensation, and other possible expenses which we'll neglect here. But even so, this employee's productive thirty hours' time that you sell costs at least $264.20/30, or $8.81. That is simply your direct cost of his time.

If you have indirect (G&A) expenses of $30,000 a year and sell 6,000 hours of service, it's costing you $5 in G&A overhead for each hour you sell. If you add that to $8.81, you get $13.81 in cost for each hour of labor sold! You'd better be billing the employee's time at a greater price than $13.81 an hour! (Many beginners in repair service businesses run on a rule of thumb of unknown origin that you bill a worker's time at twice his hourly rate. In this case it would be $12 or a loss of $1.81 for each hour billed; that's a total loss of $10,860 on 6,000 hours sold!

A service business derives profit from parts sales. Ignore those profits in developing your service-hour billing rate. Then, when you do your total profit planning, include parts profits to arrive at total planned profit.

> POINT 11-4: You are paid only for service labor billed. Therefore, develop a price for labor billed with allowance for idle time, your FICA contribution, fringe benefit costs, general overhead, and profit.

REVIEW EXERCISES 11-A

1. Discuss the four basic ways in which profit can be increased in a business.
2. Discuss the interactions between some of the elements that influence profit. Highlight changes that can have offsetting interactions.
3. A given product sells for $2 in quantities of less than twelve, $1.90 in quantities of less than forty-eight, and $1.80 in larger quantities. You sell ten units a month. If you sell the product for $3.50 a unit, what is the gross margin per unit if you buy in quantities of (a) ten, (b) twelve, (c) forty-eight. If you can buy thirteen and take the 2 percent/ten-day cash discount

or buy forty-eight but not take the discount, which is the most attractive alternative? Explain the reasons for your decision.

4. You own an air-conditioning sales and service business. Your building is 30' X 80'. You use 1,000 square feet for display and sales, 100 square feet for office, and the balance for shop and storage. You pay $300 a month rent. If you segregate expenses according to sales, shop, and G&A, how much rent expense would you allocate annually to each category?
5. You have a general garage. Your *body shop* and *general-repair* departments show a combined profit of $16,000. But your *front-end* department has shown a loss of $2,000 last year and $3,000 this year. Discuss your alternatives and make the qualified decision.
6. Discuss the differences in composition of cost of goods sold for retail, manufacturing, and service businesses.

COST, VOLUME, AND PROFIT

The cost/volume/profit concept and break-even analysis is used most frequently in manufacturing operations. But the concepts and techniques are applicable to retail, wholesale, and service businesses as well, and they find a wide range of application in business and financial decision making. The usefulness of these concepts and techniques is limited only by your imagination in applying them.

Fixed and Variable Costs

A *fixed cost* is a cost that tends to be insignificantly affected by the level of sales or business activity. Thus rent, depreciation, and utilities tend to remain relatively constant from month to month regardless of sales or business activity.

A *variable cost,* on the other hand, tends to vary with quantity produced or with sales. Typical variable costs are *cost of goods sold* and *sales commissions,* which vary with sales. The relationship is usually a direct relationship, or sufficiently direct to be assumed so for all practical purposes.

Assume that you're operating a small woodworking manufacturing company. Your G&A overhead is $300 a month. Your shop overhead is $200 a month. You manufacture decorative plaques that cost you $2 each for materials and direct labor. You can manufacture 1,000 units a month. What should you sell them for?

First, what are your fixed costs? G&A is $300 a month. What about the factory (shop) overhead of $200 a month? We said earlier that it was part of manufacturing cost of goods sold. Does that make it a variable cost? No. It's still a fixed cost. Don't confuse cost/volume/profit analysis with income accounting. Your fixed cost is $500. This is shown graphically in Figure 11-1a. Quantity is plotted along the horizontal axis and total cost along the vertical axis. Note that whether you make 10, 100, or 1,000 units, the fixed cost is still $500, as evidenced by the straight horizontal plot at the $500 total cost level.

Your variable costs are $2 a unit. If you make 10, the total variable cost is $20; if you make 1,000, the total variable cost is $2,000. This is shown graphi-

FIGURE 11-1 Cost vs. volume

(A) Fixed cost

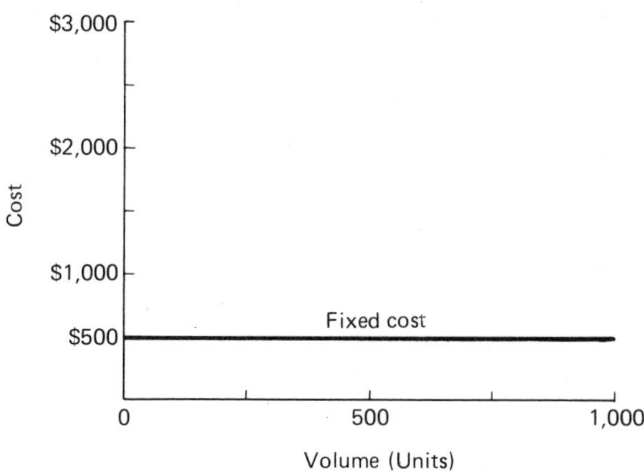

(B) Variable cost

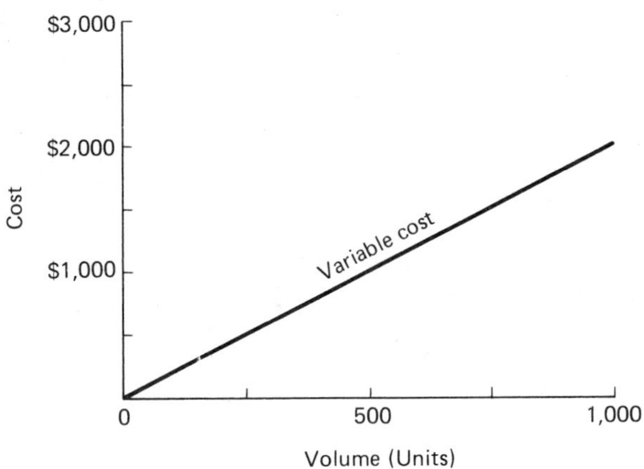

(C) Composite fixed and variable cost

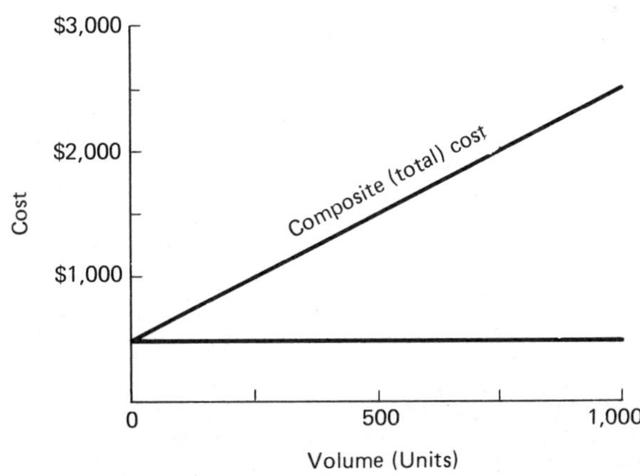

cally in Figure 11-1b. To plot the cost graph, you simply place a dot that coincides with 1,000 units on the horizontal scale and $2,000 on the vertical scale. Then you draw a straight line from zero to the dot. Now, you can pick any quantity on the horizontal axis, go straight up to the plotted line, and then straight across to the vertical axis to get the total cost. Thus, variable cost for 500 units is easily found to be $1,000. You can of course get the same result by computing 500 X $2 = $1,000.

Now, how do you make this do something more useful? Suppose we took the graph of Figure 11-1b and superimposed it, without the vertical scale, on Figure 11-1a *but* with the origin starting at the $500 mark as shown in Figure 11-1c. Now the cost of zero units is $500! And the cost of 1,000 units is $2,500. We've combined fixed and variable costs for any quantity to 1,000 units. Thus 10 units cost $520, 100 units cost $700, 500 units cost $1,500 and 1,000 units cost $2,500.

If we make 10 units, the average unit cost is $520/10, or $52 each; 100 units cost $700/100, or $7 a unit; 500 units cost $1,500/500, or $3 a unit; 1,000 units cost $2,500/1,000, or $2.50 each. This shows the cost-saving effect of high-quantity production.

This technique provides a valuable aid in arriving at a sound and profitable price. If you make only 100 units a month you must price them at $7 a unit plus profit. If you make 1,000 units a month you can sell them for considerably less since you must only price them at $2.50 a unit plus profit, and you can afford a smaller unit profit on the increased quantity.

This technique may be used to analyze a retail sales operation. One approach is to plot dollars along each axis to the same scale, with the horizontal corresponding to sales and the vertical to cost. Say fixed expense is $10,000 and your percentage cost of goods sold is 60 percent. The plot is shown in Figure 11-2.

FIGURE 11-2 Cost vs. volume

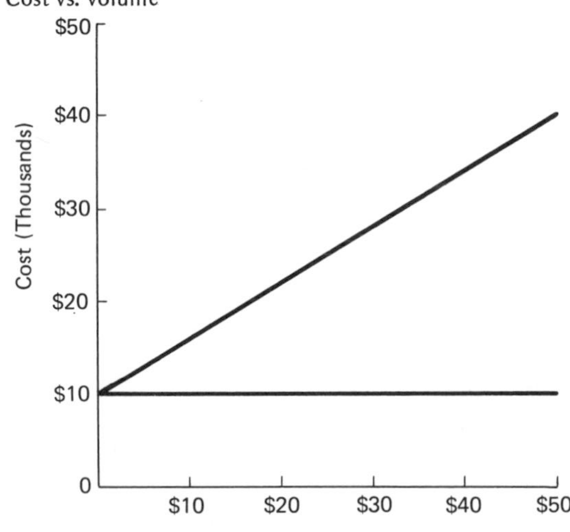

The fixed expense is plotted in at the $10,000 level. It is fixed regardless of sales volume. Your variable cost is 60 percent of sales cost, or zero for zero sales; and 60 percent of $50,000 for $50,000 sales, or $30,000 variable cost. You must add fixed costs to each of the variable costs to get total cost for each level, thus:

Total cost of zero sales = $10,000 + 0 = $10,000

Total cost of $50,000 sales = $10,000 + $30,000 = $40,000

You locate the dot for zero sales at $10,000 on the vertical axis, and go up from $50,000 on the horizontal till you reach $40,000 on the vertical axis to locate the second dot, and connect them.

POINT 11-5: Business costs (expenses) can be classified as fixed and variable. Fixed costs must be spread across the total volume produced or total volume sold, while variable costs vary directly with quantity produced or total sales.

Break-Even Analysis—Graphical

Example 1. Our graphical approach to total cost has neglected pricing thus far. In this subsection we introduce pricing. We start from Figure 11-1c by plotting a price line over our data. What if you decided to price the plaques at $4 each? How many would you have to sell to break even? How much would you make if you sold 1,000 plaques a month?

To plot the price line, one terminal will be 0,0 because zero sales at $4 a unit is zero. The second terminal dot for 1,000 units is $4 × 1,000 = $4,000. You plot the point at 1,000, $4,000. Connect the points with a dotted line. The result is shown in Figure 11-3.

FIGURE 11-3 Break-even analysis, example 1

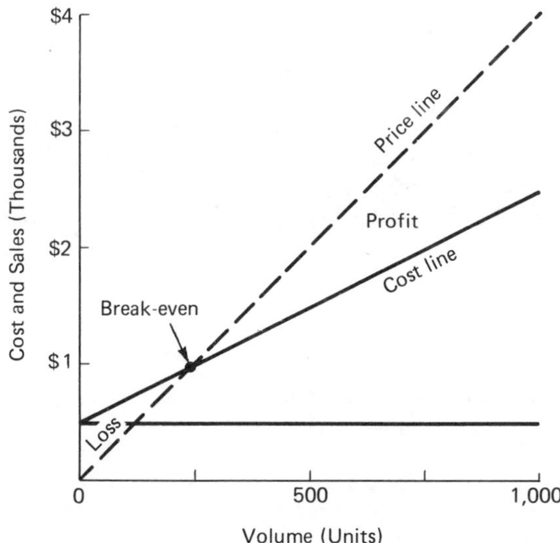

The point of intersection is the *break-even* point. It occurs at 250 units, for which total cost is $1,000 and total sales are $1,000. You can determine the profit for any quantity above break-even or the loss for any quantity below break-even by taking the *difference between sales and cost.* Thus, if you sell 1,000 units a month, profit is $4,000 minus $2,500, or $1,500.

Example 2. Examine the sales situation illustrated in Figure 11-2. The sales line is simply a 45-degree sloped line. The line starts at the graph origin (0,0) and the other plotting point is $50,000, $50,000. Draw the dotted line and you have Figure 11-4. The intersection occurs at $25,000, $25,000, the break-even point. Thus $25,000 in sales equals $10,000 fixed overhead plus $15,000 cost of goods sold. If sales hit $50,000, profit is $10,000, found from the graph by the method just described.

FIGURE 11-4 Break-even analysis, example 2

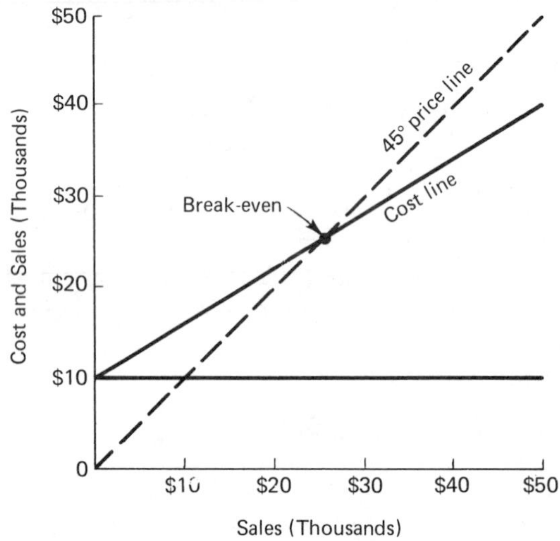

> POINT 11-6: Break-even occurs at the intersection of the price and cost lines on a cost, volume, profit graph. At that point, fixed cost plus volume times variable unit cost equals price per unit times volume.

Computational Techniques

You can perform break-even analysis without resorting to graphs. If we convert Point 11-6 into an equation we have:

1. Total Fixed Cost + (Volume × Unit Costs) = Volume × Unit Price

solving for *volume at break-even:*

2. Volume (Unit Price − Unit Cost) = Fixed Costs

3. $$\text{Break-Even Volume} = \frac{\text{Fixed Costs}}{\text{Unit Price} - \text{Unit Cost}}$$

Thus, with a fixed cost of \$500, a unit cost of \$2 and a unit price of \$4,

$$\text{Break-Even Volume} = \frac{\$500}{\$4 - \$2} = 250 \text{ units}$$

the same result arrived at graphically in Figure 11-3.

Equation 2 can be expanded to compute profit for any quantity:

4. $$\text{Profit} = \text{Volume (Unit Price} - \text{Unit Cost)} - \text{Fixed Costs}$$

Thus, with fixed cost = \$500, unit cost = \$2, unit price = \$4, and volume = 1,000 units,

$$\text{Profit} = \$1{,}000\ (\$4 - \$2) - \$500 = \$1{,}500$$

the same result as that obtained through the use of the graph.

Effects of Fixed and Variable Costs

A business with low fixed costs and a higher portion of its costs variable can operate profitably over a wide range of business levels. A business with high fixed cost and relatively low variable cost operates at a loss until a high level of business is achieved. Thus, if you can keep as many of your costs as possible variable, you minimize your risk of loss when sales are low. For example, the hourly service employee discussed earlier in this chapter was fixed cost because he was paid for a forty-hour week whether five, ten, twenty, thirty, or forty hours of his time was productive. (In the example given he averaged thirty productive hours a week.) If he had been paid only for productive hours, fixed cost would have been reduced and the business would have earned profit more directly related to time sold.

> POINT 11-7: Try to make as many of your costs (expenses) as possible variable rather than fixed for profitability over a wider range of business levels.

It isn't easy to convert some costs from fixed to variable costs. The service employee, for example, needs full pay to support a family. However, if moonlighters are available, you can usually make arrangements with them to work on direct-cost basis, for example, with a commission on billed work performed.

Another way to cut fixed costs is not to do work internally if it can be contracted to someone else. When a given type of work is infrequently required, there's no point in maintaining full-time internal capability; contract for these services as needed.

Paying commissions (rather than salaries) to salespeople is another way to convert from fixed cost to variable cost. The ups and downs of business can be smoothed out of the salesperson's income with a draw system. Under the draw system, the salesperson has a minimum weekly draw. When sales are slow, he draws more than he earns. When sales are good, he draws only his minimum until his excess commissions liquidate his earlier draws in excess of earned commissions.

REVIEW EXERCISES 11-B

1. A business has a fixed overhead of $20,000 a year. It sells goods that yield a gross margin of 35 percent. What are total costs on sales of $100,000?
2. Using the data of Problem 1, find the break-even point graphically.
3. Using the data of Problem 1, find the break-even point by computation.
4. Compute the profit with the data of Problem 1.
5. You have a manufacturing business that produces electronic precipitators. Direct cost is $2,000 per unit. Your fixed overhead is $100,000. Your selling price is $3,500 a unit. Compute break-even.
6. Using the data of Problem 5, and assuming production of 500 units per year, compute: (a) average unit cost, (b) total profit, (c) profit per unit.
7. A business that has high fixed costs relative to variable costs is called a *capital-intensive* business. Which of the following businesses are capital-intensive: (a) airline, (b) retail shoe store, (c) air-conditioning service, (d) manufacturer's representative, (e) building construction. Discuss your reasoning.
8. What can you do to convert fixed costs to variable costs in your business? Discuss.

PRICING, PROFIT, AND STABILITY

Up to this point we've examined a number of approaches for determining and controlling profit. These have included the basic profit equation (the income statement), the effects of changes in the components of the income statement (sales that involve price and volume, cost of goods sold, and expenses), cost/volume/profit analysis, and the effects of changing fixed and variable costs. Now we'll examine some additional factors in pricing and other means to increase profits and add stability to a business.

Pricing Economics

You maximize *unit* profit by reducing variable costs and fixed product costs, and getting high price. Then, you maximize *total* profit by increasing sales volume, decreasing any other fixed costs that enter into business expense, and eliminating unprofitable product lines. You further maximize *total after-tax profit* by planning investment and depreciation. This assumes you are not limited in the price you can get; but you are. The price you can get for a product is a function of variables which include:

1. The state of the economy (business conditions)
2. Competition
3. The economic characteristics of the product
4. Your marketing policy and strategy
5. Your location and market
6. Technology

The *state of the economy* determines whether the buyer or the seller most influences prices.[1] If the economy is down, buyers influence price by waiting to buy. In an ideal competitive situation, this drives prices down, and we say that it's a *buyer's market.* When the economy is booming in ideal competition, buyers compete for goods and prices are driven up. This is a *seller's market.* In reality, the market is never quite so purely competitive, and while prices fluctuate slightly, the general trend over the long term has been inflationary in the USA. Generally, you demand price increases when the economy is up without losing business, because your competitors will do likewise, and because more people have more money.

The *competition* will influence the price you can get, because if your price for a given product is greater than your competitor's *without reflecting an added value,* you'll lose some business. New competitors will enter the market and get some of it. Added value is the key for demanding and getting higher price. You add value by transforming raw materials into a product or by performing a service, such as bringing a product from producer to consumer. Your marketing strategy plays a key role in adding value.

The *economic characteristics* of the product influence the price you can ask for it. We say that demand for a product is *elastic* when a small change in price significantly changes demand. Demand is *inelastic* when changes in price do not significantly alter demand. Tobacco and liquor are classic examples of inelastic goods. People buy them in spite of heavy excise taxes that run costs up. Repair

[1] This is true for most businesses. Some businesses such as repair services and discount houses are relatively unaffected or even flourish in recessions. Prices in these businesses don't always respond to economic turns.

service is less elastic than new-car sales. When a good of considerable original value loses all its value temporarily as a result of minor malfunction, the cost of repair is generally so small compared to the original cost that the consumer orders repair without quibbling over cost. On the other hand, the consumer can live without a new car for several years by keeping the old one in repair, as evidenced by the decline in auto sales in 1974 and 1975.

Marketing policy and strategy influence the price you can demand in other ways. If you have a highly specialized line such as plumbing parts or a highly technical specialized line such as cameras, you can command a higher price by being able to give your customers expert advice in selection of purchase and "how-to-do-it" or "how-to-use-it." Other marketing strategies that add to value include stocking a broad line of merchandise to provide one source for a large number of items, many of which aren't purchased often. A customer is less likely to quibble about price on a low-priced item that he doesn't buy often. Another approach that permits high-price policy is to deal in "novelty" or "short-run" items, dropping items from your line as the novelty, demand, and price drop, and adding new items constantly. This is one of the toughest games around. Many office-supply businesses took beatings on electronic calculators because prices dropped much faster than they could unload high-priced inventory.

Your *location and market* have a major influence on pricing capability. If you're the only business of your kind in town, you have considerable pricing freedom. If you sell to a specific kind of customer and gain a reputation for servicing that type of customer, you may have plenty of pricing freedom.

Technology has a broad impact on prices. New and different technological products can generally command high prices at first, but as the technology improves, prices drop rapidly. Typical past examples are air conditioning, and more recently, electronic devices.

Don't get the impression that the basic idea in business is to get all the traffic will bear. Henry Ford summed the situation up well with this statement: "The man who will use his skill and constructive imagination to see *how much he can give for a dollar instead of how little he can give for a dollar* is bound to succeed."

POINT 11-8: The state of the economy, product characteristics, competition, sales strategy, location, market, and technology all influence your pricing freedom. Making more profit by getting higher prices is a significant challenge. An even greater challenge is to increase profits by finding ways to market products at lower prices.

Pricing for Profit

The message should be quite clear at this point. Prices must be adequate to generate profits, yet low enough to compete in the market. The nature of the influencing factors vary with product and type of business.

Here are some guidelines to follow in pricing for profit in a small business:

1. Standard branded merchandise usually has well-advertised prices. Sell at these prices unless you can add a service that increases value.
2. Specialized or unusual merchandise doesn't have widely advertised prices. Set your prices to provide a profitable return based on the analytical methods presented in this chapter.
3. Repair services are inelastic. Set your prices for profit based on the rule-of-thumb and analytical methods presented.
4. Manufactured products enjoy a special position if there is sufficient product differentiation with respect to other similar products or if they are sufficiently novel. Go for high margins. Use the analytical methods presented to price for profit as sales fall.

You must know your costs to price intelligently. And that means *all* of your costs and their nature. (The beginner in business is likely to overlook and to underestimate costs. Don't fall into this trap!)

SBA's *Small Marketers Aids,* No. 105, "A Pricing Checklist for Managers," asks almost fifty questions that will help to stimulate your thinking about pricing and pricing policy. It's free for the asking.

Competitive bidding was discussed in Chapter 4. While it would seem that competitive bidding places unusual pressure for low prices on the bidder, the situation is not too different from competing in the market with a product that has considerable price elasticity. If you're a manufacturer making a competitive bid, you'll go through the costing and pricing procedure outlined in Chapter 4. Follow the same costing procedure for a proprietary product of for a specific job that isn't sold on competitive bid. However, the market situation may give you leeway for a higher profit margin.

POINT 11-9: Price for profit by applying analytical techniques to your costs and knowing your costs. Insist on knowing true costs, and search out overlooked costs which eat profits.

REVIEW EXERCISES 11-C

1. What factors determine the maximum price you can charge for a product? Discuss.
2. What factors determine the minimum price you can charge for a product? Discuss.
3. Summarize your concept of the best way to develop profitable pricing in (a) a retail business, (b) a service business, (c) a manufacturing business.

PLANNING AND BUDGETING

Business planning and budgeting hinge on much of the knowledge and skill that you've acquired in this and preceding chapters. Your knowledge of financial statements, profitability, liquidity, return on investment, cash flow, money and interest, accounting, and analytical pricing and profit techniques all come into play in developing budgets.

Basic Planning and Budgeting

A basic approach to business planning and budgeting is to construct a pro forma income statement starting with estimated sales. This is much like what you did in the "Capital and Financing" section of Chapter 8. There, you used the representative percentage income statement for an electronics service shop to develop the capital requirements and income for a shop with $150,000 a year sales. In developing your own budget, you'd use past history of your own business, or if your business is new, a representative percentage income statement with your sales forecast (Chapter 4) for your estimate. This is a broad planning and budgeting approach.

To make the pro forma income statement approach more specific for planning purposes, you'd segregate your sales and expenses into department or product-line statements. You can expand the detail and get a more useful basis for control by preparing a monthly pro forma spread for each department or product line. (A spread is simply a tabular compilation of the income statement such as that shown for cash flow in Figure 11-5.)

POINT 11-10: The most basic financial planning document is a pro forma income statement. You can make it more specific and useful by separating product classifications and spreading it by months.

Income and Cash Flow

Income and cash flow are two separate things. Income is profit, but it doesn't necessarily rest in the business in the form of cash; it may be invested in accounts-receivable, inventory, or in retiring debt.

A simple example will illustrate the point. You borrow $5,000 to start your business. Your monthly payments are $161.34, and on the first payment $41.67 goes to interest and $119.67 to principal. Your projected sales for the first month are $2,000, cost of goods sold $1,200, and expenses other than interest are $400. You plan to increase inventory by $200 a month. The budget for the first month, *based on income,* is:

FIGURE 11-5 Cash budget

	CASH BUDGET	JAN.	FEB.	MAR.	APR.
A	Sales Forecast				
	Credit Sales, 20% Sales	1400	1600	2000	2400
	Cash Sales, 80% Sales	5600	6400	8000	9600
	Total Sales	7000	8000	10000	12000
B	Cash Collections				
	Cash Sales, this month	5600	6400	8000	9600
	Credit Sales, last month		1400	1600	2000
	Total Cash Collections	5600	7800	9600	11600
C	Purchases				
	End Inventory, this month	20000	21000	22000	23000
	Cost of Goods Sold, 60% Sales	4200	4800	6000	7200
	Total needs	24200	25800	28000	30200
	Beginning Inventory	19000	20000	21000	22000
	Total Purchases	5200	5800	7000	8200
D	Purchase Payments				
	50% Purchases, this month	2600	2900	3500	4100
	50% Purchases, last month		2600	2900	3500
	Total Payments	2600	5500	6400	7600
E	Other Variable Expense, 5% Sales	350	400	500	600
F	Fixed Expenses	2000	2000	2000	2000
G	Repayment of Debt Principal	200	200	200	200
H	Cash Beginning	5000	5450	5150	5650
I	Cash Collected, B	5600	7800	9600	11600
J	Total Cash Available	10600	13250	14750	17250
K	Cash Paid, D+E+F+G	5150	8100	9100	10400
L	Cash Balance	5450	5150	5650	6850
M	Borrowings – Short Term	—	—	—	—
N	End of Month Cash	5450	5150	5650	6850

Sales	$2,000.00	
Cost of goods sold	1,200.00	
Gross profit		$800.00
Expenses (including interest)		441.67
Net profit		$358.33

But the *cash flow* is quite different:

Sales	$2,000.00	
Purchases	1,400.00	
Cash before expense and debt service		$600.00
Expenses	$ 441.67	
Payment of principal on debt	119.67	
		561.34
Cash increase		$ 38.66

Thus, although a profit of $358.33 is projected, the bank account only grows by $38.66. The reason is that $200 went into inventory and $119.67 went to payment of debt principal.[2]

So, it's important to prepare a pro forma cash-flow projection type of budget *in addition* to the income-based budget discussed in the previous subsection.

> POINT 11-11: Income and cash flow are different quantities. Cash flow is total cash received minus total cash paid out during the period.

Cash Budget

Now we'll prepare an expanded cash-flow projection budget, or *cash budget,* for a business that sells on open account, buys on open account, and has debt in its financial structure. This is the generalized case, and although you may use cash-basis accounting in your business, you'll have to consider accounts-payable, notes-payable and accounts-receivable in your cash budget in order to estimate your cash position at the end of any month.

Refer to Figure 11-5. This is the first four months' portion of a cash budget. The sales forecast produces the number for total sales. Credit sales are estimated at 20 percent of total sales. This estimate will differ from business to business, and item A would show only total sales if all sales were for cash. Next, in item B, total cash collections consist of this month's cash sales plus collections on last month's credit sales. If collections are slower, this item might include, for example, 70 percent of last month's credit sales and 30 percent of credit sales for the month before that.

Item C develops purchases needed. Here it has been assumed that the inven-

[2] Depreciation is a source for additional cash flow since this expense does not require present cash. You may include it in expense on the cash flow pro forma if you offset it with "cash generated by depreciation." It is simpler not to include depreciation in the expenses thus leaving the cash balance unaffected.

tory should grow at the rate of $1,000 a month from the $19,000 starting inventory. Item D, purchase payments, assumes 50 percent of purchases are paid in the current month, and the balance in the next month. Other expenses, items E and F, are estimated as variable at 5 percent of sales (item E) with a $2,000 a month fixed base (item F). It has been assumed that expenses are paid immediately, but they can be handled on an open-account basis and treated in the same way purchases have been treated. Repayment of debt principal, item G, is shown as a separate item, because it is a separate balance-sheet item and because it may vary considerably.

Items H through N involve starting cash and the data developed under previous items. Item J, cash available, is simply starting cash plus cash collected. Item K is the sum of D, E, F, and G, all expense payments plus debt payments. Item J minus K gives the cash balance L. If this balance falls below a predetermined cash level, which in this case might be $5,000, you would borrow and show this under item M. End-of-month cash, item N, is simply L plus M.

In this example, sales have grown significantly from January's level of $7,000 to $12,000 in April. The income profit on January sales is as follows:

Sales	$7,000
Cost of goods sold	4,200
Gross profit	$2,800
Expenses	2,350
Profit	$ 450

It is mere coincidence that starting cash plus profit is equal to end-of-month cash. The April profit picture is much rosier:

Sales	$12,000
Cost of goods sold	7,200
Gross profit	$ 4,800
Expenses	2,600
Profit	$ 2,200

Note, however, that over four months of operation, forecast cash has only grown by $1,850 in spite of greater forecast total profits. The reason for this is that $1,000 a month is going into inventory growth. If a decline in sales were forecast for the later months of the year, you'd expect a decrease in inventory. You don't need a bigger inventory when sales decrease; the cash conservation that results keeps your cash position up, consequently maintaining a strong "acid-test" liquidity position.

POINT 11-12: A cash budget is essential in business planning to assure adequate liquidity and to plan financing.

REVIEW EXERCISES 11-D

1. Why should a budget be detailed with product lines and spread by months?
2. Why is a pro forma income statement spread inadequate for financial planning by itself?
3. What is the purpose of a cash budget?
4. What is the fundamental parameter on which a budget is based?
5. Why do income and cash budgets show different end numbers?

CASE: AN INVESTMENT DECISION INVOLVING PRICING AND PROFIT

Miriam Hooper wanted to go into the mail-order business. Her product was to be a booklet on home gardening. Her fixed cost for the booklet was to be $400 for typesetting. Her variable cost for printing the booklet was 35 cents a copy in quantities of 1,000 or more and her mailing costs were 15 cents a copy. She reasoned that $500 a month in classified ads in national magazines might bring in as many as 400 orders a month. She thought that she might attribute $1.25 in variable advertising costs to each booklet, but thought better of the idea. She set her fixed costs at $6,400 (the sum of the typesetting costs and the advertising costs for one year) and her variable costs at 50 cents a copy (printing plus mailing). She reasoned she had no further overhead because this was to be a moonlight operation conducted from her home. She felt that if she could break even on sales of 250 copies a month, the venture was worth pursuing. Instructive booklets of this type sell for $1 to $3 by mail order. After she analyzed the figures, she decided that the venture was questionable and decided not to pursue it.

REVIEW EXERCISES 11-E

1. Why did Miriam Hooper decide not to go into the mail-order business? Justify your answer with computations.
2. Do you believe Miriam's assumptions were correct? Discuss and justify the assumptions you would have made. Would your approach have altered the decision?
3. How might Miriam have altered her approach to make the venture more attractive? (Put your marketing hat on for this one.)

SUMMARY

Profit is essential for the continuing life and growth of a business. Profit can be maximized by increasing prices, increasing volume, decreasing cost of goods sold, and cutting expenses. Price increases are limited by the state of the economy, competition, the economic characteristics of the product, sales strategy, location and market, and technology. You can command higher prices by adding value.

Decreasing the cost of goods sold is limited by your purchasing ability, management capability, and external aspects of the market. Expense reduction is limited principally by your ability to manage, but has practical bottom limits where further reductions affect sales.

Improvements in each of the profit-maximizing factors can best be made by segregating activities and allocating expenses. This highlights the profitability of each activity so that poor producers can be improved or eliminated. Further opportunities for decreasing cost of goods sold and expenses can be highlighted by applying cost/volume/profit analysis.

Break-even analysis enables you to assess the effect of pricing and cost reductions on profit. Low fixed cost with major cost directly tied to sales provides stability. High fixed cost makes a business vulnerable to the ups and downs of business.

Profit and cash are two different things. Your business can be very profitable but can be cash-poor if profits are plowed into inventory, accounts-receivable, debt service, and fixed assets too rapidly. Therefore, you must concern yourself with cash flow as well as profit. Your planning should include income planning for profit and a *cash budget* for assuring yourself of adequate cash. Plans and budgets are only as good as your sales forecast, since sales are the fundamental parameter of any profit plan or budget.

KEY TERMS

Break-even
Cash budget
Cash flow
Elasticity
Finished goods
Fixed cost
Profit
Raw material
Unit cost
Unit price
Variable cost
Volume
Work in process

QUESTIONS AND PROBLEMS

1. Under what conditions can you charge higher unit prices for the products you sell?
2. Your appliance business contains an appliance sales department, a large-appliance repair department, and a small-appliance repair department which contribute $10,000, $7,000, and $2,000 respectively to total profit. Discuss the effects that eliminating the small-appliance repair department might have on total business and profits. There can be negative as well as positive effects.
3. Fixed costs are $1,000, variable costs are $1 per unit, and sales price is $2.50 per unit. What is the break-even point?
4. Using the data from Problem 3, how many units must you sell to make $1,000?
5. If the fixed cost in Problem 3 is $10,000, what is the break-even point?
6. Fixed expenses are $20,000. You can achieve $100,000 in sales with a 30 percent margin, but sales drop to $80,000 with a 40 percent margin. At which margin will you realize greater total profit?
7. Discuss price elasticity of goods and services. Give examples of highly elastic and inelastic goods and services.
8. What are the benefits and disadvantages of business specialization?
9. Extend the cash budget of Figure 11-5 for May assuming sales of $2,000, and knowing that an end-of-month cash position of $5,000 is to be maintained.
10. Is it likely that a cash budget would show such as sudden a dip in sales as that projected in Problem 9? If so, in what types of businesses and at what times of the year?
11. Compute income for the months of February and March using the data in and concerning Figure 11-5.

FIELD INVESTIGATION AND PROJECTS

1. Do research on budgeting and cash budgeting in a textbook on managerial accounting. Prepare a report.
2. (a) Prepare a cash budget using the ground rules and starting data used in developing the cash budget for Figure 11-5 for months January through June with sales as follows: January $5,000; February $6,000; March $8,000; April $7,000; May $10,000; June $9,000. Show repayment of short-term borrowings in brackets under item M.

(b) Determine the profit (or loss) for each month.

3. SBA's *Small Marketers Aids,* No. 146, deals with budgeting in a small firm. Obtain a copy, study it, and prepare a report.

*4. Develop a cash budget for the first year for the business you intend to start.

Purchasing, Inventory, and Expense Control

12

Profit can be increased by minimizing expenses. Expenses include cost of goods sold as well as the other expenses of doing business. Purchasing at lowest price, reducing inventory costs, and reducing other expenses all contribute to increased profits. Look for answers to these questions in this chapter:

1. How can I find sources for products, parts, supplies, and services?
2. How can I get best prices from suppliers?
3. What other methods can I employ to cut cost of goods sold?
4. How can I maintain adequate inventory without overstocking?
5. How much and how often should I order?
6. What methods and techniques can I use to cut expenses?
7. How can I maintain control of expenses?

PURCHASING

Astute purchasing is the key to decreasing the cost of goods sold, supply expense, and cost of fixed equipment. This involves finding sources, investigating prices, negotiating, buying merchandise that sells, and developing creative approaches for buying.

How to Find Sources

The first step in finding sources of supply for your business is a thorough study of your telephone directory Yellow Pages if you're located in a metropolitan area. If you're located in a small town in an outlying area, do your research in the Yellow Pages for the nearest large town. You can search for sources by

1. Product classification
2. Brand-name classification under products

In any event, your search begins under the appropriate product classification. Brand-name products usually appear under the appropriate classification with a 1- to 3-inch heading ad that lists the wholesaler or distributor followed by a list of retailers. If you're looking for products only without regard to brands, you'll usually find "wholesale," "distributor," and "parts and supplies–wholesale" listings. This research will provide the names of nearest suppliers.

Your next approach is through ads in trade magazines and journals. Manufacturers and distributors advertise in these.

Don't overlook the possibility of visiting people in a business similar to the one you're going to start, preferably in another town so that they won't regard you as a competitor. You may pick up business ideas as well as leads on sources of supply.

Chambers of commerce in larger cities can also be helpful. However, the Yellow Pages will probably yield as much or more information.

Your problem of supply takes on a more national flavor in some retail lines and in most manufacturing pursuits. For information on a broad array of national suppliers of merchandise as well as machinery and industrial equipment, make a trip to your library. Consult the *Thomas Register*[1] and *MacRae's Blue Book.*[2]

You can establish contact with wholesalers and distributors if you belong to local trade associations in larger cities. The suppliers usually maintain memberships and have representatives who attend the meetings. Vendor salespeople can often direct you to sources of products that they do not handle; don't overlook them as a source of information.

Offbeat sources of supply such as dealers in used equipment, surplus sellers, and liquidators can be located through the Yellow Pages, classified newspaper ads, and ads in trade papers. Some research in your library will produce the names of likely trade papers.

There are many sources of supply that do not advertise much. You usually find them by word of mouth from people in businesses similar to your own.

[1] *Thomas Register of American Manufacture* (New York: Thomas Publishing Co., published annually).

[2] *MacRae's Blue Book* (Western Springs, Ill.: MacRae.)

Trade shows provide another means for finding sources of suppliers. Suppliers rent booths manned by company salespeople with products on display and abundant supplies of giveaway literature. These shows are generally listed in trade papers.

Large cities generally have "merchandise marts" in which manufacturers, wholesalers, and distributors maintain showrooms year-round. Some cities have several marts, some devoted to specific kinds of goods such as apparel. These marts provide easy access to a large concentration of suppliers.

Although the emphasis in this section is on the mechanics of purchasing, bear in mind that you also wear a marketing hat in a small business. You have to select merchandise that will sell. In a repair service business, you must maintain higher stocks of parts that wear out most frequently. In a retail business, maintain highest stocks in fastest-moving items.

POINT 12-1: The Yellow Pages, trade papers, other businesses in your field, newspaper classified ads, and word of mouth will signal local sources of supply. Use your Library, the *Thomas Register,* and other directories for in-depth searches for sources.

Shopping and Negotiating

Your shopping begins after you've identified sources of supply. Prices are generally equal for a given branded product. However, you'll often find considerable difference in supplies and materials. You'll also find differences in selections. Some middlemen specialize in wholesaling and do not retail. Others do some retailing and operate "semi-wholesale"—that is, they sell below list, but not as low as the net you can get from a straight wholesaler. This is especially prevalent among small supply houses for plumbing, electrical, electronic, and automotive parts.

Your negotiating strength is practically zero with a wholesaler or distributor, but you may be able to do some good by buying in quantity. You can negotiate price on used equipment, large purchases, closeouts, purchases from individuals, and services furnished by moonlighters.

One approach to astute purchasing that many new businesspeople overlook is *pooling of purchasing power.* This approach was discussed in Chapter 3.

Negotiation is a give-and-take proposition. Chapter 3 should have provided considerable insight to this subject. The fundamental concept in negotiation is that *the first terms offered are unacceptable* and a counterproposal must be made. The *counterproposal* must call for better terms and conditions than you would accept, yet be sufficiently reasonable to keep the other party in the negotiations. A fundamental part of the psychological give and take is to demand some terms that you'll gladly forego, focus attention on these, and lose some of them gracefully while retaining the terms you really want. These are some of the things you can negotiate:

1. Price
2. Fast service
3. Who pays shipping, closing, or other supplemental costs
4. Quantity
5. Terms of payment including time, interest rates, and cash down payment
6. Guarantees and warranties
7. Renewals, extensions, and options

POINT 12-2: Shop for sources of supply that sell at low prices and provide good service; pool purchasing power to cut cost of goods sold and other expenses; negotiate for best terms wherever possible.

Factors Affecting Price

The prices you pay for services, equipment, supplies, and merchandise are functions of many factors. Delivery date can be a primary factor. For example, printed advertising material ordered on a rush basis would usually cost more than some material negotiated for thirty-day delivery with the printer working it in on "slack" time.

Quantity has already been noted as a factor affecting cost. Standardization is another factor. Standardized parts that will fit many makes and models cost less than specially made parts bought in small quantities. So if you're going to design a product for manufacture, you can cut costs by using standard parts already in production for other purposes.

Surplus military and industrial parts and products are available at a fraction of the production cost. If you can use surplus parts in products you manufacture or for services you provide, you can cut costs considerably. One possible problem is finding adequate sources for continued production. If you're in a large city with major production plants, you'll find that most of them operate surplus departments that dispose of surplus by auction, sealed bid, and negotiated sale. These outlets, incidentally, are good sources for used office, testing, and production equipment.

Season may have an effect on prices. For example, air-conditioning distributors generally put systems on sale to dealers in the fall and early winter to convert inventories into cash. Discounts may range from 5 to 25 percent of wholesale, depending on general business conditions, model changes, distributor's size of inventory, distributor's financial health, and special programs initiated by the manufacturer. Manufacturers and distributors also run special promotions, and you can save on merchandise purchases when these occur.

Substantial savings in equipment investment can be realized by purchasing used or reconditioned capital equipment. Sometimes "junked" equipment can be bought at junk prices and repaired with very little effort at colossal savings.

Demand affects price. When demand is down, prices usually drop; when demand increases, prices usually increase. If you can buy in periods of low demand, you can usually save.

To take advantage of many of the conditions that lower prices, you must buy in advance of need or in quantity. This runs contrary to the high-liquidity, high-cash preferences that add financial stability to business. Many businesses go under because of excess equipment and excess inventory. Not too many fail because they missed some good buys.

Service is another factor. If the distributor stocks a wide range of products and parts, if he delivers, and if he provides fast service, you may have to pay a premium. It may well be worth it if speedy service enables you to operate with a smaller inventory.

POINT 12-3: Demand, quantity, season, business conditions, vendor's condition, inventory levels, promotions, service, availability of surplus, closeouts, and specials all affect and determine the price at which you can buy.

Special Deals

The special-deal possibilities have been signaled in the previous subsections. Nevertheless, the subject merits additional attention.

Special-deal possibilities that have not been discussed include:

1. Barter
2. Lot purchases
3. Salvage

Barter is generally overlooked by larger businesses. The small businessperson, too, has forgotten much about the advantages of barter realized by his ancestors. If you can't sell for cash, why not barter for goods and services you need? The worst you should do in a barter deal is get dollar-for-dollar value for what you trade (including profit on your merchandise). You may do better. Thus, why not trade merchandise or services for store signs, store decorating and remodeling supplies, automotive and factory equipment, office equipment and supplies, and other business needs. In effect, you are lowering your expenses because you're getting profit you otherwise wouldn't realize and you're converting it directly into goods and services you'd have to buy anyway.

Lot purchases are sometimes risky, to say the least. You buy an assortment of merchandise or material that contains some product that you can use in your manufacturing operations or resell in your merchandising operations. You will not be able to use or sell some of it in your normal operation. A "lot" of merchandise is usually sold way below unit cost. The unusable part of the lot may be donated to a charity, sold wholesale, or sold at low-down promotion prices. For example, you might buy a lot consisting of 500 pairs of shoes. Half of them might be sufficiently out of style to be unsaleable. You donate these to charity and sell the rest at a big profit.

Salvage operations generally involve the cannibalization of unused obsolete equipment to recover valuable components and materials that can be used in manufacturing another product or for repairs of existing products. This involves more than mere purchasing, but the technique is worthy of note.

POINT 12-4: Innovative approaches to purchasing can reduce cost of goods sold and capital equipment. These include barter, lot purchases, salvage, and other innovations.

Paperwork

Purchasing paperwork need not be highly formalized for a small business. However, written purchasing records are essential. At a minimum, a purchase order should be written for each order placed. Most small businesses use duplicate order books obtained at office-supply stores. A purchase order is written even if the order is phoned in or given verbally to a salesperson who writes it up in his or her order book. Whether the order is mailed, phoned, or placed with a salesperson, the carbon duplicate is retained. It provides an accurate account of what has been ordered, and can be used to check against incoming merchandise shipments. When an order is received the purchase order may be filed as a filled order.

As a business grows, it must adopt more formalized purchasing procedures. The most complex and formal purchasing systems are generally found in large manufacturing concerns. Let's examine the procedures of a larger manufacturing purchasing department.

The process begins with *specifications* for materials, parts, or whatever else is to be ordered. The specification may be in the form of a brand name and number; it may refer to other specifications that are standard in the industry; it may also contain blueprints or samples or define performance requirements. A specification may be voluminous such as that for a locomotive or for a new building. Specifications for commonly used items are usually on file.

A *requisition,* shown in Figure 12-1, is submitted to the purchasing department by the department that is placing the order. The requisition specifies the item, quantity, and required delivery date. The purchasing department may place the order directly with a vendor, may solicit quotes by phone and place the order with the lowest bidder, or may go out for formal bids with a *request for quotation* (RFQ) or a *request for proposal* (RFP) in the case of a large and

FIGURE 12-1 Purchase requisition form

PURCHASE REQUISITION

ROUTING:

INITIATED BY	DELIVER TO	PURPOSE
APPROVAL — DEPT.	DATE WRITTEN	SUGGESTED SOURCES
FINAL APPROVAL	DATE NEEDED	
PURCHASING AGENT		

QUANTITY	ITEM NUMBER	DESCRIPTION	✓	✓	UNIT COST	COST

AUTHORIZED SIGNATURE	DEPT.	P.O. NO.	TOTAL COST

complex product or project. The *bids* are evaluated, and a *purchase order* is placed, or in some cases negotiations are continued until a *firm contract* is developed.

In the case of a complex product or project, the purchaser may make trips to the vendor's plant to assure himself that the project is on schedule and that specifications are met. *Acceptance testing* by the purchaser may be part of the contract.

A purchasing department maintains files of catalogs, lists of acceptable sources of supply, requests for quotations, bids, and purchase orders. Your mini-business purchasing activity should do the same, on a smaller scale of course.

POINT 12-5: Purchasing records are essential to keep track of orders and prevent overordering.

REVIEW EXERCISES 12-A

1. Discuss the methods you would use to discover sources of supply for your business.
2. Describe the kinds of purchases and the kinds of sellers that are most susceptible to negotiation.
3. What factors influence prices?
4. Discuss barter, lost purchases, salvage, and purchase pooling.

5. What is the minimum purchasing paperwork required for a small business? How is it used?
6. Describe the steps and alternatives in purchasing practiced by larger companies.

INVENTORY

You should have an aversion to building a large inventory, since this ties up cash—we've emphasized this point steadily. You should also be aware of the possible economies of quantity, lot, and special buys. And, you don't want to run out. These considerations tend to fight low inventory. This section will address the problems of inventory costs, economic order quantity, when to order, and inventory records.

Cost of Inventory

Inventory is a substantial part of capital investment in your business. Inventory may run as high as 50 to 60 percent of total assets in a well-run retail business. You certainly don't want to tie up more money in inventory than is necessary.

The costs of carrying inventory are high. They include these items:

1. Interest on inventory investment
2. Depreciation, obsolescence, and pilferage
3. Internal handling costs
4. Taxes and insurance
5. Storage costs

The *cost of carrying inventory* is in the 10 to 25 percent range of actual inventory cost. So, you not only have money tied up in inventory; the inventory also "eats" by incurring expense.

You can decrease the amount of inventory required by increasing the number of times that you turn it. Thus, a $50,000 inventory turning once a year at a 20 percent inventory carrying cost would eat up $10,000, while a $10,000 inventory turning five times a year would eat up only $1,000 in carrying costs. However, if the inventory is inadequate, you'll run out of stock and lose sales. There also is a cost of ordering attached to each order, and if you reorder too frequently, ordering costs may become excessive. Expedited orders occasioned by low inventories are more costly than routine orders, and hence tend to force ordering costs higher. Since the process of ordering, transmitting the order, getting it filled, having it delivered, and placing it in stock takes time, significant business can be lost during out-of-stock periods.

This highlights an important consideration in selecting suppliers. A supplier located close to you—one who has his own delivery service and processes orders quickly—is a valuable aid in maintaining low inventories, keeping inventory carrying costs down, and in holding transportation costs down. If his price is not always the lowest, he still may be the best choice as a primary supplier.

POINT 12-6: The goals of maintaining low inventory, being able to maintain adequate stock, and minimizing ordering costs conflict. A compromise that caters to all three requirements must be developed.

Ordering Computation

The matters of when to order, how much to order, and how often to order can be reduced to mathematical formulas. These formulas are of maximum value in large operations where large varieties of goods and large quantities are involved. They are useful to you as a small businessperson in developing ordering levels for your fastest-moving goods; and whether you use the formulas or not to establish *economic order quantities,* number of *orders to place,* and *ordering point,* they provide a valuable insight to inventory behavior.

Figure 12-2 shows idealized inventory behavior. Assume an item for which you've established a maximum inventory level of twenty-five units. You want to maintain a safety stock of five units. You can reorder when inventory falls to ten units and ordinarily expect delivery by the time you're down to five units. So you order twenty units each time.

The *economic order quantity* (EOQ) is the quantity that can most economically be ordered at a time, considering sales in units per year (U), cost per order (O), unit price (P), and percentage carrying cost of goods (C). The formula is:

FIGURE 12-2 Inventory behavior

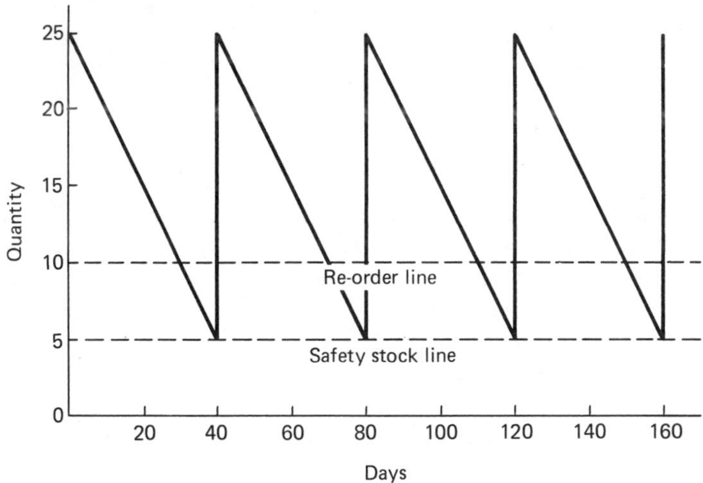

$$EOQ = \sqrt{\frac{2UO}{PC}}$$

As an example, assume that 180 units a year are sold (U), cost per order is $1 (O), unit price is $6 (P), and carrying cost is 15 percent (C). Then:

$$EOQ = \sqrt{\frac{2\,(180)\,(1)}{(6)\,(.15)}}$$

$$EOQ = \sqrt{\frac{360}{.9}}$$

$$EOQ = \sqrt{400}$$

$$EOQ = 20 \text{ units}$$

Figure 12-2 shows the behavior for this example.

Average inventory is EOQ divided by two plus safety stock. In this case, average inventory is fifteen units. The number of orders per year is U divided by EOQ, which is 180/20, or nine orders per year in this example.

Sales per day is 180/360, or one unit every two days. If it takes ten days to fill an order, you would sell five units during the time the order is being filled, so the reorder point is at ten units (allowing for five units safety stock).

Total cost of ordering for the year is order cost times number of orders: 9 X $1, or $9. Total annual carrying cost is the number of inventories (orders) times the average unit cost times carrying cost: 9 X 15 X $6 X .15, or $121.50.

POINT 12-7: You can compute economic order quantity (EOQ) to maximize tradeoffs between order cost and carrying cost. You can also develop order-point quantity, average inventory, number of orders per year, and total order and carrying costs by the methods shown.

Inventory Records and Management

Inventory record systems are detailed and sophisticated in large businesses. Most small-business beginners use hit-and-miss "guessing" methods for placing orders. Some method is essential if you want to hold inventory costs down and avoid losing sales. Method tends to make reordering more routine and prevents running out of stock by signaling a need for reorder.

Inventory management consists of getting materials or merchandise of each kind needed into the plant or store when they're needed, and in being sure that the inventory is being applied to produce a profit. So, you need to know:

1. What to order
2. How much to order

3. When to order
4. Price you can pay

Records are fundamental to knowing these things.

The system that most businesses use to keep inventory records that provide reorder signals is the ***perpetual inventory system.*** In this system, a card such as that shown in Figure 12-3 is used for each item detailed by size, color, and so forth. Receipt of merchandise and sales are posted on the card and the balance on hand is available at a glance. Sales can be recorded from sales slips or tags attached to the merchandise (these are detached by the clerk when the merchandise is sold). The amount of work and time required is great. Large businesses reduce the labor with automated inventory systems.

FIGURE 12-3 Perpetual inventory record form

INVENTORY RECORD CARD

No.	Monthly Value								
Item	Jan.	$		May	$		Sept.	$	
	Feb.	$		June	$		Oct.	$	
Cost Per Unit	Mar.	$		July	$		Nov.	$	
Selling Price Per Unit	Apr.	$		Aug.	$		Dec.	$	

Date	Rec'd	Sold	Balance	Date	Rec'd	Sold	Balance	Date	Rec'd	Sold	Balance

Small businesses can sometimes use a monthly physical inventory system with greater ease and effort than is involved in a perpetual system. A monthly inventory would develop data as shown in Figure 12-4. This data can be filed for later use in developing better ordering patterns.

Another alternative is a combination of the perpetual system, the physical system, and the visual method. The perpetual system can be used for slower-

FIGURE 12-4 Physical inventory

	Item 1	Item 2
On hand Feb. 1	20	15
Received during month	12	15
Total	32	30
On hand Mar. 1	13	16
Sold During Month	19	14

moving merchandise, the physical system for faster-moving merchandise, and the visual system for fastest-moving merchandise. The visual system can be used for merchandise that stacks neatly on shelves where all inventory of a given item is shelved as received. With this method, reorder point and order size is printed on the shelf price tag. The merchandise is scanned periodically, say once a week, and whenever merchandise on the shelf is at or below the reorder point, a new order is placed.

The *trouble with informal systems* is that they don't provide records and your chances of maintaining optimum inventory is small. The *trouble with formal systems* in a mini business is that they can be cumbersome and involve an inordinate amount of time.

Merchandise that deteriorates with time poses a special problem. You can cope with it by dating it. Thus 3/7 would indicate the merchandise was received in March 1977. Merchandise that has a very short shelf life might be dated 3/7 to indicate receipt March 7 of the current year. The oldest merchandise is sold first. In a self-service situation, new merchandise is stacked beneath the older merchandise on the premise that the customer picks up merchandise on the top of the stack.

POINT 12-8: Records and inventory management are essential for adding to profit through inventory and expense reduction. However, the effort required to develop formal inventory control systems may cost more than it is worth in a very small business. An informal system, at least, is essential.

Inventory Turnover

Rapid inventory turnover is a major goal in any business. In Chapter 7 we determined inventory turnover to be

$$\frac{\text{Cost of Goods Sold}}{\text{Average Inventory at Cost}} \text{ or } \frac{\text{Sales at Retail}}{\text{Average Inventory at Retail}}$$

Our interest in Chapter 7 was in the total picture. In inventory management and control, you're interested in the turnover of each part of your inventory. An item-by-item manual analysis might be too cumbersome for a small business. But a reasonable division into departments or type of activity is easy to handle and will prove useful.[3] Thus, a business selling and servicing vacuum cleaners, sewing machines, and air-conditioning equipment might have the following situation:

	Cost of Goods Sold	*Average Inventory*	*Turnover*
Sewing machines	$ 40,000	$10,000	4
Air-conditioning equipment	15,000	5,000	3
Vacuum cleaners	30,000	5,000	6
Sewing-machine parts	4,500	1,500	3
Air-conditioning parts	10,000	2,000	5
Vacuum-cleaner parts	4,000	1,000	4
Composite	$103,500	$24,500	4.22

If the turnovers under 5 can be increased to 5, the total turnover will increase.

Thus, if inventory is decreased to $8,000 in sewing machines, $3,000 in air conditioning, $900 in sewing-maching parts, and $800 in vacuum-cleaner parts—the inventory values that would result in turnover ratios of 5 for these respective lines—total inventory reduction would be $2,000 plus $2,000 plus $600 plus $200, or $4,800. *This is the amount of money that would be freed for other uses.* It would also result in an inventory carrying-cost reduction. The new turnover ratio on the composite would be $103,500 divided by $19,700, or 5.25 as compared to the previous 4.22. Note also that the decreased investment causes the percentage rate of return on investment to increase.

Practical limitations might make reductions in inventory impractical in some of the lines. For example, reductions of the sewing-maching parts and vacuum-cleaner parts might be impractical because a wide range of parts is required. However, these inventories aren't too significant a part of total inventory, and have a very small effect on total inventory investment and the composite turnover. The reductions in the sewing-maching and air-conditioning equipment inventory would have substantial effects on turnover ratio.

A dramatic story of what can be accomplished through the use of data and astute inventory management was told in an IBM ad that appeared in the July 15, 1976 issue of the *Wall Street Journal.* The story concerned Fingerhut Corporation, a Minnesota mail-order house that cut inventory by about 60 percent—from $48 million to $19 million—in two years. Over that two-year period, the

[3] Activity segregation is essential in the analysis of a business. This approach is used repeatedly in business in assessing profitability, rate of return, floor-space productivity, turnover, and other business parameters. For this reason we emphasize this approach in several chapters.

company was able to cut its total debt by about $57 million! About $29 million of that came from inventory reduction, and some of it from inventory carrying-cost savings.

POINT 12-9: Optimize turnover ratio to increase return on inventory investment. Break activities into lines or departments to highlight differences in turnover and to make improvements.

REVIEW EXERCISES 12-B

1. Why should inventory costs be held to a minimum?
2. What are the components of inventory carrying costs?
3. What is the danger of carrying too low a level of inventory?
4. How can you determine when to order?
5. You sell 300 units of a given item a year. The cost per order is $5, unit price is $20, and carrying cost is 20 percent. What is the economic order quantity?
6. Using the data of Problem 5, safety stock is ten units. What is average inventory?
7. Discuss the goals of inventory management.
8. Discuss the pros and cons of using formal and informal inventory record systems in mini businesses.
9. Why is it important to examine inventory turnover behavior on a department or line basis in your business? Discuss.

EXPENSE CONTROL

In the previous sections of this chapter we've concentrated our efforts on reducing the cost of goods sold and reducing expenses associated with inventory handling and merchandise purchasing. In this section, we'll attack the broad spectrum of expense reduction.

Interim Income Statement Signals

Interim income statements are the first broad step in developing business control information. Monthly income statements present the financial facts of your business and provide breakdowns in expense data that permit you to analyze costs and cut them.

As a first step, you can compare your interim income statements to your pro forma income statement plans (discussed in the previous chapter). Investigate deviations from the plan. If a given item of expense exceeds your budget, try to find out why.

The next step is to convert your interim income statement into a percentage income statement and compare it to industry standards. Any significant upward deviation in any of your expense items from industry standards should be examined. Although standard ratios may not give true apples-to-apples comparisons for reasons noted in Chapter 8, they shouldn't be overlooked.

A month-to-month comparison should be made also. This will highlight expenses that are out of line or increasing and enable you to establish seasonal trends over the years.

POINT 12-10: Prepare monthly income statements and analyze them to detect and reduce out-of-line and rising expenses.

Cutting Location and Utility Costs

Location costs can be held to very low figures for manufacturing, repair service, and wholesale operations because they can be housed in low-rent locations. A substandard location or an old building usually isn't a liability for businesses of this type because they don't rely on store traffic. Many businesses get started in old buildings. Digital Equipment, now a sizable computer company, started in a factory building about a hundred years old in the late 1950s. There are rental bargains around in old retail buildings, garages, service stations, and warehouses. Owners of these buildings generally are willing to rent them at substandard rates just to have some income and to have someone taking care of the building. You won't often find these low-rent buildings advertised in the classifieds. You generally find them either through "for rent" signs on the buildings or by checking the city or county tax departments for the owner of a given address where you've determined there's a vacant building.

Your possibilities are generally better in a larger town. However, you may find a smaller town where the old business district is semi-deserted. If you find one of these, you'll find unusually low rents. You can often find several small towns with almost empty old business districts scattered within fifty miles of most cities and county seats.

We've mentioned sharing a building. And, of course, there's always your garage, attic, or basement if your business is small enough and zoning doesn't limit you.

Finding a low-cost location for a retail business is generally a little more difficult. You want to be where the people are, and the rents are usually higher in these locations. However, some retail businesses do well in old houses in areas that have been rezoned "business," "commercial," or "central area." Some old service station sites have been successfully converted to other uses.

Repair service businesses can often locate within a retail business free or by trading some service for rent. For example, a furniture dealer who sells appliances may permit a appliance repair person to locate in the back of his store free just to have someone available for quick service.

If you locate in a low-rent district, you may still be able to present a top-notch appearance to the public by dressing up the front of the building and creating an attractive front office or display room. Another approach of doing retail business in a low-rent district is to advertise "low overhead."

What does rent cost? It depends on your local area. In the Dallas-Fort Worth Metroplex in 1977, rents in smaller industrial parks (usually 10 percent office and 90 percent warehouse type buildings) ran from about $1 to $3 a square foot per year. Retail space in suburban downtown areas ran from about $2 to $5 per square foot per year. Shopping-center space ran from $4 (in small centers) to $12 (in the large centers) a square foot per year with percentage of sales kickers in some cases.[4] The cheapest deals (low-rent district locations) ran as low as about 50 cents a square foot a year on buildings needing some repair at tenant expense. These deals are not easy to find.

Mail-order businesses, manufacturer's rep operations, and service businesses in fields such as insurance can be located in your home in some situations or in upstairs offices in older buildings at low rents. Better office space (with utilities and janitorial service furnished) ran from about $4 to $10 a square foot a year in the Dallas area in 1977, but there was some space in older buildings available for as little as $2 a square foot!

Utility costs can be cut if you

1. Turn services off when they are not in use
2. Practice proper maintenance of fixtures and system
3. Use energy-conserving devices and systems

You can lose substantial money on utilities. Dripping faucets (especially hot water faucets), incandescent lighting, inadequate wiring, inefficient air-conditioning systems, poorly insulated buildings, and large glass areas can run utility bills way up. Cost-saving moves include repairs of leaks, replacement of faucet washers or faucets when drips occur, use of fluorescent lighting, adequate wiring, high-efficiency air-conditioning systems, regular cleaning of air-conditioning condenser and evaporator coils, adequate building insulation, operation of heat at 66-degree thermostat setting, operating of cooling at 74- to 76-degree thermostat setting, use of minimum-security lighting at night, time switches on electric signs, and reflective treatment of glass spaces not utilized for display purposes.

[4] The figures cited were supplied by real estate brokers active in space leasing.

POINT 12-11: Location and space cost savings can be realized for manufacturing and service operations by locating in low-rent districts. Retail operations generally require more expensive locations to be successful.

Cutting Wage and Salary Costs

There are several approaches to cutting wage and salary costs. The first step is to analyze each job and determine whether or not it is necessary. If it isn't, eliminate it, and combine minor functions that must be performed into other jobs. Work that occurs at infrequent intervals or requires special skills can often be contracted to someone else at substantial annual savings.

The key to salary and wage savings is to try to tie costs directly to productive effort. If you can hire sales and service employees on a commission basis, you've made a step in this direction. Temporary help can be hired to handle peak loads without strapping your payroll for a whole year. Moonlighters can be employed to provide special skills and do work that will utilize your facilities after regular working hours.

Avoid organizational frills. Too often a small businessperson gets overly optimistic about his or her business, sets up a fancy organization chart, and fills the jobs at high fixed salaries. Many of the people in the organization are unnecessary and don't really have much to do. They waste the time of others by "conferencing" and unless the owner gets smart, he'll ultimately be in bankruptcy. Often, unnecessary personnel will "make work" just to keep busy and justify their jobs. Keep your organization lean, and expect everyone, including yourself, to work productively. If employees can respect you, and if they have the basic traits you want in your employees, they will respond and prosper with the business. Promote the loyal, hard-working employees, and let them know verbally and by action that you appreciate them. Get rid of deadwood fast!

Other Expense Reductions

You can reduce your operating costs by making your equipment work longer and harder. This can be done by using shifts if feasible, and by maintaining equipment properly to avoid expensive repair bills and to prolong life. Cut waste wherever possible. Sell scrap and junk to a dealer rather than throwing it away. Watch for salvageable material that may be going out the back door as scrap. For example, if you ship or deliver merchandise, save corrugated cardboard boxes from incoming shipments to use again for outgoing merchandise. Chemical drums, large cans, and other containers may be worth salvaging. Factory and repair-shop sweepings often contain dropped and spilled hardware that may be worth salvaging. Sell it in assortments if separating would be too costly.

Office supplies including printed forms, stationery, and paper can account for large unnecessary expenses. To keep these costs down, keep your inventory low to maintain better control. Pencils, pens, and other office supplies tend to "walk off" faster when there's a plentiful supply. Paper and printing costs are especially high. Get forms organized correctly before you have them printed, to avoid costly revisions and reprinting. Encourage employees to use the back of out-of-date circulars and forms for scratch paper rather than expensive bond or stationery. Protect office supplies from dirt and unnecessary handling to avoid spoilage. File folders are expensive and can be used again if you paste clean labels over the old tabs.

Study your methods of handling materials and merchandise, your storage system, your manufacturing or service methods, and your paper procedures to locate methods for cutting costs. The possibilities of cutting operating costs in manufacturing and service businesses are usually great because of the repetitive nature of the work and the direct overhead costs involved.

You can keep telephone costs at a minimum by holding down long-distance calls, using direct dialing station to station, and avoiding information calls. Sometimes a long-distance telephone call is cheaper and more effective than a letter. Letters are costly, and local communications should be handled by phone whenever possible.

It is possible to cut transportation costs and improve employee efficiency by grouping service calls geographically. Salespeople should also be encouraged to organize their calls geographically.

Cut money costs by discounting bills and avoiding bank mimimum deposit or overdraft charges. Borrow only as required and only as much as is needed to minimize interest charges. If you have an unusual cash build-up and no immediate need for the money, put it in CDs or Treasury bills so that it can earn interest. See your banker for details.

There are untold possibilities for cutting expenses in a business. While those listed here may be helpful as starting ideas, the only way you can minimize expenses in your business is by constant surveillance, review, and control. Some of the points cited here may seem trivial. But the sum of numerous trivial savings can add up to a large amount.

Expense control doesn't always call for elimination or reduction of an expense in the absolute sense. Such items as rent, advertising, and salespeople's expenses should be considered in terms of their effectiveness. Thus, higher rent is justified if the location more than pays the difference in extra business generated. The same applies to advertising and salespeople's expenses. If $100 in advertising only generates enough profit to cover its cost, it's ineffective. If $100 in advertising generates $1,000 in profit, it's very effective.

POINT 12-12: Cut expenses by examining and reviewing all expense items continuously; by controlling supplies, waste, and scrappage; and by finding cheaper ways to do things.

REVIEW EXERCISES 12-C

1. Discuss the use of interim income statements and your pro forma income statement budget in finding and correcting excessive expenses. What are the strengths and weaknesses of this method?
2. Discuss the use of industry income statements and ratios in evaluating your interim income statement performance. What are the strengths and weaknesses of this method?
3. How can you reduce employee costs in your business?
4. List specific preventative maintenance measures you can take to prolong the life of the following: (1) a truck, (2) an air conditioner, (3) a typewriter, (4) a motor-driven mechanical machine such as a drill press or a lathe.
5. Some expenses cannot be reduced without hurting business. List expenses in this category and discuss what you can do about them.
6. How can you manage your cash to cut expenses and increase profits?

CASE: SPECULATION IN PURCHASING

Steve Robertson had been in the building materials and lumberyard business for two years. He had been buying materials on a slow hand-to-mouth basis and rarely had anything in inventory over forty-five days. He was turning good profits, but in 1973 prices began to rise rapidly. Steve passed the price increases on to his customers and did not lose any customers as a result. One evening as he was going over the latest price increases, Steve decided that he could make much more money if he bought in large quantities at the current prices and then increased his retail prices, still working from inventory obtained at the lower current wholesale prices. The next day he arranged with his suppliers to increase his open-account credit from $40,000 to $80,000 and he simultaneously arranged a $50,000 line of credit with his bank based on prime rate plus 1½ percent. He also borrowed $10,000 from a finance company at a stiff interest rate, using his personal automobiles and boat as collateral. He slowed payment on his payables and speeded collection of his receivables. He was able to order $175,000 worth of materials (his normal inventory was $50,000) and felt that he could handle payment with the increased profits, and borrowed funds, and the accelerated cash inflow and slowed outflow. He placed $175,000 in orders the next day. He spent $5,000 on storage sheds for the additional material.

Prices advanced a month later and Steve found himself earning extra profits. He ordered more and extended himself further. Prices advanced again the next month, and then something happened. Sales went down as his customers put off remodeling and repair projects in the face of high prices. This didn't bother

Steve too much because his total gross profit was as good as it had been before his purchase. But the interest on his debt service reduced his net. He decided not to order except to replace out-of-stock items.

Prices didn't increase the next month as sales skidded further and two months later prices dropped. By this time Steve was falling behind on his payments to the bank, and was unable to replace out-of-stock items in his inventory. The next month retail prices dropped again, but sales were still skidding. Steve felt he was in trouble and went to see his banker. The banker suggested he hold a big clearance sale to keep from losing his business. He did, and the results were poor but adequate. With the proceeds and a renegotiation of the balance on his loan at the bank, he squeaked through.

Steve Robertson is the shrewdest buyer in Dallas County these days, and 70 percent of his inventory turns every thirty days.

REVIEW EXERCISES 12-D

1. Should a businessperson speculate in the raw materials he uses in manufacturing or in the goods he sells? Explain your answer.
2. Is there any way a businessperson can protect himself against price changes? *Hint:* Look up "hedging."
3. Did Steve violate any rules of financing? Explain.
4. Is a forty-five day inventory turnover in a building supply business excellent, average, or poor? Back your answer with evidence.
5. What do you think about Steve's reasoning that if prices are going up, they'll continue to go up? Discuss. Is there any way to predict price trends that you know of or think of as plausible?

SUMMARY

Astute purchasing cuts cost of goods sold. Locate sources with the help of the Yellow Pages, *Thomas Register, MacRae's Blue Book,* discussion with other businesspeople, newspaper classified ads, and trade journal ads. Buy in quantity and negotiate for best price whenever possible. Consider the value of special services and advantages such as fast service, free delivery, and broad stocks when evaluating a wholesaler's prices.

Purchasing records are essential for inventory control and management. Written records should be kept even if the order is phoned in or taken by a salesperson.

Inventory management should strive to maintain the lowest possible inventory and yet avoid "running out." The cost of carrying inventory is 10 to 25 percent of the cost of inventory. However, it costs money to order. An approach to optimizing inventory and ordering expense is the economic order quantity (EOQ). You can use a perpetual inventory system to maintain up-to-date inventory information, but a mini business cannot always afford this. Other methods for keeping track of inventory include monthly physical counts, or a combination of physical count, visual reorder, and perpetual system with portions of the stock under the most appropriate system. Rapid inventory turnover adds to profits. You can increase turnover by minimizing stocks of slow-moving items.

You can control other expenses by developing departmentalized interim income statements, analyzing them, and taking timely corrective measures. Location costs can be minimized by using low-rent locations for businesses such as manufacturing and some service operations that do not rely on walk-in traffic. Space pooling is another approach to low rent. Mail-order businesses and manufacturer's rep operations can be run from low-rent locations, and in many cases from your home.

Utility costs can be cut if preventative maintenance and surveillance is exercised. Supply costs can be cut by control of supply ordering and use. Office-supply and paper costs in particular can get out of hand in a small business if they're not controlled. Wage and salary costs can be reduced if compensation is directly related to billings wherever possible, and if jobs that do not come up frequently are subcontracted. Avoid overstaffing and overformalization of a small organization to further cut salary expense.

You should salvage scrap that can be reused in the business or sold. Containers used for incoming shipments such as corrugated cardboard boxes and drums can be used again. Floor sweepings may contain parts and hardware of value.

KEY TERMS

Barter
Cost of inventory
Economic order quantity (EOQ)
Interim income statement
Inventory
Inventory turnover
Lot purchase
Overage inventory
Perpetual inventory system
Purchase order
Requisition
RFP
RFQ
Salvage
Specification

QUESTIONS AND PROBLEMS

1. What are the fundamental rules of successful negotiation?
2. List five items you can negotiate.
3. What steps can you take to buy at lowest possible prices?
4. Is the lowest price always the most economical price? Explain.
5. List and discuss the carrying costs that make up total inventory carrying cost.
6. Draw a graph of idealized inventory behavior and explain it.
7. You sell 1,000 units of a given item per year. Your order cost is $10, unit price is $15, and your inventory carrying cost is 15 percent. What is the EOQ?
8. Figure average inventory, using the data of Problem 7, if safety stock is forty units?
9. What is the minimum of purchasing records that you should maintain in your mini business?
10. What are your options for having or obtaining current inventory information in your mini business?
11. What can you do to move oldest goods on the shelf first?
12. Your average inventory is $10,000. Your annual cost of goods sold is $50,000. What is your inventory turnover?
13. If the inventory in Problem 12 increases to $15,000 average, what is the turnover?
14. If inventory carrying costs are 20 percent, how would an increase from $10,000 to $15,000 in average inventory change annual expenses?
15. Discuss location cost-saving possibilities for various kinds of businesses.
16. What steps can you take to prolong the life of equipment?

FIELD INVESTIGATION AND PROJECTS

*1. Determine the potential suppliers of merchandise and equipment (that you'll need in your intended business) and visit at least three of them to determine margins, delivery arrangements, and so forth. Prepare a report. (This project bears some similiarity to Project 2, Chapter 2.)

2. Visit the manager of (a) a chain food supermarket, (b) a small individually-owned convenience food store, (c) a chain variety store, (d) a large discount store. Determine how each keeps track of inventory and display stock. Report.

*3. Call several real estate brokers in your area and obtain rental figures on (a) retail, (b) office, and (c) industrial space. Scan the classified ads under "Retail for Rent" in your newspaper and list the locations offered. Phone for information on at least three of these. Report.

Management

13

The preceding chapters have dealt with business disciplines and skills. The emphasis was on the employment of these skills for effective small-business *management,* although the word "management" was used sparingly. The business disciplines were presented first, because they're essential to management and are in fact the tools of management. To study management before learning the disciplines is like trying to become a good carpenter without using tools. Now, with the business disciplines learned, you're ready to start putting them together with your study of management.

Management in a one-person company may be difficult to visualize. Often, we think of management as "getting things done through other people." But management is much more. In a one-person business you manage money, materials, equipment and facilities, your time, and your relations with your customers. So management is much more than working through other people. *Management is the job of getting the right things done by using the business's resources to best advantage.* The resources of the business include everything that shows on the balance sheet, plus your time and talent, plus accrued good will, plus *human resources.*

Human resources (employees) are added as the business grows. This chapter dealing with management will make some reference to human resources, with further discussion in Chapter 14. Chapter 15 will deal with your business in the economic environment and your business's growth. These chapters will round out your study in starting and managing a small business.

Much of the material in these final chapters deals with the growth of your business and the problems of growing businesses. To provide an effective bridge, big-business ideas are introduced and then adapted to the growing mini business in several instances. This material will become continually more important to you as your business grows.

These are some of the questions this chapter will help you answer:

1. What are the principles of practical planning that create plans instead of unattainable guesses and dreams?
2. How can I meet the needs of growth without getting overorganized and strangled by high overhead?
3. What are the practical steps that I can take to operate within my available funds, provide the quality of service and product that wins repeat business, and meet the schedules that I've set?
4. What techniques do big-business managers use that I can employ in my mini business?
5. How can I develop the ability to come up with good ideas that will increase my profits and growth?
6. If I get in trouble with my business, how can I turn it around?

MANAGING YOUR BUSINESS

There are many theories and approaches to management. Figure 13-1 shows these approaches and their proponents. The *behavioral* approaches emphasize satisfaction of the worker. The *empirical* school fosters practical approaches with skills developed through case studies of actual experiences. The *decision theory* school asserts that decision making is the primary job of the manager. The *quantitative* approach to management is a mathematical approach, and the term "operations research" is applied to the methods presently employed and advocated. None of these approaches alone fully encompasses the job of management. The *management process* school contemplates "what managers do," *the functions of management.* This approach–sometimes called the *functional, traditional,* or *universalist* approach to management–comes closest to meeting the needs of a mini-business manager. It is the most widely accepted approach, and you've been exposed to the functions it emphasizes throughout this book. The basic functions of management are *planning, organizing, staffing, directing,* and *controlling.* Some management scholars add *innovating, coordinating, reporting, representing,* and *budgeting* to this list.[1] The discussion of staffing will be adequately covered in Chapter 14 and will not be further discussed in this chapter.

[1] Ernest Dale, *Management: Theory and Practice* (New York: McGraw-Hill Book Co., 1965), pp. 3-8.

FIGURE 13-1 Development of organization and management theory

BEHAVIORAL

	Human Relations	Social Systems	Empirical	Decision Theory	Quantitative	Management Process	
1900		Weber	Harvard "B" School —Am. Mgmt. Assn.—Practitioners		A. Marshall		Practitioners
1905							
1910					Taylor		
1915					Gilbreths	Fayol	
1920					Gantt		
1925							
1930	Hawthorne Studies					Mooney	
1935	Mayo					Urwick	
1940	Roethlisberger			Barnard			
1945				Armed Forces	J. Dean		
1950		Homans Maslow			Von Neumann		
1955	K. Davis	Argyris Simon					
1960	McGregor	Herzberg Likert	Dale	March & Simon Cyert & March	Schlaifer Hitch	Koontz Terry	
1965			Learned	Simon		Newman etc.	
1970							

Present-Day Organization and Management Theory

(Source: Robert G. Murdick and Joel E. Ross, *Information Systems For Modern Management*, 2nd ed. [Englewood Cliffs, N.J.: Prentice-Hall, Inc., 1975], p. 46.)

Planning

Planning is the most important part of the job of making your business succeed, and yet excellent planning can be totally useless!

Why? Because in order for a plan to succeed it must be translated into action. Many new-business starters make excellent plans but fail dismally because they never *work* the plans. Here's an example:

Lester Smith decided to go into a wholesale chemical (cleaning and disinfectant chemicals) business in July. He laid his plans as follows:

July 1 —Develop plan
July 2 —Find vendor sources
July 3 —Make financial arrangements

July 6 –Find a store location, order utilities
July 10–Finalize all needed permits and licenses
July 11–Place orders for initial inventory
July 12–Order stationery, forms, and advertising
July 15–Move in and open

The dates shown were the target completion dates. Lester had additional details in his plan and it was quite adequate. But Lester's wife talked him into taking a few days off to go to the lake over July 4th. He spent the 2nd getting ready for the trip, left on the 3rd, and returned on the 5th—very tired. He took the 6th off to rest up, and on the 7th he revised his schedule. All of his deadlines were moved ahead eight days.

On July 7th, the president of the local Jaycees group, of which Lester was a member, asked Lester to be chairman of the Labor Day parade committee. Lester looked at his plans, thought about the honor and what this chairmanship might mean to his business, and decided to take the job. Needless to say, his schedule slipped again, this time by two months! He never did get his business plan implemented and at last report was still working for someone else.

POINT 13-1: A plan is vital to success, but it's useless if it isn't implemented. *Plan your work, work your plan.*

Now, let's get academic for a moment and see what planning can accomplish. Planning is the process of constructing a roadmap to accomplish your goals. Planning can

1. Provide a guide (blueprint) for action
2. Provide a standard by which results can be measured
3. Stimulate creative thinking in yourself and your employees
4. Enable you to test ideas on paper so you can avoid costly mistakes
5. Make employees feel a part of the business and thus be motivated to make the plan work
6. Make possible the enthusiastic participation and cooperation of your employees, your accountant, your lawyer, and others

Formulating a good plan is not a clear-cut, easily accomplished task. It begins as a broad and nebulous thing. As you proceed, the generalities dissolve and specific, concrete goals begin to emerge. The steps in developing a plan are as follows:

1. Establish broad target objectives
2. Determine intermediate objectives (stepping stones to the broad target objectives)

3. Establish parameters (boundaries or rules within which the plan must be worked)
4. Set a preliminary course of action
5. Develop alternate courses of action
6. Evaluate, sift, and revise the courses of action and intermediate goals until you achieve a practical, workable plan

In laying out your plan, think in terms of *what, when, who, how, how much, where,* and *why*. In this way, you take all resources available to you into account. This will help you fill in the details and make your plans more specific and meaningful. Always back the words with the "how much"—the numbers. This means budgets and pro formas. A plan that is not specific is likely to be a meaningless daydream.

During the planning process, you may have to take side trips for investigation, study, and research. You can speed the process, after you have several employees, by assigning some of this study and research to others on the planning team. Keep the importance of *perspective, practicality,* and *vision* (in the planning process) in mind. These characteristics were introduced in Chapter 1.

Your study of this book or course probably came about as a result of a plan. You may not have thought of it as a part of a plan, and you may not have developed a written plan when you started. But subconsciously, you were planning. You started to commit your business plans to writing in doing the end-of-chapter projects. Your plans began to take form. You may have changed them several times. Written plans provide a defined base that can be revised and improved; this tends to eliminate needless rehashing and rethinking of the same subjects.

Larger businesses prepare a number of planning documents. The basic document for the operation of a business is the *policy statement.* The policy statement is a general, long-life document that says, in essence, "what we believe in and how we get things done around here." Don't get policy confused with *procedures.* Procedures provide guidance for getting specific, often trivial, things done. Policy sets parameters that affect planning.

In big business, plans are classified in terms of the period covered by the plan, by product, and by the specific area of the business to which they apply. *Long-range plans* may cover three to twenty years, depending on the industry, but five-year long-range plans are more common. *Short-range plans* usually cover a year or less. Some companies have *intermediate plans,* which cover one to three or one to five years, with anything longer classified as long-term. The shorter the term of the plan, the more detailed and specific it should be. *Your mini business can benefit from a one-year and a three-year plan.*

The overall or company plan is the result of the combination of numerous more detailed plans for specific areas of the business and/or the various product lines in the business. Recall that we discussed market forecasting and planning in Chapter 4, tax planning in Chapter 9, and budgeting, cash flow, and profit planning in Chapter 11. A general business plan should include all of these facets and possibly others, depending on the nature and size of the company. Thus, the larger company's plan would include personnel, facilities, and inventory planning in addition to those cited.

A formal plan makes any endeavor more likely to succeed. The formality, detail, and complexity of the plan can vary with the size of the business. A less formal, less detailed plan is in order for your mini business, but it should include *at least a market forecast, a market plan, a cash flow budget, and a pro forma income statement.* A plan without numbers is of doubtful value. If you don't have a budget or don't stick to it, there's a good chance that next year you won't even have a business to plan for.

POINT 13-2: A formal plan increases the chances of success of any endeavor. A plan provides a blueprint to work by and a standard to measure by; it also provides other benefits, including a prod to thinking and a result orientation on the part of employees participating in the planning. A good plan includes a market forecast, market plan, a pro forma income statement, and *always,* a cash budget.

The fundamental objectives of business introduced in Chapter 1 should be kept in mind during every step of the planning process. They are: (1) to make a profit, (2) to grow, and (3) to attain a position of leadership. If planning served no other purpose than to focus the attention of you and your employees on earning a profit and growing, it would serve its purpose. But it does much more. Plan, refine your plans, and make them work.

Organizing

A plan is written to be implemented. Organization of resources enables you to implement plans in an orderly way. The definition of organization is *the subdivision of functions and assignment of responsibility for each function to an individual without duplication of effort, all directed to a common goal.* The *organization chart* forms a schematic skeleton for organization. *Job descriptions* specify what each employee is to do and thus add flesh to the skeleton. Organization helps you work your plans; it helps you get things done on time and with efficiency. A major objective of organization, though it isn't stated explicitly in most definitions, is to make the organization function smoothly on an almost automatic basis. Thus, if 90 percent of the work in your business is performed routinely, you can focus more attention on the less routine 10 percent of the work that contains the major problems. This is the concept of "management by exception." Organization charts, job descriptions, policy, procedures, and plans all contribute to making management by exception more realistic.

The classical theory of organization is based on principles of

1. A clearly defined objective
2. Specialization of work

3. Coordination toward the objective
4. Top boss with line of authority to everyone in the organization
5. Authority commensurate with responsibility.[2]

In big business, these principles are used to develop *an organization chart.* An organization chart lists functions that different persons perform and/or positions of authority that they hold, and shows who reports to whom.

Suppose you start a motor repair business with two employees. You're the owner, manager, salesperson, purchasing agent, and production manager. You supervise both of the employees yourself. Your organization chart is shown in Figure 13-2 (a). After a year, you have five employees, and you place one of them in charge of production so you can devote more time to your other functions. The organization chart takes the form shown in Figure 13-2 (b).

In year 3 your business has grown to eight employees and you've added new motor sales to your service. You designate one of your employees as sales manager and another as office manager. Your organization chart now takes the form shown in Figure 13-2 (c).

By year 6, your business has grown to thirty employees. You have a sales manager, an office manager, a controller, a purchasing agent, a production manager, and two supervisors. Your organization chart will now look like the illustration in Figure 13-2 (d).

All of this is very applicable to your business as it grows, but there may be some question in your mind about how you can "organize" your starting business with few or no employees. We've emphasized organizing yourself in Chapter 1. You can best apply the principles of organization to your small company by thinking of yourself as several persons, because you'll wear a number of hats till your business grows. Thus, you list the functions in your business and put your own name in each function. This will emphasize your numerous roles and act as a reminder of the ground you have to cover. Carry this responsibility and keep your organization lean until growth demands expansion and profits can support it. You may find it helpful to set a few hours aside each day to concentrate on one specific function until you can afford help. Thus, you might concentrate on sales for a few hours on Monday, finance on Tuesday, planning on Wednesday, and so on. Of course, you won't be able to schedule a full forty hours each week of "what" you'll concentrate on "when." But you can set aside a few hours each day for a specific purpose. Most successful executives spend some time at the end of each day listing the things to be done the next day. This is a good approach to personal organization.

When your business grows to the point where you need help, add it slowly and deliberately. Add to your team only when the addition will contribute to profits and growth. If the addition simply allows you to take it easier, and it doesn't contribute to the profits, the expansion is unwise; if it will free you from

[2] *Ibid.*, p. 234.

FIGURE 13-2 Growth of a company's organization (a, b, c, d)

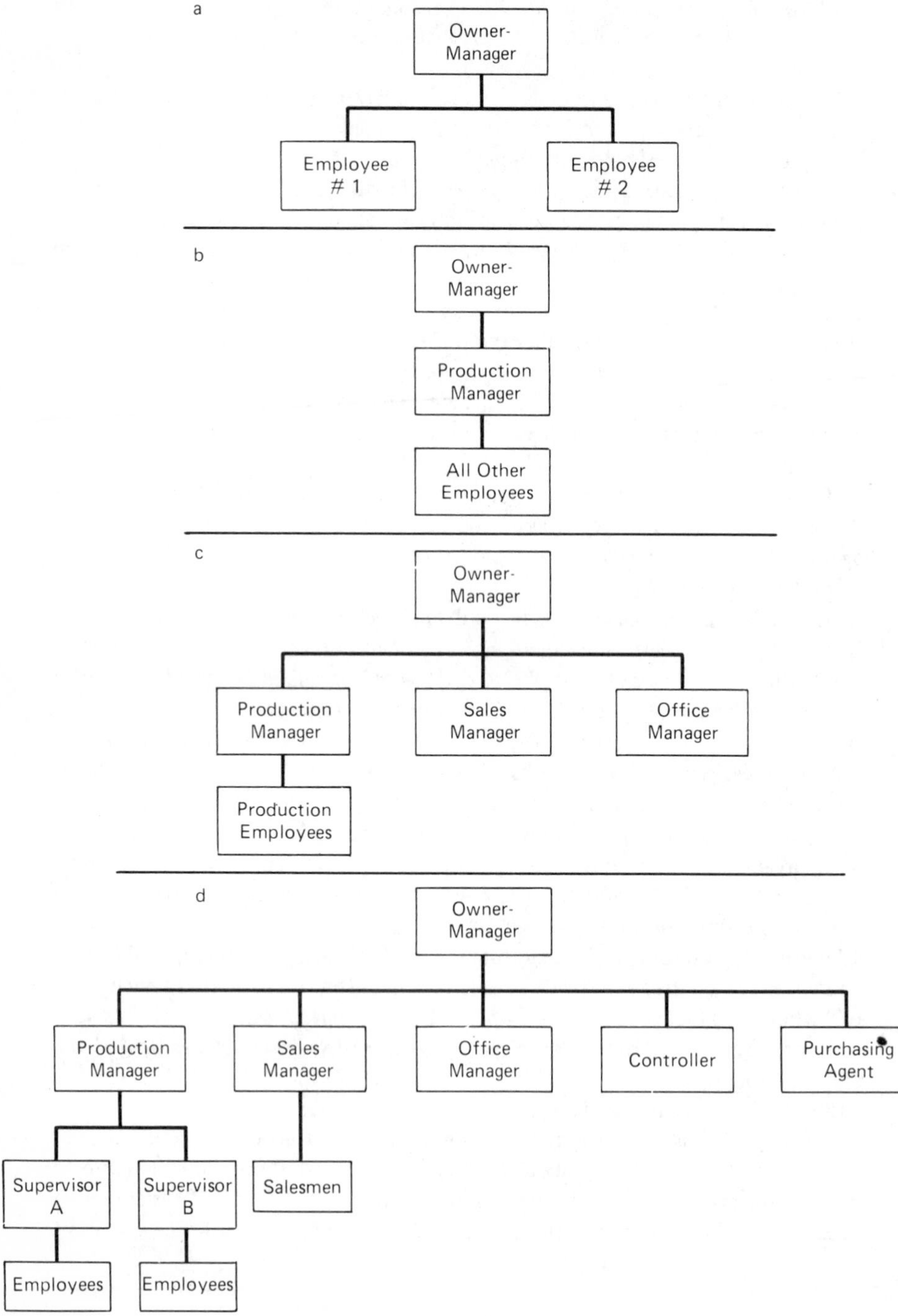

a

Owner-Manager

Employee # 1

Employee # 2

b

Owner-Manager

Production Manager

All Other Employees

c

Owner-Manager

Production Manager

Sales Manager

Office Manager

Production Employees

d

Owner-Manager

Production Manager

Sales Manager

Office Manager

Controller

Purchasing Agent

Supervisor A

Supervisor B

Salesmen

Employees

Employees

routine work for more profitable activity, it's wise; or, if a new employee will produce a contribution to profit, the addition is a good idea.

POINT 13-3: The principles of organization employed in larger companies can be used in a mini business if you'll remember that you fill several slots in the small organization. Set aside an hour or two each day to concentrate on one of your functions, shifting to another function each day. When you must add employees, do so carefully and deliberately.

Directing

With your business organized and staffed to perform its work, the next step is to get people to do the work. Organization is aimed at making it easy to do the work—getting it done as automatically as possible. But it takes more than planning and organization to get things done. People must know what to do, how it is to be done, and when it is to be done. If they are doing the work incorrectly or inefficiently, changes must be made. If they create problems as a result of personal behavior or attitudes, they must be corrected to continue to be of value to the business. Sometimes you may need to make changes in fairness to your employees. You have to *listen* as well as tell. These are the things that make up the job of direction. How you do this job has been and still is the subject of considerable discussion and evolution.

The earliest approach was force and punishment. Later, increased financial rewards for greater productivity were used in an attempt to get things done. Then came the behavioral approaches founded on human relations and social system concepts. These approaches address direction from the viewpoint of the worker's goals, motivations, and interests, and their concept of their boss. The stress now is on motivating the employee rather than on giving him orders. The behavioral schools contend that employees work well when they can achieve satisfaction in their work. They're most satisfied when they work in pleasant surroundings, do not have monotonous jobs, are recognized and accepted by you and their co-workers, know what you expect of them, have your respect, have a say in how the work is to be done, and can realize personal goals and satisfactions through their work.

To put this into perspective in a mini business, let's say you own a ladies' apparel store. All three of your employees are women. Salesperson A doubles as a window dresser, salesperson B also does in-store displays, and salesperson C doubles on alterations. Your store hours are 10 A.M. to 6 P.M. The employees come in at 9:45 and leave at 6:15. They have 30 minutes for lunch with staggered lunch periods. On Mondays, Tuesdays, and Wednesdays you operate with two employees only to give each employee a day off. Everyone has Sunday off and they trade weekdays off so that each employee has a Sunday-Monday off period every three weeks. Each employee has a week of vacation with pay during the summer, with vacations staggered. The employees are happy with these working hours.

The store atmosphere is relaxed and informal. The employees work together in keeping the store shelves and racks stocked. You pay the employees forty dollars a week plus 5 percent commission on sales. Your total sales are $6,000 to $10,000 a week and each of your employees usually sells at least $2,000 worth of merchandise per week.

So far, how does this stack up as an arrangement for good direction? It appears that you've provided the basic elements. Your employees have suitable working hours, a congenial atmosphere, incentive to sell and to perform their secondary functions, and each feels a sense of accomplishment in doing both the selling and the secondary job. Each contributes a specific individual service in the secondary role.

Now, suppose one of the employees begins arriving between 10:05 and 10:15 instead of at 9:45. How should you handle it? A good human relations approach is to speak to the employee (privately of course), tell her that she's been coming in late and that it disrupts operations—all this in a nonaccusing, matter-of-fact fashion. Then is the time to find out the reasons for her changed behavior. She may be having problems at home, with her transportation, or it may be just a series of different complications that have led to the series of tardy appearances. When you know her problem, ask her how she thinks she can rectify the situation. She'll usually have a solution and will promise to do better. If not, offer some suggestions on ways that she can solve her problem. Note that this situation is being approached with a counseling approach—the employee is asked questions and guided to her own solution. She is not "dressed down" or criticized, but is made aware of her responsibility. The same approach can be used in most situations in which an employee requires correction.

POINT 13-4: Use the questioning-counseling approach to correct employees. Avoid criticism. If the employee does not react favorably, you may have to resort to more forceful methods.

Suppose the employee does not react favorably to your questioning-counseling approach? What's next? If you can't reach an amicable solution quickly, you may have to use different measures. In the case of the tardy employee, daily 9:45 meetings may do the trick. Having employees sign in may work, but it may be resented. If this procedure fails, you may have to resort to cutting pay, giving a day off without pay so the employee can "think it over," and possibly even dismissal. You can elect to live with the employee's tardiness. If you do, it may result in deterioration of your ability to direct your entire working force.

There's an art to giving orders in the course of routine business. Most workers expect orders from a manager. The way they're issued may make the difference between willing obedience and surly resentment.

When all the work that should be done isn't getting done, the questioning-counseling approach with an "I'm asking your advice" flavor is useful. It often will highlight problems and evoke plausible solutions.

The attitude of your employee toward you is a key factor in your success at directing. A democratic leader ("How shall *we* do it?") generally has the respect of his or her employees. An autocratic leader ("Do it like this") who is fair to his employees can also have their respect. If your employee feels that you're fair with him, he'll usually respect you regardless of your style, as long as you aren't curt and rude. (More about this in Chapter 14.)

A ten-minute morning meeting on your plans for the day may be fruitful. It enables you to communicate definitely what each person is to accomplish during the day, and it gives your employees a chance to participate. Whenever the employee participates in planning his work, the prospects of his getting it done—and getting it done well—increase.

POINT 13-5: You can direct employees more effectively when they respect you. A brief morning meeting to plan the day's work is an effective direction tool.

Controlling

Controlling is the process of determining whether and how well your plan is being implemented, determining why deviations have occurred, and correcting the causes of the deviations so that future work is done on schedule and within budget.

Information concerning what has been done with respect to what should have been done (variance) is an essential part of control. The term "reporting" is sometimes used to refer to this part of the control function. Large manufacturing companies use computers to accomplish the reporting function. This provides data on a daily or weekly basis that is always relatively new and of maximum use. Manual reporting systems generally do not provide data as quickly, and variances may continue to pile up for some time before a manager is fully aware of them. You can't afford the luxury of a fancy control system in a mini business, but you can't afford *not* to have controls.

POINT 13-6: The primary requirement of a control system is provision of a means of reporting variances from plans and budgets quickly so that you can correct and adjust before things get out of hand.

In manufacturing operations you set standards in terms of time and materials cost for each job. There's usually some variance, but after some practice, you'll get a pretty good feel for normal variances and ignore them, so you can concentrate your attention on correcting abnormal variances. In a retail business, control focuses on sales, margins, and expenses. If sales are down in a given department, the report calls this to your attention, and you determine why it occurred and how it can be corrected. The cause might be poor displays, an inadequate number of salespeople, ineffective salespeople, or ineffective ads, to name just a few of the possibilities. *You attempt to identify the cause and remove or correct it.*

It is common to think of control as a financial or an accounting function dealing with budgets, cash flows, operating pro formas and actuals. Why? Because these activities go right to the bottom line—to profit. But the other facets of daily operations in a business are the functions that determine the amount of money coming in and going out of a business. Consequently, control must focus on costs, schedules, and quality in all areas of a company. As your own marketing or sales manager, you exercise control (attempt to meet sales targets and schedules) by monitoring the performance of your salespeople, results of advertising, relative sales of various products, and other pertinent factors. When a salesperson's performance falls, or advertising effectiveness falls, or sales dip on a given product, you attempt to discover why and take action to correct the situation. You have a similar responsibility related to each specific area of your business that someone else isn't managing. If you perform the control function well, your profit, growth, and leadership goals can be readily attained.

Now, *what are some of the typical things that go wrong (need controlling) in a mini business?* Here are just a few possibilities:

1. Merchandise is not reordered soon enough to provide for an adequate stock supply
2. Work is not completed by the promised delivery date
3. Collection of overdue accounts-receivable is neglected
4. A defective tool or machine slows production and causes losses
5. Bills are not paid in enough time to allow you to take cash discounts
6. Ineffective ads are left running
7. Insurance policies are allowed to lapse
8. Reports to IRS and regulatory agencies are late
9. Retail prices are not adjusted to reflect wholesale price increases
10. Water leaks run up utility bills

All these problems, if they are not corrected, contribute to reduced sales or added expenses and reductions in profit. The most effective ways to spot them in a small business that can't afford a more formal control system are to use checklists, to study accounting records of actual performance against plans, and to use some of the simplified reporting techniques discussed in the section on "Reporting." Thus weekly checks of shelf stock, deliveries, equipment, and accounting records provide control over most of the problems cited.

POINT 13-7: Control ultimately focuses on the bottom line. This implies control of costs, schedules, and quality in detail because these factors influence sales, cost of goods, and expenses—the factors that determine profit—in day-to-day operations.

REVIEW EXERCISES 13-A

1. Define management in your own words.
2. What are the goals of business?
3. Under what conditions is a good plan useless?
4. Discuss the benefits of planning.
5. What are the steps in the evolution of a plan?
6. It has been said that a poor plan can lead to success if everyone gets behind it. Discuss.
7. Define "management by exception."
8. What is "direction"? How do you intend to direct your employees? Give examples for some specific situations.
9. What are the elements of a control system?

OTHER FUNCTIONS OF MANAGEMENT

Planning, organizing, staffing, directing, and controlling are the fundamental functions of management. The list of functions has been expanded to include *innovating, coordinating, representing, budgeting,* and *reporting.* In this section we will discuss each of these functions briefly.

Innovation and Creativity

Innovation is essential to make a mini business grow. A manager must be innovative—he (or she) must find new approaches and ways of doing things simply in order to make the business function. But innovation also suggests invention, discovery, revolution, change, creation, novelty, and new ideas. An innovator may earn the title by inventing a product, process, or technique; by harnessing and exploiting existing technology in a new way; by developing more effective organizational concepts; by developing and exploiting new marketing concepts; or by other new approaches to the way we live and do things. Most businesses that have grown large from mini-business starts have grown as a result of innovation.

Creativity and innovation go hand in hand. Innovation must have a creative idea as a seed, but the innovation occurs only when the idea is put into action.

Because creativity is essential to innovation and because innovation can make your business success prospects skyrocket, the subject of creativity is worthy of further study.[3]

[3] These books will provide ideas and inspiration for creative thinking and innovation: Alex Osborn, *Your Creative Power* (New York: Charles Scribner's Sons, 1948); G. Polya, *How to Solve It* (Princeton, N.J.: Princeton University Press, 1945); Forrest H. Frantz, Sr., *The Miracle Success System–A Scientific Way to Get What You Want in Life* (West Nyack, N.Y.: Parker Publishing Co., Inc., 1967), see particularly pp. 47-60.

Breakthroughs and great ideas rarely come by accident. They're the result of a process that follows this general pattern:

1. *Problem or Need Recognition:* You perceive a problem or a need and assimilate information that bears on it.
2. *Solution Hunting:* You juggle the information looking for a solution, but the pieces may not fit—perhaps there's a piece missing.
3. *Incubation:* The problem and pertinent information are stored in your mind to ripen. From time to time you may pull this information out, look again for a solution, and then "store" it again.
4. *Illumination:* The solution comes to you. The pieces of the puzzle all fall together or you find the missing piece that makes everything fall in place. Illumination may occur while you're performing step 2, or it may occur with the speed of lightning while you're engaged in completely unrelated activity.

There are a number of ways that you can stimulate your creative output. One is to solicit your mind for problems and list them on paper. Then search for and list the possible solutions for each of the problems. Put the list away, and pull it out in a week or so; add to the list of possible solutions. Extend your approach beyond the use of words. Try to draw pictures and diagrams of possible solutions. A graphic approach often aids thinking.[4] Variations of this approach include an assault on a specific problem in a darkened room with a tape recorder to collect your ideas, or the "brainstorming" technique in which a number of people spew out ideas that are recorded on a blackboard. The basic principle is to record all ideas regardless of how impractical they may seem, since one or more impractical ideas may trigger a practical idea.

The employee suggestion system provides another avenue for innovation. Large companies employ a suggestion system with forms and suggestion boxes throughout company facilities. Employees are rewarded for their suggestions on the basis of savings or profits realized. The fundamental principle is that the person nearest the work is most likely to recognize problems and have practical solutions and improvement ideas. You can easily implement this system in a very small business. By encouraging creativity and innovation on the part of your employees, you multiply your chances for greater business success.

POINT 13-8: Creativity and innovation are needed to achieve solutions to day-to-day problems, but can also produce dramatic results in the growth and development of a business. You can multiply the results by encouraging the creative and innovative efforts of your employees.

[4] Forrest H. Frantz, Sr., *Parametrics–New Key To Successful Take-Charge Management* (West Nyack, N.Y.: Parker Publishing Co., Inc., 1968).

Coordinating

Coordinating is the process of putting things in proper order and position to make the actions of the organization mesh smoothly into a desired final result. With proper coordination work delays and idle time are avoided, customer orders are shipped on time, out-of-stock situations are avoided, and the business runs smoothly with a minimum of foul-ups. The need for coordination increases as the number of employees in a business grows.

The amount of individual personal coordination required in a business can be reduced through proper organization. Well-disseminated plans, policy, operating procedures, and working papers (work orders, requisitions, routing slips, and schedules) aid the coordinating process. But personal coordination is still required and it is accomplished through the directing function. Occasional meetings (conferences) are helpful in developing good coordination with any working group. But the use of meetings can be overdone with respect to number of meetings, who attends, and duration. Organize and control your meetings by preparing an agenda, sticking to it, and controlling verbose participants.

Representing

You *represent* your business externally and internally. You represent your business in external contacts with the general public, the financial community, governments, civic and religious groups, customers, suppliers, and others. This function includes the use of public relations principles discussed in Chapter 5 and the negotiation principles discussed in Chapter 3.

You also represent your business internally with your employees. The opinion your employees hold of the business will pretty much coincide with their opinion of you. The representation function requires tact, courtesy, and understanding.

POINT 13-9: You and every one of your employees represent your business. This representation forms the image of your business in the minds of your public. Your employees should be advised of this and you should make good representation a key objective.

Budgeting and Reporting

Budgeting is dollar planning and is usually grouped with the planning function. The budgeting portion of the planning function was discussed in the last section of Chapter 11. Review that section.

Reporting is the process of letting the boss know what you've done, that you've completed an assignment, how well you performed in doing a job, or that you've failed to get a job done. As long as you're the sole owner of your business, you won't be reporting to anyone else. When you incorporate, you'll have to report to your board of directors. You'll rely on reports from your subordinates, and they in turn will depend on reports from their subordinates. Reporting is essential to the control function.

Reporting facilitates the control function because it allows you to stay up to date on what's going on, what has and hasn't been done, and so on. Through the reporting process, you acquire data on how your subordinates have performed. You don't have to ask for this information–ideally, it is part of the expected procedure. The direct reporting process can be simplified with a form that your subordinates fill in to report their day's activities. Even if you work principally through a verbal system, let your subordinates know what you expect them to report on. Otherwise you'll either get too few reports or when your business gets large, you may spend too much of your time on trivia.

REVIEW EXERCISES 13-B

1. How are innovations and creative ideas related to the day-to-day functioning of a mini business? To its growth?
2. Describe the creative process.
3. List and discuss some of the activities that require coordination in a retail store; a service business.
4. Compile a list of businesses that have been founded on innovation; justify your choice.
5. How can you get the benefits of a reporting system in a small business while retaining simplicity?
6. Develop a daily reporting form for salespeople to use in a small hardware store. What can it report besides sales?

CASES: TYPICAL SMALL-BUSINESS MANAGEMENT PROBLEMS

Diversifying an Ice Cream Store

The Hunter Valley Ice Cream Store was located in a city with a population of 100,000 and was part of a chain. The owners of the chain decided to close down operations and liquidate the assets. The fixtures and inventory of the Hunter Valley store, as well as the Hunter Valley trade names, were bought by the owner of the building in which the store was located. The new owner purchased ice cream from another supplier and operated the store just as it had been operated by the previous owners, except that he closed the store during December, January, and February. He was an absentee owner and paid very little attention to the business. In 1974, sales were $32,500; cost of goods sold was $19,000; expenses were $11,000; and net profit was $2,500. In 1975, sales were $34,000; cost of goods sold was $23,000; expenses were $12,300; and net loss was $1,300.

(If you set up the information given as an income statement for each year, and compute the percentage cost of goods sold, expense, and net profit to understand what was wrong, it will be apparent that percentage cost of goods sold and percentage expenses increased considerably in 1975 to produce a loss, although sales were higher.)

Early in 1976, the ice cream store's prices were increased to increase gross margins. In late summer, sandwiches were added to the store's product line. In the fall, hot chili and "stew-to-go" was added to the line. This diversification allowed the store to stay open year-round and increased sales in 1976 to $41,000; cost of goods sold was $23,000; expenses were $13,000; and net profit was $5,000. Anticipated sales for 1977 were $54,000; with expected cost of goods sold $29,000, expenses $14,000, and an expected net of $11,000.

This is an example of early poor management on the owner's part. He didn't pay attention to the business in the first two years. His first attempt at control was made only after he found he'd lost $1,300 in 1975 as he scanned his tax return. He immediately increased prices to bring up the gross margin on sales. He should have installed a control system that gave him timely information on profits. A monthly income statement would have shown him when losses started to occur early in 1975. There was a more obvious signal—the price increase his supplier put on the ice cream. Whenever your supplier increases his prices, increase yours.

The rent and minimum utility cost (to avoid frozen pipes) during the three months the store was closed was $930. This was less than the store would have lost by being operated only as an ice cream store during these three months. The addition of the sandwiches and later the chili and "stew-to-go" brought sales up to a profitable level for the winter months and increased sales in other months as well. A low food cost (about 40 percent) contributed to a better gross margin. Expenses on the operation were reasonable and the increases were due to utility rate and other cost increases. (Most food businesses strive for 35 percent cost.)

POINT 13-10: A business requires attention and management to operate properly and profitably. Seasonal reductions in business can be offset by diversification.

The Small Manufacturing Company Turnaround

A small (40 employees) precision aircraft components company was acquired by a larger (300 employees) metal fabricating and machining company. The smaller company's equipment and about ten employees, including the manager and a supervisor, were moved several thousand miles and installed in the larger company's plant. The smaller company was to operate as a subsidiary. Its equipment was massive, and a considerable amount of work was in process at the time of the move. The move and downtime left the operation in chaos at the new location. Work that was in process was unmarked and scattered all over the shop. Deliveries were lagging and customers were taking a large amount of the management's time trying to find where their orders stood. The production control manager was spending all of his time trying to find work in process and had no control whatsoever on what was going on. Shop equipment was down more than it was operating. Employees could not be hired fast enough or kept long enough to staff the plant. Employee morale was low. Quality was poor and scrappage was high. The small company's manager was frustrated and the president of the acquiring company called a consultant in to see what he could do with the operation. He was given a one-month assignment.

When the consultant met with the small-company manager, the manager described the problem as principally one of morale, lack of identity, limited freedom, and shortage of competent workers. The consultant spent a few days talking to people and assessing the situation. He took steps, which we'll classify according to the functions of planning, organizing, staffing, directing, and controlling.

Planning. The consultant listed these objectives:

1. Physical organization, including the location and identification of parts and work in process in the shop
2. Development and implementation of a simple work-in-process routing, identification, and control system
3. An assault on production rate, including reductions in machine downtime, employee acquisition, training, and reduction of scrappage and rework
4. Physical and organizational identification of the smaller company within the larger company and morale improvement
5. Reduction of production harrassment by irate customers and improved customer relations

A detailed plan was developed to meet these objectives.

Organizing. A meeting was held, with all supervisors and seasoned employees attending. Two field days were announced for finding and identifying parts and work in process, with all supervisors and seasoned employees attending.

Large schedule boards visible from a considerable distance were made, one to be placed in each department. Figure 13-3 shows the sign format with provisions for incoming, work-in-process, and outgoing status. Plates that could be hung on hooks on the signs were provided. Production control provided the plate with the job number on it and furnished it with the work routing slip. When work came into a department the plate was hung under "incoming" and the received

FIGURE 13-3 Status board

GRINDING DEPARTMENT				
INCOMING			IN PROCESS	OUTGOING
JOB NO.	IN	DUE OUT	JOB NO.	JOB NO.
731	9/1	9/7	697	706
723	9/3	9/10	699	702
705	9/5	9/10	701	
			653	

and due dates were entered. When the department began work on the job, the plate was moved to "in process"; and upon completion, the plate was moved to "outgoing." Thus, production control and supervision had a prominent display of the location and status of each job.

Work-force needs were assessed and job descriptions were prepared for each position.

A schedule for maintenance work was developed to reduce machine downtime.

Staffing. In assessing the work-force needs, the consultant concluded that a chaser was required in production control to keep the work flowing from one area to the next, at least till the work force was trained and stabilized. An additional maintenance employee was needed on a permanent basis and two more were required on a short-term (two-month) basis. The two short-termers would pick up the more routine, less specialized work, while the existing maintenance staff and new permanent employee would concentrate on getting the production equipment in tip-top shape to reduce downtime.

The parent company had had several layoffs during the last three months. Its pay rates were higher than those of the acquired company. Arrangements were made with the parent company's personnel department (which functioned for both companies) to call in laid-off employees in groups of ten to fifteen for a briefing on the acquired company. The plant manager and several supervisors brought in samples of the work and explained operations, company history, and objectives. After the briefing, those who wished to explore further were interviewed. This filled the worker-level requirements within a week. Specialized workers were recruited through classified ads in cities in which similar plants were located.

Directing. The field days were supervised by the plant manager and key supervisors. During one weekend, about 90 percent of the work in process was located, identified, and placed in the proper department with routing slips and plates on the status boards. One employee was assigned to perform these tasks for the remaining unidentified work.

Job descriptions were prepared and disseminated and an on-the-job training program was implemented.

Quality control exercised closer coordination with the line functions to reduce scrappage and rework time, and all supervision placed more emphasis on quality.

Closer attention to production, quality, and training, plus the added maintenance effort, reduced machine downtime and scrappage to negligible levels.

Marketing handled all customer visits to limit interference with production, and the status boards enabled customers to see where their jobs stood. The new arrangement and the obvious progress reassured customers and employee morale increased drastically as well. Larger and better signs were installed to identify the plant, and a separate set of offices was provided for the company's management. Arrangements were made for a front-page company story in the local paper. Employee morale soared and the company's operations moved further toward management by exception.

Controlling. The status boards in the plant and the other actions performed did much to provide control visible to all. Weekly status reports on work and machine downtime provided the necessary data for control. At a weekly meeting of management and supervision, status, costs, solutions, and improvements were discussed. Thus, each manager and supervisor's action and progress was laid on the table and control was emphasized.

Results. By the end of the first month, shipments had tripled, downtime was reduced from about 40 percent to less than 10 percent, the shop was well organized, and employee morale had greatly improved. The company had moved from a large monthly loss position on operations to break-even. The impetus developed by the effort led to continuing improvement.

POINT 13-11: A common-sense approach to management, correct problem identification, and concentration on solving problems in the face of day-to-day distractions is essential to successful business management.

REVIEW EXERCISES 13-C

1. How do you think the ice cream store's problems could have been avoided?
2. Would you have approached the ice cream store case differently than the way the owner actually did? State your approach.
3. Why do you suppose an owner of a business might tend to it as carelessly as did the ice cream store owner? State several plausible reasons.
4. Would you have attacked the small manufacturing company problem any differently than the consultant did? State your approach or any differences you would include in your approach.
5. What weaknesses did the manager of the small manufacturing company possess? Do you think he should have been fired or kept? Justify your answers.

BEHAVIORAL APPROACHES TO MANAGEMENT

Figure 13-1 listed a number of schools of thought on management. The management process approach has been emphasized in this chapter because it is the most important approach to managing a mini business. The process approach is also dominant in larger businesses, but the other approaches begin to assume more importance in larger businesses. This is particularly true of the behavioral approaches. While space here permits only brief mention, you should have some knowledge of the behavioral approaches. Before we discuss these, it should be noted that Frederick Taylor pioneered the scientific approach, now considered the forerunner of the *quantitative approach*. His emphasis was on reducing the amount of energy consumed by a worker to perform a given task, and to reward the worker according to his production. The result was increased productivity, but the worker was dehumanized.

The start of the human relations movement is generally associated with the Hawthorne Experiments conducted from 1927 to 1932 in Western Electric's Hawthorne Works by Elton Mayo, J. F. Roethlisberger, and others. The "test-room studies" involved changes in illumination. As intensity of illumination was increased, output increased. But when illumination was then decreased, output continued to rise! Other experiments produced similarly confusing results.

The results of these experiments were the recognition of the worker as a complex being motivated by more than money; the importance of individual attitudes in determining behavior; the importance of the role of supervision in morale and production; the importance of team play and worker satisfaction; and recognition of the existence of informal work groups that influence individual behavior.

The Lippitt experiment, conducted some thirty or forty years ago, separated boys into groups supervised by *authoritarian* (I'm the boss; do exactly as I say), *democratic* ("Let's figure out how to do this and get it done"), and *laissez-faire* ("Do it and if you need any help, ask me") leaders, respectively. The group led by the authoritarian leader did its job well, but the work bogged down whenever the leader left. The group led by the democratic leader got its work done satisfactorily, but output was below that of the group with the authoritarian leader. The group led by the laissez-faire leader was least productive of the three, and was disorganized, frustrated, and generally discontented.[5]

Douglas McGregor's theory of management, treated in detail in the *Human Side of Engerprise,*[6] posited that the *Theory X* type of management conforms to the old-line concept that work is done out of economic necessity and there is no satisfaction in the work itself. According to this view, people do not want to work and are basically lazy and unambitious; employees must be positively directed—perhaps even goaded—to do work.

Theory Y, on the other hand, typifies the modern human relations approach. According to this idea, people like to work, can exercise initiative and self-direction, will assume (even seek) responsibility if they're motivated, and find satisfaction in achieving meaningful results.

McGregor's human relations approach focuses on the idea that management is "getting things done through people." The manager therefore must understand human relations and be capable of interacting smoothly with people. The focus is more on the individual than on the social nature of the organization. Closely related to this approach to management is the *social system approach.* However, here the emphasis is on the social nature of the organization, including formal, informal, and cultural relationships. Environment and changes come into play.

Abraham Maslow, one of the social school pioneers, developed the "hierarchy of needs," shown in Figure 13-4. According to Maslow, human beings first seek to satisfy their *physiological* needs (such as food, shelter, and sex). When these are satisfied people seek *safety* (security). The physiological and safety needs of most Americans are satisfied, so they look to higher needs. These include the *social* (sometimes called "love" or "belonging") *needs,* the *esteem needs* (which include the need for self-esteem, recognition, respect of others, and prestige), sometimes called egoistic needs, and the need for *self-actualization* or *self-fulfillment* ("doing your own thing").[7]

Whenever one of the lower-order needs is fulfilled, a person strives for fulfillment of the next-higher need. Conversely, if a lower need is not fulfilled, the person continues his quest for fulfillment of that need and hence does not aspire

[5] Ronald Lippitt and R. K. White, *Child Behavior and Development* (New York: McGraw-Hill Book Co., 1943), pp. 484-508.

[6] Douglas McGregor, *The Human Side of Enterprise* (New York: McGraw-Hill Book Co., 1961).

[7] A. H. Maslow, *Motivation and Personality* (New York: Harper & Row, Publishers, 1954).

FIGURE 13-4 The hierarchy of needs

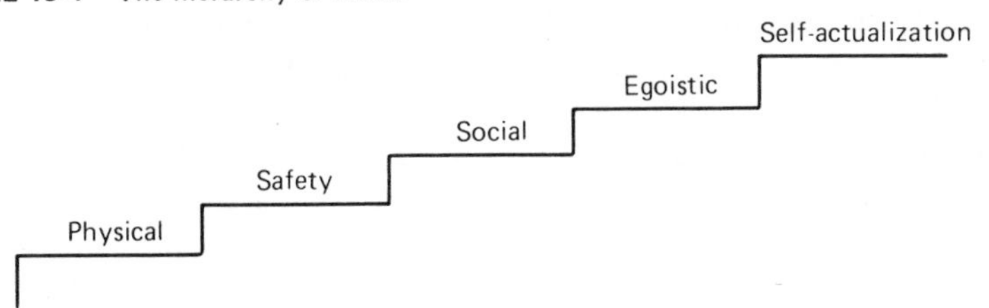

to the higher needs. Thus, in a primitive culture the emphasis on finding food and erecting shelter leaves little time to think of higher needs. In an advanced, prosperous culture the physiological and safety needs are readily filled and people strive to satisfy the social, esteem, and self-fulfillment needs in turn.

You will be able to work more effectively with other people if you can determine which of these needs each person seeks most aggressively. Hence, if a worker is striving hard for recognition, you can expect greater cooperation if your conversations with him reflect your recognition of his capabilities.

Chris Argyris, another pioneer in the social movement, takes the basic position that classical formal organization tends to stifle the need for self-actualization. The authority channels, formal structure, and specialization of the classical organization tend to make the employee passive, submissive, and prone to use his less important abilities rather than higher, more potent capabilities that might surface in a better organizational environment.[8]

Frederick Herzberg, another leader in the social approach to management, developed the *motivation-maintenance theory*. The essence of this theory is that motivation is two-dimensional. There are job factors, which, if they are not present, create *dissatisfaction;* if they are present, however, they do not motivate strongly. These are called *maintenance* or *hygiene factors.* The second set of job factors called *motivators,* builds a high degree of job *satisfaction* and *motivation* when they are present, but dissatisfaction is not necessarily present if they are missing.[9]

Herzberg's *maintainers* include pay, working conditions, security, company policy, supervisor's behavior, and interpersonal relationships with peers and superiors. His *motivators* include achievement, work content, responsibility, growth, and advancement.

SUMMARY

The functions of management as described in this book include planning, organizing, staffing, directing, controlling, innovating, coordinating, representing, budgeting, and reporting. This approach to management, "what managers do," is

[8] Chris Argyris, *Personality and Organization* (New York: Harper & Row, Publishers, 1957).

[9] Frederick Herzberg, "One More Time: How Do You Motivate Employees?" *Harvard Business Review* (January-February 1968).

called the *functional, traditional,* or *universal* approach to management. Since you've had exposure to many of these functions in earlier chapters as well as this one, the individual functions will not receive repeated treatment in this summary.

Management is a common-sense process of using available resources and information to best advantage for achieving profit and growth. The old faithful *why, what, where, when, how, who* questions, plus *how much,* will help you plan, organize, staff, direct, and control your business. The thinking must be translated into action. The emphasis should be on results rather than effort, but effort properly directed is essential to result achievement.

KEY TERMS

Controlling
Coordinating
Creativity
Directing
Innovation
Long-range plans
Management by exception
Management process approach
Organizing
Planning
Quantitative approach
Representing
Short-range plans
Staffing

QUESTIONS AND PROBLEMS

1. List and discuss the various approaches to management theory. Which do you think is the most important approach? Explain.
2. Discuss the ways in which the *why, what, when, where, who, how much,* and *how* questions facilitate performance of each of the five major management functions.
3. Discuss permanent company documents and their use in performing each of the five major management functions. Would any of these be useful to you in your mini business?
4. The business objectives of profit, growth, and leadership have been stressed throughout this book. Do you think your business should have additional objectives? Discuss them. How do they relate to the three objectives cited?
5. What is management by exception? Explain.
6. Do you agree that a questioning-counseling approach to employee problems is better than a hard-line approach? Justify your answer.
7. What is a standard? A variance? How are they used to achieve control?

8. Discuss the ways in which each of the following applies the functions of management to his or her job: (a) production manager, (b) manufacturing sales manager, (c) retail store owner, (d) repair service business owner, (e) independent insurance agent.
9. Describe the creative process.
10. In "The Small Manufacturing Company Turnaround" case you'll note some overlap of most of the actions into several management function areas. Can actions be chosen that will satisfy one function without having impact on another function? Explain your position.
11. Can you think of any other actions that should have been taken in the manufacturing case? List and discuss.
12. Briefly, tell in your own words how you intend to plan, organize, staff, direct, and control your own business.

FIELD INVESTIGATION AND PROJECTS

*1. Develop a report on management *functions* through library research. Relate your report to the business you intend to start.
2. Develop a report on "management by objectives" through library research.
3. Many management case-study textbooks have been published and are available in college libraries. Choose a case from one of these books and prepare a report on it. A suitable report would contain a summary of the case, an analysis, a statement of the problem(s), your recommendations or action, and a justification of your recommendations or action.

Human Resources

14

The most valuable asset you can have in your business derives from human resources. Human beings are endowed with the capability to think rationally as well as emotionally. Because they can think rationally, they can create new ideas and products and develop more profitable approaches to business. Because of their feelings and emotions they can sometimes be motivated to produce seemingly superhuman results; conversely, with poor motivation, they can be turned off emotionally and perform very poorly.

Thus, efficient, capable, motivated employees can make your business grow and your profits soar. An inefficient, inept, or unmotivated employee can kill potential business, waste your resources, and otherwise erode your profits and stunt your business growth.

The importance of good employees, properly motivated, places a severe burden on you as a business owner. You'll have to recruit, select, place, and train new employees. You'll have to keep employee records and make reports. You'll have to decide on methods and amounts of compensation, develop job descriptions, and perform many other functions that weren't required before you had employees. And, you'll have to have paychecks ready and covered on payday.

This chapter will provide you with guidelines for accomplishing these things. While you are learning about them, try not to lose sight of the fact that the name of the business game is profit and growth. But remember too that human resources, your most valuable asset, must be treated with considerably more care than cash, facilities, inventory, and other nonhuman resources. As you read this chapter, you will find answers to these questions:

1. How do I go about finding potential employees with special skills?
2. How can I pick the better applicants?
3. What training should I provide for new employees?
4. How can I direct my employees for greatest productivity?
5. What is motivation all about, and how can I best motivate my employees?
6. What is a job description and what practical purposes does it serve?
7. What are incentives, and how do they work?

BRINGING EMPLOYEES INTO YOUR BUSINESS

Even if you start your business as a one-person effort, there'll come a day when you'll need help if your business is successful. Personnel costs are usually the greatest expense next to cost of goods sold in a retail or wholesale business. Personnel costs also are usually the greatest expense in cost of goods and services sold in a manufacturing or service business. It behooves you to attract, select, place, train, and motivate employees to produce results that contribute to profit. Because human beings have a broad range of possibilities, human resources can make or break a business in spite of everything else that is done.

Recruiting

Recruiting employees is more difficult for a small, struggling business because such a business cannot compete with large companies in salary, fringe benefits, and apparent stability. Potential employees often do not see the opportunities for advancement that exist in the small company, and they may have doubts about the future of the business. Yet the chance of unusual opportunity is one of the leading recruiting assets of a small business. The possibility of failure ordinarily doesn't deter a young go-getter who can visualize potential for advancement and growth in your company.

Another recruiting asset that most small businesses have is a less formal, less monotonous working atmosphere than in a larger company. Although this generalization isn't always true, it is what attracts many people.

The key points in your recruiting advertising and recruiting efforts should be

1. The job, with a brief description of the work and the required (or desired) applicant qualifications. Pay can be stated or omitted in want ads.
2. The opportunities for advancement and growth with your company.
3. The pleasant working conditions provided and the challenging, interesting nature of the job.

You may go first to the classified "Help Wanted" ads in your local newspaper. Choose the classification that best fits the job described in your ad. Make your ad as specific and accurate as possible to avoid being swamped with unqualified applicants—this will just waste your time.

Other sources of applicants are the state employment services, which offer over 2,000 offices around the country[1] (no fees); placement offices in schools and colleges (no fees); private employment agencies (fees charged, paid by employee or employer depending on situation); the personnel departments of larger businesses (which may know of impending layoffs or retirements); word-of-mouth referrals; and drop-in applicants.

If this course of action seems like a lot of trouble, give it some thought. If you were buying a $10,000 machine for your business, you'd give the matter considerable attention. You'd probably devote several days to the effort and compare a number of machines. When you're hiring an employee, your potential investment can reach half a million dollars! (That's an average of $12,500 a year for forty years.) Does it seem wise to try to rush an investment of this potential size?

POINT 14-1: Your recruiting ads and efforts should be specific about the job, qualifications, and opportunities for advancement, with some mention of the pleasant working conditions and challenge within your small company.

Selection

When an applicant appears, you need to be ready to give him or her consideration. The first step is to have him or her complete an *application blank,* which provides pertinent personal information, educational and experience qualifications, work history, and references. If the potential employee applies in person, (s)he should be asked to fill in the application and should be given a courtesy screening interview. A typical application form is shown in Figure 14-1. You can probably find standard application forms in a stationery store and avoid the effort and expense of preparing your own. Submitted applications should be evaluated, and only those reasonably qualified should be invited in for in-depth interviews. (Extend the courtesy of calling or writing the others to indicate that you don't have employment for them at this time.) If a significant number of applications are received, it may be necessary to arrange screening interviews before final, extensive interviewing.

An *interview* gives you an opportunity to learn about the applicant's qualifications, motivations, and preferences. It also gives the applicant an opportunity to learn about the job, about your business, and about you. Remember that an employee can become an excellent long-term investment. Time and effort devoted to selection can pay off handsomely. On the other hand, a hasty selec-

[1] Charles E. Odell, "How The Public Employment Service Helps Small Business," *Management Aid, No. 41* (Washington, D.C.: Small Business Administration, 1971).

FIGURE 14-1 Employment application form

(A) Page 1

AN EQUAL OPPORTUNITY EMPLOYER

EMPLOYMENT APPLICATION

CODE # ______ DATE ______ NAME ______

PLEASE READ BEFORE COMPLETING THIS APPLICATION

The Bank does not discriminate in hiring or employment on the basis of race, color, religion, national origin, sex or ancestry or on the basis of age against persons whose age is between forty and sixty-five. No question on this application is intended to secure information to be used for such discrimination.

This application will be given every consideration, but its receipt does not imply that the applicant will be employed. In processing this employment application, the Bank may request that an investigative consumer report be prepared, which may include information as to your character, general reputation, police report, personal characteristics and mode of living. You have the right to request that the Bank completely and accurately disclose to you the nature and scope of the investigation requested. Such a request must be made in writing to the Personnel Section within a reasonable time after you complete this application.

I hereby authorize First National Bank in Garland to contact all previous employers for the purpose of an employment reference and release all persons and companies from any liabilities in responding to such requested information.

I HEREBY ACKNOWLEDGE THAT I HAVE READ AND UNDERSTOOD THE FOREGOING DISCLOSURE.

Signature	Date

Form No. 20011

(B) Page 2

PLEASE ANSWER EVERY QUESTION ON THIS APPLICATION

PLEASE PRINT IN INK

Name (first) (middle) (last)	Social Security Number
Street Address Apt.	Telephone Number
City State Zip	Length of Time at this Address
Maiden Name - If Married	Date of Birth

List Previous Addresses Within The U.S. (except military) If Address Changed During Past 8 Years.

No.	Street	City	State	Zip	(Date) From	(Date) To
No.	Street	City	State	Zip	(Date) From	(Date) To

Type of Work Desired	Salary or Wages Expected	Date Available for Work
Have You Ever Been Refused Bond? ☐ YES ☐ NO	Are You a United States Citizen? ☐ YES ☐ NO	If Not a Citizen, Do You Have The Legal Right To Remain Permanently in The U.S.? ☐ YES ☐ NO

EDUCATION

NAME	ADDRESS CITY STATE	MAJOR COURSE OR SUBJECT	CIRCLE LAST YR. COMPLETED	IF GRADUATED MONTH & YEAR	DEGREE
High School or Preparatory			1 2 3 4		
Business School			1 2 3 4		
College			1 2 3 4		
Graduate School			1 2 3 4		

List Scholastic Honors, Offices Held and Activities in High School and College.

Are You Planning to Pursue Further Studies? ☐ YES ☐ NO ☐ DAY SCHOOL ☐ NIGHT SCHOOL	If So, When, Where and What Courses?

GENERAL INFORMATION

Use this space to describe your interest in banking and the skills and aptitudes that you feel may qualify you for a position at the bank. You may wish to include civic and community activities, professional societies in which you participate, special training or skills such as typing, shorthand, accounting, etc.

Do You Consider Yourself in Good Health? ☐ YES ☐ NO	Describe Any Physical or Mental Handicap You May Have.		Do You Smoke? ☐ YES ☐ NO	If You Smoke, What Amount Daily?
Have You Been Employed Here Before?	Have You Ever Applied Here Before?	Name Any Relatives Or Friends In The Bank.		

Have you ever been convicted of a criminal offense involving dishonesty, breach of trust including (but not limited to) robbery, theft, embezzlement, forgery, perjury, tax evasion, etc.? ☐ YES ☐ NO If yes, describe: ____________

WORK EXPERIENCE

List the last five positions you have held beginning with most recent, or all positions held for the past five years. Include self employment, summer and part-time jobs. If you do not have enough space, you may give more complete and detailed information on a separate sheet of paper. Accuracy of dates and addresses is essential.

NAME AND ADDRESS OF FORMER EMPLOYER	DATES EMPLOYED	SALARY	
Company Name ____ Number And Street ____ City And Street ____ Zip ____ Phone ____	Beginning ____ Ending ____	Beginning $ ____ Ending $ ____	Supervisor ____ Your Title ____ Duties ____ Reason For Leaving ____
Company Name ____ Number And Street ____ City And State ____ Zip ____ Phone ____	Beginning ____ Ending ____	Beginning $ ____ Ending $ ____	Supervisor ____ Your Title ____ Duties ____ Reason For Leaving ____
Company Name ____ Number And Street ____ City And State ____ Zip ____ Phone ____	Beginning ____ Ending ____	Beginning $ ____ Ending $ ____	Supervisor ____ Your Title ____ Duties ____ Reason For Leaving ____
Company Name ____ Number And Street ____ City And State ____ Zip ____ Phone ____	Beginning ____ Ending ____	Beginning $ ____ Ending $ ____	Supervisor ____ Your Title ____ Duties ____ Reason For Leaving ____
Company Name ____ Number And Street ____ City And State ____ Zip ____ Phone ____	Beginning ____ Ending ____	Beginning $ ____ Ending $ ____	Supervisor ____ Your Title ____ Duties ____ Reason For Leaving ____

If Presently Employed, Why Do You Desire To Change Your Position?	If Now Employed, May We Contact Your Present Employer? ☐ YES ☐ NO

MILITARY SERVICE RECORD

Have You Served In The Armed Forces Of The United States? ☐ YES ☐ NO	Date of Entry in Service	Rank at Entry	Branch of Service and Special Training
Date of Discharge	**Rank at Discharge**	**Type of Discharge**	**Are You at Present in Any Active or Inactive Reserve or The National Guard?** ☐ YES ☐ NO

tion can result in a loss to you, if you hire a dishonest, immoral, or incapable employee.

During the early stages of your mini-business growth when all employees re-

no personnel Man.

(D) Page 4

PLEASE READ BEFORE SIGNING—IF YOU HAVE ANY QUESTIONS REGARDING THIS STATEMENT, PLEASE ASK THEM OF AN EMPLOYMENT INTERVIEWER BEFORE SIGNING.

In the event of my employment to a position in the Bank, I will comply with all rules and regulations as set forth in the Bank's policy manual or other communications distributed to all employees. I understand that such employment is conditioned upon a favorable health evaluation which may include a physical examination by a doctor selected by the Bank. Additionally, I authorize the Bank to supply my employment record in whole or in part, and in confidence, to any prospective employer, governmental agency or other party with a legal and proper interest.

I certify that the facts stated on my application for employment are true and correct. I understand that a misrepresentation or fabrication (including health condition) will disqualify me from further consideration of employment, or if employed by the Bank, will subject me to immediate termination.

As a condition of employment, I agree to take a polygraph test and be fingerprinted as required, prior to or during employment with First National Bank in Garland.

I further understand that at any time during the first 90 days of employment my work progress is subject to appraisal and if not satisfactory could call for immediate termination with salary paid through last day worked.

If accepted as an employee of First National Bank in Garland, I do hereby pledge myself to observe in confidence and not disclose any information relating to First National Bank in Garland business with any person, firm or corporation, except such matters that I may have express authority from an authorized officer of the Bank to disclose.

SIGNATURE OF APPLICANT DATE

PERSONNEL USE ONLY

(Courtesy First National Bank, Garland, Texas.)

port to you, you'll interview applicants yourself. When your business has grown to the point where one of your employees has reached the status of second-in-command or business confidant, it would be wise to have him or her interview applicants as well. *An interview and evaluation by two persons is likely to provide more information and a more thorough evaluation than a one-person approach.* When your business grows further, the person to whom the potential employee would report should conduct the principal interview and perhaps even make the final decision.

Conducting the Interview

Here are some guidelines for conducting a job interview:

1. Be natural and make the applicant feel at ease. Hold the interview privately and without interruptions.
2. Encourage the applicant to tell you about his (or her) previous work experience and training. Be prepared to lead him with questions but make the questions sufficiently *indirect* to encourage him to talk freely. Avoid direct questions that turn the interview into a question-and-answer period. For example, *say,* "You've been working for Ferguson Tool Company for three years, and you've had considerable previous experience. I'd like to know more about you and your working experience." *Don't ask,* "What was your first responsibility at Ferguson?" The approach to encouraging the interviewee to talk freely is called *nondirective* interviewing. (*Directive* interviewing, on the other hand, employs direct questions and encourages specific answers, thus tending to confine the conversation boundaries.)

   Once the nondirective interview is launched, you can keep the applicant talking with comments such as "I agree," "That's great," "Certainly," and "You finished that job in three hours?" Restatement of the interviewee's conversation in question form, as well as your verbal and nonverbal responses, tend to keep him talking.

   Your big job is to listen, and to listen well. It's preferable *not* to make notes in the applicant's presence because this tends to make some interviewees uneasy. Make notes after the interview out of the applicant's sight, and place them in the applicant's file. This will help you to recall the individual and the interview when you prepare to make your final selection or wish to take any other action in the matter. This information will also be useful if the applicant is not selected for the job at hand but is to be considered for a future opening.
3. Have copies of the job description and specification available to show and to discuss with the applicant. Be sure that he understands what's expected and that he knows enough about your company and you to reach an intelligent decision if a job is offered.
4. If the talk turns to pay or incentives, let the person know the specific pay if it's nailed down. If otherwise—for example, if pay is to be based on the applicant's experience, present salary, and so forth—say so and indicate that any offer, if made, will specify the pay.
5. Keep the objectives of the interview in mind. They are to determine the applicant's experience, ability, integrity, attitudes, fit to the job, and fit to your organization. You may have additional objectives. Again, employ nondirective techniques in exploring these areas.

Other Selection Action

If the position to be filled is highly technical or requires special skills, you may wish to resort to formal testing. If possible, it's preferable in a mini business to "examine" the applicant verbally during the interview. Formal testing is time-consuming, and can be expensive. Some tests have been challenged as discriminatory. Big business sometimes uses testing services. A mini business can justify the absence of formal tests on the basis of economy. Inexpensive tests for technical jobs can be developed from questions in the Schaum Publishing Company *Outline Series,* the ARCO Publishing Company *Tutor* series, and similar publications available in college book stores.

Testing should be utilized only if there is a valid reason for using it. A simple criterion is, "Do I know what this employee brings to the job relative to what he must be capable of performing?" If you cannot learn this in the interview, testing may be in order.

If the applicant appears to be promising at the interview, his or her previous employment and references should be verified. The two or three most promising candidates may be called in for additional interviews if you feel it will be helpful in the final selection. Don't discourage any of these people, because your first choice may not accept your offer, and you may want to make an offer to one of the others.

A physical examination is always a good idea because it may save you the experience of hiring someone, training him, and then having him leave for health reasons. A physical is especially advisable if the employee will be doing strenuous work.

POINT 14-2: Have applicants complete an application form; interview the most promising candidates by nondirective methods; verify employment and check references of those who appear promising from the interviews. Make a selection or schedule additional interviews for final selection.

Placement and Pay

If you're hiring to fill a specific job and don't have any other openings, the matter of placement and pay are usually predetermined. However, if you have a number of openings, the applicant may be qualified for any of several. In this case, placement and pay are not so clear-cut. You may want to have the applicant interview for each of the possible openings. A group interview followed by short individual interviews may be productive. You'd ordinarily want to place the applicant in the job in which he is qualified to earn the highest pay. Sometimes the spectrum of available applicants makes it impossible to do this, and placement and pay must be based on the convenience of the business.

Lower-skilled, lower-paid people should be used for jobs requiring lower skills and for sales jobs involving lower-priced merchandise. Businesspeople are sometimes likely to hire more skilled people than the job requires. A glaring example is the high-priced pharmacist who must sell inexpensive items in a drug store because there aren't enough considerably lower-paid salespersons. This results in higher costs. However, this is sometimes justified in a small business in which the more skilled employee can "wear several hats" effectively, and hence reduce the number of employees required.

The *hourly wage* and the *periodic* (weekly, monthly) *salary* are the most common methods of employee compensation. The *commission* method or a *combination of base salary and commission* is frequently employed to compensate salespeople and repair service workers. When the commission method is used, the employee often has a flat periodic *draw against commissions.* For example, a salesperson may earn commissions of $50, $150, $250, and $300 in four succeeding weeks, but have a weekly draw of $100. At the end of the four weeks his draws of $100 per week total $400, but he's earned a total of $750. The difference, $350, is paid to him then, and the process is repeated. Another method of compensation, *piecework,* is based on rate of production. There are variations of these methods of compensation which cannot be covered here. Some of the variations take the form of incentives and fringe benefits, which will be covered in a succeeding section.

Commission and piecework are ideal arrangements from your standpoint as the employer; both methods tie employee compensation costs to business income. The conversion of an expense from a fixed to a variable cost is advantageous to you because you can exercise more effective control. However, most workers prefer an hourly wage or a periodic salary, and some refuse to work on a commission or piecework basis. Combinations of base pay and commission or piecework payments are more acceptable to workers, but by and large, most people would rather be paid an hourly wage or salary.

While, from a pure dollar standpoint, the lowest possible hourly wage or salary for a given job might seem most attractive to you as an employer, *the low-pay approach is usually a loser for you.* Pay your employees adequate wages compatible with wages in your area. Increase their pay and offer incentives as their usefulness and period of employment in your business increases. People are motivated by more than money, but they want to feel that they're getting what they're worth. If they feel that they're underpaid, they may feel that you're cheating them and you'll lose performance.

Temporaries, Moonlighters, and Others

Temporary or part-time help may be advisable when peak loads occur or when a specialized talent is not required full-time. For example, you may need extra salespeople in a retail store during Christmas season, or you may need a bookkeeper just one day a week.

To get this kind of help at lowest cost, build a resource file of people available to help on a temporary or part-time basis. Recruit part-time help with classified ads. Interview and build files classified by skills, hours during the day available, season available, and desired pay. Call these people for help as needed, or hire them on a continuing moonlight basis if required.

Another approach to temporary help for peak loads is to use a temporary help service such as Task Force, Employer's Overload, Greyhound Temporary Personnel, Kelly Services, or Manpower. These temporary help services are listed under "Employment Contractors" in the Yellow Pages. This kind of help costs more by the hour, but you're freed of the task of building your own resource files, calling around to see who's available, and handling the payroll with the attendant record keeping. You get a straight tax-deductible expense billing that requires only one journal entry.[2]

You can free yourself of record keeping and simplify your marketing department (if you're in manufacturing) by using independent sales reps. This also tends to make your major sales costs a direct percentage of sales.[3]

The independent sales rep, often called a manufacturer's agent, enables you to start small in a manufacturing business because he or she can function as your sales department. The independent sales rep is usually paid a straight commission, so you can enjoy the benefit of sales costs proportional to sales—that is, you have sales costs only when you have sales. Commissions vary, but 10 percent to 20 percent is a fairly common range. The rep pays his expenses out of his commissions under most arrangements. He usually carries several lines of complementary but noncompetitive lines so he can make sales for several of his principals to each customer he calls on. The principal (you) and the sales rep generally enter into a written contract. Get your attorney's opinion if you have any questions.

POINT 14-3: Use temporary help and moonlighters for peaks and partial loads to increase operating profits. If you're in a manufacturing business, consider the use of an independent sales rep to tie selling costs directly to sales.

REVIEW EXERCISES 14-A

1. How can you attract job applicants to your business?
2. Why should even a very small business use a job application form?
3. What steps can you take to make the best possible selection among applicants for a job?

[2] William Olsten, "Pointers on Using Temporary-Help Services," *Management Aid, No. 205* (Washington, D.C.: Small Business Administration, 1970).

[3] Edwin E. Bobrow, "Is the Independent Sales Agent for You? *Management Aid, No. 200* (Washington, D.C.: Small Business Administration, 1974).

4. Discuss the purpose of the job interview and discuss how it should be conducted.
5. Under what circumstances should temporary help be employed?

WHEN YOU HIRE AN EMPLOYEE

Whenever you elect to employ a resource in your business, you want to use it as wisely as possible. You devote management time and administrative effort to do so. In order to use your human resources well, you'll have to devote management time and administrative effort to this cause. This section will address administrative requirements, job descriptions, employee development, performance evaluation, incentives, fringe benefits, and promotions.

Paperwork

Chapters 9 and 10 introduced you to the essential employee records for IRS and other regulatory requirements. A full listing of the desirable and the required paperwork is essential at this point:

1. Start a file on the employee when he's hired. Put his application form, his résumé or other material submitted, the notes or reports on his previous employment and references, notes on interviews, and his job description in his file. Include copies of the job offer, acceptance, pay-scale data, and information on promised incentives and fringe benefits.
2. If his job requires a certificate, license, or special authorization, place it or other acceptable evidence of it in his file.
3. If a medical examination is required, a copy of the examination report should be placed in his file.
4. As part of his employment processing, the applicant should fill in an IRS form W-4 (Figure 9-4) and the necessary insurance forms (if you have a group hospitalization or life insurance plan). Copies of these should be placed in his file. Originals of the insurance forms must be submitted to the insurance company, and the W-4 is simply held in the file for record.
5. Enter the employee's name and pertinent data on rosters to be used for payroll preparation. Information for IRS Forms 941 (filed quarterly) and W-2 (filed at the end of the calendar year) will be derived from payroll data. The Form 941 and a copy of the W-2 is submitted to IRS; the employee receives a copy of the W-2 in duplicate. Payroll data is also used to develop information for the IRS form 940 (filed annually) and state unemployment tax reports (filed quarterly).
6. Additional reports may be required if your state has a state income tax.
7. Performance evaluation reports, employee awards, reprimands, promotions, raises, and other events or status changes pertinent to the employee should be recorded in his file as they occur.

FIGURE 14-2 Care of employee records and reports

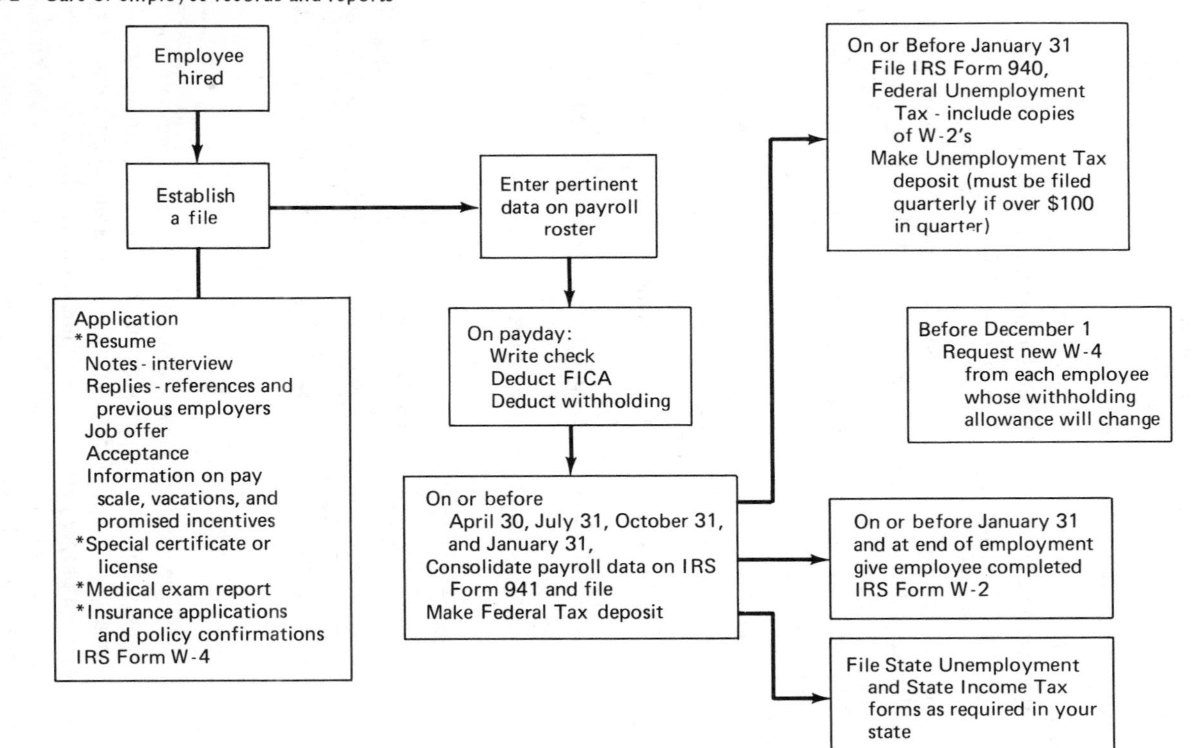

Employee hired
Establish a file
Application
*Resume
Notes - interview
Replies - references and previous employers
Job offer
Acceptance
Information on pay scale, vacations, and promised incentives
*Special certificate or license
*Medical exam report
*Insurance applications and policy confirmations
IRS Form W-4
Enter pertinent data on payroll roster
On payday:
Write check
Deduct FICA
Deduct withholding
On or before
April 30, July 31, October 31, and January 31,
Consolidate payroll data on IRS Form 941 and file
Make Federal Tax deposit
On or Before January 31
File IRS Form 940, Federal Unemployment Tax - include copies of W-2's
Make Unemployment Tax deposit (must be filed quarterly if over $100 in quarter)
Before December 1
Request new W-4 from each employee whose withholding allowance will change
On or before January 31 and at end of employment give employee completed IRS Form W-2
File State Unemployment and State Income Tax forms as required in your state

*If applicable.

Figure 14-2 shows the steps in employee record keeping and reporting for easy reference and checking. If there are additional local requirements in your area, add them to this chart for future reference.

Job Descriptions and Specifications

A *job description* for each position for which a person is hired is part of any efficient organization plan. A job description summarizes the duties and functions to be performed, the responsibility and authority that goes with the job, and the upward and downward line reporting channels. The organization chart (discussed in the last chapter) merely presents a broad view of who performs given functions and the general reporting channels. With the job descriptions, each person's part of the operation is defined and described. The job description is also useful in interesting and selecting personnel for a given job, teaching the worker his job, telling the worker what's expected of him, and helping the worker set his goals.

Job descriptions should be specific, adequate, concise, and written in plain English that the worker can understand. Unfortunately, job descriptions are often too wordy and so are meaningless to the employee. Figure 14-3 shows job descriptions that are brief and easy to understand, and adequately detail the jobs described.

A *job specification* outlines the desired qualifications for a job. It is used primarily as a guide for placing recruiting ads and evaluating applicants. The qualifications in the specification include experience, education, and personality requirements.

> POINT 14-4: A job description and job specification should be prepared for each job in your business. The job description shows the worker what is expected of him, assures you that every facet of organization is covered, and is useful for training and evaluation.

Employee Development

As your business grows, your success depends more and more on your employees. Your requirements for supervisory and managerial employees grow as your business expands. It's a good idea to develop and promote internally if you can. Some of your employee development comes automatically, with employees doing their jobs and learning more about the business by observation. You can and should aid the process by indoctrinating employees, coaching them, providing employee training, subsidizing employees for trade and college courses that expand capability, and by attempting to promote employees to higher responsibilities as they become capable of handling them.

FIGURE 14-3 Job descriptions

(A) Junior buyer

BUYER — JUNIOR

WORK PERFORMED

Negotiates the purchase of materials from vendors based on approved requisitions from responsible managers, supervisors, or foremen. Negotiations may be conducted by telephone, written correspondence, in-plant interviews, and occasionally out-of-plant visits.

GENERAL DUTIES

1. Reviews purchase requisitions.
2. Interviews vendors to obtain information relative to products, ability, price, service, and delivery.
3. Reviews proposals from vendors and negotiates with acceptable vendor for contract.
4. Buys raw materials, parts, supplies, services, equipment, machinery, etc., necessary for operation of business.
5. Has the responsibility for keeping records pertaining to items purchased, costs, and inventory.
6. Reviews rejection reports on defective materials and takes corrective action.
7. Is responsible for delivery of material by date required.
8. Approves invoices for payment.

WORKER SPECIFICATIONS

1. Must have a high school education or the equivalent, with some college credits desired.
2. Must have at least two years experience in a Purchasing Department.
3. Must have the ability to read blueprints, write requisitions for quotations, interpret specifications.
4. Must possess a knowledge of various materials, supply sources, and have the ability to negotiate prices of goods.
5. Must have the ability to use directories and find new sources of supply.

WORKING CONDITIONS

Normal to a Purchasing Department Office.

(B) General machinist

OCCUPATION: GENERAL MACHINIST

POSITION DESCRIPTION

WORK PERFORMED:

Plans and performs a variety of tasks associated with checking, setting up and operating machine tools and fitting and assembling parts to make or repair metal parts, mechanisms, tools or machines. Performs most duties with a minimum of supervision.

GENERAL DUTIES:

1. Analyzes drawings and sketches and recommends changes when necessary.
2. Analyzes methods and sequences of machining and assembly operations and recommends changes when necessary.
3. Sets up and operates any and all machine tools such as lathes, milling machines, drills, shapers, and grinders.
4. Operates a machine tool, observes its operation or tests it with inspection equipment to diagnose malfunctions or to test repaired machine and set ups.
5. Solves problems relative to jigs, fixtures, materials, machine settings, tools, product specifications, and fabrication methods.
6. Reads prints or job order and tooling instructions for specifications and makes complex and experimental parts.
7. Measures, marks and scribes dimensions and reference points to lay out stock or parts for machining.
8. Secures specified tools and fixtures and operates machine controls to set cutting speed and feed rates.
9. Positions and secures parts on surface plates or work tables, assembles parts and verifies conformance to specifications.
10. Guides and instructs lower level machinists and machine operators.
11. Works with engineers, designers, supervisors and vendors on machining problems.
12. Maintains a relatively clean work station, practices safe working habits, and observes all safety rules and regulations.
13. Performs other duties as assigned.

OCCUPATION: GENERAL MACHINIST (cont'd)

WORKER SPECIFICATIONS:

1. Equivalent to a high school education.
2. Special training in advanced shop mathematics and basic metallurgical technology.
3. Physical ability to lift tools and materials weighing up to 60 pounds manually, and heavier pieces using power equipment.
4. Over five years experience as a machinist and the ability to effectively analyze and accomplish machining operations.

WORKING CONDITIONS:

1. Normal shop conditions.

(Courtesy: Intercontinental Manufacturing Co., Inc., Garland, Texas.)

You'll want a new employee to become productive as soon as possible. You can accelerate the process by devoting time to initial indoctrination to the business and initial training in his job. If you're hiring several employees at a time, you can resort to group indoctrination. You should have an indoctrination checklist of items that you cover with every new employee. Each employee's *initial training* should cover his job description and the actual mechanics of doing his job. Initial training might take a day or less, but may require more time depending on the complexity of the job. This is usually followed by a week or more of *on-the-job training.* The amount of training is a function of the job complexity, the employee's previous experience, and his aptitude.[4]

As an example, consider the initial indoctrination and training of a sales employee in a very small retail and repair service business. The process should include a tour of the merchandise in the store; this will provide information on where the merchandise is, what the prices are, how the prices are marked and coded, and how inventory and order information is obtained. Show the new employee how to make out a sales ticket, how to determine sales tax, and how to handle purchases by check and by credit card. Let him (or her) prepare several sales tickets for hypothetical sales and check them for correctness. Show him how to reconcile the cash drawer at the end of the day, how to handle merchandise returns, how to receive shipments, how to tag equipment coming in for service, and how to handle customer in-store pick-ups. Tour the service shop and show him some of the common repairs and charges, explain the policy on estimates, and define the kind of equipment that is accepted for repair. Provide literature and other study material on the major merchandise sold, rehearse sales pitches with him, and instruct him in suggestion selling. Explain store policies, the way to greet customers, and any specific duties his job includes (such as dusting the merchandise, or restocking the shelves in free time).

Training is a continuing part of the employee development process. Periodic internal training sessions, coaching on the job, attendance at manufacturer and distributor sponsored courses and clinics, and seminars and formal courses provide additional training opportunities. A reasonably stocked *library* of books on pertinent business and technical subjects related to your business is a good training resource. By speaking enthusiastically about the books and by encouraging employees to check them out and use them, you can give an extra push to your training efforts at very low cost.

The question of training on business time vs. training on personal time may come up. If you're generous with training on business time and don't emphasize the distinction, the question probably won't be raised and you'll find employees willing to take courses on personal time. The question may arise concerning who pays for courses taken on personal time. If the employee is taking the courses on his own initiative and they're *not* related to his work, they're his expense. If

[4] For ideas, see Leonard J. Smith, "Checklist for Developing a Training Program," *Management Aid, No. 186* (Washington, D.C.: Small Business Administration, 1974).

they're related to his work but part of a formal education program, you're still on reasonably safe ground to let him bear the expense, unless you offer to pay for them as an incentive to the employee. While larger businesses can afford to pay for formal courses for employees, few mini businesses can afford the expense.

Specialized seminars and courses which you suggest or strongly encourage employees to attend are another matter. In these cases, your business should bear the expense. If the training isn't worth the expense, it shouldn't be provided.

> POINT 14-5: Provide initial indoctrination and training for your employees to make them productive faster. Provide employee development opportunities through continuing training, coaching, and the encouragement of outside study.

Performance Evaluation

The tools available for providing motivators and helping your employees fulfill their needs include performance evaluation and promotion.

Performance evaluation began as a method for selecting managers, promoting, and deciding who gets a raise. Currently, performance evaluation is also used as a coaching and training device. Some personnel experts feel that "merit raises" should be separated from performance evaluations. We proceed with the view that merit raises, when given, will be related to performance reviews.

Your employees need to know when they're doing a job well. A positive evaluation from you has considerable meaning for them. So does a promotion (an enlargement of responsibility). Pay increases are also meaningful as a way of keeping score in the human success game.

If, on the other hand, the employee is not doing well, the evaluation interview gives you an opportunity to find out why. If you can find the difficulty, you may be able to convert the individual into a more useful and valuable employee. Use the nondirective interviewing technique to discover problems. If, after repeated efforts, you cannot bring the employee around, take appropriate action, which at the worst involves dismissal.

Performance evaluation is best performed by measuring the employee's work record alongside the job description according to a reasonably structured format and discussing the evaluation with the employee. The emphasis should be on the positive, with encouragement to improve the negatives. Don't take performance evaluation lightly!

> POINT 14-6: Performance evaluation can be used to coach and encourage employees. It also provides a means of rating the employee or giving him/her a raise.

Incentives, Fringe Benefits, and Promotions

Fringe benefits can include such things as paid vacations, paid holidays, paid sick leaves, paid or partially paid health and life insurance programs, purchase discounts, free courses, paid tuition, and such privileges as after-hour use of company vehicles and club memberships, to name some of the most common ones. The very small business usually doesn't go much beyond paid vacations and holidays. Group health and life insurance programs with the employee paying the low premiums available on these group programs are well worth considering in a small business.

Incentives include commissions, bonuses based on results, profit-sharing programs, contests, special awards, and other reward arrangements. The purpose of incentives is to help the employee relate his or her personal success to the success of the business.

Beginning mini businesses usually don't get into bonus and profit-sharing programs immediately, and some never do. This may be due to lack of understanding of the benefits to the business and inability to structure a program. You'll do well to learn more about bonus and profit-sharing programs used in larger businesses and to develop a variation that might fit yours as it grows.

Contests and special awards are inexpensive and can produce results worth many times their cost. Sales, production, and quality contests are typical. The prize might be a savings bond or a suitable item of merchandise. The keys to successful employee contests are meetings with pep talks, some good-natured rivalry, and daily score keeping with results prominently displayed for competing employees or teams to see. But employee rivalry can backfire. Tread cautiously!

Awards may be presented for outstanding accomplishments not connected with contests. An award might include a certificate or letter of appreciation and some tangible gift such as a savings bond or a watch.

Promotions are usually made on the basis of need and/or the qualifications, capability, and loyalty of the person promoted. A promotion should carry increased responsibility and increased pay, and often includes additional fringe benefits. A pay increase doesn't necessarily involve a promotion. Pay increases are granted to reward results and loyalty or to meet increasing costs of living.

POINT 14-7: Mini businesses often overlook the advantages to be gained from fringe benefit and incentive programs. Contests and awards provide inexpensive incentives, but in using them, avoid antagonistic rivalries. Incentive pay systems include commission and piecework arrangements and bonuses for above-standard performance.

REVIEW EXERCISES 14-B

1. List items that should be included in an employee's file and explain the reason for including them.
2. What is a job description? What is its primary purpose? What are the secondary uses?
3. Develop a simple indoctrination and initial training program for a combination secretary and office manager in your chosen business. (You can assume the employee can type and has studied bookkeeping.) Develop the program along the practical lines of the salesperson's indoctrination example presented in this section.
4. What are the purposes of employee performance evaluations?
5. Discuss fringe benefits and incentives.

WORKING WITH AND THROUGH PEOPLE

The management functions–planning, organizing, staffing, directing, and controlling–all involve *working with and through people.* Working through people has been introduced in Chapter 13. This section will build on that introduction. The treatment is very limited by space and it is hoped that you'll study this subject further in the future.[5]

Approaches To Leadership

The approaches to working with and through people are myriad. The favored approaches in most management and supervisory literature are those of the behavioral schools (human relations and social), briefly discussed in Chapter 13. These approaches are more prevalent in big business, where *salaried managers* and supervisors tend to depend on others and to *not* "rock the boat." The situation is different for owners in small businesses. Even in big business the "as we say" and the "as we do" often aren't the same thing. The old hard-line autocratic "Do it now" managers aren't extinct (and are very much alive in small businesses). Most of the top entrepreneurs, the people who've built big businesses from scratch or mini-business beginnings tend to be tough-minded, demanding, often autocratic, and at times even obnoxious!

[5] These books are suggested for the student who wishes to delve deeper: George Strauss and Leonard R. Sayles, *Personnel: The Human Problems of Management,* 3rd ed. (Englewood Cliffs, N.J.: Prentice-Hall, Inc., 1972); and Ralph W. Reber and Gloria E. Terry, *Behavioral Insights for Supervision* (Englewood Cliffs, N.J.: Prentice-Hall, Inc., 1975).

To sum it up, there isn't a single blueprint for all successful manager-leaders. Every leader has his or her own style. And you'll develop your own style as you learn to manage your business.

What are some of the approaches to leadership? Let's visit with some typical leaders:

Democratic Leader: "OK, gang, we should reach $20,000 in sales this month. How can we do it?"
Participative Leader: "OK, gang, we've got to reach $20,000 in sales this month. We want everyone to share in this. How will each of you help to achieve it?" (These leaders are very much alike.)
Autocratic Leader: "You sell $4,000 this month, Harry. Billy, you sell $6,000. Florence, you sell $6,000 and Larry, you sell $4,000. No excuses. Here's how I want you to do it–(details)."
Laissez-Faire Leader: "The sales goal is $20,000 this month. Go to it. If you need any help, let me know."

Those are the most often seen types of leaders. Here are two others who don't get quite as much publicity.

Optimistic Leader: "OK, gang, there's $100,000 in sales out there. Our goal is only $20,000 this month, and of course that's going to be easy as pie to exceed. Here's the general plan–"
Motivating Leader: "Our sales goal is $20,000 this month. This is a wonderful opportunity for all of us to excel. The person who achieves highest sales will receive a $25 savings bond, and if we exceed the goal by $5,000 or more, we'll have a celebration party."

There are quite a few similarities and overlaps between some leadership styles. The extremely optimistic, autocratic, and laissez-faire styles are generally regarded with less favor than the others. Successful leadership depends not only on the style of the leader, but on the *character of the leader* and *the confidence and respect that he or she earns* from associates and subordinates. You can earn your employees' respect if you

1. Treat them fairly
2. Live and work with reasonable moral standards
3. Possess a reasonable degree of technical competence in your business
4. Respect those who work for you

You can earn additional respect if you are considerate and understanding of human needs. This trait, *empathy,* is the ability to sense and experience the thoughts and feelings of another as though you were the other person. In other words, empathy is the ability to put yourself in the other person's shoes. This trait will go a long way in leading and dealing with your employees. In fact, it is a valuable resource in *all* your interactions with others.

POINT 14-8: There are many styles of leadership. Regardless of your leadership style, you can lead successfully if you have the respect of your employees and if you respect them. If you can put yourself in the other person's shoes, you'll enhance your ability to lead and work through people.

Communications

The ability to communicate effectively is a primary requisite for working with and through people. Communication consists of *encoding* messages (translating ideas into words, tone, and facial expression), *transmitting* messages (physically stating and acting encoded messages), *receiving* messages (listening to the words and tone and seeing the accompanying nonverbal cues), and *decoding* messages (converting the words, tone, and nonverbal cues back into ideas). When the initial receiver becomes the sender and responds with a message to the initial sender (who is now the receiver), the communication process has come full circle. See Figure 14-4.

FIGURE 14-4 The communication process

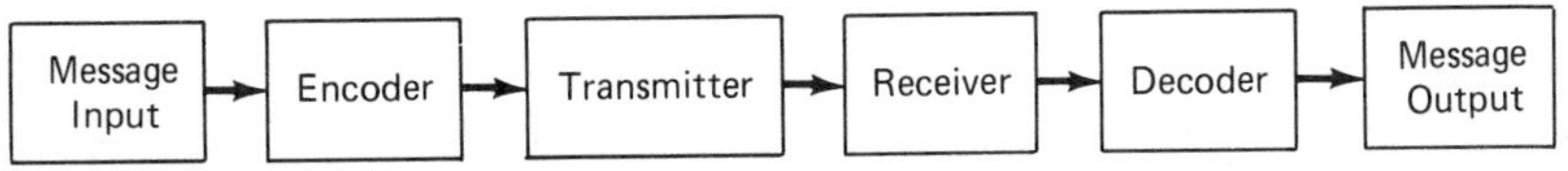

There are several points about this process that are worthy of note. *First,* an idea can be encoded in a number of ways. You can put too many or too few words into the message. You can choose words that are too weak or too strong. Poor choice of words can distort the meaning. The tone and inflection you use adds to the meaning, and provides another possibility for clarification or distortion. Finally, the physical accompaniment (particularly facial expressions) perceivable by the eye can clarify or distort the intended meaning. The transmitted message, in other words, can convey all, a part of, or more than the idea originally intended by the sender to the receiver. Thus, the statement "Management is getting things done through people" can be transmitted with different meanings depending on the vocal emphasis. "Management is *getting things done* through people," and "Management is getting things done *through people*" convey two different ideas. Note how the mere shift of emphasis changes the message.

You can say to an employee, "Ship twenty soldering irons to Frank Jones," or "Ship twenty soldering irons to Frank Jones by the fastest method," or "Ship twenty soldering irons to Frank Jones by the most economical method." The first message is incomplete if you intended either of the other two. If you say, "Ship twenty soldering irons to Frank Jones by the fastest and the most economical method," you're sending a confusing message because "fastest" and "most economical" aren't necessarily the same. And if you want "most economical method" but say "parcel post" instead, (on the assumption that it's the most economical method), you may be sending the wrong information; another means may be more economical.

The messages "Verify the total shipments today," "Check your figures on today's shipments; I'm out of balance," and "You must have fouled up again on the shipping figures—do them again and do them right," convey considerably different meaning to the receiver, yet the same incident might result in any of these messages being sent. The first one is a bit brief and doesn't convey a "why," which often helps the receiver know what to look for. The second one explains "why" and doesn't have the demoralizing slant the third message contains. Inflection, volume, and facial expression can make any of the three forms come off better or worse.

POINT 14-9: Communication consists of translating an idea into a message, transmission, reception, and conversion of the message back into an idea. The words, the way they're said, and your nonverbal cues all contribute to the message content.

The original idea can lose its meaning through poor encoding and transmission on the sender's part and *through poor reception and decoding on the receiver's part.*

This leads to the *second* point—that receiving and decoding (listening, observing, and interpreting) is as important in the communication process as sending the message. Communications skill is a key tool in sales, and the best salespeople are those who develop the art of competent listening, observing, and interpreting. These abilities are just as essential to you (as a manager) in dealing with employees. Thus, the message, "I'd like to take Tuesday off to take my daughter to college," can come through to you as any of these ideas:

"I'd like to take Tuesday off."
"I'm tired and need a rest. I want Tuesday off."
"I want Tuesday off for my convenience; the heck with the business."
"I love my daughter and getting her off to college for the first time is a very special event in our family. I'd like to take Tuesday off to do it."

If you're a good listener you'll hear the original message completely and the employee's tone, inflections, and facial expressions will tend to convey any of the rest of the meanings cited. Your own attitude and regard for people will have something to do with your interpretation; clearly, the last interpretation shows empathy on your part. Finally, the employee's past performance and your individual regard for him or her will influence your interpretation.

POINT 14-10: Listening and observing is an important part of communication and a key managerial skill. Listen and look for the whole message.

The *third* point in the communication process is that communication is not complete until the initial sender and receiver change roles and a response to the original message is received. This response "closes the loop" and should let the original sender know if his message was received, if it was correctly received and understood, and the probable resulting action he can expect from the original receiver.

Thus, the message, "Ship X to Mr. Y," might trigger one of these responses:

"OK."
"I'll do it right away."
"Any special handling?"
"Fastest or cheapest way?"

The first response says "message received; it will be done." The second response adds "now." The third and fourth response add "give me this additional information so I'll do it the way you want it done." Again, more than words enter the communication in the response. The responder's tone, pauses, and nonverbal cues such as facial expression add to the communication.

You'll use your communications skills in *directing* people and in *getting things done.* You can get things done with *established routines, on order,* and with *employee initiative.*

Job descriptions, written procedures, and working practices are the basis for established routines. Established routines take care (or should) of getting most things done in a business. These are a form of communication. *Orders* are required to get things done that aren't routine (and sometimes things that should be done routinely but aren't). There are many ways to give orders. Some of these ways have limited effectiveness at the time the orders are given and can lead to deteriorating relations in the long run.

When you have highly motivated, loyal, and experienced employees, you'll get most of your best results through employee initiative. Employees who display a high degree of initiative are your potential top-management candidates.

Your contact with your employees will involve considerably more than giving orders. You can improve employee communications by encouraging your employees to participate in planning, soliciting their suggestions, and by discussing business and working matters with them. At times, personal problems may affect their work. In such cases employees may ask you for help, or you may have to initiate a discussion. Friction or conflict between employees, between an employee and a customer, or between an employee and a vendor may require your attention. Any of these situations may call for discussion or counseling. We've discussed the counseling approach in Chapter 13 and the nondirective interview technique in the first part of this chapter. Both of these approaches deserve your attention. *Empathy* is a primary key to success in human relations.

Coaching is an effective direction and training technique that also puts your communications skills to work. When you see an employee doing a good job, take time to tell him so occasionally. If he's doing something wrong, suggest the right way or a better way to do it, and if showing him how will help, do so. You can correct him tactfully and gracefully. *Counsel,* don't criticize.

> POINT 14-11: Your dealings with employees will involve direct and indirect order situations, correction, counseling, coaching, and arbitrator roles. Communication skills and empathy are essential.

As your business grows, you'll conduct and participate in more and more *meetings* or *conferences.* The purpose of a meeting is to *plan, reach a decision, resolve a conflict,* or *accomplish a specific piece of work* in a situation in which several people are involved. Properly used as a communications tool, the meeting saves time and can produce more coordinated results. Overused, poorly organized, and overattended, the meeting is a costly and almost useless affair.

The keys to getting the most out of a meeting are to

1. Prepare an agenda in advance of the meeting
2. Estimate and allocate a reasonable amount of time to each item on the agenda
3. Invite only those who can contribute to the meeting or will be affected by the outcome
4. Try to schedule the meeting when it will provide least interference with the day's routine business
5. Start the meeting on time
6. Follow the agenda and control participants who deviate from the subject matter or who tend to get windy.

Needless to say, all of those invited to the meeting should be told what it's about, and should be asked to bring any reports or other information that they'll be expected to supply. Until your business becomes relatively large, you'll have few meetings and they'll be quite small. A short, informal communications meeting of employees at the start or end of each business day to review a day's business and plan the next can be very productive in a business with as few as three or four employees.

Motivation

This subject has been mentioned in connection with selling, advertising, managing, and dealing with employees throughout this book. Now, let's put it together and check your motivation quotient:

1. People are more likely to respond (do what you want them to do) if they see a benefit in responding. *Do you offer benefits in your dealings with people?*
2. There is a short-term response (to do a specific thing now to receive a specific benefit) such as buying in response to a sales presentation or hitting a production goal in response to a promise of a specific benefit. *Do you offer specific and adequate benefits in individual people transactions?*
3. There is a long-term response that is based on a longer-term arrangement (such as employment) which will continue and grow as long as there is continuing reinforcement. *Do you reinforce long-term relationships and build loyalty with continuing motivation?*

FIGURE 14-5 Needs, motivations, and applicable human relations skills

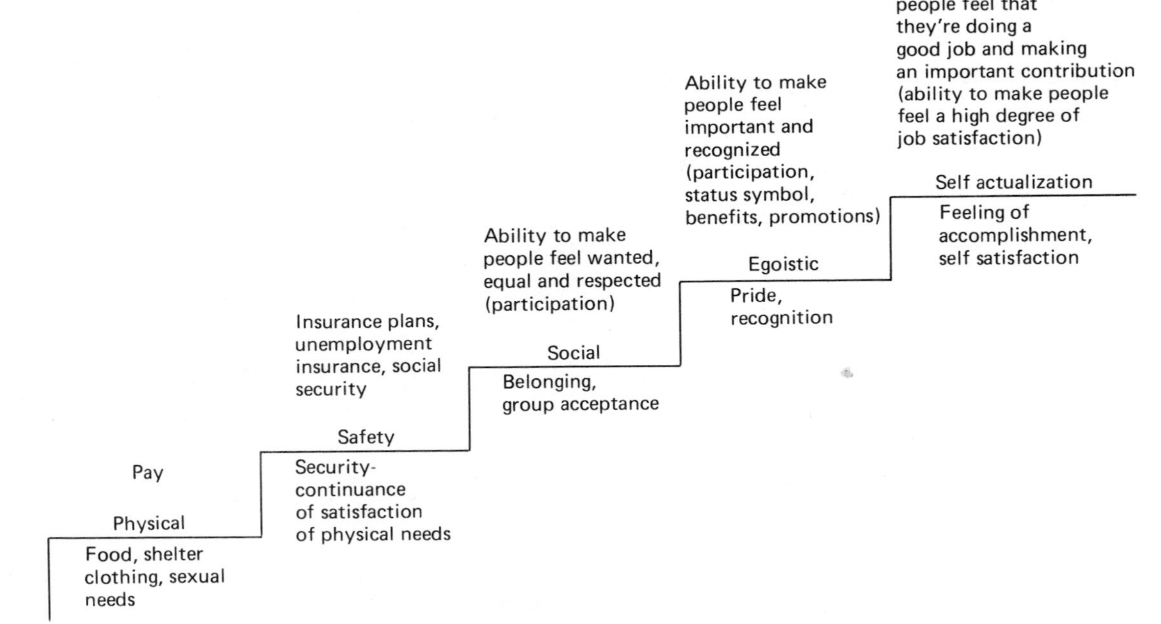

4. A person first strives to attain the *physical* needs, the benefits of shelter, food, clothing, and sexual needs. These needs are easily satisfied and are practically guaranteed in our society. Next a person aspires to *safety* (or security) *needs,* which are simply some assurances that physical needs will continue to be met. At this point, the individual tries to meet the *social needs* (belonging and being accepted), *egoistic needs* (receiving recognition from others), and *self-actualization needs* (feeling a sense of accomplishment). This is Maslow's *hierarchy of needs.* You'll motivate more effectively if you know where your workers stand in the hierarchy of needs. Figure 14-5 shows the hierarchy and the motivation skills and actions that you can apply. *Do you understand and practice the motivation needs indicated by the hierarchy of needs?*
5. People like to participate in planning, making decisions, and getting things done. You'll increase your motivation quotient by encouraging participation to the greatest extent practical. *Do you encourage people to participate in planning, and decision making, and in feeling a sense of accomplishment in the success of your business?*

If you scored four or more "yeses," you're doing well. Regardless of what you scored, there's always room for improvement. Frequent review of this material and that on the behavioral theories at the end of Chapter 13 is recommended.

POINT 14-12: Employees, after physical and safety needs are satisfied, successively aspire to social, egoistic, and self-actualization needs. You enhance your ability to deal with people if you understand motivation principles and practice them.

REVIEW EXERCISES 14-C

1. Describe and discuss leadership styles.
2. What are the steps in the complete closed-loop communications process?
3. Why is the ability to be a good listener important in the communications process and in managing your business effectively? Discuss this from the standpoint of employee, customer, and vendor relationships.
4. What is empathy? Why does empathy play such an important role in working with and through people?
5. Why is employee participation an important part of the motivating process?

CASE: A LESSON IN HIRING

Laurie Swift owned a picture-framing business. She had started it from scratch, prospered, and after two years took in a friend as an employee. All went well and the business continued to grow and thrive. Laurie needed an additional employee a year later. She placed a classified ad in the local newspaper and was swamped with phone calls. She scheduled twenty interviews over the next two days, canceled the ad and told the twenty-first and subsequent applicants that the job was being filled.

After two days of interviews, with only ten applicants showing up, Laurie was confused. She could hardly remember what the applicants looked or sounded like and couldn't match people to her somewhat jumbled notes. Finally, after a day of poring through her notes, she eliminated six of the applicants who had appeared. She couldn't remember all she wanted to about the four she wanted to consider and decided to ask them back in. When she called them, two had taken other jobs, a third wasn't interested, and the fourth agreed to come in. When the applicant appeared, Laurie had a formal application blank for him. After the interview, which didn't sell Laurie on the applicant's capability, Laurie checked his references and previous employment. The references were guarded in their comments but didn't discredit the applicant's capability or integrity directly. Laurie was desperate for help and hired him. He was slow in catching on to his job and displayed no initiative. After two weeks Laurie realized he wouldn't work out and gave him a two weeks' notice with pay.

She started the recruiting process all over, but when calls started coming in, she handled them differently.

REVIEW EXERCISES 14-D

1. How do you believe Laurie handled her hiring problem the second time around? List her probable steps in detail.
2. If the employee Laurie hired initially was paid $3.50 an hour for 160 hours of work and Laurie's shop overhead is $2 per hour per employee, what was the probable total cost? (Don't forget Laurie's contribution to FICA, employment insurance, etc.)
3. Laurie spent the equivalent of three eight-hour days hiring this employee. If an hour of her time contributed to the business is worth $10, what did this part of the hiring cost amount to? (Many business owners overlook the value of their time. Laurie's hiring fiasco was costly!)

SUMMARY

Wages and salaries are *a* major (and in some businesses *the* major) expense. It is important to attract high-caliber, efficient employees and utilize them at their most productive level of capability. You can recruit employees through advertising, referrals, and employment services. Make your advertising specific to attract qualified applicants. Use an adequate job application form, interview promising applicants, and check references and previous employment. Make the applicant feel at ease during a nondirective interview and encourage him to talk about previous work experience and training. Use the job description and specification in the interview. Try to place the applicant in the job that utilizes his maximum capability if he is qualified for several openings. If the applicant won't be reporting directly to you, have his potential supervisor interview him.

Your long-term investment in an employee is substantial. It will pay to provide thorough indoctrination, training, and continuing development opportunities.

It is desirable to keep good employees. This requires some knowledge of (and skill in) human relations. The worker is a complex entity motivated by more than money. The supervisor's role has an important bearing on morale and production; team play and satisfaction with the work are important; and informal work and social-group pressures come into play.

Leaders tend to lean toward *autocratic* (do as I say), *democratic* (let's see how we can do it), or *laissez-faire* (let me know if you need help) leadership styles, or variations of these styles. Any leadership can be effective as long as the leader has the respect of the employee and treats him fairly.

Performance evaluation should be conducted periodically. Incentives, fringe benefits, and promotions are tools for satisfying and motivating employees. They can be harnessed even in a very small business. The addition of employees adds a substantial amount of paperwork and administration to your managing job. Maintain good employee files for ease in administration and future personnel decisions.

Communication is a key management skill. Saying what you mean through words, inflection, and nonverbal cues all impart meaning to the messages you send. The reply, in the same terms, reflects what message was received and *how* the message was received. The ability to listen well is as important as the ability to express yourself well.

People are motivated by benefits. Benefits are satisfaction of needs. Physical and safety needs are fundamental. When these are fulfilled, people successively pursue *social, egoistic,* and *self-actualization* needs until each is satisfied. You enhance your ability to work with and through people as you develop your understanding and skill in motivating.

KEY TERMS

Autocratic leadership
Coaching
Communication
Democratic leadership
Empathy
Employee development
Fringe benefits
Hierarchy of needs
Incentives
Job description
Laissez-faire leadership
Leadership
Motivation
Nondirective interview
Organization chart
Participation
Performance evaluation
Recruiting
Selection
Training

QUESTIONS AND PROBLEMS

1. What are the steps in finding an employee and putting him or her to work?
2. What is the purpose of the job application form?
3. What are the steps in the employee selection process?
4. Discuss directive and nondirective interviews. Under what circumstances other than an employment situation would the nondirective interview be useful?
5. Why is it important to make notes after the interview?
6. What is a job description? What purposes does it serve?
7. Under what circumstances would you test a job applicant?
8. Discuss the different compensation plans that can be used to pay employees.
9. Why should you have an employee development program? What are the avenues available for employee development?
10. Why is an independent sales rep worth considering in a small manufacturing business?
11. List and describe the paperwork that must be completed on a new employee.
12. Define and discuss (a) counseling, (b) coaching, (c) training, (d) indoctrination.
13. What are the important attitudes and abilities for a leader to possess? Do they necessarily have anything to do with his or her style categorization? Justify your position.
14. Describe the ways in which choice of words, tone of voice, gestures, and other actions can turn the simple phrase, "Clean your machine at quitting time every night," into (a) a well-received order, (b) a resented order.
15. Why is a response from the employee desirable on receipt of an order? What is the difference between a "response to an order" and a "report"?
16. This chapter has stressed the importance of listening and listening well. Make a list of what you consider to be the key rules for developing good listening and interpretive ability.
17. Discuss the hierarchy of needs, and explain how you intend to use this knowledge to motivate your employees.

FIELD INVESTIGATION AND PROJECTS

1. Interview several retailers who employ between five and twenty people, a retail chain store manager who employs fewer than fifty people, and the industrial relations or personnel manager of a manufacturing company concerning hiring and employee procedures and practices. Prepare a report.

*2. Develop a personnel plan for the business you intend to start. Include the topic headings in this chapter that fit logically into your plan.

Economics, Business Cycles, and the Growth of Your Business

15

Your efforts comprise the major determinant of the success of your business. But there are external factors that can affect it too. You cannot control these factors, but if you understand them, you can cope with them and thus enhance your chances of continued success.

Local economic events–such as a plant or military base closedown–can shatter your business. National economic conditions–such as a recession–can slow your business down. Actually, the national economy is cyclic–that is, it alternates between prosperity and recession. This alternation is known as "the business cycle." There are indicators that predict the cycle swings, and the businessperson who understands them can capitalize on these swings.

Businesses go through cycles of growth. Unfortunately, most small businesspeople come to understand the business growth cycle too late. The last part of this chapter discusses this subject.

Although some of this chapter tends to move away from the mini-business base of the earlier chapters, the material presented is important to you and will serve you well. An understanding of the business cycle and economics is an essential part of any entrepreneur's business tool kit that too many small-business textbooks avoid.

This chapter should provide answers to the following questions:

1. What local economic events can have an effect on my business?
2. How do government spending, taxation, and interest rates affect business?
3. How do consumption and investment differ? Why do they compete with each other?
4. How does the nation's economy affect a mini business? How can I use national economic statistics in running my business better?
5. How does the business cycle work? What makes it behave as it does?
6. What are some of the indicators of impending prosperity or recession?
7. What is the growth pattern of a business?
8. Are changes in form of entity, personnel, organization, product line, and/or other changes likely to take place as my business grows?

HOW ECONOMIC CONDITIONS AFFECT BUSINESS

External conditions affect business. The economy, government policy, social values, the physical environment, international events, and natural events can exert a profound impact on a business. The focus in this chapter will be on economics. We will hardly scratch the surface of the subject matter in the limited space available. The goal is for you to learn enough about economics to enable you to run your business better.

Local Conditions

"New York Firm Moves Headquarters To Dallas"
"Dress Factory Moves From Rhode Island To Mississippi"
"Military Base Closed"
"General Motors Lays Off 16,000 Workers"
"College To Be Located In Mesquite"

These headlines report events that will affect the local economics of each of several towns or cities. When a large industrial plant or headquarters leaves a town or city, it pulls spending power out. The closing of a military base pulls spending power. If the withdrawal is from a small town that is heavily dependent on that single activity for employment, the town undergoes recession, businesses fail, and in the extreme case, the town may wither and die. There's a very practical business lesson in this.

> POINT 15-1: You may be taking a big chance if you establish a consumer business (retail or service) in a town that is heavily dependent on a single industry or a single government activity.

A new industry moving to a town, or the opening of a new college or government facility increases local employment, brings new families into a town, and boosts local spending. In agricultural areas, good crop years stimulate the local economy. And the national economy has substantial impact on small towns with manufacturing plants. Another kind of activity that can cause fluctuations in a local economy is a temporary activity such as a highway construction project. Local activities have a direct impact on business in the community. In choosing your location and in making your continuing business plans, keep these factors in mind.

What are some of the signs of a community's economic stability? A diversified payroll base is a good sign. If the community has a number of manufacturing activities in unrelated fields, plus one or more substantial nonbusiness activities such as a college, a medical center patronized by out-of-towners, established tourist attractions, or a stable government installation, the local economy will tend to be relatively stable. A local or nearby transportation terminal such as an airport or a distribution center (warehouse-trucking complex) tends to add stability.

What about business growth potential relative to local economic conditions? If the community is growing, the chance of retail and service business growth in the community is enhanced. Direct income-growth statistics are not always available. You may have to use indirect indicators. Some of the indirect indicators of community income growth are *population growth rate, payroll growth rate,* and *bank-deposit growth rate*. A 10 percent annual growth in population (doubling about every seven years) indicates reasonably progressive and stable growth. A greater rate of population growth is a plus if there are indications that the growth is stable. Growth in payroll and bank deposits at a rate of more than 20 percent per year also indicates business-growth potential.

The rules of thumb presented in this section are subject to qualifications, as is the case for any general statement or rule of thumb. Accept these as general guidelines, not as iron-clad rules. For example, proximity of a small town to a large city might result in a large part of the community's consumer spending going to the large city. This would reduce the effect that income growth in the community would have on retail sales in the community.

Other local indications of business stability and growth potential are continuing acquisitions of new manufacturing plants, the progressiveness of town government, and the level and direction of activity of the chamber of commerce.

These indicators are not as important in choosing a location for most manufacturing, distribution, or service businesses that aren't dependent on local consumer purchases. The availability of adequately skilled employees at a reasonable pay rate and the availability of an adequate facility at low cost are primary considerations for these kinds of businesses. Proximity to prime manufacturers may be a consideration in the case of the manufacturing job shop or a component fabrication plant.

POINT 15-2: Local economic stability and growth should be considered in locating a business. Stability is generally indicated by payroll diversification; growth potential is generally indicated by population, payroll, and bank-deposit growth.

National Conditions

National economic conditions are the composite of many local economic conditions. National economic conditions are measured by statistics and indicators that are widely publicized. This publicity has psychological effects on consumers in your town and hence the state of the national economy has an additional effect on your mini business. The state of the economy is measured by the *Gross National Product* (GNP). GNP is the annual output at market value of all goods and services produced by an economy. GNP is measured in dollars. It can be computed in terms of total expenditures or in terms of income produced. The expression of GNP in terms of total expenditures is the more commonly used form.

The quantities which make up GNP include:

1. *Personal consumption expenditures*—what people spend for housing, shelter, clothing, food, and other goods and services for final use
2. *Government spending*—what federal, state, and local governments spend for defense, improvements, services for the public, administration, and other purposes
3. *Investment*—domestic private investment for purposes of producing goods and services including plants, equipment, and other expenditures for goods and services that will produce other goods and services rather than be consumed for individual satisfaction
4. *Exports*—goods and services sold outside of the country or to nationals of other countries, adding to the income of the exporting country
5. *Imports*—goods and service brought into this country or bought by nationals of this country abroad.

Government spending, investment, and exports all cause money to flow into the American economy. If the government spends more money or cuts taxes (the equivalent of spending more money, as far as individual cash for spending is concerned), more jobs are created and income is added to GNP. If industry invests more in new plants, more jobs are created, and income is added to GNP. If exports and expenditures by foreign nationals in the U.S. increases, income is added to GNP. These contributors to GNP increase are called *injections* by economists.

GNP equals spending for consumption plus injections by government spending, investment, and exports *minus* the outflow of money due to import spending. But these injections are recycled in the economy and produce additional effects.

POINT 15-3: GNP is the sum of injections into the economy (government spending, domestic investment, and exports) and consumption, less imports. Injections into the economy create additional spending for consumption and investment that magnify the effect of the original injection.

It takes several years to finalize and publish accurate GNP statistics. The statistics for 1974 published in 1976 were as follows:[1]

Consumption	$ 876.7 billion
Government spending	309.2
Investment	209.4
Net exports (exports minus imports)	2.0
GNP	$1,397.3

Of what use is knowledge of the GNP? First of all, GNP can be used as an indicator of economic growth from year to year. Figure 15-1 shows GNP from 1960 to 1974 in current dollars (dotted line) and in 1958 constant dollars (solid line). The constant dollar is adjusted for inflation (or deflation) of the dollar's value owing to price increases. The economic growth rate has been developed and is shown by the bars. Note the recessions in 1970 and 1974 which made economic growth go negative. Note also that the dotted and solid lines tend to diverge with time, indicating growing inflation. Viewed in current dollars, we can compute (by means beyond the scope of this text) average annual economic growth over the fourteen-year period as being about 8.5 percent per year. But this is growth plus inflation. If we view the growth in terms of 1958 constant dollars, the average annual economic growth rate was just slightly over 4 percent. (The bars on Figure 15-1 are based on 1958 constant dollars. Hence we must conclude that average inflation over the fourteen-year period was about 4.5 percent. But inflation was less than 1 percent till 1964. In 1974 it was about 9 percent!

FIGURE 15-1 Gross national product

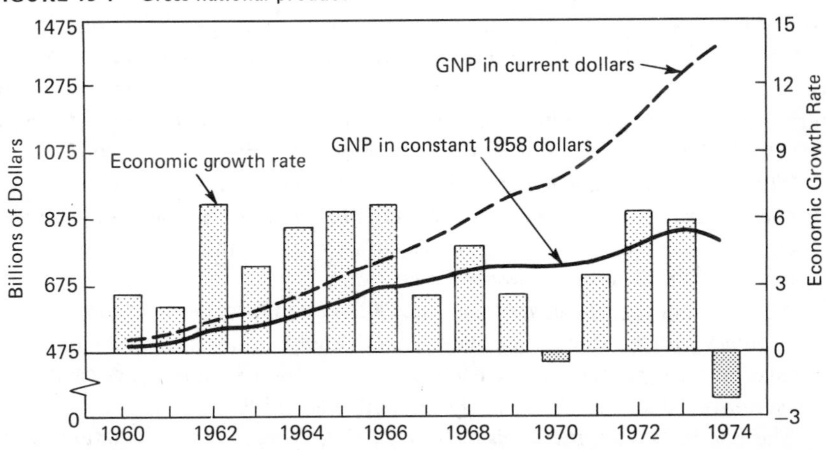

(Source: *Statistical Abstract of the United States* [Washington, D.C.: U.S. Department of Commerce, 1975], p. 379.)

[1] Statistical Abstract of the United States (Washington, D.C.: U.S. Department of Commerce, 1975), p. 380.

GNP growth and inflation rate should be part of your computations in preparing your marketing forecasts. You can assume that sales will be influenced by GNP plus inflation on growth rate. Use the average rate for the last five years of data available to you for forecasting purposes until experience enables you to adjust this factor.

In our discussion of GNP we emphasized that changes in injections had additional effects. One of these effects is the multiplier effect.[2] Assume $100 billion is "injected" into the economy, either by government spending, investment, or monetary expansion. The recipients of this $100 billion might save $40 billion and spend $60 billion. This $60 billion "echoes" as another "injection." The recipients of this $60 billion might save $24 billion and spend the rest, $36 billion. This is another injection–a percentage of which will be saved, and the rest spent. The process will continue until the "echoes" approach zero. The net result of the initial injection then is multiplied by subsequent spending cycles. In this case, the $100 billion injection into the economy will cause GNP to rise by $250 billion! The multiplier effect does not occur instantaneously. It takes time for the money to circulate and produce the added income on each successive go-around.

Monetary and Fiscal Policy

Fiscal policy is the government's spending policy. From the definition of GNP, it is apparent that the government can stimulate the economy by spending more money. It can also restrain the economy by reducing spending when the economy is overheated.

When the economy is running at high heat, supply of goods usually cannot keep up with demand, and prices increase as people with more money are willing to pay more for scarce goods and services. This is *demand-pull inflation*–goods cost more; the dollar buys less. (Another form of inflation is *cost-push inflation,* caused by special-interest groups forcing costs up, such as labor demanding higher wages.) *The government can either cut expenditures or increase taxes (or both),* which has the effect of reducing the money people have to spend.

When the economy is underproductive with high unemployment, *an increase in government spending or a tax cut fuels the economy* by increasing employment and putting more spending money in people's hands. So, fiscal policy can be used to exert some control over the economy.

Another tool that the government uses in an attempt to regulate the economy is *monetary policy*. Monetary policy is the increase or decrease of the money in circulation with accompanying decreases or increases of interest rates through the actions of the Federal Reserve (commonly called the "Fed").

The Fed has several mechanisms for changing the money in circulation, which include:

[2] For further study of economics, these may be helpful: In the PLAID series, Lloyd G. Reynolds, *Principles of Economics: Macro,* and *Principles of Economics: Micro* (both Homewood, Ill.: Learning Systems Company, 1973); and Robert L. Heilbroner and Lester Thurow, *The Economic Problem,* 5th ed. (Englewood Cliffs, N.J.: Prentice-Hall, Inc., 1977).

1. Open-market operations
2. Changing member bank reserve requirements
3. Discount rate changes
4. Interest ceilings on time deposits
5. "Jawboning" (persuasive talk, usually pressuring in nature)

A discussion of these mechanisms is beyond the scope of this text. It is sufficient to say that these actions can make money scarcer and drive interest rates up (making businesspeople less willing to borrow). Or it can make money more plentiful and reduce interest rates to cause the opposite effect.

Are fiscal and monetary policy effective in preventing runaway booms and in cushioning recessions? Yes, to a point. Certainly, the exercise of fiscal policy can have a pronounced effect on the economy either in heating it up or in cooling it off. But it takes time to pump money into the economy, circulate it, and feel the results of the multiplier. Sometimes the intended restraint on a boom takes hold only after the economic downswing has begun. This kind of backfire exaggerates booms and recessions.

Monetary policy is usually a more effective tool for restraining the inflation caused by a boom than it is for pulling the economy out of recession. Higher interest rates restrain some business activity even in an optimistic period. But lower interest rates don't usually encourage business to expand as readily during a period of recession and pessimism. Monetary policy has some of the delay drawbacks of fiscal policy, but a change in interest rates can be implemented much more rapidly than a massive government spending program.

POINT 15-4: Government exercises some control of the economy through fiscal (government spending) and monetary (money supply) policy. Government attempts to control can backfire and add to the problem that was to be cured.

REVIEW EXERCISES 15-A

1. What influence do local economic conditions have on growth opportunities for a business? The stability of a business?
2. What is the difference between consumption and investment?
3. State the composition of GNP and discuss the effects of changes in the contributions.
4. Define and discuss fiscal and monetary policy.
5. What are the factors of production?

BUSINESS CYCLES

Business has its ups and downs. The changes in business activity behave in a pattern that we call the *business cycle.*

The Nature of the Business Cycle

The business cycle follows the pattern shown in Figure 15-2. In reality, it is not so symmetrical, the magnitude of the excursions vary from one cycle to the next, and the period of time for a cycle varies, though the average in recent history seems to have been about four or five years. The expansion or *upswing* (ABC in Figure 15-2) has taken three to four years in recent history and the contraction or *downswing* (CDE) has lasted a year or a little more. Business cycles before World War II were longer and there were violent *troughs* (AE) in 1857, 1893, and 1929 of "depression" proportion. The less violent troughs of business cycles are called "recessions."

FIGURE 15-2 The business cycle

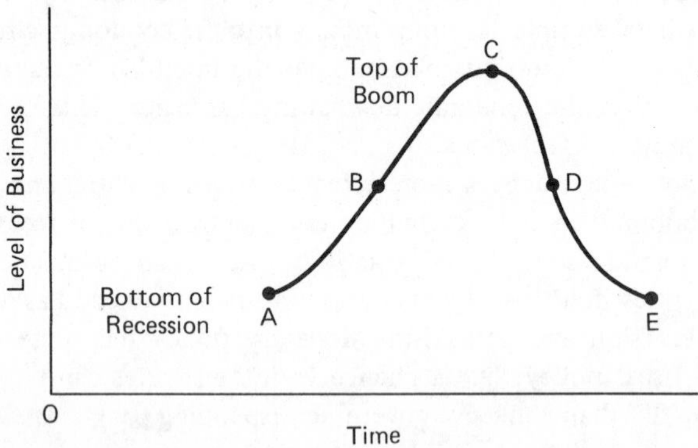

Of what importance is the business cycle to you? First of all, it gives you an idea of when to expect better business and when to expect poorer business as a result of overall economic activity. It also tells you when you should be building inventory and production or sales capacity, and when you should slow down on buying and expansion. Further, it provides clues as to when you'll need financing and what form your financing should take. In short, it helps you to know how to run your business better.

The Upswing

Point A on the business cycle (Figure 15-2) is the *trough* of the business cycle, also known as the lower turning point. A long period of poor business has depleted business inventories during curtailed purchasing. Machinery not replaced during the downswing and this period of low business is wearing out. Consumers have held back on buying. Cars, clothes, and appliances are wearing out. Interest rates have dropped to a very low point owing to lack of loan demand. Many workers have been laid off during the downswing. Housing starts have been low–people haven't been buying because of high mortgage interest rates, but interest rates are coming down.

Smart businesspeople, sensing the bottom of the trough, begin to replace worn-out equipment and build inventories for the upswing. These purchases give the upswing a slow-momentum start. A few laid-off workers are called back to work while those who were retained are put on overtime. The public begins to feel confident because the stock market, which bottomed some months before, has started to move up.

Money starts to move faster as consumers spend more. The multiplier begins to work. Businesspeople borrow at the bank, taking advantage of low-interest loans for the working capital needs they see in the months ahead. The upswing gains further momentum and moves up to point B in Figure 15-2. Consumer confidence soars as workers are called back to work and businesspeople begin to build inventory in anticipation of increasing prices. Large businesses go to the bond market to obtain long-term debt financing for new plants and equipment before interest rates rise significantly. Deliveries on orders lag; demand exceeds supply, and prices increase. No one cares and everyone continues to buy and spend. Business expands to meet demand. The cycle passes point B and moves toward C. Interest rates increase, and large corporations tap the equity markets with stock offerings because earnings are high and the market will pay high prices for stocks. The stock market approaches its peak, then slows down and signals the impending peak of business cycle. Now, the flood of goods from the increased capacity begins to catch up with demand, and business begins to level off.

The Peak

As production catches up with demand and sales drop, businesspeople sense the approaching peak. They reduce ordering. Investment in plant and equipment has been adequately committed to meet future needs. The multiplier acts to slow the upswing and turn it around. Interest rates are high and business is reluctant to borrow at the high rates. This also causes those who would borrow to buy homes and cars to put off purchases. The business cycle has hit point C. Businesses reduce production and workers are laid off. The government will have resorted to fiscal restraint by this time. Business profits are under pressure as sales drop and costs increase. The business cycle has passed point C and is turning downward.

The Downswing

The stock market has signaled the downswing by a decline started six months or so ago. Consumer confidence begins to erode. Businesspeople cancel orders and do not commit new funds to plant expansion. There are more layoffs as production is canceled in response to decreased demand. The multiplier and the accelerator work to speed the downswing. The downswing moves through point D in Figure 15-2. As prices fall, the value of collateral falls below the value of loans and loans are called. Collections on accounts slow. Some businesses are forced into bankruptcy. Smart businesspeople cut expenses to the bone, resulting in further decreases in demand and more layoffs. Unemployment benefits for workers laid off early are used up, and income (and spending for consumption) decreases further. Now, most manufacturers and retailers are doing most of their business out of accumulated inventories. The general pessimism causes further reduction in sales as individuals and businesses strive to become liquid. Interest rates drop, and the government applies fiscal and monetary policy to cushion the recession. The downswing begins to slow as it approaches point E.

The Trough

Now, as the downswing approaches point E, inventory levels are dropping toward the lower safety level. Equipment is wearing out and is in need of replacement. There is an adequate demand for consumer necessities to put additional braking on the downswing. The downswing slows. Businesses trimmed lean during the downswing begin to realize some profit improvements. The stock market, sensing the impending trough and upswing, begins to pick up volume and stock prices start to firm up and increase. Smart businesspeople sense the bottom of the trough and begin to gear up for the coming upswing.

And that was where we started. The cycle repeats itself again.

POINT 15-5: The business cycle goes from trough through upswing, peak and downswing, usually over a period of four or five years. The multiplier plays a key role in its behavior. Knowledge of business-cycle behavior can guide you in making business decisions.

Indicators

The National Bureau of Economic Research and the Department of Commerce have chosen a number of indicators which signal or confirm changes in the business cycle. These indicators are classified as *leading, coincident,* and *lagging.* The leading indicators signal impending changes in advance of occurrence. The coincident and lagging indicators confirm that changes are taking place or have taken place.

The *stock market* is a relatively reliable leading indicator that usually turns four to eight months in advance of the business cycle. *Average work week (manufacturing), new building permits, new orders for consumer goods (in 1967 dollars), and orders for plant and equipment (in 1967 dollars)* are some other leading indicators. The 1967 dollar is used as a reference because subsequent inflation has caused dollar value to fluctuate from year to year.

The coincident indicators include *GNP, personal income, unemployment rate,* and *retail sales,* among others. Lagging indicators include *total manufacturers' inventories, plant and equipment expenditures* (note that orders are coincident; expenditures lag), *and consumer installment debt,* among others.

The rationale of the indicators will become more evident if you'll go back through the business cycle.

The indicators are published by the government and are generally reported in business publications such as *Business Week* and the *Wall Street Journal.*

POINT 15-6: Leading indicators, of which the stock market is one, signal future changes in the business cycle. Coincident and lagging indicators confirm business-cycle behavior. Use indicators to recognize changes in the cycle.

Harnessing Business-Cycle Knowledge

Now that you know how business cycles behave, how do you put this knowledge to work in your business?

First of all, you watch the leading indicators for signs of impending turns. You try to adjust your expenditures and your finances so that you'll be liquid during the downswing. Reduce inventory and all expenses during the downswing. At the trough, begin to build inventory and replace worn-out equipment, driving for hard bargains with suppliers who are hungry for business. Begin to look for employees, who will be needed during the upswing, before the best workers are put back to work by others. Meet financing needs with bank loans while short-term interest is still low.

As the upswing begins, make major plant and equipment expenditures, using long-term financing while long-term interest rates are still low. Build inventory rapidly early in the upswing before prices start to rise. If you're in a repair and sales business, shift emphasis to sales. Watch the leading indicators for signals of the upper peak. If you're going to sell a business or sell equity in a business, do so in the upswing as near the peak as possible for maximum yield.

At the first signal of the approaching of the peak, cut inventory building and try to work out of your inventory as much as possible. Halt further expansion and make plans for layoffs and other cash-conserving moves to be implemented before the turnaround occurs. If you're in a repair and sales business, keep your emphasis on sales during the early part of the downswing, but be ready to increase repair-service capacity as the downswing begins in earnest. Operate on low inventory during the downswing and try to hold as liquid a position as possible.

Increase prices as the upswing gets underway and your sales increase. This will help you to avoid profit erosion, because the cost of goods sold tends to increase during an upswing. Be prepared to drop prices during the downswing to increase your share of the market. If you're a retailer, go heavy on sales promotions during the downswing and at the trough.

Much more can be said about business cycles than space permits. Some additional study of the subject will be well worth your while.[3]

[3] For more information on business cycles and forecasting, see George A. Christy and Peyton Foster Roden, *Finance, Environment and Decision* (San Francisco: Canfield Press, 1973) and William F. Butler, Robert A. Kavesh, and Robert B. Platt, *Methods and Techniques of Business Forecasting* (Englewood Cliffs, N.J.: Prentice-Hall, Inc., 1974).

REVIEW EXERCISES 15-B

1. Explain the business cycle in detail.
2. Discuss and list several leading indicators.
3. Discuss and list several coincident and lagging indicators.
4. Explain the rationale of the indicators listed in Problems 2 and 3 above in terms of the business cycle.
5. Explain how you can apply your knowledge of the business cycle to buying and inventories, financing, hiring and laying off workers, replacing and expanding plant and equipment, and pricing.

YOUR GROWING BUSINESS

As businesses grow, changes take place. Your advance knowledge of the growth cycle–which few businesspeople learn very early in their careers–can help you promote the continuing growth of your business.

The Growth Cycle of a Business

A business has a life and a growth pattern. The life and growth pattern for each kind of business is different in detail from the others. But there are some general overall patterns that are similar in character for all businesses that succeed. In order to develop these ideas, let's start first with the growth cycle of an industry, as shown in Figure 15-3.

FIGURE 15-3 Life cycle of an industry

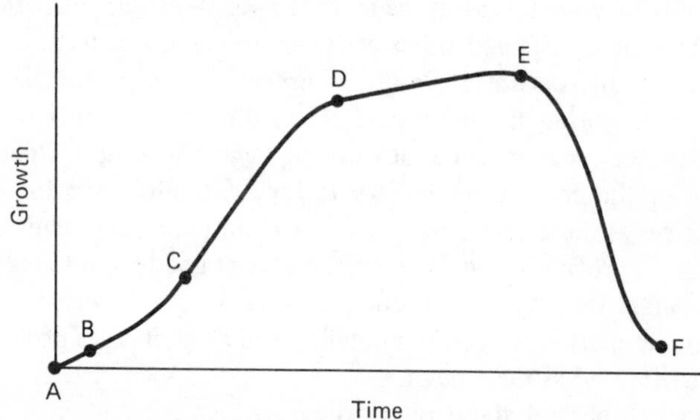

The new industry generally begins as the result of a technological development. Typical examples are rail transportation, automobile transportation, air transportation, and data processing. The start is slow while development is underway. As the technical innovation becomes more practical to use, massive investments are made and the industry moves from point B to point C in roughly a decade or two. During that period of time vast improvements are made, the novelty wears off, and the development becomes a necessity and a part of our way of life or of doing business. During the next roughly three to seven decades the industry grows from point C to point D. By now the industry is highly developed and growth tends to level off to point E. This period may last for about two to five decades. Then, the industry declines to point F. The decline may take two to five decades. Thus, rail transportation would seem to be somewhere between point E and F; auto transportation, including trucking, somewhere between D and E; air transportation between D and E; and data processing between C and D.

Now that we have a feel for the growth and decline of an industry, let's look at a business. First of all we are considering only businesses which are adequately conceived, financed and managed to be successful over a relatively long period of years.

Figure 15-4 shows a typical growth pattern of a business. The business is founded at point A. The dominant requirement is growth in sales and effective management at this point. Sales grow increasingly till a plateau is reached, owing to limitations in facilities and personnel. At point B financing (usually debt) is obtained to make the necessary expansion. Sales begin to increase until a plateau is reached and again expansion in personnel and facilities is required. At point C, the owner may incorporate the business and take in a few stockholders to obtain *equity* capital for the necessary expansion. Sales grow again until the next plateau is reached. At point D, the owner might decide to issue additional stock and "take the company public" (increase the number of shareholders considerably) to obtain necessary expansion financing. Again, sales grow rapidly at first, and then more slowly. At point E, the company may be sold or merged into a larger corporation, or may continue as is. The problem at point E is often that the

FIGURE 15-4 Life cycle of a business

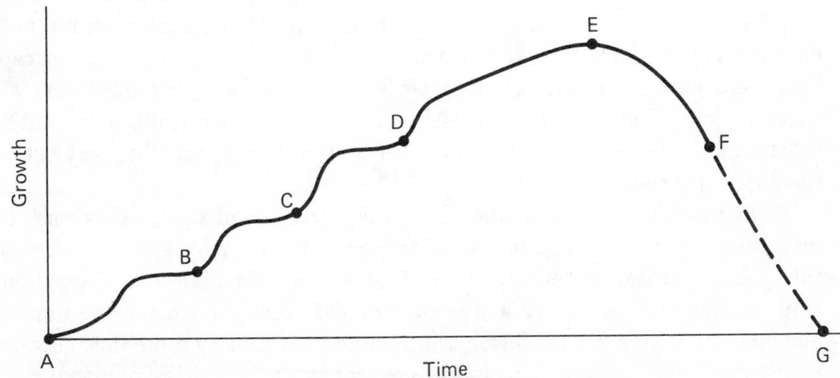

manager is the entrepreneur who started the business, and he's reached his level of adequacy, is getting too old to actively run the business, or may have died. If the company is not merged or sold, or still hasn't brought in new management, the company's sales begin to drop. Somewhere along the line, the stockholders may blow the whistle, say at point F. New management may be brought in, the company may be sold, or it may be merged. If not, it may continue to deteriorate to point G and go bankrupt.

The period of time covered by this drama ranges from twenty to two hundred years, though it's probably more like five to fifty years for most small businesses. Every business is unique and the situations are different, but they all start at some point in time and are sold, merged, or die at another point in time.

Changes in Requirements

Now let's have another look at the needs of the business to see how they vary with time. Getting your business started involves financial pressures. Once you surmount the hurdle of financing the business, the stress is on your management ability to put the business together and open the doors.

After you open the business, the pressure focuses on sales. *Most businesses that fizzle in the first year simply cannot build adequate sales to cover overhead and compensate the owner.* Proper management can reduce overhead to a point, but sales and margins must be sufficient to cover this minimum amount of overhead and provide bread and butter for you and your family. The required level of sales for profitable operation is difficult to achieve, and this will probably be your major concern in the early years of your business.

Once you achieve adequate sales, the momentum carries your business to a point at which sales tend to level off owing to lack of facilities, personnel, or because of change in the location environment. Often, this is the point at which you buy or build a business building instead of renting. You'll probably use *debt financing* to make the necessary changes and expansion on this go-around. The preferred financing is *long-term* debt since the funds are to be applied to long-term needs. However, you may have an opportunity to resort to equity financing. Factors connected with implementation of the expansion might make equity financing attractive. If, for example, you need a special talent or capability and have an individual available with the necessary qualifications who wants a piece of the action, you might wish to incorporate at this point and sell a share of the business to him or her. Talented personnel may be a key need in this first expansion.

After the first expansion, the stress will again be on sales, advertising, and promotion to make adequate use of the expanded capacity and capability. At this point, you should become more conscious of public relations. You should firm up your business image and begin to build broad contacts in the financial community. Your next expansion will require considerably more financing, and you'll need more personnel, including several extremely competent management people. At this point, you should also begin to "fine-tune" your long-range plans. You may want to consider diversification of your business, financial diversification through outside investments, or you may want to consider merger or acquisition in your next expansion. Changes in products, markets, and consumer mores may alter the way you run your business, too. The need for more astute management and a broader range of business knowledge grows continually as your business grows.

If you have not incorporated by the time you reach this point, it is probable that this step will become a part of your plans. You can incorporate without transferring equity outside of your family. This places you in a position to sell equity to the public in the future. Your business profits should have grown by this time to the point at which incorporation would give you tax advantages.

As the years pass and you go through successive expansions, you'll become increasingly aware of the need to provide continuity in your business. Too many people wait until they're very old before they think about providing continuity in their businesses.

You may want to cash in and sell your business before you're faced with demands to provide continuity. Many businesspeople do this. If your end objective is to sell the business, sell it when it's performing well and be assured that the buyer can operate it successfully. Otherwise, unless you sell for cash, you may have it back with reduced business and lower value than it had when you sold it.

POINT 15-7: The requirements and stress on knowledge and resources change as a business grows. Stress is successively on sales, financing expansion, personnel and staffing, change in entity, and long-range plans. Ultimately, there's a need for providing continuity or selling the business.

Development of Continuity

Many businesses die with the owner; some die before the owner does. In both cases, the reason may be that the owner didn't provide for continuity. Once you get your business going, it behooves you to hire people who can grow with the business and step up into successively more demanding positions. Help these people to grow and to realize their full potential in your company. If you do this, you'll be able to fill new positions created by expansions, and somewhere among those who are advancing you'll have one or more candidates to succeed you. Relinquish your responsibilities gradually and allow a year or two of overlap operation for your successor before you retire.

Mergers and Acquisitions

One corporation may buy another, usually a much smaller one, and operate it as a division or subsidiary, or otherwise absorb it into its operations. The process is called *acquisition.* The buying corporation may purchase for cash, may trade debt notes (bonds or debentures usually), or may exchange some of its stock for the stock of the acquired corporation (held by its shareholders).

When the sizes of the two corporations are more nearly equal, the combination of the two corporations is usually referred to as a *merger*. The resulting enlarged corporation may take the name of one of the merging corporations, a name including the names of both of the merging corporations, or a new one.

REVIEW EXERCISES 15-C

1. Why is it important to develop employees as your business grows?
2. If a business with owner's equity of $10 million merges with a business with owner's equity of $5 million, what is owner's equity in the new business? Why?
3. Why is a change to the corporate entity form almost mandatory at some point in a growing company's life? Don't limit your answer to this chapter's discussion. Explain.

CASE: PROFITING FROM THE BUSINESS CYCLE

Steve Robertson (see the case in Chapter 12, p. 327) was having lunch with Professor Mel Fair of Tri-State Tech and mentioned his experience with price changes and purchasing speculation.

"You know," Professor Fair said, "you were a victim of the business cycle. You apparently didn't know about the cycle, or you would have speculated more conservatively, and you would have been borrowing and buying earlier than you did. You would have been paying debts and reducing inventory about the time you actually borrowed and bought."

Professor Fair explained the workings of the business cycle in detail. He ended with, "Since you can't always predict the duration of the cycle and its components, it's a good idea to exercise reasonable restraint in using it. Your borrowing and buying, if held to half of what you did, based on business-cycle knowledge would have earned you a reasonably tidy addition to profit."

That evening Steve went to the library and scanned the *Wall Street Journal,* several issues of *Business Week* and *Forbes,* and some books on finance and economics. The stock market had started rising three months ago and had risen 300 points in the interim.

Steve placed $25,000 in orders above his regular ordering level the next day and arranged a loan for facility expansion and future inventory increases.

REVIEW EXERCISES 15-D

1. How does Steve's new program differ from his original one? Is it better? Discuss.
2. Is Steve's speculation at this time a prudent move? Explain.
3. From the information given in the case in Chapter 12 and here, what do you estimate Steve's monthly sales to be? Show your calculations.
4. Are there any marketing moves that Steve can make to help his speculation pay off?

SUMMARY

Local economic conditions, including the stability and growth of the local payroll base, can have a decided effect on a small business. Locate in a community that has a stable, growing economic base to enhance your chances of survival and growth.

Gross National Product measures total national output and is equal to the sum of consumption, government spending, domestic investment, and exports minus imports. GNP keeps score on an economy, permits the measurement of growth, and provides considerable information about an economy.

Fiscal (government spending and tax cuts) policy and *monetary* (control of money in circulation and interest rates) policy are used by the government to exercise some control of the economy. Monetary policy is exercised principally through "Fed" open-market operations, the discount rate, and bank-reserve requirements.

Supply and demand determine prices in an ideal market economy. Injections of money into the economy have a *multiplier* effect. (Another effect, the accelerator effect, was not discussed in this chapter.)

Business has ups and downs that behave in a cyclic pattern. When inventories are depleted and durable goods wear out, the cycle has hit bottom (the *trough*), and as business is forced to buy materials for production and to replace worn-out equipment, the upswing begins. This small trickle into the economy creates jobs and increases consumption. Consumers begin to replace durable goods and the upswing gains momentum. Demand soon outstrips supply. As new production capacity comes on line, supply begins to catch up with demand, and plant expansion and inventory building slackens. The multiplier acts to slow the upswing and the peak is reached. The downswing begins as layoffs increase, businesses decrease inventories, and buyers' resistance increases. A general air or pessimism takes hold and everyone strives to become liquid, cut expenses and expenditures, and the trough is reached. Sales increase when inventories are depleted and machinery and durable goods wear out, the economy turns, and the upswing begins again.

Business cycles have lasted four to five years in more recent times, with upswings taking longer than downswings. *Leading indicators* signal turns in the cycle, and the stock market is one of the most reliable. *Coincident* and *lagging* indicators confirm business-cycle behavior.

Businesses have life and growth patterns ranging through a series of expansions; change in entity; changes in operations; and possible sale, acquisition, or merger. Requirements in personnel, facilities, and financing change as well with growth. Astute long-range planning will smooth these successive transitions.

A successful company may become an acquirer or an acquisition target. Be sure that you and your associates own enough of your company's stock to retain control so you can pick your buyer and make your own terms.

KEY TERMS

Acquisition
Business cycle
Consumption
Fed
Fiscal policy
GNP
Indicators
Investment
Merger
Monetary policy
Multiplier

QUESTIONS AND PROBLEMS

1. Discuss local business conditions and indicators of these conditions that you can investigate to evaluate a town for location of your business.
2. Discuss and explain Gross National Product, its components, and its value to small businesspeople.
3. If consumption is $900 billion, government spending $400 billion, investment $250 billion, exports $50 billion, and imports $45 billion, what is GNP?
4. How do national economic conditions affect local economic conditions? Explain.
5. Explain what you will do about financing your company's needs at the various points on the business cycle when your business has grown to the $5-million-a-year sales level.

6. At what points in the business cycle would you resort to overtime for employees rather than increase the work force? Explain why.
7. At what points in the business cycle would it be prudent to catch up on housekeeping (painting, small plant or store improvements, etc.), preventative maintenance, and supervisory training? Why?
8. If you're engaged in the manufacture of proprietary products, at what point in the business cycle should you start new-product development? Why?
9. In the growth cycle of a business, which of your publics is likely to become your primary target in each of these periods: years 1 to 3, years 3 to 6; years 6 to 10. Discuss. (Review Chapter 5 if necessary.)
10. Discuss business financing at various stages of a business's growth.
11. How can you try to assure the continuity of your business?
12. List and discuss the points of negotiation that you think should be brought up in the merger of two small corporations.
13. When in a company's life is merger or sale of the business an advantageous move? Justify your answer.

FIELD INVESTIGATION AND PROJECTS

*1. Research business cycles in the library and prepare a report. Relate the effects of the business cycle to the kind of business you intend to start.
2. Pick an issue of *Business Week* and scan it for references to economics, business cycles, indicators, fiscal and monetary policy, the Fed, mergers and acquisitions. Make notes on the page, subject, and general gist of each story or set of data. Report.
3. Research the merger and conglomeration era of the 1960s. You'll find plenty of books and references to the "goings-on" in business periodicals of the late 1960s and early 1970s.

INDEX

A

Accelerated depreciation, 252-54
Acceptance testing, 315
Accountants, 159
  in checking price formula for new business, 64
  finding businesses through, 61
Accounting:
  accrual vs. cash basis of, 140
  See also Bookkeeping
Accounting cycle, 154-56
Accounting equation, 148, 150
Accounts
  chart of, 148-49
  description of, 149-54
Accounts payable, 191
  disbursement of, in double-entry bookkeeping, 147
  as short-term financing, 214
Accounts-payable memo file, 142
Accounts receivable, 191
  insurance on, 277
Accounts receivable *(cont.)*
  pledged to banks, 216
  turnover in, 196-97
Accounts-receivable memo file, 140
Accrual basis of accounting, 140
Acid test ratio (quick ratio), 193-94, 199
Acquisitions, 405-6
Activity ratios, 193, 196
Activity segregation, 321*n*
  and profit, 285-87
Adjusted gross income (AGI), 243, 245, 248
Ad valorem taxes, definition of, 241
Advantages
  of corporations, 34, 35-36
  of owning a business, 6
  of partnerships, 33-35
  of proprietorships, 32-33, 34
Advertising, 110-23
  classified, *see* Want ads
  free, 112
  layout, position, and size in, 119-20

Advertising *(cont.)*
measuring results of, 122-23
principles of writing, 113-19
profit from, 326
types of, 110-13
warning about, 112
"After-hours" sales, 129
Agency, law of, 263-65
Agents as middlemen, 7
AGI (adjusted gross income), 243, 245, 248
Air-conditioning business, example of promotion for, 125-26
Amortization tables, 65, 66*n*
Annual percentage rate (APR), 217-18, 271
Annual Statement Studies, 199, 203
Annual Survey of Buying Power, 85
Appreciation, 70
Approach in selling process, 94
APR (annual percentage rate), 217-18, 271
ARCO Publishing Company *Tutor* series, 367
Argyris, Chris, 335, 355
Asset accounts, 149
Assets
on balance sheet, 191
current, 191
definition of, 8, 56
fixed
depreciation of, 186
financing of, 212
types of, 191
long-term, definition of, 212
pledged as collateral, 62
return on, 197
Auctions, 129
Automobile repair shops
minimum starting capital requirements for, 208
See also Repair shops
Automobiles
dealer franchises in, 67
elasticity of sales of, 298
insurance on, 276-77
Awards to employees, 378
Aztech International, Ltd., 114

B

Bait and switch, 101
Balance sheet, 190-92
formula for, 56
for loan applications, 226
owner's equity on, 182, 191-92
Ballpoint pens with ads, 112
Bank-balance reconciliation, 163
Bank of America, 47-48, 206, 208
Bankruptcy, annual number of failures from, 5
Banks, 46
CDs of, 267-68, 326
compensating balances by, 236
finding businesses through, 61
loans by, 223-27
short-term, 216, 219
tax deposits by, 236
Barbie Dolls, 75
Bargains in buying businesses, 60-61
Bars
product liability insurance for, 266
state regulation of, 271
Barter, 313
Baumback, Clifford M., 70
Bearer bonds, definition of, 267
Behavioral approaches to management, 334-35, 353-55
"Believe It Or Not" window display, 128
Bids
preparation of, 102-3
pricing of, 299
requests for, 314-15
Billboards, 113
Bills (invoices), 142, 146
Bills of lading
definition of, 267
"sight" drafts with, 268
Binders, insurance, 274
"Bingo" cards, 132
Blank endorsements, 268
Bobrow, Edwin E., 369*n*
Bonds
definitions of, 216, 267
fidelity, 277
Bonuses, 378
Book value, definition of, 59
Bookkeeping
accounting cycle in, 154-56
"books" for, 156-59
chart of accounts in, 148-54
double-entry, 140-47

Bookkeeping *(cont.)*
diagram on, 141
expanding system of, 148-54
opening entries in, 157-59
work sheets for, 159, 160
simplified systems for, 173
See also Record keeping
Branded merchandise, prices for, 299
Break-even analysis, 293-96
Brokers, 7, 90
finding businesses through, 61-62
Budgeting, 300-303, 347
Building codes, 272
Burglary, protection against, 165
Business cards, 112, 133
Business conditions, *see* Economic conditions
Business cycles, 17, 397-401
indicators for, 500-501
planning and, 12, 86, 398-400, 401
pricing and, 297
Business entity, form of, 32-36
Business failures, 261
annual number of, 8
definition of, 8
reasons for, 9-10
Business law, 262-69
agency, 263-65
contracts, 262-63
form of entity, 32-36
negotiable transactions, 267-69
property, 265-66
sales, 266-67
security, 269
Business Operations, 47
Business Profiles, 47
Businesses
life cycles of, 403-4
new, *see* New businesses
total number of, 4
types of, 7
Butler, William F., 85*n*, 401*n*
Buyer's market, 297
Buying a business, 56-66
investigation and analysis in, 62-64
negotiation in, 64-66
price formula for, 63-64
profit considerations in, 59-61
reasons for, 56-59
search in, 61-62
transaction assistance in, 66
Buying of goods, *see* Purchasing

C

Calendars, advertising, 112
Capacity, credit policy and, 170, 223
Capital
in credit policy, 170, 233
definition of, 21, 205
how much needed, 206-13
long-term, 212-13
net working, 194, 199, 205
new business' need for, 22, 23-24, 39, 45-46
short-term, 214, 216, 219
sources of, 219-21
See also Loans
Capital (account), 152
Capital accounts, 149
Capital gains, 71
on income-tax return, 245
Capital goods, 21
Capitalization method of business valuation, 59-60
Cash, petty, 164
Cash (account), 150
Cash basis of accounting, 140, 159
Cash budget (cash-flow budget), 302-3, 338
Cash-drawer reconciliation, 163-64
Cash flow
income distinguished from, 300-302, 338
projection of, 45
for loan application, 226
Cash Over and Short (account), 153
Cash registers, protection for, 162
Cash sales in double-entry bookkeeping, 143-44
CDs, *see* Certificates of deposit
Census of Business, 85
Certificates of deposit (CDs), 326
definition of, 267-68
C.F. contract, law of, 266
Chambers of commerce, 126, 134, 310
Character, credit policy and, 170, 223
Charge accounts, 166
revolving, 167
Charge sales in double-entry bookkeeping, 144
Check protectors, 162
Checking accounts, interest on, 218-19
Checklist for buying a business, 62-63
Checkpoints in planning, 14

Checks, 142, 145
  definition of, 267
  payroll, 145, 236-40
Child Protection and Toy Safety Act (1969), 270
Christy, George A., 212*n*, 401*n*
Circular E (IRS), 236
Circulars (handbills), 111
Classified ads, *see* Want ads
Clayton Act (1914), 270
Closing the sale, 94, 99-100
Coincident indicators, 400-401
Coinsurance clauses, 274, 276
Collateral, 216-17
  assets pledged as, 62
  in credit policy, 170, 223
  law of, 269
Collection agencies, 172
Collections, 172
  law of, 269
Commissions, *see* Sales commissions
Communications with employees, 381-84
Community relations, 133-34
Competition
  assessment of, 44-45
  pricing and, 297
Computers, reporting by, 343
Concept development, 37
Conditional sales contract, 167
Conferences with employees, 384
Consideration in contracts, 262
Consignment, law of, 266
Construction businesses, 75-76
"Consumer Electronics Centers" profile, 208-11
Consumer goods
  classification of, 89
  definitions of, 21, 89, 90
  distribution channel for, 90
Contemporary Marketing, Inc., 116
Contests for employees, 378
Continuity in business, 405
Contractors, minimum starting capital for, 208
Contracts
  bidding for, *see* Bids
  law of, 262-63
    negotiable instruments, 267-69
Control, 14-15, 343-44
  of expenses, 322-26
Control *(cont.)*
  internal, 162-65
  reporting and, 343, 348
Convenience goods, definition of, 89
Cooperative advertising programs, 112
Cooperative arrangements, 67-68
Coordinating, 347
Copyrights, 271
Corley, Robert N., 262*n*
Corporations
  advantages and disadvantages of, 34, 35-36, 405
  definition of, 32
  income-tax forms for, 242
  mergers and acquisitions by, 405-6
  short-term investments of, 267
  Subchapter S (tax-option), *see* Subchapter S Corporations
  total number of, 4
Cost-of-freight (C.F.) contract, law of, 266
Costs
  break-even analysis of, 293-96
  fixed and variable, 290-96
  of goods sold, 290
    decreasing of, and profit, 284, 309
    in manufacturing business, 288
  locations, 323-24
  See also Expenses
Courses given by stores or shops, 127
Creativity, 345-46
Credit
  application form for, 170, 171
  financing of, 214-15
  5Cs of, 167-70, 222-23, 226
  insurance for, 277
  lines of, 220
  middlemen for, 90
  policy for, 167-72
  types of, 166-67
  See also Installment sales; Loans
Credit cards, 167, 215
Credit unions, 220
Cundiff, Edward W., 82*n*
Current ratio, 193, 199
Customer surveys, 85
Customers
  daily relations with, 133
  services to, *see* Special services
  unreasonable demands by, 17

D

Dale, Ernest, 334*n*
Dallas-Fort Worth Metroplex, rents in, 324
Deadbeats, 17, 172
Dealer franchises, 67-68
Debentures, definition of, 216
Debt financing, 404
  definition of, 71
Debt-to-equity ratio, 195
Debts
  securing of, 216
  See also Capital; Loans
Deductible clauses in insurance, 275
Deductions from federal income tax, 245-48, 255
Default, 269
Defective merchandise, borrower's right to refuse to pay for, 267
Deficiency judgment, 269
Delivery date, price and, 312
Demand
  elasticity of, 297-98
  price and, 313
Department of Commerce, 400
Deposit slips, 142, 143
Depreciation
  accelerated, 70, 252-54
  definition of, 185, 186
  straight-line, 251
  tax laws on, 251-54
Depreciation Expense (account), 153
Depressions, 398
  See also Business cycles
Digital Equipment, 323
Direct mail, high expenses of, 110
Direction, 13-14, 341-43
  communication in, 381-84
  leadership in, 379-80
Disabilities as no barrier to starting a business, 24-25
Discount houses, business cycle and, 297*n*
Discounts, seasonal, 312
Discounts Earned (account), 152
Dishonest employees, 165
  insurance against, 277
Distribution channels, 90
Distributors, 7, 90
  advertising aids from, 112
Diversification, disadvantages of, 89
Door-to-door salespersons, 90
Drafts
  definition of, 267
  "sight," 268
Drugstores, price rule of thumb for, 64
Dun & Bradstreet, 199, 211
  on causes of business failure, 9

E

Earning power, insurance against loss of, 274
Economic conditions, 391-401
  credit policy and, 170, 223
  governmental policy and, 396-97
  See also Business cycles
Economic order quantity (EOQ), 317-18
Elasticity, demand, 297-98
Electric Wastebasket Corporation, 117
Electronic service shops, capital needed for, 208-11
Empathy, 113, 380, 383
Employees (human resources), 39-40, 359-88
  as agents, 263-64
  communication with, 381-84
  directing of, 341-43
  dishonest, 165
    insurance against, 277
  fringe benefits for, 378
  incentives for, 378
  job descriptions for, 371, 373-75
  job specifications for, 371
  leadership of, 379-80
  motivation quotient for work with, 384-85, 386
  part-time and temporary, 14, 368-69
  payroll checks for, 145, 236-40
  performance evaluation of, 377
  promotion of, 378
  record keeping on, 370-71, 372
  recruiting and selection of, 360-69
    application form, 362-65
    interview, 361, 365-66
    physical examination, 367, 370
    tests, 367
  tax records for, 19, 236-41
  training of, 376-77
  wages of, *see* Wages
Employer identification number, 236

Employer's Tax Guide (IRS), 236
Employment agencies, 361
Employment application form, 362-65
Employment Taxes (account), 153-54
Endorsements on negotiable instruments, 268
Entity, business, form of, 32-36
Enterpreneurship, meaning of, 22
EOQ (economic order quantity), 317-18
Equipment (account), 151
Equity (owner's equity; net worth)
  on balance sheet, 182, 191-92
  capital needs and, 211
  in example of income statement, 57
  formula for, 56
  leverage and, 195-97
  return on, 58, 188, 195-96, 199
  source of, 212
Equity financing, definition of, 71
Estimated taxes, 242-43, 248
Excise taxes, 242, 298
Exclusions from federal income tax, 243
Expansion of a business, 404-5
Expense accounts, 149, 153
Expense—Invoice Received, Not Paid, in double-entry bookkeeping, 147
Expense Paid, in double-entry bookkeeping, 146
Expense statement, 207
Expenses
  control of, 322-26
  decreasing of, and profit, 285, 309
  on income statement, 184-85
  income-tax deductions for, 255
  See also Costs
Expenses in Retail Business, 206
Experience
  lack of, as cause of business failure, 9-10
  from mistakes, 15
Extended-coverage endorsement on fire insurance, 276
Exterior of store, 96

F

Factors (middlemen), 90
  accounts receivable sold to, 216, 220
Factors of production, 21-22
Failures, *see* Business failures
Fair market value, 242
Feasibility study, 41-45
Federal Housing Administration (FHA), 221
Federal income taxes, *see* Income taxes
Federal Income Taxes (FIT) Withheld (account), 151
Federal regulation, 270-71
Federal Reserve (Fed), 396-97
Federal Trade Commission, 270
Fee simple, definition of, 265
FICA, *see* Social Security taxes
Fidelity bonds, 277
Field warehousemen, 90
FIFO valuation, 150, 255
Finance capital, 21
Finance companies, loans by, 220
Financial statements, 154, 156
Financing
  debt, 404
    definition of, 71
  long-term, 212-13, 404
    off-balance sheet, 213
  out-of-the-business, 214-15
  short-term, 214
Fingerhut Corporation, 321-22
Finished goods, inventory of, 288
Fire insurance, 276
Fire regulations, 272
Fireproof buildings, 273
Fiscal policy, 396
5Cs, 167-70, 223, 226
Flammable Fabrics Act, 270
Floor planning, 217
Florists, price rule of thumb for, 64
F.O.B., law of, 266
Food and Drug Administration, 270
Ford, Henry, 298
Forecasting
  business cycle and, 12, 86, 398-400, 401
  market, 85-87, 338
Forms, tax, 234-43, 370
  Form 1040, 244-47
Four Ps, 87
Franchises, 67-70
  how to investigate, 70
  reasons for, 68-69
Frantz, Forrest H., Sr., 345*n*, 346*n*

Fringe benefits for employees, 378
Funds statement, 159
Furniture stores, minimum starting capital for, 208
Future expenses, insurance against, 274

G

Gain from Sale of Assets (account), 152-53
Garages, 128
Gentry, James A., 148*n*
GNP (gross national product)
  in forecasting, 85, 394-96
  quantities used in, 394
Goal setting, 11
Good will, 58, 265
Goods, *see* Consumer goods, Defective merchandise; Industrial goods; Property; Purchasing
Govani, Norman, 82
Government financing, 220-21
Grand opening, example of, 125-27
Green, Paul E., 84*n*
Gross margin, 189
Gross national product, *see* GNP
Group buying arrangement, 285
Growth of a business, 15-16
  changing requirements due to, 404-5
  cycle of, 402-4

H

Handbills, 111
Hanzen, James M., 64*n*
Hardware stores, ratios for, 196, 199-200
Harrod's of London, 127
Hawthorne Experiments, 335, 353
Headlines, principles of writing, 115-18, 120
Health insurance, 277
Hedging, 273
Heilbroner, Robert L., 396*n*
Herzberg, Frederick, 335, 355
Hewlett-Packard, 75
Hierarchy of needs, 354-55
Hiring of employees, *see* Employees—recruiting and selection of
Holder (of negotiable instrument),
Holder *(cont.)*
  definition of, 268
Home service, 127
Horngren, Charles T., 159
Hourly specials, 128
Hourly wages, 289, 368
Human-relations approach to management, 354
Human resources, *see* Employees

I

Illiquidity, 8-9
Image, 130-31
  definition of, 130
Incentives for employees, 378
Income
  cash flow distinguished from, 300-302
  formula for, 56
Income statements, 56, 156, 182-87
  examples of, 57, 185
  interim, and expense control, 322-23
  for loan applications, 226
  in manufacturing businesses, 288
  percentage, 189-90
  pro forma, for budgeting, 300, 338
Income taxes
  account for, 151
  estimated, 242-43, 248
  in negotiating for buying a business, 65-66
  new business' problems with, 19
  planning for, 251-56
    summary points listed, 255-56
  preparing federal returns for, 243-50
    basic formula for, 243-44
    deductions, 245-48, 255
    lists of schedules, 245, 248
    property taxes, 242
    whether to do own return, 159, 250
  on Subchapter S Corporations, 36, 71, 242
Incompetence as cause of business failure, 9
Independent sales reps, 369
Indicators in business cycles, 400-401
Industrial goods

Industrial goods *(cont.)*
definitions of, 89, 90
distribution channel for, 90
Inelasticity, demand, 297-98
Inflation, 395-96
demand-pull vs. cost-push, 396
monetary policy and, 397
Innovation, 345-46
Insolvency, definition of, 8
Inspections, governmental, 271
Installment sales, 167
law on, 271
Insurance, 273-77
automobile, 276-77
coinsurance clauses in, 274, 276
deductible clauses in, 275
dishonesty, 277
fire, 276
liability, 274, 276
product liability, 266
mutual, 274
Insurance companies, loans from, 220
Insurance selling, prospecting in, 95
Intangible goods, definition of, 265
Interest
on negotiable instruments, 267-68
rates of, 217-18
Interest (account), 154
Interior of store, 96
Internal control, 162-65
Internal Revenue Service, 233
booklets of, 236, 242, 250
forms of, 236-41
See also Income taxes; Taxes
Interviewing prospective employees, 361, 365-66
Inventory
assets of, 191
categories of, in manufacturing businesses, 288
cost of, 316-17
dating of, 320
methods of valuation of, 150, 255
new business' requirement for, 39
ordering computation for, 317-18
purchasing and size of, 313
records and management of, 318-20
turnover in, 196, 316, 320-22
Inventory-Merchandise (account), 150
Investment
Investment *(cont.)*
fair returns on, 9
short-term, for idle cash, 267-68
tax laws and, 70-71
Investment capital, 21
Investment credit, 70, 249, 254
Invoices (bills), 142, 146

J

Job descriptions, 371, 373-75
Job specifications, 371
Jobbers, 90
Johnson, Glen L., 148*n*
Joint tenancy, 265
Journals
definition of, 154
example of pages of, 154, 158

K

Kaman Aircraft Corporation, 75
Kavesh, Robert A., 85*n*, 401*n*
Kelley, Pearce C., 70
Keys, issuance of, 165
Kursh, Harry, 70

L

Lagging indicators, 400-401
Land, definition of, 21
Laws
demands on owners from, 17
See also Business law; Public regulation
Lawson Hill Leather and Shoe Co., 118
Lawyer, Kenneth, 70
Lawyers, finding businesses through, 61
Layout of ads, 120
Layout of premises, planning of, 48-51
Leadership, 16, 379-80
Leading indicators, 400-401
Leasehold, definition of, 265
Leases
analysis of, in buying businesses, 62
cost of, 324
Texas city property, 263, 264
Ledgers, 154, 156
Leverage, 193, 195-97

Liabilities
on balance sheet, 191
current, 191
definition of, 8, 56
long-term, 191
Liability accounts, 149
Liability insurance, 274, 276
product liability, 266
Library, 376
Licenses
local, 271-72
state, 271
Life insurance, 277
loans on, 216
LIFO valuation, 150, 255
Lines of credit, 220
Lippitt, Ronald, 354
Liquidated business inventories, 285
Liquidation value, 60
Liquidity, 193-95
Loan application form, 170, 171
Loans, 216-28
cost of, 217-18
how to get, 222-27
renewals of, 221-22
term, 212
See also Credit; Installment sales
Local economic conditions, 392-93
Location, 41-42
costs of, 323-24
Long-term capital gain on income tax return, 245
Long-term financing, 212-13, 404
off-balance sheet, 213
Lot purchases, 313-14
"Low overhead," 324

M

McGregor, Douglas, 335, 354
Macrae's Blue Book, 310
Mail-order businesses, 90
Management, 333-56
basic functions of, 334
coordination by, 347
definition of, 333
"by exception," 338
functions of, 11
innovation and creativity as function of, 345-46
planning and, 334-38
Management *(cont.)*
representing by, 347
theories of, 334-35, 353-55
See also Control
Manufacturer's representatives (agents), 8, 90
Manufacturing businesses, 75
control in, 343
federal regulation of, 270
income statement for, 288
increasing efficiency in, 285
inventory categories in, 288
low-cost locations for, 323
pricing strategy for, 299
product liability of, 266
Markdown cancellations, definition of, 288
Markdowns
definition of, 288
net, 288
Market forecasting, *see* Forecasting
Market plan, 338
Market research, 82, 84-85
Market segmentation, 82-83, 87
Market survey, 42-44
Marketing, 82-89
definition of, 82, 84
strategy and tactics in, 87-88, 298
Marketing mix, 82-84
Markup cancellations, definition of, 287, 288
Markups (markdowns)
additional, 287, 288
definition of, 288
net, 287-88
Maslow, Abraham, 335, 354-55
Mattel, Inc., 75
Mayo, Elton, 335, 353
Meeting with employees, 384
Mehta, Dileep R., 194*n*
Merchant middlemen, 74, 90
Mergers, 405-6
Metcalf, Wendell O., 34*n*, 43*n*
Middlemen, 7-8, 74, 90
product liability of, 266
Miller, Jerome S., 273*n*
Mini businesses, definition of, 4, 5
Mistakes, experience from, 15
Monetary policy, 396-97
Mortgages, 216, 220, 269
Motivation-maintenance theory, 355

Motivation quotient, 384-85, 386
Multiplier effect, 396, 399

N

National Appliance and Radio TV Dealers Association, 208
National Association of Bank Loan Officers and Credit Men, 199
National Bureau of Economic Research, 400
National Cash Register Company (NCR), 206
  "Peg-n-Post" systems of, 173
Needs, Hierarchy of, 354-55
Negligence, claims for, 276
Negotiable instruments, law of, 267-69
Negotiation
  in buying a business, 64-66
  in purchasing, 311-12
Neiman-Marcus store, 127
Net profit, 22-23, 182, 186-87
Net profit margin, 188, 199
Net working capital, 194, 199, 205
Net worth, *see* Book value; Equity
New businesses
  bases for, 5, 7
  capital needs of, 22, 23-24
  income-tax problem of, 19
  planning of, *see* Planning–of new business
  profit expectations of, 22-24
  sales as first need in, 404
  with small investments, 8
  whether to start or buy, *see* Buying a business
"New products" columns, 132
Newspapers
  ads in, 111-23
  free publicity in, 131-32
  See also Want ads
Notes, *see* Promissory notes
Notes payable, 191
  as short-term loans, 214
Notes-Payable (account), 152
Notes receivable, 191
Novelty items, 298

O

Objectives
  of business in general, 15-16
Objectives *(cont.)*
  setting of, 11-12
Occupational Safety and Health Administration (OSHA), 261, 270
Odell, Charles E., 361*n*
Off-balance sheet financing, 213
"Off-day" sales, 129
Office supplies, savings in, 325-26
Oil companies, dealer franchises by, 67
Olsten, William, 369*n*
Omni Offices, Inc., 121
Open accounts, 166
Operating businesses, classification of, 72
Operating expense statement, 207
Orders, 382-83
Organization, 12-13, 338-41
  theory of, 334-35
Original sales price, definition of, 287, 288
Osborn, Alex, 345*n*
OSHA (Occupational Safety and Health Administration), 261, 270
Out-of-the-business financing, 214-15
Overcoming objections, 94, 100-101
Owner's Draw (account), 152
Owner's equity, *see* Equity
Ownership of property, law of, 265

P

Parking regulations, 272
Partnerships
  advantages and disadvantages of, 33-35
  definition of, 32
  general vs. limited, 33
  income from, on income tax returns, 243
  income-tax forms for, 242, 245
  total number of, 4
Part-time employee, 14, 368-69
Patents, 265, 271
Payment received on account, in double-entry bookkeeping, 146
Payments, slow, 17
Payroll, temporary employees and, 369

Payroll checks, 145, 236-40
Peg systems, 173
Pension and trust funds, loans from, 220
Percentage income statement, 189-90
Percentage lease, definition of, 62
Performance evaluation of employees, 377
Perpetual inventory system, 319-20
Personal financial statement, 224-25
Personal property
  definition of, 265
  taxes on, 241-42
Petty cash, 164
Petty Cash (account), 151
Physical examinations of employees, 367, 370
Piecework compensation, 368
Planning, 11-12
  budgeting of, 300-303
  business cycle and, 12, 86, 398-400, 401
  example of, 350
  long-range vs. short-range, 337
  management and, 334-38
  of new business, 37-51
    feasibility study, 41-45
    final plans and action, 45-48
    of layout, 48-51
    marketing questions, 88
  tax, 251-56
Platt, Robert B., 85*n*, 401*n*
Policy statements, 337
Polya, G., 345*n*
Postal money orders, endorsement of, 268
PR, *see* Public relations
Pre-approach in selling process, 93
Presentation, 94
Press releases, 132
Price breaks, buying and, 285
Price fixing and discrimination, 270
Price for buying a business, 63-66
Pricing
  Ford's advice on, 298
  profit and, 284
    economics of, 297-98
    guidelines, 299
    marketing strategy, 298
  retail terms in, 287-88
Principal-agent relationship, 263-65
Prize drawings, 125
Procedures, policy distinguished from, 337
Product knowledge, selling points based on, 92-93
Product liability, law of, 266
Production, factors of, 21-22
Professional Management, 47-48
Profit, 15, 283
  activity segregation and, 285-87
  capitalization of, 59-60
  cost analysis for, 290-96
  equation for, 284-85
  gross, 22-23, 182, 183-84
  "income" used for, 56
  net, 22-23, 182, 186-87
  net profit margin, 188, 199
  new business' expectations of, 22-24
  pricing and, *see* Pricing–profit and
  time required to reach, 23-24
  venture, 9
Profit (account), 152
Profit-sharing programs, 378
Profitability, 182
  measures of, 187-90
Promissory notes, 268
  for defective merchandise, 267
  definition of, 267
Promotions, 123-29
  definition of, 124
  by distributors, 284-85
  events suitable for, 124
  how to succeed in, 124-27
  ten ideas in, 128-29
  types of, 124
Property
  insurance against loss of, 274
    See also Insurance
  law of, 265-66
Property Tax Expense (account), 153
Property taxes, 241-42
Proposals, *see* Bids
Proprietorships
  advantages and disadvantages of, 32-33, 34
  definition of, 4, 32
  income-tax forms for, 242
  total number of, 4
Prospecting, 93, 95
Public bulletin boards, 112

Public regulation
 federal, 270-71
 local, 271-72
 state, 271
Public relations (PR), 129-31
 definition of, 130
Public service, 133-34
Publicity, 129, 131-32
 definition of, 130
Purchase orders, 142, 144, 314, 315
Purchasing, 309-15
 barter instead of, 313
 finding sources for, 310-11
 by lot, 313-14
 negotiating in, 311-312
 paperwork in, 314-15
 price factors in, 312-13
 salvage, 314
 savings in, 284-85
Pure Food and Drug Act, 270

Q

Qualified endorsements, 268
Questioning-counseling approach, 342
Quick ratio, 193-94, 199

R

Radio spots, 111
Ratios, 198-200
 current, 193
 as measures of profitability, 187-90
 quick (acid test), 193-94
Raw-materials inventory, 288
Real property
 definition of, 265
 taxes on, 241-42
Reber, Ralph W., 379*n*
Receipts, fake, 165
Recessions, *see* Business cycles
Record keeping, 47
 on employees, 370-71, 372
 for inventory, 318-20
 need for, 17, 19
 for purchasing, 314-15
 for taxes, 19, 234-43; *see also* Income taxes
 See also Bookkeeping
Recording the sale, 94
Refinancing, 221-22
Registered owners of bonds, 267
Rented property, *see* Leasehold; Leases
Repair shops
 advertising stickers for, 112
 billing of parts at, 284, 289
 business cycle and, 297*n*
 home service by, 127
 layouts of, 50
 low-cost locations for, 323, 324
 minimum starting capital for, 208
Replacement cost, 59, 60
Reporting, 343, 347-48
Repossession of merchandise, 172
Representing the business, 347
Request for proposal (RPF), 314
Request for quotation (RFQ), 314
Requisitions, 314, 315
Restaurants
 product liability insurance for, 266
 public regulation of, 271, 272
Restrictive endorsements, 268
Résumé in applying for loans, 226
Retail businesses, 73-74, 90
 analysis for "sell" by, 95-97
 control in, 343
 layout for, 50
 low-cost locations for, 323-24
 pricing terms in, 287-88
 product liability insurance of, 266
 profit format for, 287-88
 prospecting by, 95
 special services by, 127-28
Retired people, new businesses by, 25
Retirement from business, 405
Return on assets, 197
Return on equity, 58, 188, 195-96, 199
Revenue accounts, 149
Revolving charge accounts, 167
Reynolds, Lloyd G., 396*n*
Riegel, Robert, 273*n*
Risk
 classification of, 274, 275
 four ways to meet, 273
 speculative vs. pure, 261, 273
 See also Insurance
Robert, William J., 262*n*
Robert Morris Associates, 199, 203
Robinson-Patman Act (1936), 270
Roden, Peyton Foster, 212*n*, 401*n*
Roethlisberger, F. J., 335, 353
Route salespersons, 90

Routines, 383
Ryan, William T., 82*n*

S

Safety laws, 261
  federal, 270
  local, 271-72
  state, 271
Salaries, *see* Wages
Sales
  as first need, in new business, 404
  law of, 266
  volume of, and profit, 284
Sales (account), 152
"Sales" (promotions), 124
  ideas for, 128-29
Sales and Marketing Executives International, 107
Sales commissions, 368
  to independent sales reps, 369
  as variable cost, 290
Sales Management, 85
Sales promotion, *see* Promotions
Sales Tax Collected (account), 151
Sales taxes, 19, 234-36
Sales tickets, 140, 142
Salespersons
  list of rules for, 91-92
  transportation costs of, 326
  See also Selling
Salvage
  purchasing of, 314
  selling of, 325
Salvage value, 251-52
Sayles, Leonard R., 379*n*
Schaum Publishing Company *Outline Series,* 367
Schedule A, 245
Schedule B, 245
Schedule boards, 350-51, 352
Schedule C, 242, 243
Schedule D, 245
Schedule E, 243
Schedule R, 245
Schedule X, 248
Schedule Y, 248
Schedule Z, 248
Scrap and junk, selling of, 325
Searching for business opportunities, 61-62
Security, law of, 269
Self-control, 14-15
Seller's market, 297
Selling, 91-104
  analysis of place of business for, 95-97
  process of, 93-95
  six steps to, 97-100
Selling agents, 90
Series analysis, 85-86
Service businesses
  categorization of, 72-73
  source of profit in, 289
  successes in, 6
  See also Repair shops
Service offices, layout of, 51
Service stations (filling stations), tie-ins by, 128
Service to customers, *see* Sepcial services
Sewing-maching businesses, 127
Shopping goods, definition of, 89
"Sight" drafts, 268
Sign ordinances, 272
Single-mindedness, 11
Small business
  attributes one should have for, 10-16
  headaches of, 17
  U.S. definition of, 4
Small Business Administration (SBA), 199
  definitions of, 4
  loans by, 221
  as source of information, 47-48
Small Business Bibliography, 206
Small Business Reporter, 47, 206, 208
Small-claims courts, 172
Small Marketers Aids, 47, 299
Smith, Leonard J., 376*n*
Social Security taxes (FICA)
  accounts for, 151, 153-54
  how to pay, 236-40
Social Security Taxes (FICA) Withheld (account), 151
Special endorsements, 268
Special services, 127-28, 133
  price and, 284
Specialization, advantages and disadvantages of, 20, 88-89
Specialty goods, definition of, 89
Specifications
  job, 371

Specifications *(cont.)*
in purchasing, 314
Speculative risk, 261, 273
SS-4 form, 236, 237
Standards, 14
Starting and Managing, 48
State regulation, 271
Statistical Abstract of the United States, 44-45, 85, 206
Status boards, 350-51, 352
Stigelman, C. R., 70
Still, R., 82*n*
Stock market as business-cycle indicator, 400
Stocks
definition of, 267
dividends from, income-tax exclusion of, 243
Strauss, George, 379*n*
Subchapter S Corporations, 36, 71
income from, on individual tax returns, 243
income-tax forms for, 242
Success, ingredients of, 10-16
Success science, 91
Suggestion selling, 94, 101-2
Suitability of person for business, 16-21
test for, 18
Surplus products, purchasing of, 312
Surprise "Giveaway" sale, 129
Survey of Current Business, 85
Sweat equity, 5

T

Talks, free, for sales promotion, 128
Tangible goods, definition of, 265
Target market, 82-83
Tax credits, 248-50
Tax deposits, 236, 238
Tax Guide for Small Business, 242, 250
Tax-option corporations, *see* Subchapter S Corporations
Tax Reform Act of 1976, 36
Tax shelters, 71
Taxes
accounts for, 151, 153-54
investment and, 70-71
in negotiating for buying a business, 65-66
Taxes *(cont.)*
records on, 19, 234-43
See also Income taxes
Taylor, Frederick, 335, 353
Technology
growth cycle and, 402-3
prices and, 298
Teenage sale, 129
Telephone costs, holding down, 326
Temporary employees, 368-69
Tenancy, in-common vs. joint, 265
Term loans, 212
Terry, Gloria E., 379*n*
Test-room studies, 353
Tests of prospective employees, 367
Texas
sales and use tax return of, 234, 235
standard city property lease in, 263, 264
Theft, *see* Dishonest employees
Thomas Register of American Manufacture, 310
Thurow, Lester, 396*n*
Ticket marking sales, 128
Time as valuable resource, 13
Time clocks, 162
Title to goods, law of, 266
Tort, definition of, 276
Toys, federal regulation of, 270
Trade papers, "bingo" cards in, 132
Trade shows, 311
Trademarks, 271
Trading on the equity, 196
Training of employees, 376-77
Trial balance, 159
Truth-in-Lending Act (1969), 271
Tull, Donald S., 84*n*
Turnover ratios, 193, 196

U

Unemployment taxes, 240-41
Uniform Commercial Code (U.C.C.), contracts under, 262, 266
Retail Installment Contract, 167, 168
Unsought goods, definition of, 89
Urban Business Profiles, 206
Used equipment, purchasing, 313
User, definition of, 89
Utility costs, reduction of, 324

Utility Deposits (accounts), 151

V

Veterans Administration (VA), loans by, 220-21

W

W-2 form, 236, 240, 370
W-4 form, 236, 239, 370
Wages
- cutting costs of, 325
- hourly, 289, 368
- increases in, 378
- minimum 270-71
- piecework, 368
- *See also* Sales commissions

Wall Street Journal, 61, 321
Want ads (classified ads)
- business opportunities in, 61
- use of, 111, 122
  - for hiring employees, 360-61

Warehouse receipts, 216, 268
- definition of, 267

Western Electric, 353
White, R. K., 354*n*
Wholesalers, 7, 74, 90
- layout of, 50-51
- low-cost locations for, 323
- profit format for, 287

Williams, C. Arthur, Jr., 273*n*
Wilson Jones forms, 156
Window displays
- "Believe It Or Not," 128
- example of, 125

Withholding taxes, 236-40
Work in process, inventory of, 288
Work sheets, 159, 160

Y

Yellow Pages
- finding temporary employees from, 369
- placing ads in, 110-11
- purchasing from, 310

Your Federal Income Tax Return-For Individuals, 250

Z

Zoning, 271-72